Practical

Internetworking

with TCP/IP and UNIX

Practical

Internetworking

with TCP/IP and UNIX

Smoot Carl-Mitchell

John S. Quarterman

Texas Internet Consulting
tic@tic.com

 Addison-Wesley Publishing Company

Reading, Massachusetts • Menlo Park, California • New York
Don Mills, Ontario • Wokingham, England • Amsterdam • Bonn
Sydney • Singapore • Tokyo • Madrid • San Juan • Milan • Paris

This book is in the **Addison-Wesley UNIX and Open Systems Series**
Series Editors: Marshall Kirk McKusick and John S. Quarterman

Deborah R. Lafferty: Sponsoring Editor
Thomas Stone: Senior Editor
Patsy DuMoulin: Associate Production Supervisor
Bob Donegan: Marketing Manager
Roy E. Logan: Senior Manufacturing Manager
Marshall Henrichs: Cover Designer
Jaap Akkerhuis: Troff Macro Designer
Laura K. Michaels: Copy Editor

Library of Congress Cataloging-in-Publication Data

```
Carl-Mitchell, Smoot.
    Practical Internetworking with TCP/IP and UNIX / Smoot
  Carl-Mitchell, John S. Quarterman.
      p.   cm.
    Includes index.
    ISBN 0-201-58629-0
    1. Computer networks.  2. TCP/IP (Computer network protocol)
  3. UNIX (Computer file) I. Quarterman, John S.  II. Title.
  TK5105.5.C36   1993                                    92-41015
  004.6--dc20                                                CIP
```

The programs and applications presented in this book have been included for their instructional value. They have been tested with care, but are not guaranteed for any particular purpose. The publisher does not offer any warranties or representations, nor does it accept any liabilities with respect to the programs or applications.

UNIX is a registered trademark of UNIX System Laboratories in the United States and other countries. Many of the designations used by manufacturers and sellers to distinguish their products are claimed as trademarks. Where those designations appear in this book, and Addison-Wesley was aware of a trademark claim, the designations have been printed in initial caps or all caps.

1 2 3 4 5 6 7 8 9 10–MA–959493

This book is dedicated to
Charlotte

UNIX AND OPEN SYSTEMS SERIES

Network Management:
  A Practical Perspective

Allan Leinwand
Karen Fang

UNIX, POSIX, and Open Systems:
  The Open Standards Puzzle

John S. Quarterman
Susanne Wilhelm

Practical Internetworking
  with TCP/IP and UNIX

Smoot Carl-Mitchell
John S. Quarterman

Programming under Mach

Joseph Boykin
David Kirschen
Alan Langerman
Susan LoVerso

Series Editors
John S. Quarterman
Marshall Kirk McKusick

Series Foreword

Marshall Kirk McKusick
John S. Quarterman

Addison-Wesley is proud to publish the **UNIX and Open Systems Series.** The primary audience for the Series will be system designers, implementors, administrators, and their managers. The core of the series will consist of books detailing operating systems, standards, networking, and programming languages. The titles will interest specialists in these fields, as well as appeal more broadly to computer scientists and engineers who must deal with open-systems environments in their work. The Series comprises professional reference books and instructional texts.

Open systems allow users to move their applications between systems easily; thus, purchasing decisions can be made on the basis of cost-performance ratio and vendor support, rather than on which systems will run a user's application suite. Decreasing computer hardware prices have facilitated the widespread adoption of capable multiprocess, multiuser operating systems, UNIX being a prime example. Newer operating systems, such as Mach and Chorus, support additional services, such as lightweight processes. The Series illuminates the design and implementation of all such open systems. It teaches readers how to write applications programs to run on these systems, and gives advice on administration and use.

The Series treats as a unified whole the previously distinct fields of networking and operating systems. Networks permit open systems to share hardware and software resources, and allow people to communicate efficiently. The exponential growth of networks such as the Internet and the adoption of protocols such as TCP/IP in industry, government, and academia have made network and system administration critically important to many organizations. This Series will examine many aspects of network protocols, emphasizing the interaction with operating systems. It will focus on the evolution in computer environments and will assist professionals in the development and use of practical networking technologies.

Standards for programming interfaces, protocols, and languages are a key concern as networks of open systems expand within organizations and across the globe. Standards can be useful for system engineering, application programming, marketing, and procurement; but standards that are released too late, cover too little, or are too narrowly defined can be counterproductive. This series will encourage its readers to participate in the standards process by presenting material that details the use of specific standards to write application programs, and to build modern multiprocess, multiuser computing environments.

Newer operating systems are implemented in object-oriented languages, and network protocols use specialized languages to specify data formats and to compile protocol descriptions. As user interfaces become increasingly sophisticated, the level at which they are programmed continues to evolve upward, from system calls to remote procedure call compilers and generic description environments for graphical user interfaces. The effects of new languages on systems, programs, and users are explored in this series.

Foreword

Vinton G. Cerf

This book is the product a great deal of work by two very dedicated Internauts, Smoot Carl-Mitchell and John S. Quarterman. Their labor is indicative of a rising interest in and demand for international computer communications services by an extraordinarily wide range of users, many of whom would find it hard, indeed, to get their day's work done without the use of the Internet or networks based on its technology.

The authors concentrate on the most widespread protocol suite used in the Internet: TCP/IP but it is important to note that the Internet itself and many of its private clones have become multi-protocol in nature. Commercial routers support many protocols concurrently to meet the needs of users living with very diverse platforms requiring a variety of protocols. This diversity of need does not appear likely to abate, but readers will find in this book a particularly helpful emphasis on the practical challenge of setting up the most typical and commonly-needed environment associated with the UNIX operating system (or its variants and derivatives).

There are myriad reasons why internetworking is important to the business, academic and public sectors, but I would like to focus on one key proposition here. I think it is increasingly true that our daily work is supported by and even critically dependent upon computer-based applications. The results of our work are often manifested in forms which are only useful when viewed through the lens of application software (e.g. spreadsheets, multi-media documents, etc.). As we rely more on these tools, it becomes more important that we be able to communicate the results of our work to others in "machinable" form. The spread of personal computing and workstations thus engenders a concomitant demand for computer networking.

Although one can expect to build up personal files of valuable information, this trend has already led to the accretion of such large databases that it is impractical to copy all the material relevant to our work and to maintain it locally. Consequently, on-line archives and information services are becoming a common fixture in the networking world. With increasingly powerful workstations and personal computers, it is not uncommon for programs to run in the background to service our electronic messaging needs, search for data in file and data servers around the network, carry out various transactions with service providers on the net, all while running one or more interactive applications to help us with our immediate needs. Concurrent communication needs are driving interest in packet switched networking which permits multiple processes in a single computer to interact with other processes in many other computers scattered around the network.

On the social side, the global linking of our computer resources is truly creating electronic communities with ties that transcend national boundaries and which often rival arbitrary geopolitical borders in the strength of their binding power. Common interests and experiences are powerful forces comparable in the social dimension to the binding forces of the subatomic particles deeply hidden within the nuclei of atoms.

In the last two decades, networking technology has emerged from its academic cocoon, metamorphosing and taking flight. It has become the basis for a new information infrastructure, a global economic engine of incalculable potential. This book will help you get ready for your journey on the electronic highways of the future: fill up . . . and lift off!

Preface

This book is a practical guide for building TCP/IP networks with the UNIX operating system, and for using both TCP/IP and UNIX to integrate other network protocols and operating systems into a distributed computing environment. The book is not a protocol theory book, not a programming text, and not a user tutorial. It is about how to make whole networks actually work in practice.

The Networks

The TCP/IP protocols are used in tens of thousands of networks to connect millions of machines throughout the world. The largest of the collection of networks that use TCP/IP is the Internet. The Internet is the world's largest computer network and has been doubling in size each year since 1988. It had perhaps ten million users by 1993: researchers and academics, corporate employees, librarians and politicians, schoolteachers, and the general public. This global network commune has no central authority. The Internet works because of general agreement on network protocols used and because of cooperation among the users for the good of the network.

Much of the growth of the Internet is in **local area networks (LANs)** inside both private and public organizations, as opposed to **wide area networks (WANs)**. Some of these organizations are universities, government agencies, or government contractors, which were the historical research and academic base of TCP/IP. Other LANs are privately owned enterprise networks inside commercial companies. Many enterprise networks are not interconnected directly with the Internet proper, or are deliberately firewalled from it, so that only authorized corporate users may have access.

The LANs, whether interconnected with the Internet or not, are growing very rapidly, and more of them appear daily. Many of the organizations behind these networks, especially private companies, do not have a tradition of TCP/IP expertise. This is not surprising, because the number of qualified technical personnel in any area does not tend to double annually. The exponential growth of the use of

TCP/IP has outstripped the capability of the traditional support community to cope.

Most of these LANs use Ethernet (or IEEE 802.3) technology with TCP/IP. Other LAN technologies, such as FDDI, are even more capable and are growing in use. FDDI, for example, is not yet widespread, and organizations using it tend to be very familiar with it, often having been involved in its development. The predominant LAN technology is still Ethernet, and this is the first LAN technology an organization new to TCP/IP is likely to use, if for no other reason because all the major UNIX workstation vendors sell their computers with a built in Ethernet interface. For these reasons, this book emphasises Ethernet as the local area network technology of choice.

The Book

There are many books about network protocol theory, a few about the networks constructed from those protocols, and some about writing network applications. *Practical Internetworking with TCP/IP and UNIX* is about making the most widespread protocol suite and the most widespread general purpose operating system work together in a practical distributed computing environment.

This book is geared towards the knowledgeable UNIX administrator and user who lack a clear idea of what TCP/IP is and how it can be used. We cover a range of topics that are needed in setting up a working network. Also included is some background material on the history of TCP/IP and the Internet.

Since TCP/IP and the Internet are living systems which continue to grow and evolve, we also briefly cover the Internet Standards process as well as other topics relevant to the functioning of the Internet community. This book avoids going into extreme detail on all topics, in the interests of space. Also this book is not written as a reference book, but rather as a guidebook with enough practical examples to emphasis the points being made.

Organization

The book is organized in three parts, **Theory**, **Practice**, and **Advanced Topics**, plus a foreword, this preface, appendices, a glossary, and an index. References are included at the end of each chapter.

- **Forewords**   In addition to the series foreword, the foreword by Vinton G. Cerf explains the significance of the book.

- **Part 1, Theory**   The first part, which consists of five chapters, describes how the IP protocol suite is supposed to work. The first chapter provides an overview of the entire TCP/IP protocol suite, including lists of the protocols, and some information on how their specifications are produced. The second chapter gives a quick sketch of TCP/IP services. The third chapter describes the key protocol, IP itself. The fourth chapter examines the functions of transport protocols, such as TCP and UDP. The last chapter discusses the standard resource naming system used in the Internet community.

- **Part 2, Practice**   The second part of the book examines how UNIX implementations of the TCP/IP protocols actually work. The three chapters in the part treat setting up basic network services, setting up and managing electronic mail, and other network services.

- **Part 3, Advanced Topics**   The third part of the book discusses advanced topics, in three chapters on integrating Apple Macintoshes and IBM PCs, network management, and network debugging.

- **Appendices** Two appendices provide information on where to find protocol specifications and the numerous software packages mentioned in the book, as well as most of the programming examples used in the book.

- **References, Glossary, and Index**   Numerous bibliographic citations occur in the text, and the actual references are gathered at the end of each chapter. The glossary defines major (and many minor) terms and acronyms. The index indicates where they are used in the text. Expansions of acronyms are given both in the glossary and in the index for easy reference.

Readers

Beginning UNIX network system administrators will want to read the whole book, in order.

Readers already familiar with the TCP/IP protocols will probably also find much useful information in the first part of the book, but may want to skip directly to the practical details in the second part.

Experienced system administrators may want to skip directly to the advanced topics in the third part.

Familiarity with network protocol theory will be most helpful to all readers. We include some detail on the theory of how TCP/IP works, but we must assume some basic networking concepts.

Terminology

The book is written in American English. Some familiarity with networking and UNIX is assumed, but jargon is explained when used. The glossary contains definitions of difficult terms.

Acknowledgments

We would like to thank the reviewers, John Amason, Wayne Hathaway, Doug McCallum, Eugene Pinsky, Clyde Poole, William Selmeier, Barry Shein, Kean Stump, and Edward Vielmetti. All of them gave us valuable insights in how to better present the subject. We would also like to thank Laura Michaels, the copyeditor, who also added much to the clarity of the final book. And finally, we thank the editorial and production staff of Addison-Wesley, Tom Stone, Debbie Lafferty, and Patsy DuMoulin.

Contents

Appendix A   Access   **409**

Appendix B   **Program Listings**   **429**

Glossary   **449**

Index   **469**

Practical

Internetworking

with TCP/IP and UNIX

## PART 1

Theory

## CHAPTER 1

What is TCP/IP?

The **TCP/IP (Transmission Control Protocol/Internet Protocol)** protocol suite supports **the Internet,** the single largest computer network in the world. The Internet is not a single network. Rather, it is an **internetwork** consisting of many smaller networks. The Internet (note the definite article and the capital "I") is unique for it contains more than 11,000 networks and a million hosts. It is a multiprotocol internet, since protocol suites other than TCP/IP also are used. However, the TCP/IP protocol is by far the most widely used.

The TCP/IP protocol suite makes internets like the Internet possible by providing common services over a diverse set of underlying protocols and physical network hardware. The key protocol in the suite is the **Internet Protocol (IP),** which provides a common address space and routes packets across an entire internet. The **Transmission Control Protocol (TCP)** allows extremely reliable data transmission over IP. Another protocol, the **User Datagram Protocol (UDP),** transmits discrete packets of data, without any guarantee of delivery. Both TCP and UDP require IP, and all other TCP/IP protocols depend on it. Note that the acronym IP is often used to refer to the whole protocol suite.

In Chapter 3 and Chapter 4 we discuss IP, TCP, and UDP in more depth. In this chapter, however, we place TCP/IP in context of the history of computer networks, the design of network protocols, its place in the development of hardware and software technologies, and its user community. We also define some basic terminology that will be used throughout the rest of this book.

First, we discuss the ARPANET, which preceded and led to the Internet and on which many important network protocol concepts were developed. We follow with discussions of related networks and of the Internet itself. We also review protocol layering, network reference models, protocol suites, protocol stacks, and application program interfaces. Because protocols must be standard in order to be useful, we describe the processes used to produce Internet Standards. And finally, because these protocols and standards are constantly evolving, as is the Internet, we describe some of the central bodies that produce them.

1.1   The ARPANET

Before the Internet, there was the ARPANET (1969–1990). The **Advanced Research Projects Agency (ARPA)** of the U.S. **Department of Defense (DoD)** created the ARPANET as an experiment in packet-switched computer networking [Quarterman 1990]. The first ARPANET nodes were installed in 1969. However, the first protocols used on the ARPANET were not TCP/IP. Rather the TCP/IP protocols were invented using the ARPANET. Although the ARPANET is the precursor to the Internet, they are not the same. The ARPANET, however, was the first transcontinental backbone network in the Internet. Decommissioned in 1990, it was made obsolete by the newer network technologies it in part helped create.

The ARPANET was a direct product of the Cold War. ARPA itself was formed in response to the Soviet Union's Sputnik satellite in 1957. It was intended to ensure the U.S. got ahead in military research and stayed there. As DoD urgently wanted military command and control networks that could survive a nuclear war, ARPA was charged with inventing a technology that could get data to its destination reliably even if arbitrary parts of the network disappeared without warning as a result of a nuclear attack.

Traditional telephone technology, called **circuit switching,** wouldn't work for it had a serious drawback. In circuit switching, a route for data to get from one place to another is set up by using relays to make physical connections among pieces of cable. This works fine for analog voice circuits under ordinary conditions. However, if part of the circuit fails, a new circuit must be set up. Doing this is slow but not especially difficult under ordinary conditions. However, because a telephone network is likely to be set up with as few links between regions as possible (to save money), if a whole region vanishes, any other regions that normally route through that region are permanently disconnected.

The ARPANET used a different kind of technology, called **packet switching.** In packet switchng, data to be sent over a network is divided into many discrete parts each of which is called a **packet.** Each packet is routed from one computer to the next across the network until it reaches its final destination. Dedicated computers are normally used to route packets from place to place, much like a smart relay. Each of these relays is called a **router,** these computers are connected to each other by a physical data carrier, such as a copper cable, a fiber optic cable, or a microwave relay. This physical connection between two routers is called a **link.** and each networked computers that people actually use directly is called a **host.** A host is connected to the network in the same way as a router, but the usual difference is a host has a single link to one network, while a router has several links. In the ARPANET, hosts were connected to a local router, so the host needed to know only how to send data to the router; it wasn't involved in the packet routing decisions.

The basic ARPANET protocol was called **Network Control Protocol (NCP)** and the protocol for a host to communicate with a router over a local link was called **BBN 1822,** after the technical report that specified it. Other networks, particularly local area networks (LANs) permit hosts to share links directly. We have more to say about various network topologies in Chapter 6.

A networked computer that is not used directly by people but that provides some sort of service, such as large amounts of disk space, is called a **server.** The same machine can be both a host and a server, so for simplicity we will use the term host when we don't need to be more specific. A general term for a computer that may be a router, host, or server is **node.**

Each node has an **address,** which is a type of identifier, usually numeric. (IP addresses actually identify interfaces of links to nodes, not the nodes themselves, but most nodes have only one interface, so let's ignore that distinction for the moment.) A node that wants to send a packet to another node uses the address of the destination node to tell the intervening routers where the packet should go. As a packet travels through the network, it traces a **path,** or **route,** among the nodes of the network. A router decides which link to send a packet on next. For more about addressing and routing in the TCP/IP protocol suite, see Chapter 3.

Each ARPANET router was called a **Packet Switch Node (PSN)** in the declining days of the network, but they were originally each called an **Interface Message Processor (IMP).**

Once you have divided data into packets, there are two basic ways you can route them to their destinations: through virtual circuits or as datagrams.

A **virtual circuit** is a connection that is established when one node begins to send packets to another node. All packets between the two nodes pass over the same route as long as that connection lasts. This method of packet routing is much like traditional circuit switching, except that virtual circuits are set up in software, rather than with hardware relays, and routers can normally multiplex more than one virtual circuit over a given physical link or path. Virtual circuit switching can be efficient because the routers along the virtual circuit path can make routing decisions only once and not have to repeat them for each packet. The address of the destination node may even be omitted from most packets sent over a connection; an identifier for the virtual circuit might suffice. Virtual circuits also can provide dependable bandwidth, since routers can allocate sufficient buffers and other resources and keep them available during the lifetime of the connection. A protocol that implements a virtual circuit is called a **connection-oriented protocol.**

A fast, efficient, dependable virtual circuit becomes none of those things when a node or link along its path fails. Just as in hardware circuit switching, a virtual circuit must be reconstructed once it fails. This is not a problem if failures are rare. If failures are unpredictable in location, extent, or duration, you might as well route each packet separately. Since such unpredictability is exactly what one would expect in a war, ARPA chose to route packets individually. A packet that can be routed in a self-contained manner is called a **datagram.** Each packet must include a destination address. Intervening nodes don't usually allocate resources specific to packets traveling between a pair of nodes because any given packet may take a different route, bypassing a node that other packets traversed. This sounds inefficient, but need not be. Once you accept that each packet may be routed individually, you can choose to reroute packets for reasons other than node or link failures. For example, a link or node might become overloaded. A router then can choose to reroute some packets around the heavily loaded link. Use of datagrams thus permits load balancing throughout the network. This kind of dynamic reconfiguration is useful not only when nodes or links degrade or fail due to enemy action, but also during ordinary hardware or software overloads or failures, or simple human error. The ARPANET was mostly built out of datagram technology because of its inherent fault tolerance. A protocol that uses datagrams without virtual circuits is called a **connectionless protocol.**

Which approach is better: connection-oriented or connectionless? Proponents of both have been debating that question for 25 years. Some say virtual circuits are better because they are dependable; other say datagrams are more dependable because of their adaptability to changing conditions. The OSI protocols, which we will describe later on in this chapter, were built around virtual circuit switching. IP uses datagrams; however, TCP implements a kind of virtual circuit over IP datagrams, and the OSI protocols now include a datagram protocol much like IP. We discuss how IP uses datagrams in Chapter 3 and how user processes set up services using connection-oriented and connectionless protocols in Chapter 4.

The ARPANET was the first packet-switched network with nodes in several widely dispersed geographical locations. Many important computer networking concepts, such as the division of protocols into layers to reduce complexity and the ability to substitute one protocol for another at the same layer, were either invented or at least in part developed on the ARPANET. Almost all later networks and network protocols are indebted to the ARPANET.

Some of this debt is direct. The original intended use of the ARPANET was to allow remote login to fast computers so that ARPA would not have to buy a computer for each research locations it was funding. Bulk file transfers from one site to another also were important. The main protocols developed for these purposes were **TELNET (Virtual Terminal Protocol)** and **FTP (File Transfer Protocol).** With a few modifications and additions, the NCP versions of TELNET and FTP were converted for use with TCP/IP. Today, TELNET and FTP are two of the most popular protocols on the Internet and continue to provide the basic services of remote login and file transfer.

1.2   The Internet

The Internet evolved from the ARPANET, and sometimes people still confuse the ARPANET with the Internet. This confusion results probably because the ARPANET was the first backbone network of the early Internet and remained a part of the Internet until it was retired in 1990.

Early Internet Experiments

The proper name, the Internet, was first applied to a research program in 1973, with the first workable system demonstrated in 1977. This first implementation of the Internet involved four networks: a packet satellite network, a packet radio network, the ARPANET, and an Ethernet at the XEROX research center in Palo Alto, California [Cerf 1992].

The TCP/IP protocols and the Internet built from are mostly associated with the U.S. research community. However, the research has not been limited to just the U.S. for quite some time. Norway and England were connected from the earliest days of IP development and considerable technical input for IP and TCP came from France and the United Kingdom. For example, the original TCP retransmission algorithm was known as the **RSRE (Royal Signals and Radar Establishment)** algorithm for the organization in the United Kingdom that developed it [Partridge 1992].

The Early Internet

By 1983, the ARPANET had become so successful that ARPA no longer considered it experimental and so passed operational control of it to the **Defense Communications Agency (DCA)** (now known as the **Defense Information Systems Agency (DISA)** A nonexperimental internet, known as the ARPA Internet, began in January 1983 when DCA required all nodes to use TCP/IP. Simultaneously, DCA mandated the split of the original ARPANET into two networks: ARPANET (for continued research) and MILNET (for military operations).

Much of the early popularity of TCP/IP can be traced to the implementation of those protocols in the 4.2BSD version of the UNIX operating system. 4.2BSD was funded in part by ARPA to develop an operating system to serve as a research platform. Other funding came from the State of California, since 4.2BSD was developed at the **University of California at Berkeley (UCB)** by its **Computer Systems Research Group (CSRG).** Because of the public source of its funding, 4.2BSD was made available at the cost of its distribution and so its use spread quickly. Coincidentally, the 4.2BSD implementation became available at the same time as the inexpensive microprocessors such as the Motorola 680x0 series and the Intel 80x86 chip sets. Startup and established companies took advantage of the combination to build systems, mainly workstations, incorporating both the newly available inexpensive processors and 4.2BSD. Because of this, the development of UNIX and TCP/IP became intimately intertwined.

ARPANET and MILNET were the two early transcontinental national backbones in the developing network, with others added by government agencies such as the **National Aeronautics and Space Agency (NASA).** As the participation of other government agencies increased, the name of this composite internet changed, from ARPA Internet to the Federal Research Internet to TCP/IP Internet and finally to its current name of just the Internet.

NSFNET

In 1984, the **National Science Foundation (NSF)** established an office for networking and implemented several versions of its **NSFNET** national backbone network: in 1986 (DS-0, 56Kbps), 1988 (T-1, 1.544Mbps), and 1990 (T-3, 45Mbps). In addition to the NSFNET backbone, NSF provided seed money for the NSFNET mid-level networks, which are commonly known as the NSFNET regionals. These regional networks (now all mostly self-supporting) provide extensive connectivity for campus networks at educational institutions, government agencies, and commercial businesses.

The NSFNET backbone, the regionals, and other networks took advantage of the increasing availability and lowered cost of fiber optic bandwidth from interexchange carriers and telephone companies. High bandwidth wide area networks had become much less expensive to build and as a result became more common.

1.3   The Internet and the Matrix

The Internet is not the only computer network in the world. It is related to, and often confused with, several other networks.

Other Networks and Electronic Mail

The ARPANET became so popular and useful to researchers that several networks, such as CSNET, BITNET, UUCP, USENET, and FidoNet, sprang up partly in imitation of it. One of the earliest of these was **CSNET (Computer Science Network)**. Established in January 1981, it was intended to facilitate research and advanced development in computer science and engineering by providing a means for increased collaboration among those working in the fields. Most CSNET hosts didn't use TCP/IP; instead, many were connected by telephone dialup protocols that permitted essentially only one service — **electronic mail,** also known as **e-mail** or simply **mail.** Mail permits network users to send textual messages to one another and became the most popular service on the ARPANET even though it hadn't been planned. Researchers who wanted to discuss their research discovered they could avoid telephone tag by using the network to exchange messages. We have more to say about mail in Chapter 7 and Chapter 8. They even invented the **mailing list.** A mailing list is a list of names and addresses that has a single name. A network user then can send mail to the name of the list and software will automatically forward the message to everyone who has subscribed to that list, thus the sender avoids the need to keep track of who is on the list and reduces typing errors. We say more about mailing lists in Chapter 8.

BITNET (Because It's Time Network) was formed in May 1981 and uses the **Network Job Entry (NJE)** protocol and software that had been developed by IBM for its internal uses, principally as a part of the VM/370 operating system. NJE supports several services, including electronic mail, sending files, and relaying brief interactive messages. BITNET, like CSNET, interconnects mostly universities. But while CSNET tended to go to computer science departments, BITNET usually linked computation centers. In 1989, BITNET and CSNET merged administratively under the name **Corporation for Research and Education Networking (CREN)** and subsequently CSNET was retired when the NSFNET regionals subsumed its function. BITNET and CREN continue, however, although it appears that BITNET is being absorbed into the Internet.

The **UUCP mail network** began in its earliest form in 1978. Named after its protocol, **UNIX to UNIX Copy (UUCP),** which was first distributed with **UNIX Seventh Edition** in 1978, it since has come packaged with most versions of UNIX. UUCP mostly runs over ordinary dialup telephone lines and is therefore very inexpensive to implement. All you need is a phone line and a modem. Under favorable conditions and with similar versions of UNIX, you can actually transfer files through several UUCP links. But the only service you can really depend on getting through the UUCP network is electronic mail. We have more to say about how UUCP mail works and interacts with TCP/IP based mail services in Chapter 7 and Chapter 8.

USENET (Users' Network) began in 1979 and carries a service called **news.** A news message is called an **article** and looks much like an electronic mail message. But whereas an electronic mail message is ordinarily addressed to a single person or a relatively small group of people, a news article reaches everyone on USENET who subscribes to a particular discussion topic, called a **newsgroup.** Newsgroups were invented in imitation of ARPANET mailing lists but are much more efficient and can reach much larger groups of people. We have more to say about setting up a news system in Chapter 9.

USENET and UUCP are often confused but are not the same. USENET is not really a network; rather it's just the collection of all computers that carry USENET news. USENET news is carried not only over UUCP but also over other networks, including BITNET, FidoNet, and the Internet. Today, most USENET hosts are now on the Internet.

FidoNet was invented in 1983 to connect computers running MS-DOS. It uses the **Fido** protocols, which have many of the functions of UUCP but which are completely different internally and more efficient. The name, Fido, is not an acronym; it is a common pet name for a family dog and was intended to reach the masses with their personal computers. Fido, like UUCP, usually is used for telephone dialup connections, although either can be used over dedicated connections. FidoNet was invented somewhat in imitation of UUCP and USENET, which were invented somewhat in imitation of the ARPANET, so the ARPANET has at least one unexpected grandchild.

The Matrix

The existence of all these networks can create confusion, but just remember that each has its own niche and each serves a purpose [Quarterman 1991a]. All can exchange electronic mail with each other. All of them together, plus other networks and computers, form **the Matrix,** which consists of all interconnected computer networks that exchange electronic mail or news [Quarterman 1990]. The Internet is often confused with the Matrix. The Internet is the largest and perhaps the fastest-growing network in the Matrix, but it is not the Matrix, which also includes USENET, UUCP, FidoNet, BITNET, thousands of enterprise IP networks within corporations, and numerous other entities [Quarterman 1992a; Quarterman 1992b].

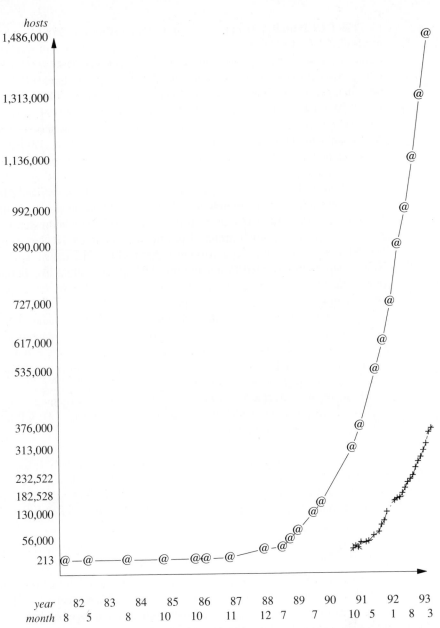

@ Worldwide (see RFC 1296), by Mark Lottor <mkl@nisc.sri.com>.
+ Europe, for RIPE (see RFC 1181), by Marten Terpstra <terpstra@ripe.net>.

Figure 1.1 Internet hosts, worldwide and in Europe.
Adapted from Quarterman, "Sizes of Four Networks in the Matrix," Matrix News,
Vol. 2, No. 2, MIDS, Austin, mids@tic.com, July 1992. Copyright © 1992 MIDS.
Reprinted with permission.

Some of these other networks are being absorbed by the Internet. For example, most USENET news traffic is now carried over the Internet (although much is still carried over UUCP, FidoNet, and BITNET). Also, the backbone of BITNET in the U.S. is carried over the Internet, as is also the case with the related **European Academic and Research Network (EARN).** Some FidoNet traffic across the Atlantic is carried over the Internet. Some whole national segments of the UUCP network pass and receive most of their mail traffic to the outside world also over the Internet. The Internet has become the core of the Matrix.

If a host or network can only exchange mail, it's not on the Internet. FTP can be used to define the extent of the Internet: To be on the Internet, a host must have direct interactive IP connectivity to the Internet. So if you can FTP to a host known to be on the Internet, such as *is.internic.net, ftp.psi.com,* or *ftp.uu.net,* your host is also **on the Internet.** If you can't do that, but you can send mail to one of those hosts, your host is not on the Internet but is still **in the Matrix.**

DNS: The Domain Name System

The Internet often is confused with the hosts and networks that use the Internet DNS, which defines and implements domain names like *tic.com,* so that (among other functions) mail to addresses like *tic@tic.com* works.

DNS is intended primarily to map between domain names and IP addresses for use by machines that are directly connected to the Internet. The deployment of DNS in 1986 was important because it freed the Internet from dependence on the old centralized ARPANET host table that had previously been used to map hostnames to addresses. However, DNS also can support domain names for machines that are not on the Internet. For such a machine, DNS can provide a domain name of a mail forwarder that is on the Internet and that knows how to reach the machine that is not on the Internet.

DNS names are widely used on UUCP, BITNET, FidoNet, and other networks. One name for all hosts that use DNS names for their hosts and that interchange mail is the **DNS Mail System.** Also sometimes called the **Internet Mail System,** this designation too easily confuses it with the Internet itself and leads people on mail-only networks to expect Internet services they can't get, such as FTP or TELNET. The DNS Mail System is closely related to the Internet, but it is not the Internet. It is larger, and many of the hosts on it cannot provide Internet services such as FTP for file transfer or TELNET for remote login. We say more about DNS and how it is implemented in Chapter 5 and Chapter 6.

1.4   Internet Growth

The Internet is growing exponentially and diversifying rapidly, hence the exact form of its future is unpredictable. Beginning about 1986, the size of the Internet has been more than doubling every year and promises to continue doing so for quite a while. The approximate numbers of hosts on the Internet from 1981 to 1993 are shown in Fig. 1.1 [Lottor 1992]. Growth of this magnitude does not happen by accident. Five key factors triggered this massive and sustained exponential growth:

- The reference implementation of TCP/IP in 4.2BSD in 1983 (later updated in 4.3BSD and 4.4BSD)

- Inexpensive microprocessors, beginning from about 1983

- Inexpensive wide-area fiber optic bandwidth, beginning from about 1984

- The NSFNET backbone and regional networks, beginning from 1986

- The deployment of DNS in 1986

None of these factors were enough alone to cause rapid growth. However, all came together in about 1986, thus producing the exponential growth.

The operating system used on most Internet hosts is probably UNIX. However, the Internet is not a UNIX network. TCP/IP is implemented on nearly every known operating system, and examples of most are connected to the Internet; in particular, there are large numbers of MS-DOS and Macintosh machines. In Chapter 10 we discuss methods of integrating these latter two systems into a TCP/IP network.

The numbers shown in Fig. 1.1 for dates since late 1986 were produced by looking at the distributed DNS database on the Internet. They exclude domains with only mail connectivity via UUCP or some other non-TCP/IP protocol. Domains included have associated IP addresses, although whether they are actually directly connected to the Internet isn't known (this would require actually attempting to exchange traffic with each host). However, it's reasonable to assume that most are and that these numbers are probably reasonably accurate for the size of the Internet. They certainly demonstrate the extraordinarily strong and undiminished growth since 1986.

The number estimated for April 1993 was 1,486,000 hosts. Given a factor of 5 to 10 users per host (plausible in an era of more PCs, workstations, and file-servers than large timesharing machines), this means approximately 7.4 to 10.5 million Internet users worldwide, which is consistent with estimates from other sources and methods [Partridge 1991]. If we say the number of users is 11 million and doubling each year more or less, this means 22 million in April 1993, 176 million by 1996, and more than 5 billion by 2001. Such rapid growth has to slow down eventually, of course.

The Internet Today

The Internet is characterized by use of the TCP/IP protocol suite. However, it now also includes major parts that support other protocols, such as CLNP (the OSI connectionless network protocol).

The Internet is run by a federation of organizations, each with its own operational arm. The policy body for the Internet moved from DARPA to a succession of committees of government agencies. Starting in the mid-1980s the NSF has taken a leading role in setting policy for the Internet in the U.S., partly due to its funding for NSFNET. Each major federal agency or departmental networks has its own usage and other policies set by its sponsoring organizations. DARPA, **DOE (Department of Energy)**, NASA, **NIH (National Institutes of Health)**, and NSF participate in the **Federal Networking Council (FNC)**, which is the coordinating body for Internet-related issues in the federal government.

NSFNET is the most prominent of the backbones with policies set by the government. Approximately a dozen regional networks connect to it, and thousands more local networks at companies, universities, and agencies connect to the regionals. There also are several other national backbones — such as PSINet, AlterNet, and ANSnet — most of which are not run by the government. In addition, other backbones, such as EBONE in Europe or WIDE in Japan, are not controlled by the U.S. government, although they might be related to governments in other countries.

The Internet itself has grown far beyond being just a government sponsored entity of the U.S or any foreign country. Most of it consists of thousands of local, metropolitan, state or provincial, regional, and national networks that are owned and operated by a diverse array of corporations, universities, networking companies, nongovernmental organizations, and governments. In some regions, there are coordinating bodies, such as **Reseaux IP Européens (RIPE)** in Europe; RIPE was at one point part of **Reseaux Associés pour la Recerche Européenne (RARE)**, which is itself affiliated with the **European Commission (EC)**. In some countries, there is a national governmental lead organization, such as that for the national backbone network CA*net in Canada. But no organization or organizations have overall responsibility for the worldwide Internet.

Research and Educational Usage

The successor to NSFNET, at least for research purposes, will be the **National Research and Education Network (NREN)**. Although the NREN was authorized by the U.S. Congress in the **High Performance Computing Act (HPCA)** of December 1991, there has been much discussion about exactly what it should be used for [Kahin 1992]. Researchers want to build a very fast backbone network and were allocated funds to do so. Educators and librarians want much wider access to the existing Internet but were not allocated much money for this purpose. Meanwhile, interest increases in using the Internet in classrooms and in classroom teaching of how to use the Internet [Tennant *et al.* 1993].

Commercialized Use

Perhaps as much as half of the Internet is already owned by commercial companies. The Internet reaches many organizations and people beyond its original research and educational base [Malamud 1992a].

1.5   Models and Layers

A communications system is a very complex collection of cooperating software and hardware. To aid in the understanding of these systems, network practitioners have developed some standard ways to model these systems and break them down into simpler pieces. A **reference model** is a model used to explain how the various components of a system fit together and explains what the common interface specifications are between the various components. For example a video system has a reference model, so that video components like cameras, VCRs, and monitors can work together. Things like video tape formats must be described, so that different manufacturers equipment can work together. Similarly, in networking there are the TCP/IP and OSI reference models, among others. The TCP/IP protocols are the more widely used, but the OSI model is the more widely cited in academic journals. We will explain the common features and differences of both models.

Models and Protocol Suites

The specifications for TCP/IP are written by the **IETF (Internet Engineering Task Force),** which is overseen by the **IAB (Internet Architecture Board),** that was called the **Internet Activities Board (IAB)** until June 1992.

OSI standards are written by formal international standards committees [Rose 1989; Stallings 1987]. The Basic Reference Model for **Open Systems Interconnection (OSI),** or OSI Model, was specified by the **International Organization for Standardization (ISO),** which also specifies protocols in a protocol suite to fit the model. Several of the OSI protocols were originally specified by **CCITT (International Consultative Committee on Telegraphy and Telephony).** CCITT has also adopted the OSI Model. The CCITT specification numbers are always prefixed with an "X." For example, parts of X.25 have the corresponding International Standards IS 8878 and IS 7776. The X.400 series of recommendations are also specified in IS 10021, for **MHS (Message Handling System).** X.500 is Directory Services and is also known as IS 9594. Some ISO OSI specifications don't have corresponding CCITT specifications.

OSI working groups operate at the international level of formal standardization and are composed of national delegations; therefore OSI working groups are more formal than are IETF working groups. In contrast many rules and procedures of IETF working groups are only now being written down. Although there has always been international participation in specification and implementation of the Internet protocols, the Internet community has perhaps been less international than the OSI community (although that appears to be changing).

Layers

A basic feature of both models is the division of protocols into layers, done in an attempt to reduce conceptual complexity. A protocol in a given layer can be described by the services it provides to the next higher layer and by the services it uses from the next lower layer. Protocols don't have to be implemented in separate program modules for each layer (although they often are); layering is a conceptual aid not an implementation directive. OSI has seven layers (more or less), while TCP/IP has five (more or less). Yet each protocol model accomplishes similar ends.

Many machines are connected to networks that use CSMA/CD, token ring, or token bus technology. The IEEE 802 standards govern communication at this level. ISO has the corresponding IS 8802 standards. IETF working groups may produce interface or management specifications for these media level protocols, but they do not normally specify the latter directly. The one exception so far is the **Point-to-Point Protocol (PPP).** In this book, we are mainly interested in protocols at the internet layer or higher, that is, protocols that can be used across several physical networks.

Assigning a network protocol to a layer can be tricky. Is Ethernet a network layer protocol or a datalink layer protocol? Well, that depends on several factors:

• Which network layer from which model you are referring to

• Whether you consider the internet layer to be part of the network layer

• Which protocol you are using on top of Ethernet

• Which Ethernet specification you mean

Many of these arguments are more in the lines of "religion," rather than practical differences. Suffice it to say, layering is not an exact science, but should be treated as a way reducing complexity and increasing understandability.

TCP/IP Layers. The TCP/IP protocols have several traditional layers, as shown in Table 1.1 and described as follows:

Physical   The Internet protocol model is really about software, not hardware, so there is no physical layer as such. But we can call everything under the network layer the physical layer.

Table 1.1 TCP/IP layers.

Layer	Examples
Process/Applications	TELNET, FTP, SMTP
Transport	TCP
Internet	IP
Network	X.25, Ethernet, FDDI
Physical	various

Network   The network layer contains whatever IP will run over, such as Ethernet, token ring, FDDI, etc. A network layer protocol routes packets across a network. A link layer is sometimes separated out at the lower end of this layer.

Internet   The internet layer is the key layer. It has one protocol: IP. IP provides many of the same functions as the network layer, such as addressing and routing. But it provides them and a common address space across multiple lower-layer network protocols, thus permitting the construction of internets.

Transport   The transport layer handles data consistency functions. TCP and UDP are transport layer protocols. TCP provides a reliable byte stream over a connection between two processes and ensures that data arrives and that it arrives in order and without errors. UDP makes an effort to deliver datagrams but doesn't ensure order or prevent packet loss or duplication. Most TCP/IP applications, such as TELNET and FTP, use TCP. Some, such as voice and video, use UDP, since fast delivery is, for such applications, more important than consistency.

Process/Applications   The process/applications layer provides application services to users and programs.

ISO-OSI Layers. In OSI, there is a strong distinction between a **service,** which is something an application program or a higher-layer protocol uses, and a **protocol,** which is the set of rules for providing the service. Protocols can be characterized according to the services they provide. A protocol layer provides a broad characterization of the services of protocols that fit in that layer.

The seven basic OSI layers are shown in Table 1.2 and described as follows:

Physical   This layer consists of cables and connectors and is responsible for converting analog signals into bits.

Data Link   The datalink layer transmits frames of bits across a single link between two machines. The link can be a bus (as in Ethernet), a ring (as in token ring) or a simple cable with two endpoints.

Network   The network layer routes packets through a network of nodes to a destination node. Fragmentation, reassembly, and flow control occur at this level.

Transport   This layer transmits messages from a process on one machine to a process on another machine. Various transport services and protocols can be defined ranging from almost nothing (provided by the TP0 protocol) to a reliable byte stream (provided by the TP4 protocol).

Table 1.2 OSI layers.

	Layer	Examples
7	Application	VTM, FTAM, MHS
6	Presentation	IS 8822/X.216, IS 8823/X.226
5	Session	IS 8226/X.215, IS 8327/X.225
4	Transport	IS 8072/X.214 (TP0-TP4)
3	Network	X.25
2	Data Link	HDLC
1	Physical	X.21

Session   The session layer establishes and maintains a connection between endpoints.

Presentation This layer encodes and decodes data for diverse data types and machine types.

Application   The application layer delivers a service to a user or a program.

Comparison of Layering Models

User programs and implementations of distributed services are more concerned with getting bits, bytes, and data structures from here to there than with what protocol "religion" the underlying network infrastructure supports. The two main protocol models disagree on many points, even on their basic layering divisions, as shown in Fig. 1.2.

Unlike the Internet Model, the OSI model separates presentation and session functions from the application layer and into separate layers. Internet protocols such as TELNET and FTP incorporate their own presentation functions. It is easy to argue that TCP incorporates many session functions. However, TCP doesn't fit the strict definition of an OSI session protocol, since it does not provide some OSI session functions and yet does provide many transport functions. The transport layers are perhaps the most similar of the layers in the two models (although they are not identical).

The OSI model has a network layer (now including an internet sublayer) and a datalink layer, while the Internet model has an Internet layer, a network layer, and a link layer. These cover approximately the same functions. Also, ISO recently adopted three formal sublayers to their network layer, as follows:

internet   This is formally the subnetwork-independent sublayer with a **Subnetwork-independent Convergence Protocol (SNICP),** which is often null for the **Connection-oriented Network Service (CONS),** that is, over X.25, but can be **CLNP (Connectionless Network Protocol)** (also known as ISO-IP) for the **Connectionless Network Service (CLNS).**

ISO-OSI Model		Internet Model	User Model
7 Application		Process	Network
6 Presentation		/	
5 Session		Applications	Applications
4 Transport		Transport	Network
3 Network	internet	Internet	
	convergence	Network	
	subnet		
2 Data Link		Link	Infrastructure
1 Physical		Physical	

Figure 1.2 Protocol models and layers.

From Quarterman and Wilhelm, UNIX, POSIX, *and Open Systems, The Open Standards Puzzle, Reading, MA: Addison-Wesley Publishing Company, Inc.* © *1993.*

Reprinted with permission.

convergence   This is formally the subnetwork-dependent sublayer with the **Subnetwork-dependent Convergence Protocol (SNDCP).**

subnet   This is formally the subnetwork access sublayer, in which is used a **Subnetwork Access Protocol (SNAcP)** containing an encoding of the network protocol [Rose 1989], for example, the Ethernet type field.

The OSI internet sublayer corresponds to the Internet layer, and OSI CLNP (ISO-IP) has the same general functions as does the Internet Protocol (although they differ in some details such as address format). The existence of this OSI internet sublayer removes one of the major points of disagreement in the ISO OSI and TCP/IP layering models. Because IP is always encapsulated in a network layer protocol (except for some point-to-point links), the TCP/IP Internet layer might be considered to be a sublayer of the network layer, like the OSI internet sublayer within the OSI network layer. However, if we consider Ethernet, token ring, X.25, BBN 1822 (the old ARPANET network protocol), ISDN, SMDS, frame relay, and ATM all to be network layer protocols, then IP fills a separate Internet layer above the network layer [Cerf & Cain 1983; Cerf & Kahn 1974]. CCITT has not followed ISO in adopting an internet sublayer, so ISO OSI and TCP/IP are now actually closer than ISO and CCITT in this respect.

A Simpler Model

We can simplify the picture by thinking of the protocol layers as being divided above the transport layer into application protocols above and infrastructure including the transport and lower layers [Quarterman 1991b; Quarterman 1991c]. In addition, although the TCP/IP model has no formal presentation layer, presentation protocols, such as Sun's **XDR (external data representation)**. are sometimes used with TCP/IP. However, the Internet transport layer has some features of the OSI session layer. For example, FTP uses two data channels, which are handled as two transport channels. In the OSI model, these would properly be handled by the session layer, but there is no Internet session layer. One could instead argue that the application layer is handling the missing session functions. The point remains that layer boundaries are somewhat arbitrary. The important thing about layering is not the number of layers or exactly where the boundaries are but that there are layers that permit substitutable protocols and simplify understanding and programming.

1.6   Protocol Stacks

A protocol model is not much good without actual protocols, no matter how many layers in the model. A **protocol suite** is a set of protocols that fit a protocol model. However, there might be more protocols in a protocol suite than are practical for use with a particular application. Therefore a **protocol stack** — a selection of protocols from a protocol suite — is selected to support a particular application or class of applications [Malamud 1992b].

IP Stacks

As you can see in Fig. 1.3, the IP protocol is the key protocol in the TCP/IP protocol model, since all stacks include it. IP provides an internetwork address space, routing, and other services across various underlying networks and network technologies. Above IP, either TCP or UDP may be used, and most application protocols are designed to be used with one or the other of these. TELNET, FTP, and SMTP were designed for use with TCP, and NTP and NFS for use with UDP. The DNS uses UDP for most purposes, but TCP where 100% reliability is required. Below IP, a wide variety of network protocols may be used. These might require their own underlying stacks of link and physical layer protocols; however, most TCP/IP application protocols are not concerned with what is underneath IP.

A transport layer protocol might need to know the maximum transmission unit (see Chapter 3) of an underlying network protocol to facilitate tuning the size of transmitted messages. Or an application might be concerned with a particular class of service, such as broadcast, and might need to know whether the network or link layer supports it. But most details below the Internet Layer are hidden from the transport and application layers.

Layer	Protocols					
Process/ Application	TELNET (login)	FTP (files)	SMTP (mail)	DNS (names)	NTP (time)	NFS (files)
Transport	TCP			UDP		
Internet	IP					
Network	Ethernet	ISO 8802-2		X.25	SLIP	PPP
Link		ISO 8802-3 IEEE 802.3 (CSMA/CD)	ISO 8802-5 IEEE 802.5 (token ring)	ISO 7776 X.25 LAPB (HDLC)	(serial)	
Physical	(various)					

Figure 1.3 IP protocol stacks.

OSI Stacks

Various national and international bodies specify **profiles** for stacks of OSI proto-cols. In the U.S., the **National Institute of Standards and Technology (NIST)** specifies such stacks, in their **Government OSI Profile (GOSIP).** GOSIP is an acquisition and procurement profile that dictates what U.S. government agencies have to buy, although it doesn't say what they have to use. U.S. GOSIP Version 1 was approved as a draft in October, 1988, as a Full Use version in NIST Special Publication 500-187. The current version is GOSIP Version 2, which is FIPS 146-1 of 3 April 1991.

The basic GOSIP Version 2 protocol stack is shown in Fig. 1.4. The key pro-tocol is CLNP, which is essentially the Internet IP protocol with a larger address space and supports the CLNS. Above this protocol is TP4, which closely resem-bles TCP. Above TP4 are the OSI session, presentation, and application layers. **ODA (Office Documentation Architecture)** is an additional application protocol layered on top of **FTAM (File Transfer, Access, and Manipulation)** and **MHS (Message Handling System).** Other GOSIP application protocols include **VT (Virtual Terminal)** and the OSI Directory service, X.500. For each application protocol (except ODA), Fig. 1.4 shows the acronym (that is, MHS), the general type (messages), the International Standard number (ISO 10021), and (where appropriate) the CCITT recommendation number (X.400).

The protocols shown in the Data Link layer in Fig. 1.4 are often considered in other documents to be in the network layer. Here we follow the layering shown in the GOSIP document itself.

ISO-OSI Model	GOSIP Protocols			
7 *Application* what: ISO: CCITT:	VT (login) ISO 9040	ODA FTAM (files) ISO 9571 ISO 8850: ACSE	MHS (messages) ISO 10021 X.400	Directory (directory) ISO 9594 X.500
6 *Presentation*	ISO 8823			
5 *Session*	ISO 8327			
4 *Transport*	ISO 8073: TP4			
3 *Network* internet convergence subnet	CLNS ISO 8473: CLNP (ISO-IP)			
2 *Data Link*	ISO 8802-3 IEEE 802.3 (CSMA/CD)	ISO 8802-2 ISO 8802-4 IEEE 802.4 (token bus)	ISO 8802-5 IEEE 802.5 (token ring)	ISO 7776 X.25 LAPB (HDLC) ISDN
1 *Physical*	(various)			

Figure 1.4 GOSIP Version 2 primary protocol stack.
From Quarterman and Wilhelm, UNIX, POSIX, and Open Systems, The Open Standards Puzzle, *Reading, MA: Addison-Wesley Publishing Company, Inc. © 1993.*
Reprinted with permission.

GOSIP Version 2 also permits another protocol stack, shown in Fig. 1.5, that substitutes the **Connection-oriented Network Protocol (CONP)** X.25 for CLNP to support the **Connection-oriented Network Service (CONS)** in place of CLNS. GOSIP intends CONS and CONP to be used over X.25 and ISDN. The rest of the stack, from the transport layer through the application layer, remains the same. GOSIP permits use of the ISO 8602 connectionless transport protocol for applications that need it.

GOSIP also permits TP0 to be used for some purposes such as connecting to public messaging systems. That stack looks like the one shown in Fig. 1.5, except TP0 replaces TP4, and is essentially the traditional European OSI protocol stack.

We have included this material on OSI here for the orientation of those who are familiar with OSI. We will not say much more about OSI in this book, which is about TCP/IP.

ISO-OSI Model	GOSIP Protocols			
7 *Application* what: ISO: CCITT:	VT (login) ISO 9040	ODA FTAM (files) ISO 9571	MHS (messages) ISO 10021 X.400	Directory (directory) ISO 9594 X.500
	ISO 8850: ACSE			
6 *Presentation*	ISO 8823			
5 *Session*	ISO 8327			
4 *Transport*	ISO 8073: TP4			
3 *Network* internet convergence subnet	CONS ISO 8878: X.25			
2 *Data Link*	ISO 7776 X.25 LAPB (HDLC)			ISDN
1 *Physical*	(various)			

Figure 1.5 GOSIP Version 2 secondary protocol stack.
From Quarterman and Wilhelm, UNIX, POSIX, and Open Systems, The Open
Standards Puzzle, *Reading, MA: Addison-Wesley Publishing Company, Inc.* © *1993.*
Reprinted with permission.

1.7   API: Application Program Interfaces

Several UNIX programming interfaces have been developed for programming at
least at the transport layer: **sockets (Berkeley sockets)** and the **TLI (Transport
Layer Interface)** or **XTI (X/Open Transport Interface).** Most commonly, current IP applications that run under UNIX are written for one of these interfaces.
There also are higher-level programming packages, such as those that facilitate
programming using **RPC (remote procedure call).**

Standards for a common **Protocol Independent Interface (PII)** and for
related API and EEI are being produced by the **IEEE/CS TCOS-SS (POSIX)**
committees listed in Table 1.3. It's worthwhile to know about these, although
most actual UNIX TCP/IP applications are still written using one of sockets, TLI,
or XTI.

Table 1.3 TCOS distributed services.
From Quarterman and Wilhelm, UNIX, POSIX, *and Open Systems, The Open Standards Puzzle, Reading, MA: Addison-Wesley Publishing Company, Inc. © 1993.*
Reprinted with permission.

Project	Title	Committee
1003.8	Transparent File Access (TFA)	P1003.8
1003.12	Protocol-Independent Interface (PII)	P1003.12
1003.17	Directory Services API	P1003.17
1238	Common OSI API	P1238
1238.1	FTAM API part	P1238
1224	Message Handling Services (MHS)	P1224
1224.1	Message Handling Services (MHS)	P1224
(1237	Remote Procedure Call (RPC) API	into X3T5.5)

1.8   Internet Protocol Specifications

RFC: Request for Comments

Many documents related to the Internet or to TCP/IP are published online on the Internet itself in the **Request for Comments (RFC)** series of documents. That acronym originated in the early days of the ARPANET when members of the group designing and implementing the ARPANET protocols (the ARPANET Network Working Group) published RFCs to ask for input from one another and from others. The RFC series of documents contains a wide variety of material, from network demographic surveys to poetry.

RFCs are numbered and are referred to by their number. The most basic RFCs are listed in Table 1.4. For example, RFC-1360 is the "IAB Official Protocol Standards" document [Postel 1992a]. That document lists the RFCs that specify all the TCP/IP protocols. It is periodically updated in a new RFC with a new number. RFCs for additional applications and for other services are shown in Table 1.5.

STDs: Internet Standards

Some RFCs are also Internet Standards. Standards are also numbered in an STD (standards) series. RFC-1280 is also STD-1. Later updates of RFC-1280 will have different RFC numbers, but will still be STD-1. STD-1 is the authoritative source for references on Internet Standards [Postel 1992b]. An STD number generally refers to a protocol rather than to a specification, so an STD number can apply to several RFCs.

All STD numbers assigned when the STD series was begun (by grandfathering existing protocols) are listed in Table 1.4, plus those shown in Table 1.5.

Table 1.4 Some Internet Standards.

From Quarterman and Wilhelm, UNIX, POSIX, and Open Systems, The Open Standards Puzzle, *Reading, MA: Addison-Wesley Publishing Company, Inc. © 1993.*
Reprinted with permission.

Acronym	Name	MIL-STD (old)	RFC	Status (current)	STD
Model and	IAB Official Protocol Standards	—	1360	Req	1
Taxonomy	Assigned Numbers	—	1060	Req	2
Requirements	Host Requirements	—	1122	Req	3
Documents	— Communications				
	Host Requirements	—	1123	Req	3
	— Applications				
	Gateway Requirements	—	1009	Req	4
Internet Layer					
IP	Internet Protocol	1777	791	Req	5
	IP Subnet Extension	—	950	Req	5
	IP Broadcast Datagrams	—	919	Req	5
	IP Broadcast Datagrams with Subnets	—	922	Req	5
ICMP	Internet Control Message Protocol	—	792	Req	5
IGMP	Internet Group Multicast Protocol	—	1112	Rec	5
Transport Layer					
TCP	Transmission Control Protocol	1778	793	Rec	6
UDP	User Datagram Protocol	—	768	Rec	7
Application Layer					
TELNET	Telnet Protocol and Options	1782	854, 855	Rec	8
TOPT-BIN	Binary Transmission	Option 0	856	Rec	27
TOPT-ECHO	Echo	Option 1	857	Rec	28
TOPT-SUPP	Suppress Go Ahead	Option 3	858	Rec	29
TOPT-STAT	Status	Option 5	859	Rec	30
TOPT-TIM	Timing Mark	Option 6	860	Rec	31
TOPT-EXTOP	Extended-Options-List	Option 255	861	Rec	32
FTP	File Transfer Protocol	1780	959	Rec	9
SMTP	Simple Mail Transfer Protocol	1781	821	Rec	10
MAIL	Format of Electronic Mail Messages	—	822	Rec	11
CONTENT	Content Type Header Field	—	1049	Rec	11

Table 1.5 More Internet Standards.
From Quarterman and Wilhelm, UNIX, POSIX, and Open Systems, *The Open Standards Puzzle, Reading, MA: Addison-Wesley Publishing Company, Inc. © 1993.*
Reprinted with permission.

Acronym	Name	RFC	Status	STD
Application				
Layer				
NETBIOS	NetBIOS Service Protocols	1001, 1002	Ele	19
ECHO	Echo Protocol	862	Rec	20
DISCARD	Discard Protocol	863	Ele	21
CHARGEN	Character Generator Protocol	864	Ele	22
QUOTE	Quote of the Day Protocol	865	Ele	23
USERS	Active Users Protocol	866	Ele	24
DAYTIME	Daytime Protocol	867	Ele	25
TIME	Time Server Protocol	868	Ele	26
Distributed				
Services				
NTP	Network Time Protocol	1119	Rec	12
DNS	Domain Name System	1034, 1035	Rec	13
DNS-MX	Mail Routing and the Domain System	974	Rec	14
Network				
Management				
SNMP	Simple Network Management Protocol	1157	Rec	15
SMI	Structure of Management Information	1155	Rec	16
MIB-II	Management Information Base-II	1213	Rec	17
Routing				
EGP	Exterior Gateway Protocol	904	Rec	18

These tables also show the requirement status of each STD. (We describe requirement statuses in more detail later in this chapter.) The three statuses that appear in these tables are Required, Recommended, and Elective, shown as Req, Rec, and Ele, respectively. A basic status for each STD is assigned by STD-1. A protocol specification like STD-6 for TCP that is a **Technical Specification (TS)** is given a status by another document, called an **Applicability Specification (AS).**

All STDs are given statuses by STD-1; for example STD-1 specifies that TCP is Recommended. However, another AS might be needed for a given application and so might give another status. For example, a host that supports TCP/IP must conform to STD-2, which is an AS. STD-2 makes TCP Required, even though STD-1 said TCP was only Recommended.

Any AS can amend, extend, or otherwise generally modify a TS; STD-1, STD-2, and STD-3 do this. So, it's not enough to look at just the basic specification for a protocol, such as RFC-793 for STD-6 (TCP). An implementer, application programmer, or tester also must examine STD-1, as well as STD-2, STD-3, or any other AS that is relevant to the platform or application.

RFCs, STDs, and MIL-STDs

One U.S. DoD agency, formerly DCA now DISA, has produced its own specifications through the **Protocol Standards Steering Group (PSSG),** for some of the TCP/IP RFCs. Those are numbered in a MIL-STD (military standards) series. All TCP/IP MIL-STDs are listed in Table 1.4; however, you don't want to use them. Important in their time, they have been superseded by RFCs and so are obsolete. Those RFCs and many others are also STDs. All the current specifications for TCP/IP are found in RFCs, particularly in the ones that are Internet Standards, or STD documents.

Internet Draft

Another online series of documents is also available from a number of well-known Internet hosts scattered around the world. Called **Internet Drafts,** these are documents intended to be RFCs that are first put online for review. However, the IAB does not consider the Internet Draft series to be "archival" publications [Cerf 1992]. Rather it views them as volatile storage for access to working documents. When a version of an Internet Draft is published as an RFC, it is no longer available as an Internet Draft. These documents are withdrawn for other reasons, such as their authors having decided they have served their purposes or they have reached the end of their accepted lifetime (Internet Drafts are always removed after they have been online for six months).

1.9   TCP/IP Technical Bodies

In this section we describe the bodies that produce the TCP/IP protocol specifications and Internet Standards, in particular the IAB and the IETF.

Internet Society (ISOC)

The **Internet Society (ISOC)** is an international nonprofit membership organization formed in January, 1992, to promote the use of the Internet for research and scholarly communication and collaboration [CNRI 1991]. Its activities includes education about how to use the Internet and exploration of new applications.

Members include individuals, who can vote for ISOC Trustees, and several classes of institutional members, who can't vote. ISOC holds an annual meeting and publishes a newsletter, *Internet Society News*.

Internet Architecture Board (IAB)

The IAB is responsible for design, engineering, and management of the TCP/IP protocols [Cerf 1990]. The IAB does not attempt to manage the Internet built out of those protocols. Rather it limits itself to the following functions [Cerf 1992]:

1. Providing a forum for communication and collaboration among network operators; Participants may include anyone who has run networks. Typically, this means regional networks.

2. Specifying and recommending technology.

The IAB doesn't require anybody to do anything and isn't involved in the daily operation of networks. It does issue standards, but these are adhered to voluntarily. Any participant network organization could presumably issue its own mandatory operational standards, but it is not known any that have.

Unlike the U.S. NSF, IAB membership is not limited to the U.S. or any other country. It has two Task Forces, one each for Engineering (the IETF) and Research (the **Internet Research Task Force (IRTF)** Of no fixed size, it currently consists of a Chairman, an Executive Director, the Chairs of the IRTF and IETF, an RFC Editor, and six other Members. The IETF and IRTF each have Steering Groups, the **Internet Engineering Steering Group (IESG)** and the **Internet Research Steering Group (IRSG)**. The IESG consists of the IETF Chair and Area Directors. There may be more than one Director per Area. The IRSG consists of the IRTF Chair and Research Group Chairs. The IRSG has a couple of Members-at-Large with no specific areas. The Chairs of the IESG and IRSG are the Chairs of the IETF and IRTF, respectively. These relationships are shown in Fig. 1.6, and we explore them in more detail in the next two subsections.

The IAB itself is self-perpetuating. The Chair is elected for a term of two years by the IAB members, and IAB members are appointed by the IAB Chair with the advice and consent of the other members.

IETF: Internet Engineering Task Force

Although the IAB is composed of technically competent people, many of whom were intimately involved in inventing the TCP/IP protocols, the IAB itself originates no technical work; it instead originates mostly architectural and technical policy recommendations. Detailed work on TCP/IP protocols and specifications for standardization is done by the IETF. The IETF has Working Groups that handle specific design and specification projects. The IETF meets three times a year (skipping fall). In addition to meetings of each Working Group, there is a plenary of all attendees. Working Groups may also meet outside of IETF meetings, and they regularly discuss drafts of documents and other issues using electronic mail.

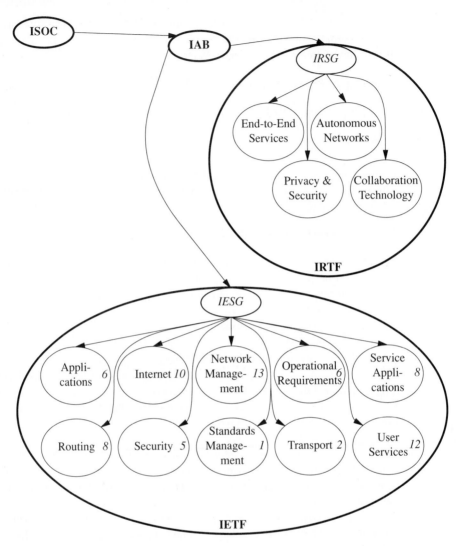

Figure 1.6 Internet working bodies, with working groups per IETF Area, 3 May 1993.
From Quarterman and Wilhelm, UNIX, POSIX, *and Open Systems, The Open
Standards Puzzle, Reading, MA: Addison-Wesley Publishing Company, Inc. © 1993.*
Reprinted with permission.

Groups are organized in technical Areas, each of which has a Director respon-
sible for coordinating the IETF Working Groups in that given technical area. The
Area Directors plus a Chair, Executive Director, and Secretary form the IESG.
The Chair of the IESG is the Chair of the IETF and a member of the IAB. The
IESG recommends actions on standardization to the IAB, which makes most
actual decisions.

The relationships among IETF, IESG, and IAB are shown in Table 1.4. The numbers in the right-hand corner of each IETF Area ellipse represent the number of IETF Working Groups in that Area, as of this writing, approximately 60.

IETF Working Groups are sometimes proposed by the IESG, but more commonly someone else, such as a researcher or vendor, comes forward with a proposal for one, usually because they want a standard way of doing something and are willing to pursue it into the IETF. The criteria for creation of a Working Group are as follows:

- A goal

- An expectation of success

- A community base (people who want the result)

- A provider base (people willing to work in the Working Group to produce that result)

Every IETF Working Group has a charter with projected milestones. Copies of that charter and related documents are kept in an anonymous FTP repository at *nri.reston.va.us* [Chapin 1992a].

Participation in the IETF is by individuals not by representatives of organizations. Membership in its Working Groups is open; simply attending IETF meetings or contributing to online Working Group discussions is enough to constitute IETF membership. According to one participant, "IETF membership is thus a state of mind" [Crocker 1992].

IRTF: Internet Research Task Force

Another IAB subgroup, the **Internet Research Task Force (IRTF)** is responsible for topics that are oriented more toward research than toward operational engineering. Research for this purpose is defined to involve either long-term or high-risk engineering or real research where the outcome is uncertain, that is, where failure is allowed [Cerf 1992]. The IRTF is structured into Areas like the IETF, although some members of the IRSG are not also Area Directors or officers.

1.10 The IAB Standards Process

The TCP/IP protocols historically have been specified and implemented with little formality. In the past, the IAB and IETF considered this informality to be a major factor in the success of the protocols. However, because there are many people who participate in creating TCP/IP protocols and still more involved in implementing and using those protocols, both have since seen the need for more formal, or at least more codified, processes. Consequently, they are modifying and codifying the historical process, although carefully to avoid killing the spirit of it. (For a more detailed examination of the current processes used by these bodies, see [Quarterman & Wilhelm 1993].)

It's worth reemphasizing that no book is the official source for procedures for any standardization process. In the case of TCP/IP standardization, the IAB document about the Internet Standards Process [Chapin 1992b] is an attempt by the IAB and IESG "to describe the procedures as we now understand them" [Cerf 1992]. "The Internet evolves, and the procedures evolve" [Postel 1992c].

States and Statuses

Internet Standards follow the IAB Standards Track, that is, they flow from being a Proposed Standard to a Draft Standard to an Internet Standard [Chapin 1992b; Postel 1992a], although some early specifications were grandfathered to standards status when the current procedures were defined. This process resembles many other other standards processes, such as that for the ISO, which has the states **Committee Draft (CD), Draft International Standard (DIS), and International Standard (IS).** But this IAB Standards Track also has an applicability status or requirement level in addition to the standardization state dimension. This leads to a two-dimensional standards track, as shown in Fig. 1.7.

Each protocol enters the IAB Standards Track with the goal of becoming an Internet Standard and eventually being used in the worldwide Internet. For this reason, IAB standardization has a very strong emphasis on implementation and testing by actual interoperation with other implementations, preferably on existing networks, where feasible. A protocol begins as a Proposed Standard and moves to Draft Standard and finally to Internet Standard, where it stays indefinitely until it is either superseded by a later protocol or otherwise retired. A Proposed Standard needs implementation by and interoperability testing between at least two groups before it is likely to be promoted to be a Draft Standard. A Draft Standard then needs widespread testing, some operational experience, and widespread comment before it can be promoted to be an Internet Standard. While this procedure might seem a slower path than for anticipatory standards, in general this isn't the case. Current Draft Standards are shown in Table 1.6.

There are other, offtrack, states. A protocol whose time has passed may be reclassified as Historic, whether or not it ever become a standard. Two states, called Informational and Experimental, are for protocols that are not intended for the Standards Track. The Informational, Internet Standard, and Historic states (shown as boxes in Table 1.6) are permanent, or at least there is no limit on how long a protocol may stay in one of those states. The others (shown as ellipses) are temporary. Classification of a protocol as a Proposed, Draft, or Internet Standard requires a recommendation from the IESG and approval by the IAB. As already mentioned, the RFC Editor may publish Informational or Experimental RFCs. A protocol may enter the final Historic state from any of the other states.

The requirement levels are, from highest to lowest, as follows:

• Required

• Recommended

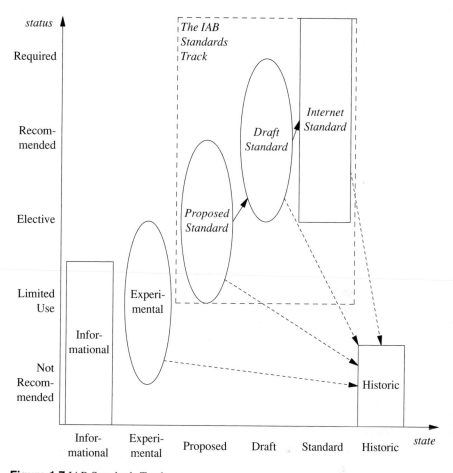

Figure 1.7 IAB Standards Track.
From Quarterman and Wilhelm, UNIX, POSIX, and Open Systems, The Open Standards Puzzle, *Reading, MA: Addison-Wesley Publishing Company, Inc.* © 1993.
Reprinted with permission.

• Elective

• Limited Use

• Not Recommended

The further along a protocol is in standardization state, the higher on this status scale it is likely to be. There are very few Required protocols and not many Recommended ones. Most are Elective.

At one time, the status of a protocol was kept in the protocol specification document. Currently, status information is kept in a related RFC called "IAB Official Protocol Standards." Because this RFC is reissued frequently as a new

Table 1.6 Draft Standards, September 1992.

Acronym	Name	RFC	Status
Application Layer			
FINGER	Finger Protocol	1288	Elective
POP3	Post Office Protocol, Version 3	1225	Elective
TOPT-LINE	Telnet Linemode Option	1184	Elective
NICNAME	WhoIs Protocol	954	Elective
Transport Layer			
TP-TCP	ISO Transport Service on top of the TCP	1006	Elective
Internet Layer			
IP-FDDI	Internet Protocol on FDDI Networks	1188	Elective
Network Layer			
PPP	Point to Point Protocol	1171	Elective
Network Management			
Concise-MIB	Concise MIB Definitions	1212	Elective
BOOTP	Bootstrap Protocol	951	Recommended
		1084	
Routing			
BGP3	Border Gateway Protocol 3 (BGP-3)	1267	Elective
		1268	
OSPF2	Open Shortest Path First Routing V2	1247	Elective

RFC with a new number, we don't suggest you depend on knowing the current RFC number [Postel 1992a]. Partly to simplify this situation, there is a new series of Internet Standard numbers. STD-1 is always the official protocol document, regardless of its current RFC number [Cerf 1992]. Assigning statuses in a separate status document avoids the need to reissue a protocol specification or other document as a new RFC just to change its status.

The requirement level of a protocol is increasingly context dependent. An RFC may also be assigned a status, or a set of statuses for various uses, by an AS. The most general AS's are the Requirements Documents, of which there are currently two, one each for hosts and for routers. An AS is basically a profile that describes how to fit protocols together to support certain applications, or certain platforms such as hosts or routers.

Table 1.7 Proposed Standards, applications, September 1992.

Acronym	Name	RFC	Status
Application Layer			
—	Representation of Non-ASCII Text...	1342	Elective
MIME	Multipurpose Internet Mail Extensions	1341	Elective
—	X.400 1988 to 1984 downgrading	1328	Elective
—	Mapping between X.400(1988)...	1327	Elective
NETFAX	File Format for the Exchange of Images...	1314	Elective
—	Replication and Distributed Operations...	1276	Elective
—	COSINE and Internet X.500 Schema...	1274	Elective
ISO-TS-ECHO	Echo for ISO-8473	1139	Elective
SUN-NFS	Network File System Protocol	1094	Elective
SUN-RPC	Remote Procedure Call Protocol	1057	Elective
NNTP	Network News Transfer Protocol	977	Elective
RLP	Resource Location Protocol	887	Elective

The IAB Standards Track

To enter the Standards Track as a Proposed Standard, such as those in Tables 1.7, 1.8, and 1.9, a protocol must have a good specification. To become a Draft Standard, the Proposed Standard must be implemented and tested by more than one organization. To become an Internet Standard, the protocol specified must be stable and must see actual use. Let's examine these three states of the Standards Track in detail, together with some interesting features of how a specification progresses through them. Although we have indicated status ranges for each of these states, usually only an Internet Standard has a fixed status. The status of a specification is given in the separate "IAB Official Protocol Standards" document [Postel 1992a], or in an AS. A protocol specification is called a TS. Either a TS or an AS can be a Proposed Standard, Draft Standard, or Internet Standard.

- To become a Proposed Standard, a specification should be stable technically and should have no known bugs or holes. For example, a basic algorithm cannot be left for later selection. There also should be sufficient community interest to predict or suggest community usage. If the nature of the specification is sufficiently complicated to be hard to understand or if the specification has an important effect on technical infrastructure, the IESG (or IAB) can require that the specification first be implemented and tested. An example of a specification with effects on technical infrastructure would be a modification to IP. How many implementations might be required is undetermined. Functionality cannot be

Table 1.8 Proposed Standards, infrastructure, September 1992.

Transport Layer			
TCP-EXT	TCP Extensions for High Performance	1323	Elective
OSI-UDP	OSI TS on UDP	1240	Elective
Internet Layer			
IPSO	DoD Security Options for IP	1108	Elective
IP-MTU	Path MTU Discovery	1191	Elective
IP-CMPRS	Compressing TCP/IP Headers	1144	Elective
IPX-IP	Tunneling IPX Traffic through IP Nets	1234	Elective
IP-SMDS	IP Datagrams over the SMDS Service	1209	Elective
IP-ARCNET	Transmitting IP Traffic over ARCNET Nets	1201	Elective
OSI-NSAP	Guidelines for OSI NSAP Allocation	1237	Elective
Network Layer			
	X.25 and ISDN in the Packet Mode	1356	Elective
PPP	Point-to-Point Protocol (PPP)	1331	Elective
IARP	Inverse Address Resolution Protocol	1293	Elective
—	Encoding Network Addresses...	1277	Elective
PPP-EXT	PPP Extensions for Bridging	1220	Elective
Link Layer			
PPP-LINK	PPP Link Quality Monitoring	1333	Elective

added once a specification becomes a Proposed Standard. A hole (a missing ancillary function) may be split into a separate specification; this might be called an extension. Otherwise, a standard that has reached Proposed state should be debugged only in that state; anything else requires reentering the Standards Track with a new specification. A protocol must stay in the Proposed state for a minimum of six months. A Proposed Standard will not normally have Required status and usually does not have a status lower than Limited Use.

• To become a Draft Standard, a protocol must have at least two independent and interoperable implementations that test all specified functions. There is no conformance certification. A protocol must stay in this state for a minimum of four months before being promoted to a Internet Standard. A Draft Standard can be Required and usually doesn't have a status lower than Elective.

• Full standards in the IAB Standards Track are called Internet Standards. To reach this state, a protocol must have had significant field use and there must be

Table 1.9 Proposed Standards on network management and routing, September 1992.

Acronym	Name	RFC	Status
Network Management			
—	Administration of SNMP	1353	Elective
SNMP-SEC	SNMP Security Protocols	1352	Elective
SNMP-ADMIN	SNMP Administrative Model	1351	Elective
TOS	Type of Service in the Internet...	1349	Elective
—	Def. Man. Objs Parallel-printer-like...	1318	Elective
—	Def. Man Objs RS-232-like...	1317	Elective
—	Def. Man. Objs. Character Stream...	1316	Elective
TABLE-MIB	IP Forwarding Table MIB	1354	Elective
FRAME-MIB	Management Information Base for Frame...	1315	Elective
SIP-MIB	SIP Interface Type MIB	1304	Elective
DECNET-MIB	DECNET MIB	1289	Elective
BRIDGE-MIB	BRIDGE-MIB	1286	Elective
FDDI-MIB	FDDI-MIB	1285	Elective
ETHER-MIB	Ethernet MIB	1284	Elective
RMON-MIB	Remote Network Monitoring MIB	1271	Elective
BGP-MIB	Border Gateway Protocol MIB (Version 3)	1269	Elective
OSPF-MIB	OSPF Version 2 MIB	1253	Elective
AT-MIB	Appletalk MIB	1243	Elective
STD-MIBs	Reassignment of Exp MIBs to Std MIBs	1239	Elective
DS3-MIB	DS3 Interface Objects	1233	Elective
DS1-MIB	DS1 Interface Objects	1232	Elective
802.5-MIB	IEEE 802.5 Token Ring MIB	1231	Elective
802.4-MIP	IEEE 802.4 Token Bus MIB	1230	Elective
GINT-MIB	Extensions to the Generic-Interface MIB	1229	Elective
OIM-MIB-II	OSI Internet Management: MIB-II	1214	Elective
CMOT	Common Management Information Services...	1189	Elective
Routing			
ICMP-ROUT	ICMP Router Discovery Messages	1256	Elective
IS-IS	OSI IS-IS for TCP/IP Dual Environments	1195	Elective

clear community interest in production use. There is no limit on the time a protocol may remain in this state and no mandatory review after a preset period; in fact, there is no mandatory review at all. An Internet Standard can have any status from Elective to Required but doesn't usually have a lower status.

The minimum time for a specification to reach Internet Standard status is 10 months and can take up to 24 months, after which time, it is "reviewed for viability."

Sometimes precision is avoided in Internet Standards to retain the human component in the process. The Internet process has succeeded because of individual effort, and the roles, skills, and integrity of the people involved in the effort are essential. Above all, interoperating protocols and systems are more important than formalities. A common phrase (attributed to David Clark) used to sum up the intent of the IETF and IAB is "rough consensus and working code."

Offtrack States

Apparently neither Informational nor Experimental RFCs have statuses [Chapin 1992a]. The following point out some features of these RFCs.

- Informational protocols are usually taken from some other source, such as OSI, or a vendor's proprietary protocol suite. This state, unlike the others, also is used for documents that don't describe protocols. Informational RFCs can describe procedures, practices, or perspectives. The only statuses permitted them are Limited Use and Not Recommended. But an AS may reference an Informational RFC and make the Informational RFC mandatory [Cerf 1992].

- An Experimental protocol is usually just that: a protocol for which its author, the RFC Editor, or the IAB thinks experimentation is appropriate. It might not be intended ever to see operational use. It is, however, intended to be of interest to, and to be used by, the participants in the experiment [Chapin 1992a]. An Experimental protocol can have Elective, Limited Use, or Not Recommended status.

- A Prototype state was recently introduced for protocols that differ somewhat from Experimental protocols. A Prototype is intended for eventual production use and is not a research experiment, whereas an Experimental protocol is not intended (or at least not ready) for moving into any production track [Cerf 1992].

- The Historic state is for protocols that are no longer (or never were) recommended for operational use. A protocol can move into the Historic state from any other state. Historic protocols may have only a status of Not Recommended.

1.11 A Final Word

The TCP/IP protocol suite is an evolutionary outgrowth of the early packet switching work of the ARPANET pioneers. With its roots firmly in the academic and research community, it has grown in both stature and commercial success well beyond the dreams of its inventors. In this chapter, we have offered you a taste of where TCP/IP came from and where it is evolving. We also have showed how the protocol has and will evolve and the necessary structures (standards committees, etc.) that give coherence to its evolution as it moves further away from its experimental roots. While it might appear at first glance that this is of little interest to a system administrator setting up a TCP/IP network using UNIX systems, most TCP/IP networks become a part of the Internet. Because the success of the Internet in turn depends on the smooth interoperability of its TCP/IP implementations, standardization is an increasingly important component in setting up a successful system.

References

Cerf 1990.   Cerf, Vinton, "The Internet Activities Board; RFC1160," *Network Working Group Requests for Comments* (RFC1160), Network Information Systems Center, SRI International (May 1990).

Cerf 1992.   Cerf, Vinton G., Personal communication (March 1992).

Cerf & Cain 1983.   Cerf, Vinton G., & Cain, Edward, "The DoD Internet Architecture Model," *Computer Networks* **7**(5), pp. 307–318 (October 1983).

Cerf & Kahn 1974.   Cerf, Vinton G., & Kahn, Robert, "A Protocol for Packet Network Interconnection," *IEEE Transactions on Communications* **COM-22**(5), pp. 637–648 (May 1974). Also in Partridge, *Innovations in Internetworking*, 1988.

Chapin 1992a.   Chapin, Lyman, Personal communication (14 April 1992).

Chapin 1992b.   Chapin, Lyman, "The Internet Standards Process; RFC1310," *Network Working Group Requests for Comments* (RFC1310), Network Information Systems Center, SRI International (March 1992).

CNRI 1991.   CNRI, "Announcing the Internet Society," Corporation for the National Research Initiatives, Reston, VA (July 1991).

Crocker 1992.   Crocker, Dave, Personal communication (3 February 1992 and 4 March 1992).

Kahin 1992.   Kahin, Brian ed., *Building Information Infrastructure: Issues in the Development of the National Research and Education Network,* McGraw-Hill, New York (1992).

Lottor 1992.   Lottor, Mark, "Internet Growth (1981-1991); RFC1296," *Network Working Group Request for Comments* (RFC1296), Network Information Systems Center, SRI International (January 1992).

Malamud 1992a.   Malamud, Carl, *Exploring the Internet: A Technical Travelogue,* Prentice-Hall, Englewood Cliffs, NJ (August 1992).

Malamud 1992b.   Malamud, Carl, *Stacks,* Prentice-Hall, Englewood Cliffs, NJ (1992).

Partridge 1991.   Partridge, Craig, "How Many Users are on the Internet," *Matrix News* **1**(3), p. 1, Matrix Information and Directory Services, Inc. (MIDS) (June 1991).

Partridge 1992.   Partridge, Craig, Personal communication (August–November 1988 and February 1992).

Postel 1992a.   Postel, Jon ed., "IAB Official Protocol Standards; STD-1/RFC-1360," *Network Working Group Requests for Comments*

(STD-1/RFC-1360), Network Information Systems Center, SRI International (September 1992).

Postel 1992b.   Postel, Jon, "Introduction to the STD Notes," *Network Working Group Request for Comments* (RFC1311), Network Information Systems Center, SRI International (March 1992).

Postel 1992c.   Postel, Jon, Personal communication (April 1992).

Quarterman 1990.   Quarterman, John S., *The Matrix: Computer Networks and Conferencing Systems Worldwide,* Digital Press, Bedford, MA (1990).

Quarterman 1991a.   Quarterman, John S., "Which Network, and Why It Matters," *Matrix News* **1**(5), p. 6–13, Matrix Information and Directory Services, Inc. (MIDS) (August 1991).

Quarterman 1991b.   Quarterman, John S., "Network Applications," UniForum, Santa Clara, CA (January 1991).

Quarterman 1991c.   Quarterman, John S., "Network Substrata," UniForum, Santa Clara, CA (January 1991).

Quarterman 1992a.   Quarterman, John S., "How Big is the Matrix?," *Matrix News* **2**(2), pp. 1,5–11, Matrix Information and Directory Services, Inc. (MIDS) (February 1992).

Quarterman 1992b.   Quarterman, John S., "Sizes of Four Networks in the Matrix," *Matrix News* **2**(7), p. 5–9, Matrix Information and Directory Services, Inc. (MIDS) (July 1992).

Quarterman & Wilhelm 1993.   Quarterman, John S., & Wilhelm, Susanne, *UNIX, POSIX, and Open Systems: The Open Standards Puzzle,* Addison-Wesley, Reading, MA (1993).

Rose 1989.   Rose, Marshall, *The Open Book: A Practical Perspective on Open Systems Interconnection,* Prentice-Hall, Englewood Cliffs, NJ (1989).

Stallings 1987.   Stallings, William, *The Open System Interconnection (OSI) Model and OSI-Related Standards,* vol. 1 of *Handbook of Computer Communications Standards,* Howard W. Sams, Indianapolis (1987).

Tennant et al. 1993.   Tennant, Roy, Ober, John, Lipow, Anne G., & Lynch, Foreword by Clifford, *Crossing the Internet Threshold: an Instructional Handbook*, 1993.

CHAPTER 2

TCP/IP Services

In this chapter we describe the most popular TCP/IP services available today. First, we sketch the client/server model that is used to build the services. We follow with an overview of IP routing and then describe the two major transport layer protocols: TCP and UDP. Next, we describe some distributed infrastructure services for naming and time synchronization. Naming protocols such as DNS are needed for most user-level services. Time synchronization is useful when using distributed file systems and necessary for secure user authentication.

Most of the chapter deals with services for direct use by end-users. We start with communication services — such as electronic mail, mailing lists, and news — and follow with resource sharing services — such as file transfer and remote login. We describe resource discovery services for people, files, documents, and general network resources. Finally, we mention protocols used to support network management functions.

In this quick overview of Internet services, we mention some services that we don't describe in detail later in the book and don't discuss some that we do describe later. The resource discovery services, for example, are quite new and are mostly used over wide-area networks (WANs) and on very large campuses, so we don't examine their technical underpinnings. In this chapter, we hope to give an idea of what kinds of services the TCP/IP protocols and its Internet infrastructure can and do support.

2.1 The Client/Server Model

Internet services are usually designed and implemented using the client/server model of computing. This model divides the service into three distinct parts, as shown in Fig. 2.1.

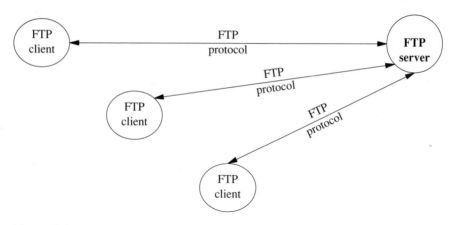

Figure 2.1 Client/Server Model.

Each of these parts performs a distinct function in implementing the client/server model, as follows:

1. The client process, which uses the service.

2. The server process, perhaps on another machine, which provides the service.

3. The protocol, which the client and server use to communicate with each other.

An Internet Standard for a TCP/IP service normally specifies the protocol and some aspects of the client and server. Most detail of the client, such as the user interface, are not described, as are implementation details of the server. A service protocol and a server may be designed to allow many client processes to use the same server process, or a server may serialize client access and field only one client request at a time.

This client/server model is not the same as the concept of Client/Server Computing that is often discussed in business schools and mainframe computing centers. That kind of **Management Information Science (MIS) Client/Server Computing** assumes that one machine is always the client and another machine is always the server. The server in that kind of computing is usually a mainframe or a dedicated fileserver that provides most of the computing resources, while the client is some much smaller machine, perhaps a personal computer (PC), that primarily just accesses resources on the server machine.

The client/server model used by TCP/IP involves processes running on machines not on dedicated client or server machines. Each host can have server processes for one or more application protocols and client processes using one or more servers, as shown in Fig. 2.2. A client process can communicate with a server process on any host that is running such a process. Also two hosts can each be running servers for the same application protocol and also each have client processes connecting to the other's server. We discuss how this works in more detail in Chapter 4.

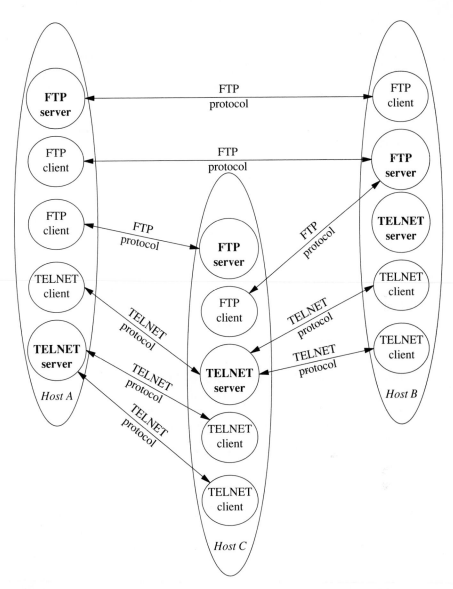

Figure 2.2 Client/Server Model.

The MIS kind of Client/Server Computing also is assumed by people familiar with personal computers such as the IBM PC and the Apple Macintosh. These are primarily machines that handle a single process at a time, so each such machine has to choose to be either a client or a server. But UNIX is a multiprocessing operating system. Processes in UNIX are cheap, and it's very common for multiple servers and clients to be running on the same machine. Many other operating systems, such as VMS, Mach, Chorus, and CMS, are also multiprocessing. The

TCP/IP protocols were invented for this kind of diverse environment of interconnected multiprocessing hosts. However, TCP/IP is also useful for personal computers. TCP/IP software for DOS and MacOS operating systems exists, and we discuss in Chapter 10 how to make it work in these environments and how to interconnect PC and Macintosh network protocols to TCP/IP.

2.2   The Internet Protocol and Routing

Routing in the Internet is accomplished essentially by a table on each host and router that indicates which interface to use to reach the destination network. Several methods are available for updating these tables, and we explore several of them in detail in Chapter 3. Here we list some of the most important, beginning with basic support protocols that handle routing error messages and address mappings and following with actual routing protocols.

Support Protocols

Support protocols handle routing redirects, routing error messages, and mappings between IP addresses and lower-layer addresses. They do not make routing decisions at the Internet layer, although they can be used by protocols that do make such decisions.

Internet Control Message Protocol (ICMP). ICMP is a required protocol that must be implemented in conjunction with IP. It handles basic control services such as sending error messages upon attempts to send packets to an unreachable host or network and other unrecoverable routing errors.

Address Resolution Protocol (ARP). Given an IP address, this protocol finds the corresponding datalink layer address by broadcasting on the local network a message that contains the IP address and then waiting for a response. Once an ARP response has been seen for an IP address, that pair of addresses is cached so that there will be no need to broadcast a request again, at least for some time (the cache entries eventually time out). ARP is commonly used over lower-layer datalink protocols that support broadcasting like Ethernet.

Reverse Address Resolution Protocol (RARP). Given a datalink layer address, this protocol finds an IP address. RARP is particularly useful for diskless workstations that need to find an IP address on startup.

Routing Protocols

These protocols make routing decisions at the Internet layer. An Internet router may be part of an **autonomous system (AS).** An AS is a collection of routers that are under a single administration. These routers run the same routing protocol, called an **interior gateway protocol (IGP).** There are several current IGPs, but all the routers in an AS normally run the same one. To communicate with another AS, a router usually uses an **exterior gateway protocol (EGP),** or an **inter-AS**

routing protocol, which doesn't know details of routing within another AS. An IGP is like a local telephone exchange, and an inter-AS protocol is like a long-distance operator.

Default Routing. Most hosts have only one network interface, and many LANs have only one router connecting them to the outside world. All a host on such a LAN needs for routing is a routing table consisting of one default route through that single router to every network. This is a standard feature of most UNIX systems.

Routing Information Protocol (RIP). The RIP is the oldest routing protocol commonly used in the Internet. It is designed for LANs and depends on broadcasting. The *routed* daemon found on most UNIX systems uses RIP.

Open Shortest Path First (OSPF). The OSPF probably will soon be the Internet Standard IGP. Unlike RIP, OSPF uses information on link speed and link state and can split traffic across multiple paths to the same destination.

Exterior Gateway Protocol (EGP). This was the first inter-AS protocol intended to connect an AS to a single core AS. It assumes the core AS has some means of routing to all other AS's. EGP is a reachability protocol; that is, it doesn't take link speed or state into account; it determines only how to get to the destination.

Border Gateway Protocol (BGP). BGP is a more current inter-AS protocol and is an update of EGP (the current version is BGP-3) and, like EGP, is a reachability protocol. The two differ primarily in that BGP supports more complex topologies than the simple core and stub AS star of EGP.

2.3   Transport Layer Protocols

Primarily two transport protocols are used with IP: TCP and UDP. We discuss how they work in Chapter 4.

Transmission Control Protocol (TCP)

TCP is a reliable two-way byte stream protocol and the most popular transport protocol. It's used for mail, file transfer, and remote login protocols. It also provides a reliable duplex byte stream, thus eliminating duplicate packets, handling retransmissions of lost packets, and ensuring data is delivered in order.

User Datagram Protocol (UDP)

UDP is an unreliable datagram protocol and is deliberately rudimentary. It doesn't ensure packets arrive in order, unduplicated, or at all. It just sends discrete messages, sometimes called datagrams, and delivers messages that arrive. The standard Internet name service, DNS, uses UDP, as do some transparent file access mechanisms.

2.4   Naming and Infrastructure

Most high-level Internet services require mapping of textual domain names to numeric IP addresses. Some other infrastructure services, such as time service, also have wide applicability. We describe only a few examples here.

Domain Name Service (DNS)

The Internet Standard DNS maps host names, such as *tic.com,* to IP addresses, such as 192.135.128.129. It is the most widely distributed service in the Internet.

The DNS namespace is partitioned hierarchically into a tree. Redundant nameservers field requests from clients for resource-name-to-resource-value mappings. Its protocol specifications define how DNS clients ask DNS servers for mappings and how DNS servers communicate with each other.

An organization not having an IP connection to the Internet nevertheless can arrange for its domain to be recognized on the Internet for the exchange of electronic mail. We discuss DNS in more depth in Chapter 5.

Network Information Service (NIS)

The NIS from Sun Microsystems provides another method of mapping domain names to addresses. It also can handle other mappings, such as user names to userids. It has some advantages over DNS on LANs but was not designed to deal with WANs. DNS should be used for domain nameservice across the Internet. More detail on NIS can be found in Chapter 5.

Network Time Protocol (NTP)

It's often useful to arrange for hosts to keep the same time of day. This can be done with NTP.

2.5   Communication Services

The most widespread use of computer networks, including the Internet, is to communicate with other people. Such services are known in the academic literature as **Computer Mediated Communication (CMC).** Since this whole book is about computers, let's just call them communication services.

Electronic Mail

The most commonly used network service is electronic mail, also commonly called email. To compose a mail message, you need a **user agent (UA).** There are many of these available on UNIX, including */bin/mail, Berkeley Mail, MH, mush, elm,* and *pine.* To actually transfer the mail message, the UA needs to communicate with a **message transfer agent (MTA),** also called a mailer. Several MTAs are popular with UNIX: *upas, smail, zmailer,* and *sendmail,* among others.

For difficult situations, the de facto standard UNIX mailer is still *sendmail*. For much more information on mail, see Chapter 7 and Chapter 8.

Simple Mail Transfer Protocol (SMTP). SMTP is the Internet Standard mail protocol. MTAs on the Internet, whether running on UNIX or not, use SMTP.

Multipurpose Internet Mail Extensions (MIME). A set of MIME have been specified recently and their use on the Internet is spreading. These extensions permit sending more than just the plain 7-bit ASCII text of traditional Internet mail by providing conventions for marking part of a message as being some kind of non-ASCII encoding.

Mailing Lists

Electronic mail is delivered to either a mailbox or a list of mailboxes. The term mailbox often applies to a single person, who then reads its contents. But mail also can be addressed to an alias, which is a mailing list that expands to many mailboxes or even to other aliases. Mailing lists provide ongoing forums for discussion of relatively specific topics. There are hundreds of such lists on the Internet [SRI 1992]. For more information on mailing lists, see Chapter 8.

USENET News

USENET news can handle very large discussion topics, called **newsgroups.** Once news is set up on a host, users of that host can access newsgroups more readily than even mailing lists. It's available over the Internet as well as other networks, such as BITNET, UUCP, and FidoNet. USENET itself is not a real network. It is simply the set of all hosts that interchange USENET news.

Network News Transfer Protocol (NNTP). The usual protocol for delivering and accessing USENET news over the Internet is NNTP. News servers use NNTP to transfer news among themselves. News clients use it to read and post news through a news server. For more on this protocol, see Chapter 9.

2.6   Resource Sharing

The original purpose of the earliest packet-switched network, the ARPANET, was resource sharing, that is, remote access to resources like supercomputers and file servers through the network. Resource sharing has also been used to justify NSFNET and NREN. While communications services might actually be more widely used, resource sharing services are quite important. It's also something that many networks, such as UUCP and FidoNet, don't have since it usually requires an interactive connection.

The traditional "big three," that is, the most-used, Internet services are the communication protocol SMTP, which we've already mentioned, and the resource sharing protocols FTP and TELNET. These are all Internet Standards and are required for Internet hosts.

In addition, 4.2BSD and 4.3BSD supplied several UNIX-specific protocols, including RCP (remote copy), RLOGIN (remote login), and RSH (remote shell). These R* (pronounced R star) protocols provide functionality similar to the Internet Standard protocols (RCP and FTP do file transfer and RLOGIN and TELNET perform remote login). But the R* protocols are quite specific to UNIX, making no allowances for different text line terminators or file formats. Their purpose was to extend basic UNIX functionality across a LAN of UNIX machines. The advantages of the R* protocols include simplified and convenient authentication and, in the case of RLOGIN, passing of more initialization parameters. We discuss these and other resource sharing services next.

File Transfer

The simplest way to access a file on another host across the network is to copy it to your local host.

File Transfer Protocol (FTP). The Internet Standard for file transfer is the FTP. It requires little setup; in fact, most vendors deliver machines with FTP configured.

A special FTP service called **anonymous FTP** requires more configuration, however. Ordinary FTP requires a remote user to have a normal user account on the FTP server host. Anonymous FTP permits any user on the Internet to access a carefully protected filesystem subtree using FTP. We discuss how this is done in Chapter 9 and how to use it in Appendix A. Anonymous FTP is particularly useful for retrieving programs and other information from the large number of Internet archive sites.

Remote Copy Protocol (RCP). 4.2BSD introduced RCP in the *rcp* command, whose user syntax is much like the UNIX *cp* file copy command. The RCP facility is designed to transfer files inside a department or organization where all machines have equivalent access to each other. Although convenient in such a situation, for security reasons it's not widely used across WANs.

Remote Login

To access a resource of a remote host, it can be convenient to actually log on to the remote host as if it were local. This can be done using the following protocols.

TELNET: Virtual Terminal Protocol. The Internet Standard for remote login is TELNET. Like FTP, TELNET is usually already configured by OS vendors.

Remote Login Protocol (RLOGIN). 4.2BSD also introduced RLOGIN. The UNIX *rlogin* command, the client side of this protocol, provides convenient local network login access. When properly configured, rlogin permits a user to log in on another host without typing a password. Access is controlled by several parameter files. Terminal type is also passed through automatically by the RLOGIN protocol. For more on this protocol, see Chapter 9.

Other Network Services

Many other Internet services are available. All those listed here are described in more detail in Chapter 9.

Inetd: the Server's Server. A host wanting to support many services could require a process for a server for each service. Even on UNIX systems, the number of idle server processes can quickly grow beyond a reasonable size, thus absorbing system resources unnecessarily, since servers typically spend most of their time waiting for connections from clients. The *inetd* server accepts connections for a range of protocols, invoking the appropriate servers when needed. This procedure reduces the number of processes, since an actual server process specific to a given protocol is needed only when inetd discovers a client request for that protocol. This mechanism also reduces the complexity of servers, since inetd can handle much of the complexity of setting up TCP or UDP connectivity appropriately.

Remote Procedure Call (RPC). The Sun **RPC (remote procedure call)** protocol is used to support Sun's NFS and NIS services. RPC also can be used to build a number of other interesting services that employ a function call interface.

Network File System (NFS). The Sun **Network File System (NFS)** provides **transparent file access (TFA)** over the network so that remote files appear as if they are local. NFS was designed for use over LANs and is widely used in such environments. It also was designed for use with many operating systems, not just UNIX. DOS and Macintosh NFS clients exist and are widely used.

Andrew File System (AFS). The AFS provides TFA. AFS was designed with efficiency over WANs in mind.

Printer Spooling. Many PC users still think erroneously that print spooling is a network's only use. The most common UNIX print spooling protocol is that of **Line Printing Protocol (LPR)** which was introduced with 4.2BSD.

User Validation. Several methods of user validation are used over networks. Traditional password protection requires the user to send the password over the network in cleartext. This can present a problem, however, because some network technologies, such as Ethernet, are very easy to monitor. The Berkeley R* protocols, such as RCP and RLOGIN, depend on lists of hostnames in a file, as we have noted. The target system then decides whether to permit a logon, which it does simply by looking at the remote user's logon name and without requiring a password. In this case, the remote system essentially trusts the local system to be secure. While better than passing passwords in cleartext across the network, it permits anyone who breaks into an account on one host to have access to any other host permitted in such a file. Newer mechanisms include **Kerberos,** which uses encryption to authenticate users.

System logging (syslog). One service users usually don't care about is system logging. It's important to system administrators, however. One common mechanism for system logging on UNIX hosts is called *syslog*, which permits logging to be directed to any host on the network.

Remote Shell Protocol (RSH). The RSH is another Berkeley R* protocol. It uses the same user validation mechanism as the RCP and RLOGIN protocols and permits the user to run a shell command on the remote machine. This is a form of remote job execution.

2.7   Resource Discovery Services

The Internet has become so big that finding a file, document, resource, or person has become a huge problem. Fortunately, recently resource discovery services have appeared. Following are some examples. Note, we don't discuss these in detail elsewhere in this book. Many of these services are new and their protocols are still evolving as the Internet community gains experience with them.

Finding People

Electronic mail is useful but only if you know the mail address of the person you want to reach. Many services have been developed to deal with this problem.

WHOIS: A centralized user database server. The WHOIS service uses a centralized database to maintain information on people who ask to be listed, such as their electronic mail address, telephone number, and postal address. This service is convenient, but only a few of the millions of Internet users are listed.

finger: A local user database server. The finger protocol allows remote users to query information about users on a specific host. This service distributes the information as locally as possible but addresses neither the problem of ensuring that everyone is listed nor that of finding the host a person uses.

netfind: A person locator. The netfind facility uses finger, SMTP, DNS, and other protocols to try to locate the electronic mail address of a person. To find people, it uses the structure of the Internet itself rather than a separate database.

X.500: Directory and Name Service. X.500 is the ISO-OSI Directory and Name Service. Although implemented in several forms on the Internet, it's not widely used.

Finding Files and Documents

Resource sharing protocols like FTP are very useful but only if you first know the resource's location.

archie: An archive index. Hundreds of gigabytes of information are available on the Internet by anonymous FTP. But how do you find the right anonymous FTP server? With archie, which polls thousands of FTP servers monthly, compiles a composite index, and makes that index accessible to users.

Prospero: Transparent anonymous FTP access. The Prospero protocol permits anonymous FTP servers to be used as if the files on them were local to the client machine. It also permits building both temporary and permanent classifications of files and directories.

Wide Area Information Servers (WAIS). Finding files is often not enough. Finding documents, or passages within documents, is often more useful. The WAIS are one approach to this problem. WAIS supports keyword searches of arbitrary textual databases without requiring markup of the documents.

Network Service User Interfaces

The various new resource discovery services each have strong points; unfortunately they also each have different user interfaces and protocols, as does FTP. Many resources are accessible only through TELNET to idiosyncratic, locally designed user interfaces; library catalogs are particularly notorious for this kind of gratuitous variation. The average user, however, just wants to find and use the resources.

gopher: An interactive menu-oriented front end. So far, the most popular solution to finding diverse resources through diverse interfaces and protocols is gopher. Called "duct tape for the Internet," a gopher server displays menus of resources, some of which can be other gopher servers. Gopher also can call archie, WAIS, TELNET, or FTP directly.

veronica: A gopher server index. Given hundreds of gopher servers, how do you know which one you want? You can walk through hierarchical menus from server to server until you stumble over the right one, or you can use veronica. Veronica, available through gopher, is an index to the names of gopher servers, much as archie is an index to filenames.

World Wide Web (WWW). WWW is a networked hypertext protocol and user interface. It provides access to multiple services and documents like gopher does but is more ambitious in its reach. WWW permits users to select words or phrases within a document that retrieves other documents, in hypertext fashion. It also requires documents it serves to be marked up with **Simplified Generic Markup Language (SGML).**

2.8   Network Management

We discuss some details of network management in Chapter 11.

Remote distribution (rdist)

This Berkeley command was originally intended as a stopgap before TFAs were available. Essentially, it copies a list of files from one system to another, suppressing copies of files that are already up to date and handling different file types.

Rdist (Remote Distribution) also is useful for keeping TFA servers up to date in situations where duplicate servers are being used for reliability.

Simple Network Management Protocol (SNMP)

The Internet uses SNMP to manage diverse components of the networks across the Internet itself. While use of SNMP is spreading, it's still mostly the province of network connectivity providers not of end users. We discuss SNMP in Chapter 11.

References

SRI 1992.   SRI, *Internet: Mailing Lists,* SRI International, Menlo Park, CA
        (1992).

## CHAPTER 3

How IP Works: The Key to Internetworking

IP is the centerpiece of the TCP/IP protocol stack. Much like the center of an hourglass, IP funnels data to and from the protocols above and below it. It lets an internetwork use many different link layer protocols and allows applications to employ different transport layer protocols. In many ways, IP is very simple. However, it has one important advantage over simpler protocols: it hides the differences between the datalink protocols from the transport protocols that end-user applications use. By doing this, it enables you to replace old datalink technologies with newer and faster technologies without having to change application codes. Thus applications written against a transport protocol interface are portable across a wide range of link layer technologies. As discussed in Chapter 1 the TCP/IP Model Link Layer is identical to the OSI Model Data Link Layer. To avoid terminology confusion, in this chapter we will use the term "datalink" when referring to a protocol at the TCP/IP Model Link Layer or the OSI Model Data Link Layer.

3.1   IP Addressing

IP defines a single virtual network address space within which each host network interface has a unique address. The Internet is part of the official and only sanctioned instance of the IP address space, which also includes a number of isolated IP networks that exist outside the Internet. An isolated network can duplicate IP addresses in use on the Internet but can interconnect with the Internet only by using an officially assigned network number.

If a machine has more than one network interface, each interface has a separate IP address. Network practitioners often refer to a *host* address when they really mean the host's network *interface* address. Hosts do not have IP addresses; network interfaces do. Unfortunately, the protocol specifications found in the various RFCs more often use *host* than *interface*, so, for consistency, we will follow the official nomenclature, even though it is somewhat misleading.

The IP address space is four bytes wide. Conveniently, four bytes is a common size for integers on most modern computer systems. Usually an IP address is written in **dotted-decimal** notation, where each byte appears as a decimal number separated by periods, arranged from high-order byte to low-order byte. For example, the dotted-decimal number 128.83.12.14 is equivalent to 2,152,926,222 decimal or 0x80530C0E. When the address is represented in base 2, the highest-order bit in each byte is the leftmost bit. Note that the byte and bit ordering are important; when an IP address is a field in a data packet, it is transmitted as a byte stream, high-order byte first.

To simplify routing, an IP address is divided into a **network number** and a **host number.** For all machines to communicate successfully, every network interface on the same physical network must have the *same* network number and a *unique* host number. Originally, IP used the high-order byte as the network number and the lower-order three bytes as the host number [Postel 1980]. Up to 254 networks were permitted, each with 16,777,214 (2^{24}–2) hosts. The network number and host number with all bits set to 0 or all bits set to 1 are always reserved, reducing by 2 the total number of usable networks and hosts.

Address Classes

Soon after IP was first specified, it became obvious there would be more than 254 interconnected networks. However, a clever encoding of the high-order bits in the high-order byte of the IP address lets the network number be 1, 2, or 3 bytes long, with the remaining byte(s) used for the host number [Postel 1981]. The encoding divides the address space into five address classes, A through E. Table 3.1 shows the five classes and bit encoding. We write the network number in dotted-decimal notation with the host portion of the address set to all 0's to distinguish it from any specific host address. Class A through class C are the most commonly used address types. Class D is used for multicast addresses. Class E is unused except for one address and otherwise is reserved for future use.

Table 3.1 IP Address Classes.

Class	High Order Bits of First Byte				Network Range		Host Range	
	0	1	2	3	Low	High	Low	High
A	0	–	–	–	0.0.0.0	127.0.0.0	0.0.0	255.255.255
B	1	0	–	–	128.0.0.0	191.255.0.0	0.0	255.255
C	1	1	0	–	192.0.0.0	223.255.255.0	0	255
D	1	1	1	–	224.0.0.0	239.255.255.255	N/A	N/A
E	1	1	1	1	240.0.0.0	255.255.255.255	N/A	N/A

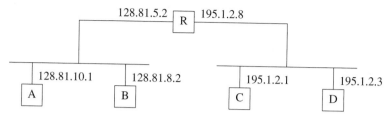

Figure 3.1 Valid IP Address Assignment.

As of this writing, several proposals are under discussion regarding changing the IP address class structure [Wang & Crowcroft 1992] and [Callon 1992]. Some of these recommend replacing IP, which would require a complete revamping of all IP software currently in the field. Others call for extending the current address structure while leaving in place the current class structure for existing machines.

When an IP address is written in dotted-decimal notation, you can easily determine the class of the address from the bit encoding simply by referring to the value of the highest-order byte. Addresses in each class are numerically contiguous. IP allows the host number to be further subdivided by using subnets. We will discuss subnets in more detail later in this chapter.

Address Assignment

Regardless of the address class, all hosts on a single physical network must have the same network number and a unique host number. For example, you could assign IP addresses to an internetwork consisting of two network segments linked by a router, as shown in Fig. 3.1. The router R in this figure has two IP addresses associated with it — one for each interface. All interfaces connected to the same physical network have the same network number. For example, if you add a new host to network 128.81.0.0, you need to use network number 128.81.0.0 and give it a unique host number. Similarly, if you add a new host to network 195.1.2.0, then its network number must be 195.1.2.0. Figure 3.2 shows an invalid IP address assignment. Note that in this figure, Host E's interface has an incorrect network number; Host E therefore will be unable to communicate with the other machines on the two networks.

Reserved Addresses

Some IP addresses are reserved for special use. For example, a network number with all bits set to binary 0 means "this network"; similarly, a host number with all bits set to 0 means "this host." By extension, an IP address consisting of all binary 0's refers to "this host" on "this network." These addresses can be used only as source addresses and not as destination addresses. A host uses them when it doesn't know all or part of its own IP address. The RARP and BOOTP protocols exploit these reserved addresses when they are used to boot a diskless client that doesn't know either its own IP address or what IP network it is attached to.

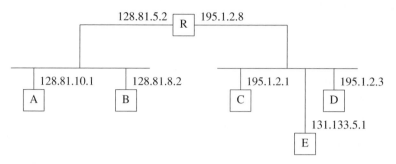

Figure 3.2 Invalid IP Address Assignment.

The host number with all bits set to 1 is reserved as a **broadcast address.** An IP packet with a broadcast destination address is sent to and processed by all hosts on that IP network. The most common broadcast address uses the network number in conjunction with an all-1's bit host part, where the all-1's host address means "any host." For example, on the IP network 128.81.0.0, the IP address 128.81.255.255 is the broadcast address. Some older software uses an all-0's host part as the broadcast address. Although this is incorrect, to ensure backward compatibility all IP implementations must recognize these old broadcast addresses when they are used as destination addresses.

The Class E address 255.255.255.255 is a special case that refers to "any host on this network." This address can be used only as a destination address, and a packet with this address will be broadcast only to hosts on the same physical network as the sender of the packet.

3.2   Message Encapsulation and Framing

The IP address space enables you to construct large internetworks concatenated from many different datalink networks. Each datalink protocol has its own addressing scheme and has no knowledge of IP addressing. All hosts using IP share the same virtual network address space. IP maps each host datalink address to an IP address. IP encapsulates a transport layer **message** into a **packet** and creates a datalink **frame** for transporting the packet on a physical network. Strictly speaking, the datalink layer frames an IP packet. Most IP implementations, however, put together much of the framing information before passing the packet to the datalink driver.

Since different higher-level transport protocols layered on top of IP can send messages that are larger than the frame size of the underlying network hardware, IP also does **fragmentation** of packets when they are transmitted on a datalink network that can't accommodate the original packet size or **reassembly** of the pieces of a previously fragmented packet.

The process of packetizing, framing, fragmenting, and reassembling are the fundamental IP operations. These operations give IP the flexibility to operate with many different physical network media and many different transport protocols.

The IP Header

IP packetizes a message by creating an IP packet for each message it receives from a transport protocol. Each packet consists of an IP header, followed by the actual transport protocol message, which, as far as IP is concerned, is simply a sequence of bytes. For example, given a message of 200 bytes, IP would create a packet consisting of an IP header, followed by the 200-byte message. Figure 3.3 shows the format of the IP header.

- *version*
  The version number of IP; currently, version number 4 is deployed.

- *hlen*
  The length of the IP header in 32-bit words. The header is always padded out to a multiple of 32-bit words.

- *tos*
  The type of service or priority for this packet. Type of service processing is not used very often, so it is almost always set to the default value of 0.

- *length*
  The length of the IP packet (including the header) in bytes.

- *fragid*, *flags*, and *fragoff*
  Used for fragmentation and reassembly control.

- *ttl*
  The maximum time in seconds — the **time-to-live** — that the packet may exist. This field is decremented by at least 1 each time the IP header is processed by a router or a host. Unless the packet is queued in a buffer for a long period of

Figure 3.3 IP Header.

0 3	4 7	8 15	16 23	24 31
version	hlen	tos	length	
fragid			flags	fragoff
ttl		protocol	checksum	
source				
destination				
options			padding	

time, this field actually indicates the maximum number of intermediate routers a packet may cross before it is dropped. Note, whenever this field reaches 0, IP must drop the packet unconditionally. This feature prevents a packet from looping around the network forever because of a routing error. As of this writing, the *ttl* field is usually set by the sending system to 30, which is currently sufficiently large, since no IP network on the Internet today is more than 30 hops from any other network.

• *protocol*
Indicates the type of protocol message encapsulated within the IP packet. The protocol field value is 6 for TCP and 17 for UDP. These are not the only possible values, however, as other specialized protocols use different values. For a list of valid *protocol* field values, see [Reynolds & Postel 1992].

• *checksum*
The 16-bit 1's complement sum of all 16-bit words in the IP header. This field checks for transmission errors that might have corrupted important header information. This is the only error-checking that IP does, other than routing errors. IP simply moves packets through the internetwork using a best-effort algorithm. Note, it is a checksum of the header only; the higher-layer protocols must handle error checking of the encapsulated message. For instance, a packet can be lost enroute to its destination because of transmission errors or a router might deliberately drop a packet because of buffer space shortage. Also, IP may deliver a packet more than once. It is up to the protocol that composed the encapsulated message to be aware of these possible problems and take the appropriate action.

• *source*
The IP address of the interface from which the packet originated.

• *destination*
The IP address of the packet's final destination regardless of the number of intermediate routers the packet may pass through. Because each IP packet contains the original source and the final destination IP addresses, the packet is self-contained and can be routed independently to its destination.

• *options*
The options an IP header may contain. Although an IP header may contain options, most do not. Options include the following:

  • *source routing*
  Enables an IP packet's route to be explicitly controlled.

  • *route recording*
  Records the route of the packet in the *options* field.

  • *timestamping*
  Adds a timestamp by each intermediate router.

  • *security*
  Includes various seldom-used security options.

• *padding*

Pads the IP header to an even 4-byte boundary. This is occasionally needed because not all IP options are even multiples of 32 bits.

Datalink Frame Creation

IP is not finished when it creates a packet; it also needs to determine which network interface to use and then pass enough information to the datalink protocol output module so it can properly encapsulate the IP packet in a datalink protocol frame. Frame formats are specific to each datalink protocol used. Ethernet, a common LAN medium, has a 14-byte frame header and a 4-byte frame trailer. The header contains the 6-byte Ethernet destination address, the 6-byte Ethernet source address, and a 2-byte type field. The trailer is a 4-byte cyclic redundancy check of the entire frame. When sending a packet on an Ethernet, IP passes to the datalink protocol output module the Ethernet destination address, the Ethernet type field value that indicates that the encapsulated packet is an IP packet, and the IP packet itself. The Ethernet datalink protocol output module in turn sets the source Ethernet address to the Ethernet address of the network interface it uses to transmit the frame and then calculates the Ethernet checksum. Figure 3.4 shows an IP packet encapsulated within an Ethernet frame. The 8 byte preamble that marks the start of each frame is not shown.

Ethernet addresses are shown as 6 hexadecimal bytes separated by colons and with the high-order byte first. In this figure, the destination Ethernet address is 80:20:5:3:2:8 and the source Ethernet address is 80:1:20:0f:1:4. The *type* field is set to 0x0800. This number identifies the frame contents as an IP packet and tells the host to give the packet, stripped of its Ethernet frame, to the IP input module for processing. Other network protocols, such as DECNet or Appletalk, use a different type field value. Thus multiple network protocols can use the same datalink protocol simultaneously.

Figure 3.4 IP Ethernet Encapsulation.

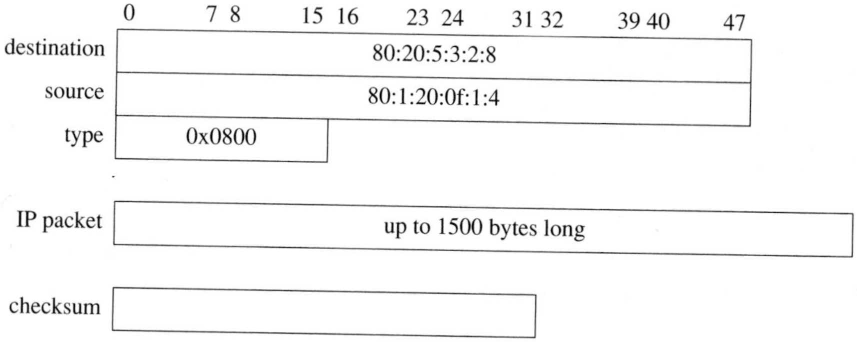

The source Ethernet address is the address of the last interface that transmitted the frame, while the destination Ethernet address is the destination address of the next Ethernet interface on the same physical network where the frame will be received. The source and destination Ethernet addresses refer only to the same interfaces as the source and destination IP addresses when the source and destination hosts are attached to the same physical network. If an interface sends the frame to an intermediate router, the destination Ethernet address is the address of the interface of the intermediate router. In this case, the destination IP address does not refer to the router's IP interface address, but rather to the interface address of the final destination.

Figure 3.5 shows how a router connecting two Ethernets reframes a packet sent from Host A on one Ethernet to Host B on the other Ethernet. The router strips the Ethernet frame from the IP packet, examines the IP destination address, and reframes the IP packet in another Ethernet frame that the router then forwards to Host B. Note that the source and destination IP addresses remain the same throughout the life of the packet.

Other datalink protocols have their own frame formats. For example, **IEEE 802.3** (a baseband network very similar to Ethernet), **IEEE 802.4** (Token Bus), and **IEEE 802.5** (Token Ring), all use the **IEEE 802.2** frame format. The primary difference between 802.2 and Ethernet frame format is that the Ethernet *type* field becomes an 802.2 *length* field, which is the number of bytes of data encapsulated in the frame. Also, 802.2 uses a **Logical Link Control (LLC)** protocol extension called the **Sub Network Access Protocol (SNAcP)** to encapsulate IP packets. In this case, a 3-byte LLC header followed by a 5-byte SNAP header is placed at the

---

Figure 3.5 IP Reframing.

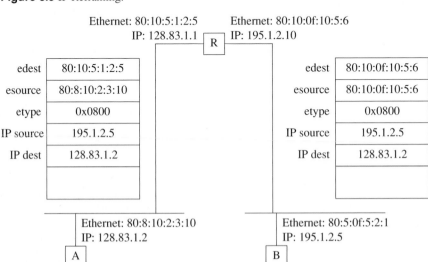

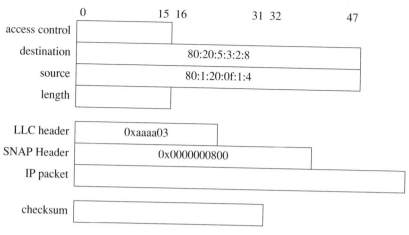

Figure 3.6 Token Ring Encapsulation Using SNAP.

beginning of the encapsulated packet. The LLC header for SNAP has the value 0xAAAA03. The SNAP header is divided into a 3-byte organization code and a 2-byte *ethertype* field. For IP encapsulation, the organization code is set to 0x000000. The *ethertype* field uses the same codes as the *type* field in the Ethernet header. Figure 3.6 shows an example Token Ring frame with a SNAP header.

Fragmentation and Reassembly

IP also fragments and reassembles packets as it passes them from one datalink medium to another datalink medium that has a different maximum frame size. An IP packet can be up to 65,536 bytes in length; the packet size is limited by the 2-byte width of the packet length field in the IP header. However, most datalink protocols support only physical frames of at most a few thousand bytes in length, which is a small fraction of the biggest potential IP packet. The largest amount of encapsulated data a network interface can transmit is called the **maximum transmission unit (MTU).** Fragmentation and reassembly bridges the difference between the large IP packets and the MTU of a specific datalink protocol.

Fragmentation divides a single IP packet into several smaller packets, each called a **fragment,** that can fit within the MTU of the datalink protocol. Each fragment has its own IP header. Fields within the header indicate that the fragment is a piece of an oversized IP packet. For example, Ethernet supports an MTU of 1500 bytes, excluding the Ethernet frame header and trailer. If IP wants to use Ethernet to send a 2000-byte packet, IP will divide the packet into two smaller packets, each of which can fit within the MTU limitation.

Suppose the original packet has a 20-byte IP header and 1980 bytes of data. IP splits the original packet into two fragments. The first would be 1500 bytes long: An IP fragment header of 20 bytes (assuming there are no IP options in the header) followed by the first 1480 bytes of data. Note, the data size must be an even multiple of 8 bytes. The reason for this is that the *fragoff* field in the IP header, which indicates the starting byte position of the fragment, is only 13 bytes long, so it counts bytes in multiples of eight ($2^{13} \times 8 = 65,536$ which is the maximum size of an IP packet). The second fragment would be 540 bytes long, which is the size of the remainder of the message (520 bytes) plus the size of the second fragment's IP header (20 bytes).

IP uses the MF flag (the lowest of the 3 bits in the *flags* field of the IP header) and the *fragoff* field in the IP header of a fragment to identify the packet as a fragment and to know where each fragment is to be placed when it is eventually reassembled. The first packet's *fragoff* is 0; the second's is 185 ($8 \times 185 = 1480$). IP sets the *fragid* field in each packet to the same unique value and uses this field to identify each part of a fragmented packet. In Fig. 3.7, both fragments have an ID of 1111. The first fragment sets the MF flag to 1; the second has an offset of 185 and since this is the last fragment, it sets the MF flag to 0.

Figure 3.7 IP Fragmentation.

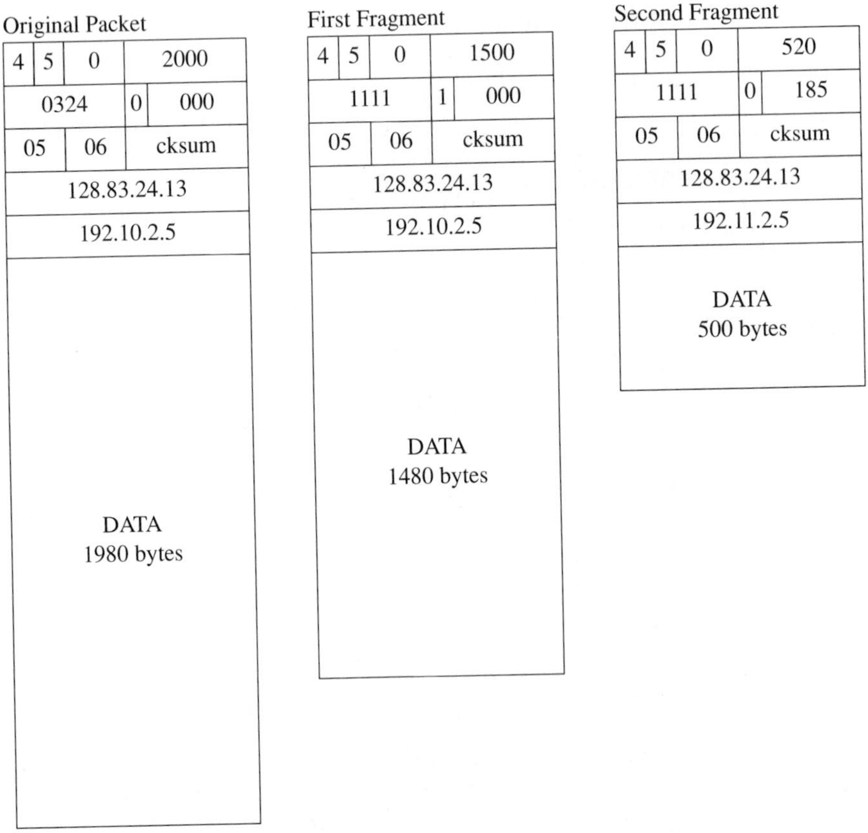

Original Packet

4	5	0	2000
0324		0	000
05	06		cksum
128.83.24.13			
192.10.2.5			
DATA 1980 bytes			

First Fragment

4	5	0	1500
1111		1	000
05	06		cksum
128.83.24.13			
192.10.2.5			
DATA 1480 bytes			

Second Fragment

4	5	0	520
1111		0	185
05	06		cksum
128.83.24.13			
192.11.2.5			
DATA 500 bytes			

Packet reassembly simply reverses the fragmentation process. When a fragment is received, IP holds it in a reassembly queue until all fragments with the same *fragid* are received. Then when the first fragment with a new *fragid* is received, it starts a timer. IP must receive all subsequent fragments before the timer expires.

IP sets the timer to an initial value of 15 seconds. Each time another fragment arrives, IP resets the timer to the greater of the *ttl* of the arriving fragment or of the current timer value. If the timer expires for a *fragid*, IP discards any fragments with that *fragid* in the reassembly queue. Once IP receives all the fragments, it reassembles the original packet and handles it like a normal unfragmented IP packet. IP usually reassembles packets only at the final destination of the packet. However, if the MTU of the outgoing interface permits, an intermediate router is free to reassemble fragments and pass them along as a larger IP packet. In practice, this is rarely done because the cost of reassembly is often higher than that of simply sending the fragments and letting the final destination handle the reassembly. The packet in the latter instance might have to be fragmented again before it reaches its final destination, which adds additional overhead. In any case, if an intermediate router does reassembly, it is completely transparent to the source or destination of the packets. Also dynamic routing may send fragments along different paths to the final destination. So intermediate reassembly is also not advisable for this reason.

Avoiding Fragmentation

For packets with a destination on the same physical network as the original sender, the MTU is known by the sending host because it is a parameter that is a part of every network interface specification. A transport protocol then can use the MTU to limit the message size it passes to IP; therefore a message will never be fragmented. When a transport protocol builds a message for a host on a different network, it has no way of knowing the route of the packet or the MTU of each physical network the packet will be transmitted over along the route.

Because of dynamic routing, the route the packet takes may change. Therefore IP must be able to fragment and reassemble large packets. Fragmentation and reassembly are expensive, however, especially on internetworks that experience frame loss. If the destination host doesn't receive even a single fragment of a packet, then all the fragments must be retransmitted or they will all be lost. Consequently, the transport protocols use a default MTU of 576 bytes when transmitting messages to a host many router hops away. A packet 576 bytes in length supports a 512-byte message plus a 20-byte TCP header plus a 20-byte IP header, with a little room left over for options. Most datalink protocols support an MTU of at least 576 bytes, which almost guarantees that a packet of 576 bytes or less is never fragmented. These simple heuristics allows IP to optimize use of the local network media (where most of the traffic occurs), while avoiding unnecessary and sometimes expensive fragmentation for long-haul traffic.

3.3   Support Protocols

Internet Control Message Protocol

An integral part of IP is the **Internet Control Message Protocol (ICMP).** ICMP sends information and control messages between IP hosts. Routers generate most ICMP messages to inform hosts either that a packet could not be delivered because of an error or that a better route exists to a particular destination. ICMP messages are sent like other transport protocol messages, that is, they are encapsulated in an IP packet. These messages set the IP *protocol* field to 1. The most common types of ICMP messages are as follows:

- *destination unreachable*
  When a router cannot find a routing table entry for the destination of an IP packet it has received, it sends a *destination unreachable* message to inform a host that no route exists to a specific network.

- *routing redirect*
  A router sends a *routing redirect* message to inform a host that a better route to a destination exists on another router. This message contains the IP address of the better router. The host is then expected to update its routing tables in response to the message and send all subsequent packets for the destination network to the new router. Note, the first router forwards the first packet received from the host to the new router before it sends the *routing redirect* message.

- *time expired*
  A *time expired* message indicates a packet's *ttl* field has reached 0. Usually, sending this message is a result of a routing configuration error or a transient routing loop caused by a malfunctioning router. IP puts the header of the expired packet into the data part of the ICMP message.

- *echo request* and *echo reply*
  An *echo request* is a message containing an arbitrary amount of data sent to a host asking that host to echo back the message in an *echo reply* message. The UNIX *ping* program enables you to send *echo request* messages to remote hosts. Using this program, you can determine whether a remote host is up and running. *ping* also timestamps each message, so it can calculate the round-trip time with a great deal of accuracy.

ICMP also is useful for network debugging. Monitoring ICMP messages can tell you a great deal about the state of a network. ICMP packets should only be generated occasionally. A high volume of these messages usually indicates a badly misconfigured network. Most UNIX operating systems keep counts of ICMP messages both sent and received. By monitoring these counts, you can tell a great deal about the state of your network. We will discuss this topic more in Chapter 12.

The Address Resolution Protocol

The IP address space is a virtual address space that has no addressing relationship to the underlying datalink protocols. Every network interface has an IP address associated with it and every network interface, except for point-to-point links, also has a datalink protocol address associated with it. Point-to-point links often do not have any associated datalink addresses since they have only a single destination. In this case, no address mapping needs to be done.

Datalink protocol addresses vary widely in format. For example, Ethernet addresses are 6 bytes in length; IBM Token Ring addresses are either 2 or 6 bytes long; ARCNET, developed originally by Datapoint, uses 1-byte addresses; and FDDI uses either 2-byte or 6-byte addresses. When IP wants to frame a packet, it needs to pass to the datalink output module the datalink address of the destination interface to which the datalink protocol will deliver the frame.

Suppose IP is sending a packet to a remote host on the same Ethernet. IP needs the destination Ethernet address to properly construct the frame header. You could manually create a table that maps an interface's IP address to its corresponding Ethernet address. Then when IP needs an Ethernet address, it could look up the corresponding IP address in the table. A manual table can be easily constructed and maintained for a small number of hosts on a network. On a large network, however, a manual table quickly becomes unmanageable because every time a new host is added to the network, you need to update the address mapping table for every host on the network.

You can automate the process of updating the address table by using the **Address Resolution Protocol (ARP).** ARP maps any network level address (such as IP) to its corresponding datalink address (such as Ethernet). The idea is to ask for and receive updates to mappings using the network itself. ARP does this by exploiting the broadcasting capability of most LAN datalink protocols.

ARP is described in [Plummer 1982]. While this particular reference talks specifically about Ethernet as the datalink protocol, the description of ARP is much more general and can be used by any datalink protocol that supports broadcasting. The reference also refers to *hardware* and *protocol* addresses. For consistency, we will refer to a hardware address as a datalink address and a protocol address as a network address. An ARP packet has the general format shown in Fig. 3.8 and explained next.

- *datalink type*

The assigned numeric type of the datalink protocol. The latest assigned numbers RFC as of this writing, [Reynolds & Postel 1992], includes a list of the datalink protocols that support AR and their datalink type. Ethernet, for example, has a datalink address type of 0x0001. Other datalink protocols use different numbers.

- *network type*

Indicates the type of network address used. For IP, this field is identical to the Ethernet type used for IP (0x0800).

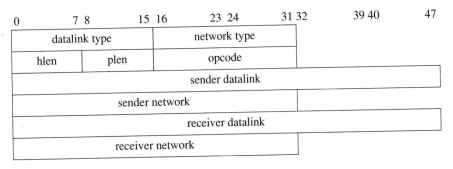

Figure 3.8 ARP Packet Format.

- *hlen*
  The length in bytes of the datalink addresses. For Ethernet, this is set to 6.

- *plen*
  The length in bytes of the network addresses. For IP, the length is always 4.

- *opcode*
  0x0001 indicates an ARP request; 0x0002 indicates an ARP reply.

- *sender datalink* and *sender network*
  For both a request and a reply, set by the sender of the ARP packet, which fills in its own datalink and network addresses.

- *target network*
  On a request, filled in with the IP address of the target; on a reply, filled in with the original sender's IP address.

- *target datalink*
  On a request, filled in with 0; on a reply, filled in with the original sender's datalink address.

An ARP packet is encapsulated in a datalink frame. For Ethernet frames, the *type* field is 0x0806; for 802.2 frames, the same value is used in the SNAP *ethertype* field. An ARP request is broadcast on the local network using the broadcast address of the datalink media being used to send the request. ARP replies are broadcast using the datalink address found in the *sender datalink* field of an ARP request. So the sequence for an ARP request/reply is as follows: A request is broadcast to all hosts connected to the datalink network and a reply is received only by the sender of the ARP request.

Suppose Host A wants to send Host B an IP packet. Both hosts have the same IP network number, and both are attached to the same Ethernet, as shown in Fig. 3.9. Host A, looking first in its IP-to-Ethernet address mapping table (also called an **ARP cache** doesn't find an entry for Host B's IP address. Host A then generates an ARP request packet and encapsulates it in the Ethernet frame shown in Fig. 3.10. The target network address is Host B's IP network interface address.

Figure 3.9 ARP on Local Network.

The target datalink address, being unknown, is set to 0:0:0:0:0:0. Host A puts its own Ethernet and IP addresses in the ARP request *sender* fields and sets the *type* and *length* fields to the correct values. The opcode field in the ARP packet is set to 0x0001 to indicate a request. ARP then broadcasts this packet to all hosts on the local Ethernet.

Each host, seeing that the type field in the Ethernet frame header is 0x0806, passes the encapsulated ARP packet to the ARP input routine. This routine on each machine in turn checks the target network address. All hosts except B will notice the IP address found there doesn't match its own IP address and will discard the packet. Host B will be the only machine to see that the target IP address matches its own IP address.

Host B then constructs an ARP reply by doing the following:

1. Fills in the sender datalink and network fields with the Ethernet and IP addresses of the network interface that received the ARP request.

Figure 3.10 ARP Request Packet.

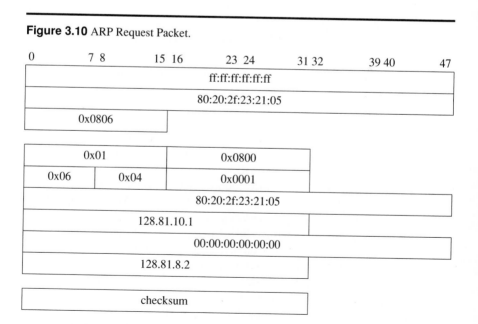

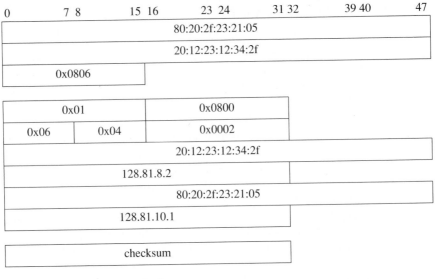

Figure 3.11 ARP Response Packet.

2. Fills in the target datalink and network addresses with the addresses found in the corresponding sender fields of the ARP request.

3. Sets the opcode to 0x0002 for a reply.

4. Encapsulates the packet in an Ethernet frame using Host A's Ethernet address found in the sender datalink address of the ARP request packet. The Ethernet frame with the encapsulated ARP reply packet is shown in Fig. 3.11.

Because it is highly likely that Host B will soon be communicating with Host A (almost all network communications are bidirectional), Host B also adds an entry for Host A in its own ARP cache using the information in the sender datalink and network fields of the ARP request packet. Host A, upon receiving the ARP reply, will add Host B's IP-to-Ethernet address entry to its ARP cache. Then, using Host B's Ethernet address, which it has now discovered, it will frame and send the original packet that generated the ARP request.

Through ARP, every host's address table can be dynamically updated. To keep the mapping table from becoming too large, ARP periodically times-out unused entries and purges them from the cache. A table entry also can become invalid if a datalink interface board is replaced (the datalink address is usually read from read-only memory on the interface board itself). In this case, when the host is rebooted with the new board and a new datalink address, other machines with ARP cache entries for that host's IP address will not be able to communicate with that machine until their own ARP cache entries time-out. Some machines avoid this problem when they boot by gratuitously broadcasting an ARP reply with its own IP and datalink addresses filled in. Then other hosts on the network receive this reply and update their own ARP caches.

Most hosts on a LAN communicate with relatively few other hosts on the same LAN either because clients normally talk to few file servers, mail gets sent to a mail gateway, or X-terminals log in to a couple of servers. Therefore communication patterns rapidly stabilize on even very large LANs. Hosts quickly add ARP cache entries for all hosts to which they normally communicate. If all hosts on a network are booted at the same time, you will see a flurry of ARP requests and replies. After a relatively short period of time, almost all IP-to-datalink address mappings are handled by cache lookups. So ARP traffic load on a properly configured network is very small. In Chapter 12, we show how ARP can cause performance problems on an improperly configured network. Excessive and continuous ARP traffic on a LAN almost always indicates a serious configuration problem.

ARP is an extremely useful support protocol. An elegant example of using the network itself to help support network communications and also ease network management, ARP is the glue that lets IP operate efficiently over a wide range of datalink protocols that support broadcasting.

Reverse ARP

ARP maps from network addresses to datalink addresses. Sometimes, however, you need the reverse mapping as well. For example, a diskless workstation or X-terminal knows its own datalink address (the address can be found by reading the ROM that holds the address on the interface card), but needs to discover its own IP address. The **Reverse Address Resolution Protocol (RARP)** handles this function. An RARP packet is identical in format to an ARP packet. It differs in that some additional operations are added. Also, the type field in the datalink header is different than that in ARP. RARP, like ARP, is also generalized for use with a wide variety of network and datalink protocols.

Unlike ARP, however, RARP requires a host server explicitly to have a datalink-to- network address mapping table. A host broadcasts an RARP request just as it does an ARP request, that is, the broadcast request asks for any server on the LAN to reply. An RARP server fills in the network address of the target and returns a reply. Figure 3.12 shows an example RARP packet request to translate from an Ethernet address to an IP address. With the exception of the *type* field (0x0835 instead of 0x0806), RARP uses the same packet format as ARP. RARP also defines two more operations, as follows. This example shows a *reverse request* that has an opcode of 0x0003. The sender of the packet fills in its own sender datalink address. The sender network address is always 0. The target datalink address of the host of interest, which is usually the same as the sender's, is filled in by the sender. The target network address is set by the sender to 0, since this is the address of interest.

Figure 3.13 shows a reply to the RARP request. In this case, the opcode is 0x0004 for a *reverse reply*. The sender of the reply fills in its own sender datalink and network address. The target hardware address is left as in the request packet, and the target network address is filled in with the requested network address.

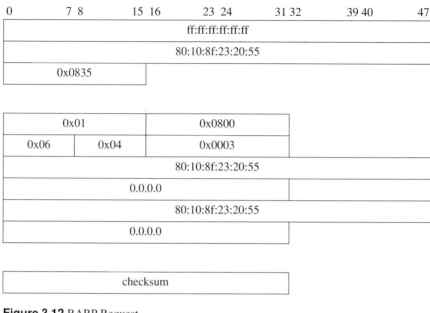

Figure 3.12 RARP Request.

RARP is usually the first step taken when a diskless workstation or X-terminal is booted. Once the host knows its own IP address, it can then proceed to load its own operating system from a network server by using a simple file transfer protocol, like TFTP.

3.4 Basic IP Routing

The IP protocol never consults the host number when routing a packet; rather, it routes packets solely by looking at the IP network number. This procedure greatly simplifies the routing algorithm, but requires that all hosts connected to the same datalink network have the same IP network number. If you could assign IP addresses at random, then the routing algorithm would have to know where every host is located, since you could attach a host with an arbitrary, but unique, IP address to any datalink network. The resulting tables would be enormous.

Knowing that all hosts on the same datalink network must have the same network address means the routing algorithm needs to know only the route to each IP network in order to reach any host address on that network. Routing to networks, rather than to hosts, decreases the size of the routing tables considerably. However, given the current size of the Internet as of this writing (more than 10,000 networks), routing to just networks also is becoming problematic because of the routing table sizes. Just as splitting an IP address into a network and host number simplified the routing to a host, a similar solution regarding IP network numbers is

0	7 8	15 16	23 24	31 32	39 40	47

80:10:8f:23:20:55
24:12:23:25:12:2f

0x0835	

0x01		0x0800
0x06	0x04	0x0004

80:12:23:25:12:2f
199.12.1.1	
80:10:8f:23:20:55
199.12.1.8	

checksum	

Figure 3.13 RARP Reply.

---

likely to take place. We discuss subnets and the OSPF routing protocol later in this chapter. At that time, you will see that the notion of a network number is extended to mean any part of an IP address. But the basic notion of IP routing on just the network part of an address is still preserved, along with the requirement that all hosts connected to the same datalink network must have the same IP network number.

The basic IP routing algorithm is shown in Fig. 3.14. The algorithm looks up routing information in a **routing table.** Each routing table entry is of the form:

```
<network, gateway, flags>
```

Every directly attached network has a routing table entry whose *gateway* field is the IP address of the directly attached network interface. The *flags* field is set to indicate the route is a directly attached network. If a packet's destination IP network address matches one of these entries, then the destination host is on that directly attached network; the packet is simply sent to its final destination. If the network supports ARP and no ARP cache entry exists for the destination IP address, then an ARP request is sent on the directly connected network to find the datalink address of the destination host.

A routing table entry to networks reachable through an intermediate router has a *gateway* entry that is the address of the next router on the path to the packet's final destination. The next router is always attached to one of the host's directly attached networks. So the host will use ARP, if supported, to discover the

```
Decrement the packet's TTL field
if a packet's TTL is zero then
    discard the packet
    send an ICMP time expired message
      to the source IP address
    return
end if
if a packet's destination address is one
  of my IP interface addresses then
    process the packet locally
    return
end if
determine the destination network number
find a routing entry to one of my interfaces
  for that IP network
if no routing entry exists then
    discard the packet and send an ICMP destination
      unreachable message to the packet's IP source address
    return
end if
if the network number is the same
  as one of my interface network numbers then
    send the packet to its final destination
else
    send the packet to the intermediate destination
      in the routing table entry
end if
```

Figure 3.14 Basic IP Routing Algorithm.

datalink address of the router's network interface on the same network as the host's interface. The host then will send the packet to the router. For these entries, the *flags* field is set to indicate the route to the destination network is through an intermediate router.

A router uses the same routing algorithm as a host. The router unframes and reframes the packet as it passes through, but the IP source and destination addresses in the IP header never change. The *ttl* field is decremented before the packet is reframed and transmitted or when the packet is buffered for more than a second (this rarely happens except on a very congested router). A router also might fragment or reassemble a packet along the route, depending on the MTU size of the datalink networks used. While the actual routing algorithm is simple, each router must have an up-to-date routing table as more than a single network path might exist between the source and destination hosts. If a link breaks, a router can reroute the packet along a different path.

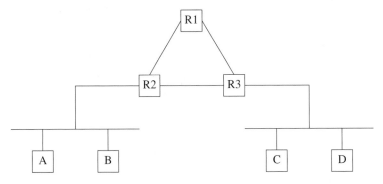

Figure 3.15 LANs Interconnected with Serial Lines.

Figure 3.15 illustrates an IP internetwork that combines several LANs using several WAN links. In the diagram, if Host A wishes to communicate with Host C two different routes exist to deliver the packets. A packet can be sent via path A→R2→R3→B or via path A→R2→R1→R3→B. Which of these routes is the most reliable or efficient depends on the reliability of the various links, the current amount of traffic on each link, and the speed of each link. Each IP packet is routed independently, so if a link fails then subsequent packets can be routed on a different path. The key to making this all work smoothly is keeping each node's routing tables up to date by distributing the appropriate routing information.

A **routing protocol** manages and updates routing tables on each network node. A routing protocol is not a part of IP. However, IP performs the actual routing, although it knows nothing about updating its own routing tables. The simplest routing protocol is to manually enter the routing table entries on each host. Like doing ARP mappings by hand, this procedure is laborious and error prone, especially for a large, complex network. If a network is static, is expected to remain static, and does not contain any redundant paths, then manual table updating will work. However, in a growing and changing network — one with redundant paths — a dynamic routing protocol is preferable. This type of protocol monitors changes in network topology and changes the routing tables when a link goes down, comes back up, or is added to the network. We will discuss some common routing protocols after describing IP subnets.

3.5 Subnets

IP allows you to divide a single IP network number into smaller pieces, called **subnets.** A description of the subnet extension to IP is found in [Mogul 1984a]. More often than not, a network that starts out as a single datalink network will grow into a network with multiple datalink network segments interconnected by routers. You then must treat each new segment as a separate IP network; the IP routing algorithm requires this. Doing this is cumbersome because when you need a new network number, you must obtain it from the central network registry. Also, if your network is connected to the Internet, each new network number must be advertised on your gateway routers so that routing will work properly. All this adds size to the routing tables.

Subnets are an alternative to registering a new IP network number each time you add a new datalink network. Subnetting allows you to logically partition a single IP network number. You then can use each logical partition as if it were a distinct IP network number.

Subnet Topology

A subnetted IP network is a group of datalink networks in which each shares the same IP network number but uses a distinct subnet number. All these networks must be fully connected. A typical subnet configuration might consist of several LANs interconnected by routers, one of which has a serial link to a WAN. Figure 3.16 shows a typical subnet configuration. In this example, each LAN uses the same Class B network number, 132.12.0.0. You can distinguish which datalink network each host is attached to by the value of the third byte of the IP address. The fourth byte is the unique host number. Network 132.12.0.0, however, needs to be registered only once. You then can divide this network into subnets at any time without consulting the central address registry. From the standpoint of a host outside this subnetted network, the network simply looks like a single IP network. Packet routing decisions within the subnetted network are made by the local routers. Routers outside the network have a single routing table entry for the entire subnetted network. External routers need not even be aware that the network is subnetted. Thus you have hidden the internal topology of the network from the outside world.

Figure 3.16 A Typical Subnet Configuration.

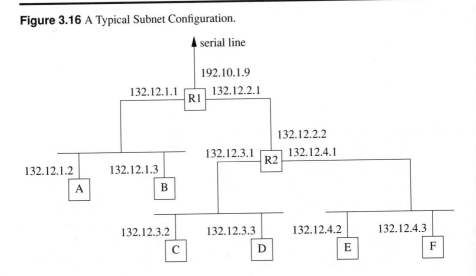

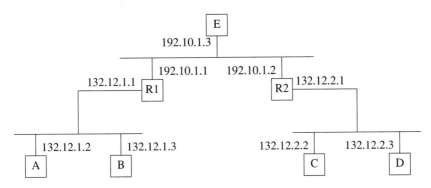

Figure 3.17 An Illegal Subnet Configuration.

A subnetted network must be fully connected. Creating two disjoint internetworks by subnetting a single IP network is not allowed. Figure 3.17 shows a subnetted Class B network interconnected by a single Class C network. This configuration is not legal. The reason for this limitation is simple. Suppose Host E on the Class C network wants to send a packet to Host B on subnet 132.12.1.0. Host E is unaware that network 132.12.0.0 is subnetted. To which router does Host A send the packet: R1 or R2? Being unaware of the subnets, Host E has no way of knowing. Worse, if the routers are running a routing protocol, both R1 and R2 will each advertise that they are on the path to network 132.12.0.0. If Host E sends the packet to R2, then R2 will see it has no path to 132.12.1.0 and will return a destination unreachable ICMP message to Host E. This is the correct behavior for R2, but it is incorrect from Host E's perspective.

Subnet Masks

IP uses a **network mask** to determine which bits in the host number are to be used as a subnet number. The mask is a 32-bit integer and is logically ANDed with the IP address of a host to determine which part of the address is used as the network part of the address for routing purposes. Thus 1-bits in the mask cover the network and subnet number; all remaining bits cover the host number. For example, a Class B network without subnetting has a network mask of 255.255.0.0 (0xffff0000); one that uses the third byte as a subnet has a mask of 255.255.255.0 (0xffffff00). The subnet part of the mask does not need to start or end on an even byte boundary or even be contiguous, but the mask must always cover the main network number. For example, the mask 0.255.255.0 for a Class B address is illegal, although its illegality is often not enforced, thus resulting in some very peculiar routing problems. The mask 255.255.255.240 (0xfffffff0) for a Class C network divides the last byte of the address into a 4-bit subnet number and a 4-bit host number (the last byte is 11110000 binary). On the other hand, the mask 255.255.255.15 (the last byte is 00001111 binary) also divides the last byte into a 4-bit subnet and a 4-bit host number, but the subnet is the lower-order 4 bits of the last byte. You also could use the mask 255.255.255.170 (170 decimal is

10101010 binary). In this latter case, the subnet number would be the alternating bit pattern. Needless to say, this could be very confusing.

In practice, the subnet mask is set so that the subnet number is adjacent to the main network number. Conventionally, a Class B network is divided into subnets by using the entire third byte as the subnet number. Doing this makes reading subnetwork addresses easy in the dotted decimal notation used for IP addresses. Because the subnet numbers of all 0 and all 1 bits are reserved just as for an unsubnetted network number, the host and subnet part of a subnetted network must contain at least 2 bits. With the reserved addresses, a single bit would leave no room for subnets or hosts.

Subnet Broadcasting

Using subnets complicates the interpretation of broadcast addresses. Given a Class B network number 131.134.0.0 that uses the third byte for subnets, that is, the subnet mask is 255.255.255.0, then a number of different broadcast addresses are possible. The network broadcast address is 131.134.255.255, while the broadcast address is 131.134.1.255 for subnet 1 and 131.134.2.255 for subnet 2. Following is the correct interpretation of these various broadcast addresses:

• The network broadcast should be sent to all subnets.

• The subnet broadcast is sent only to the specific subnet.

As a practical matter, you should confine broadcasting to a single datalink network. Therefore when a network is subnetted, you should uses the subnet broadcast address. For a full discussion of IP broadcasting with subnets, see [Mogul 1984b].

Subnet Routing

Routing in a subnetted environment is the same as for a set of unsubnetted networks. Each subnet is treated as a distinct network and the same routing algorithm is used. All host numbers must be unique and the subnet number must be the same for all interfaces connected to the same datalink network. A host on a different IP network routes to the network as a whole. The subnetted network's internal topology is hidden from the outside host, which sees the subnetted network as a single IP network. Once a packet reaches a router at the border of the subnetted environment, then that router will route the packet to the correct destination subnetwork.

The routing algorithm uses the network mask to determine if a network is subnetted. Note that a host or router knows a network is subnetted only if one or more of its own interfaces is connected to the subnetted network.

With subnets, the routing algorithm described earlier is modified as shown in Fig. 3.18. The only change, shown in italics, deals with determining if the network number is a local interface and then getting the possibly subnetted network number by logically ANDing the address with the network mask.

```
Decrement the packet's TTL field
if a packet's TTL is zero then
    discard the packet
    send an ICMP time expired message
      to the source IP address
    return
end if
if a packet's destination address is one
  of my IP interface addresses then
    process the packet locally
    return
end if
determine the destination network number
if the network number is the same
  as one of my interface network numbers then
      logically AND the netmask to the address
      to get the (possibly) subnetted network number
end if
find a routing entry to one of my interfaces
  for that IP network
if no routing entry exists then
    discard the packet and send an ICMP destination
      unreachable message to the packet's IP source address
    return
end if
if the network number is the same
  as one of my interface network numbers
    send the packet to its final destination
else
    send the packet to the intermediate destination
      in the routing table entry
end if
```

Figure 3.18 IP Routing Algorithm with Subnets.

Every interface has a network mask. The initial search for a matching interface is done using the IP network number (unsubnetted). The network mask of the first interface that matches the network number is used. For this reason, all network masks must be identical for every interface of a subnetted network. If the target network is unsubnetted, but an interface to that network exists on the host, then the subnet mask of that interface just covers the IP network number and the AND operation ends up being a null operation (it just returns the IP network number). So the subnet addition impacts only IP networks that are subnetted and that are local to the host.

The routing table search is identical to the unsubnetted case. Routing table entries must reflect the use of subnets. We mean by this that the *network* field of the routing entry should include the subnet part of the address as well as the IP network part of the address. These entries will appear only on hosts that understand subnets, that is, a host or router internal to or on the border of the subnetted network. OSPF uses a further extension of the subnet concept. We discuss in the next section how using OSPF alters the routing algorithm yet again.

Proxy ARP

Given the simple subnet topology shown in Fig. 3.19, suppose Host A does not understand subnets. The equivalent of not understanding subnets is as if you had set Host A's network mask to 255.255.0.0 for this Class B network. Host A will be able to communicate with all hosts on the directly attached datalink network, since Host A thinks that its network interface is simply attached to network 132.12.0.0. ARPing for hosts on the directly connected network will work. The other hosts on the same datalink network also will be able to send packets to Host A, since it has its third octet (the subnet number) set to 1.

However, if Host A tries to communicate with Host C, the communication will fail because Host C is not directly connected to the same datalink network as Host A but rather is connected to another subnet on the other side of the router. Host A will send an ARP packet looking for the datalink address of Host C, since Host A believes Host C is on its directly connected network, but no host will respond. Eventually, Host A will believe that Host C either does not exist or is down.

Suppose the router shown in the figure responded to Host A's ARP request for C. Then the router will appear to be Host C to Host A. Host A will add an ARP cache entry with Host C's IP address and the datalink address of the router's subnet 1 interface. Next, Host A will send subsequent IP packets to the router believing that it is sending the packets directly to Host C. When the router receives the packets, it will see they are not for itself (the destination IP address is Host C's IP address) and will forward the packets to Host C on subnet 2.

This algorithm, which allows a router to act as a proxy for an unsubnetted host in a subnet environment, is appropriately called **Proxy ARP.** This algorithm

Figure 3.19 Proxy ARP and Subnets.

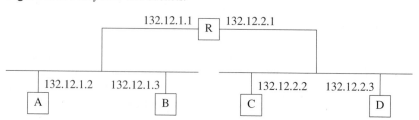

allows hosts that understand subnets to coexist with hosts that do not understand subnets; which is not uncommon, even today. A router that understands Proxy ARP will respond to an ARP request for a host that is reachable by the router and that is not on the same datalink interface as the requester. The basic algorithm follows:

```
router receives ARP packet on interface A
if the ARP request is not for a host on interface A then
    check if host is reachable by looking in routing tables
    if host is reachable then send ARP reply
end if
```

As you can see, the router "proxies" for a host on a reachable subnet. The assumption in the algorithm is that any host that is sending an ARP request for a host that is not on the same subnet does not understand subnets and therefore needs the router to stand in for the destination host. The router then can route the subsequent data packets using the conventional IP routing algorithm.

Looking carefully at this protocol, you will see that no machine, except the router, needs to understand subnets. All major IP router manufacturers support Proxy ARP, so it is widely implemented. The only requirement for its use is that the IP interface addresses of each host be organized as if they were subnetted. The subnet number that the router understands must be the same for all hosts on the same datalink network. As you can see, Proxy ARP is a very convenient support protocol for transitioning from an unsubnetted network to a subnetted one.

Subnet Routing Versus Bridging

Often LANs are interconnected using bridges. A bridge makes several datalink networks appear, to the higher-layer protocols, as a single datalink network, a scheme that is convenient and easy to implement since the interconnected cables look like a single datalink network. Bridges are also "plug and play" devices. Connecting two datalink networks by a bridge generally requires no software configuration. With most bridges, you simply connect the cables and power up the bridge. Therefore, for small installations, bridging works well. However, beyond a certain network size, bridging creates problems. Bridges do filter network traffic and perform useful traffic isolation, which we will discuss in more detail in Chapter 6. But a bridge must propagate datalink layer broadcasts to every host on every bridged network. It also must forward all datalink broadcast frames, since the bridged network is treated by the datalink layer as a single datalink network. This kind of system is very vulnerable to broadcast storms in which a very large bridged network with thousands of hosts can be severely disrupted by just a few misconfigured hosts that transmit unnecessary broadcast frames. Chapter 12 discusses this problem at greater length.

Connecting datalink networks via routers using subnets offers a way to protect against broadcast storms. A router will not pass Ethernet broadcast frames, so a broadcast storm is confined to a single datalink cable. Routers are generally harder to configure than are bridges, so greater care and knowledge is required to install them properly. Routing protocols also must be configured for the network to work properly. Generally speaking, a properly configured routed IP network is better at isolating broadcast problems created by misconfigured hosts.

3.6   Routing Architecture

IP looks up routing information in a routing table to find the next router that is in the path of the packet's final destination. Most IP implementations let you construct routing tables by hand. However, as with ARP table management, manually updated routing tables work well only in relatively small network environments. A much better choice for a network of any size is to use a dynamic routing protocol that updates a network's routers automatically.

Before we talk about some of the commonly used routing protocols, we need to discuss the overall routing management structure of the Internet today and how it is evolving. Doing this will give some insight into the complexity of managing routing in a large heterogeneous network environment.

Network Communities and Autonomous Systems

As of this writing, the TCP/IP Internet has over 10,000 connected networks, and each year, this number is at least doubling. In the early days of the Internet, every routing node knew how to get to every network and all routers in the Internet exchanged routing information. This approach quickly became impractical. Because of the sheer number of routers, routing information soon become a large percentage of the overall traffic. As a first step in administering routing, the Internet was divided into separate regions, each called an **autonomous system (AS)**. An AS is a collection of routers that are under a single administration and that run the same routing protocol, called an **interior gateway protocol (IGP)**. An IGP keeps every router within the AS informed as to the routes to all the networks within the AS. Generally, each router that is part of an AS must run the same IGP, although different AS's need not run the same IGP. Note that this requirement is not strictly true, but it is the classical and traditional definition of an AS. Suffice it to say that all routers within an AS must have a common view of the routes to all the networks within the AS. It is possible to do this with several routing protocols sharing a common set of information. For our purposes, the classical definition is sufficient.

At the routers where one AS system connects to another, an **exterior gateway protocol (EGP)** is used. An EGP is also called an **inter-AS routing protocol**. An EGP supplies routing information between AS's. To an EGP at the border of an AS, the internal topology of a remote AS is opaque. Routing decisions within the remote AS may change without affecting the EGP. By analogy, the EGP is the equivalent of a long-distance operator for packets with destinations outside an AS. It exchanges routing information with the IGP within its AS so that all routers in the AS know where the routes to networks in other AS's are located. The EGP also passes along information regarding which networks are routable within its own AS to neighboring AS's. Each AS is identified by a unique 16-bit integer that is used in an EGP routing exchange and that uniquely identifies the source of the routing information. An organization can obtain an AS number from the central Internet registry.

As of this writing, EGPs are still evolving. The original Internet EGP was appropriately enough called EGP. More modern EGP are called Border Gateway Protocols (BGPs), the latest version of which is BGP-3. AS's add a level of hierarchy to routing that simplifies routing table management within and between AS's. An AS also might, through the information it exchanges with its neighboring AS's, control traffic flow into and out of each AS. For example, an AS may choose to advertise only its internal networks with its neighboring AS's. In this simple example of **policy routing,** any route through the AS from a network outside the AS to another network outside the AS is disallowed. Traffic that passes through an AS is called **transit traffic;** that destined for or coming from a host within an AS is called **local traffic.** Of course, one AS's local traffic can be another AS's transit traffic.

EGPs are being actively researched within the Internet. In general, registering your own AS is unnecessary unless your network is very complicated and has many interconnections with other AS's or you want to selectively allow transit traffic. If you don't register the AS, you also don't have to run an EGP. If on the other hand you have a network that interconnects several AS's, you must run both an EGP and an IGP and also should keep up with the research activity in this area.

Routing Protocols

The Internet uses a number of routing protocols, which generally fall into two categories: reachability and distance vector. A **reachability protocol** tells whether a path exists to a distant network. A **distance vector protocol** calculates a distance metric to a remote network. The distance metric can be just the number of routers between the source and destination network or it can include more information about each link, such as bandwidth and load. Examples of a simple distance vector protocol include RIP. Another such protocol is OSPF, which is the soon-to-be standard Internet IGP. EGPs are reachability protocols, since reachability is really all the information required about networks outside an AS.

There is no such thing as a universal routing protocol. Each of the currently popular protocols has its own strengths and weaknesses. For small homogeneous networks, RIP is more than adequate. For larger networks with a complex topology, a more sophisticated routing protocol such as OSPF is probably required. Research continues on routing protocols that will work in very large networks. We briefly describe next a few of the more popular and implemented protocols.

Routing Information Protocol (RIP). RIP [Hedrick 1988] is an adaptation of the original routing protocol for the **Xerox Network System (XNS)** protocol family. The *routed* daemon found on most UNIX systems, for example, implements RIP. A relatively simple protocol, it calls for routing information to be exchanged by broadcasting information among hosts and routers. RIP uses UDP transport to send routing update messages. A RIP message is either a request for a remote router to send its routing table or a reply that lists the router's current routing table. Each RIP update consists of an IP address that is normally a network address and a metric associated with that network. More than a single network/metric pair can be sent within a single RIP message.

When multiple routes exists to a destination, RIP uses a simple **hop count** metric to arbitrate the best route. A route is considered best if the number of routers the route passes through is minimal compared to that of all other routes to the same destination network. Because RIP sends updates every 30 seconds, it propagates routing changes in a reasonable amount of time.

The RIP algorithm is straightforward. Each router sends a message with every network reachable from itself. Initially, this will be the directly connected networks. The directly connected networks are considered to be 0 hops away. RIP increments the hop count for reach reachable network by 1 when it sends a RIP update message to its neighbors. This message is broadcast on every network interface. As each router receives updates from neighboring routers, the list of reachable networks grows. When neighboring routers have a route to a network that is already in its routing table, the hop count allows each router to select the "best" route.

For example, consider the case of two routers connecting three Ethernets, as shown in Fig. 3.20. On startup, router R1 has two routing table entries — one for network 199.12.1.0 and another for network 199.13.1.0 with a hop count of 0. Router R2 also has two routing table entries — one for network 199.13.1.0 and one for network 199.14.1.0, also with a 0 hop count. R1 and R2 broadcast their own routing information on both Ethernet interfaces. Router R2 will receive two updates, one for network 199.12.1.0 with a hop count of 1 and one for network 199.13.1.0, also with a hop count of 1. It will discard the update for network 199.13.1.0, since it already has a routing entry for that network with a smaller hop count, and it will add the entry for network 199.12.1.0 to its routing table, since it has no entry for that network. The hop count on network 199.12.1.0 will be 1. Router R1 will receive the routing updates from R2 in the same manner, discarding the update for network 199.13.10 and adding the entry for network 199.14.1.0 with a hop count of 1.

Figure 3.20 Two Router RIP Configuration.

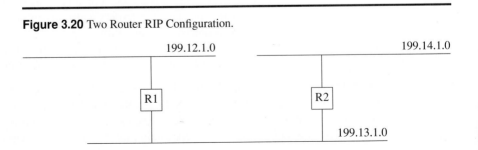

The routing tables for both routers are now stable. Each router will continue to send RIP updates every 30 seconds to advertise all their routes. Router R1 will advertise a route for network 199.14.1.0 with a hop count of 2; this routing update will be discarded by router R2, since router R2 has a route to 199.14.1.0 with a hop count of 0. Router R1 will discard router R2's update for network 199.12.1.0, since router R1 has a route to 199.12.1.0 with a hop count of 0.

RIP also supports more complicated topologies. For example, if you add a router to the previous example that directly connects network 199.12.1.0 and 199.14.1.0, as shown in Fig. 3.21, then redundant paths exist to all networks. When router R3 begins to advertise routing information, the 2-hop route from 199.12.1.0 to 199.14.1.0 through router R1 and R2 will be replaced with the 1-hop route through router R3. With all routers operational, the least hop count path from any network to any other network is obvious. If router R3 fails, then the route from 199.12.1.0 to 199.14.1.0 will fall back to the 2-hop route through router R1 and R2.

RIP is very popular primarily because it is implemented on most UNIX systems. It works reasonably well in a LAN without a complex topology. Its biggest drawback is that the hop count cannot exceed 15. Because a hop count of 16 is considered infinite, on a large network with routers more than 15 hops distant from each other, RIP will not work. One reason for the small hop count is the "counting to infinity" problem when the routing topology changes because a link went down. In some topologies, the routing tables will oscillate and form loops for a long period of time until they stabilize. During this period, hop counts to some networks will slowly increment to infinity as routing loops are resolved. A small value for "infinity" minimizes the time needed to stabilize the new routing configuration.

When routes are unstable, routing loops appear in the routing tables. If it takes too long to stabilize the routing tables, packets may be lost and a considerable amount of network traffic generated that can have a very adverse affect on network performance. Generally, you use RIP within a LAN environment. RIP exchanges routing information with one or more routers connected to a WAN that uses a different routing protocol.

Figure 3.21 Three Router RIP Configuration.

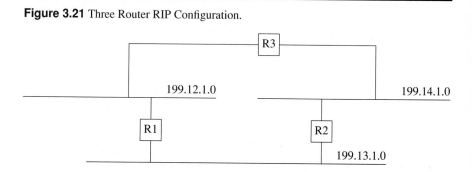

Open Shortest Path First (OSPF). The OSPF routing protocol [May 1991] is an emerging standard IGP for AS's within the Internet. OSPF incorporates bandwidth metrics to determine the best path to a network; a high bandwidth path through several routers might be a better path than a direct, lower speed link. Unlike RIP, OSPF takes link state into consideration when making routing decisions. It also supports multiple, equal-cost routes to the same destination and will split traffic among the possible routes. Further, OSPF can establish routes based on the IP Type of Service (the *tos* field value in the IP header).

Routers using OSPF exchange routing information and each builds a complete graph of the AS. The global state graph is the concatenation of every router's reachable neighbors and interfaces. Each router then builds a shortest path routing tree to every network from the global database. Routes derived from outside the AS by an EGP are seen as leaf nodes in the computed routing tree.

OSPF lets you divide a large AS into routing areas. Routing within an area is opaque to routers outside the area, thus reducing the amount of routing traffic passed between areas. A routing area is a generalization of the IP subnet concept. As a result, OSPF adds another wrinkle to the IP routing algorithm. With subnets, the portion of the IP address used for routing depended on the bits in the subnet mask for that network and are only used if the network number matches the network number of a local interface. On the other hand, with OSPF every routing table entry has an associated mask. So an OSPF routing table entry is now as follows:

<destination> <mask> <gateway> <flags>

IP with OSPF support now masks every destination address using the routing table *mask* field before it checks the target address against the *destination* field. The address entries are sorted by decreasing mask length, so a destination address will match the most specific destination address.

Figure 3.22 illustrates a network configuration using OSPF for routing. In this figure, the node R1's routing table is shown in Table 3.2. The first entry is the route to the loopback interface. The next entry is a route to a specific host attached to a serial line — the mask in this case is all 1's. The next three entries are routes to the directly connected networks. The following two entries are routes to other subnets of network 131.10.0.0. The mask distinguishes whether the high-order bit of the host number is set or not (128 = 1000000 binary). Router R1 will forward any address with the high-order bit set to R3 and any address without the high-order bit set to R4. R3 routes to subnets of network 131.10.0.0 that have the high-order bit of the third octet set, while R4 handles all the other subnets. The next entry routes packets for network 132.12.0.0 to R2. (Note that network 132.12.0.0 is subnetted using the third byte of the address as a subnet number.) R2 will forward the packet to its final destination. The final entry is the default route. Note that the default route is the last entry in the table and it will matches any IP address that has not matched a previous entry. Packets whose destinations match the default entry are sent to router R5, which is presumably the gateway router to other AS's in the Internet.

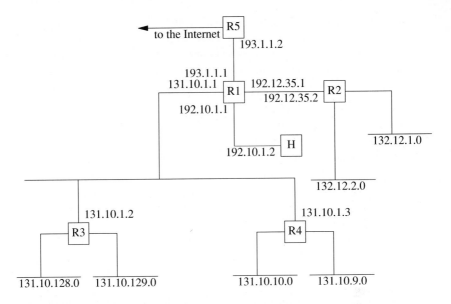

Figure 3.22 OSPF Sample Network.

Adding a mask to each routing table entry, supplemented by judicious network assignments, results in R1's routing table being smaller than it would be if RIP was used to disseminate routing information. OSPF can completely specify the routes to all the subnets of network 131.10.0.0 with three routing table entries, whereas RIP routing with subnets would require five routing table entries. Moreover, with OSPF, if a subnet is added to R3 no additional routing table entries are required on R1, provided the new subnet has the high-order bit of the third byte set to 1.

Table 3.2 OSPF Routing Table.

Destination	Mask	Gateway	Flags
127.0.0.1	255.255.255.255	127.0.0.1	UH
192.10.1.2	255.255.255.255	192.10.1.1	UH
131.10.1.0	255.255.255.0	131.10.1.1	U
192.12.35.0	255.255.255.0	192.12.35.1	U
193.1.1.0	255.255.255.0	193.1.1.1	U
131.10.128.0	255.255.128.0	131.10.1.2	UG
131.10.0.0	255.255.128.0	131.10.1.3	UG
132.12.0.0	255.255.0.0	192.12.35.2	UG
0.0.0.0	0.0.0.0	193.1.1.2	UG

OSPF is a complicated and sophisticated routing protocol. We can hardly do justice to all its features in this short section. Suffice it to say that OSPF is designed for large and complex networks. It also, as of this writing, is just now being widely deployed. Unless you are building a very large and/or complex network, most of its features would not be needed.

Default Routing. By far the simplest routing paradigm is default routing. While not strictly a protocol, default routing is very useful in relatively static network environments. A default route is one of last resort; it is coded as a route to network 0.0.0.0. When no other route exists and a default one exists, IP sends the packet to the *gateway* field found in the default routing table entry. For networks with a single outside router, default routing is quite adequate.

Figure 3.23, shows an Ethernet connected to a WAN via a single router. Hosts on the Ethernet can use a default route to the IP address of the router's Ethernet interface for all IP networks except the local network. A look at Host A's routing table (shown in Table 3.3) with the default route installed shows the gateway to network 129.12.0.0 is the local interface and the gateway to the default destination is 129.12.1.1, which is the router's Ethernet interface. IP forwards all packets not destined for the local IP network to the router. The router then forwards the packets using its own routing table, which can be updated using a dynamic routing protocol.

Using default routes in this circumstance avoids running a dynamic routing protocol that is not needed, since all network traffic is forwarded through the router for all destination networks outside of the local network. If your environment has multiple paths to the outside world or a complicated internal routing topology, then you are usually better off running a dynamic routing protocol. Where multiple routers with multiple paths to outside networks exist, you can still use default routes by simply adding a default route that points at one of the routers. Next, configure the routers to exchange routing information using an IGP. Then when a packet arrives at the default router and a better route exists on an

Figure 3.23 Default Routing Topology.

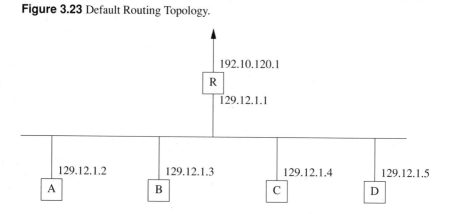

Table 3.3 Default Routing Table.

Destination	Gateway	Flags
127.0.0.1	127.0.0.1	UH
129.12.0.0	129.12.1.2	U
0.0.0.0	129.12.1.1	UG

alternate router, the default router will update the host's routing tables using an ICMP *redirect* message.

Exterior Gateway Protocol (EGP). You can use EGP [Mills 1984] to connect an AS to another AS that handles routing to all other AS's. EGP is a reachability routing protocol and is a specific implementation of a generic EGP. The topology in which EGP is used is shown in Fig. 3.24. EGP assumes a **core AS** exists (in this diagram the node labeled "Core") that exchanges routing information with each stub AS. A **stub AS** is an AS that sends all transit traffic bound for remote networks in other AS's to the core AS. Each stub AS has a single router through which all transit traffic passes to the core system. Essential EGP supports a two-level routing hierarchy with a single core transit network.

In the figure, region A is a separate AS that may contain one or more interconnected networks. Other AS's (shown as B, C, D, and E) are also attached to the core system and exchange reachability information with the core, using either EGP or another routing protocol. No transit packets from the core to another AS are accepted by any stub AS. EGP may be configured to hide networks within each stub A and not advertise them to the core system. Consequently, those networks are not reachable from remote systems, but are only reachable from within the AS.

The core in turn advertises routing information about other AS's that are reachable through the core system. EGP on A's gateway router receives this routing information and updates its own routing tables accordingly. One of region A's

Figure 3.24 EGP Configuration.

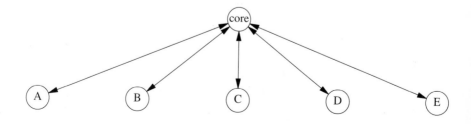

routers exchanges reachability information with a specific core router. This exchange of routing information is set up by prior agreement between the administrators of the core system and of region A.

Border Gateway Protocol (BGP). BGP is a reachability protocol [Lougheed & Rekhter 1991]. An update to EGP, it removes the strict two-level hierarchy restriction of EGP. Now in its third version — BGP-3— BGP implements a similar reachability algorithm as does EGP. It is designed, however, to work with arbitrarily complex topologies, that is, a network of AS's with arbitrary connectivity. A major goal of BGP-3 is to control transit traffic across an AS. It lets you specify whether transit traffic will be allowed at all. We can illustrate the transit traffic problem with the following simple example.

Consider five AS's with the connectivity shown in Fig. 3.25. Under normal operation, hosts within C exchanges packets with both B and D using the direct links to those AS's. This could be because of a joint project between C and B and between C and D, where direct exchange is more efficient or required for privacy, or because A might have a policy against transiting that traffic, even though if the direct link between C and B fails, the traffic could be routed via A. C's administrator uses BGP to prevent traffic between B and D from transiting the networks within C. thus forcing traffic between B and D to go through A. In the same way, traffic from E to B is be prevented from transiting C if the link between A and B fails. The policy is set for for traffic between E and D.

In this example, E is a stub AS. It has a single connection to another AS, and all traffic coming from or going to networks outside its AS boundaries flow through a single remote AS (in this case A). B, C, and D are each examples of a **multihomed AS,** that is, although each is connected to more than one remote AS, they allow only traffic that has a destination or source IP address for hosts within the AS. A is a **transit AS;** it allows traffic to pass from one connected AS to another. Effectively, BGP lets you control transit traffic when you set up connections to remote AS's. A wide variety of policies can be enforced with this mechanism. Unless you are planning to be a transit network provider (that is, a backbone network), you don't need to worry about BGP or even run the protocol.

Figure 3.25 AS Configuration with Transit Traffic.

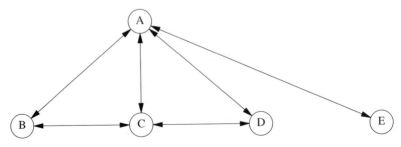

Which Type of Routing to Use?

Routing is a complicated subject and selecting among the various and myriad options can be a problem. As explained earlier, routing is more an art than a science, and considerable research efforts are underway to devise better, more robust protocols. For most networks, you should apply the KISS (Keep It Simple Stupid) principle. Don't be fancy where you don't have to be. For most small networks, static routes complemented with default routes is usually sufficient. RIP is an old and limited routing protocol and is widely implemented on UNIX systems. It remains a reasonable routing protocol choice, unless you have a complex topology — more than a few LANs or a number of WAN links — in which case, you should consider using OSPF as an IGP. Even then you can just run OSPF on your dedicated routers and distribute routing information to hosts that passively listen for routing updates from the active routing nodes. Or you could even set up most hosts to use default routes to the nearest router; because most LANs in the majority of configurations have only a single route to the outside, this works quite well. Only if your network must handle transit traffic should you ever need to run an EGP in combination with an IGP. In most cases, a default route to the outside networks is sufficient.

References

Callon 1992.   Callon, R., *TCP and UDP with Bigger Addresses (TUBA), A Simple Proposal for Internet Addressing and Routing (RFC1347)*, June 1992.

Hedrick 1988.   Hedrick, C. L., *Routing Information Protocol*, June 1988.

Lougheed & Rekhter 1991.   Lougheed, K., & Rekhter, Y., *Border Gateway Protocol 3 (BGP-3) (RFC1267)*, October 1991.

May 1991.   May, J., *OSPF Version 2*, July 1991.

Mills 1984.   Mills, D. L., *Exterior Gateway Protocol Formal Specification (RFC904)*, April 1984.

Mogul 1984a.   Mogul, J. C., *Internet Subnets (RFC917)*, October 1984.

Mogul 1984b.   Mogul, J. C., *Broadcasting Internet Datagrams in the Presence of Subnets (RFC922)*, October 1984.

Plummer 1982.   Plummer, D. C., *Ethernet Address Resolution Protocol (RFC826)*, November 1982.

Postel 1980.   Postel, John B., *DoD Standard Internet Protocol (RFC760)*, January 1980.

Postel 1981.   Postel, John B., *Internet Protocol (RFC791)*, September 1981.

Reynolds & Postel 1992.   Reynolds, Joyce, & Postel, John, *Assigned Numbers (RFC1340)*, Updated periodically, July 1992.

Wang & Crowcroft 1992.   Wang, Z., & Crowcroft, J., *A Two-Tier Address Structnure for the Internet: A Solution to the Problem of Address Space Exhaustion (RFC1335)*, May 1992.

CHAPTER 4

Transport Protocol Basics

The two major TCP/IP transport protocols, TCP and UDP, compose messages received from applications and deliver those messages using IP's packet delivery services. Because IP delivers packets only to a host, the transport protocols must add information to allow addressing to an individual process. A transport protocol may, at its option, provide for flow control and end-to-end reliability.

4.1   The Client/Server Model

The client/server model of data communication is a very useful means of conceptualizing most network services. Although not the only way two processes on a network can communicate with each other, this model is so useful that all but a few applications use it. We discussed some of the basics of the client/server model in Chapter 1. In this chapter, we will go into more specific details about how the client/server model is actually implemented using TCP/IP on a modern UNIX system.

In a client/server relationship, a server process on a machine offers services, while a client process, which usually resides on another machine, initiates a connection with the server process. The server waits for messages coming from the client, and when the proper initial message sequence is exchanged, it accepts the connection. A server can elect either to multiplex more than a single client connection or to handle each request serially.

Once the connection between the two processes is established, data passes from one process to the other in a symmetric fashion. (The asymmetry of the client and server processes exists only during the establishment of a connection.) The client/server relationship can be terminated by either process using a defined connection close message sequence.

The services a server offers a client can vary widely. Data can flow from the server to the client or vice versa. For example, the server might be transaction oriented, that is, a client sends a transaction request to which the server responds. Or, conversely, the client can download data to the server.

Because a server is a *process* and not a *machine,* a server for the same service can exist on more than one machine. Also, a machine can have many servers and clients simultaneously. The key difference between a client and a server is that a client initiates a connection with a server while a server waits for client connection requests.

Within the TCP/IP protocol family, a server can use either TCP or UDP transport. The initial message sequence for establishing a connection is different depending on which underlying transport protocol the client and server use, but the general paradigm is the same regardless of the transport protocol used.

Figure 4.1 TCP Message Format.

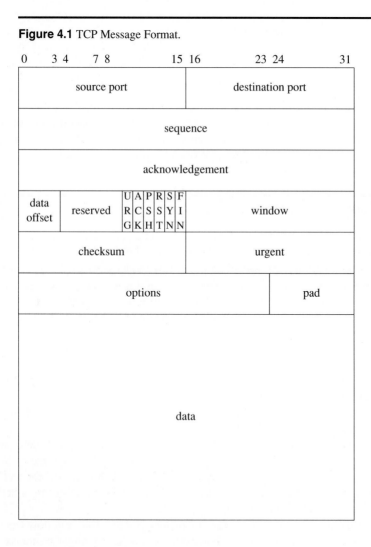

4.2   The Transmission Control Protocol

The most commonly used transport protocol is the **Transmission Control Protocol (TCP)** [Postel 1981]. A TCP connection is much like a UNIX pipe, except that it supports a reliable bidirectional byte stream. This means two processes that communicate using TCP see not underlying message or packet boundaries but rather a continuous sequence of bytes that can be read or written a single byte or many bytes at a time by either process.

TCP Messages

TCP is a fairly complicated protocol because (1) it ensures the end-to-end reliability and in-order sequencing of the byte stream and (2) it tries to optimize available network bandwidth by monitoring and managing the flow of data from the sender to the receiver. This protocol processes a stream of data from a host process and divides the data into messages that then are sent to the TCP program on the other end of the connection. This remote TCP collects these messages, recreates the original byte stream, and then passes it on to the remote process. A typical TCP message is shown in Fig. 4.1. The fields in the message are:

• *source port* and *destination port*
Along with the source and destination IP addresses found in the packet's IP header, uniquely identify the two processes associated with the connection.

• *sequence*
The relative byte offset of the first byte in the current message. The sequence number starts at an arbitrary 32-bit number that is negotiated when TCP opens a connection with a remote TCP.

• *acknowledgement*
The relative byte position of the last byte successfully acknowledged by the TCP that sent the message. TCP uses this field to acknowledge received data. The field is examined only when the ACK bit is set. (See the discussion of the *flags* field below.)

• *data offset*
The offset in bytes to the beginning of the *data* field from the beginning of the header. This tells the receiver where user data begins and indirectly the length of any TCP options at the end of the TCP header.

• *reserved*
Always set to zero. This field is reserved for future use.

• *flags*
This field is a series of 1-bit values. It immediately follows the *reserved* field. Used to pass connection state information to the remote TCP and also to indicate successful receipt of a TCP message. The following 1-bit flags are available:

- URG

  When set tells the receiving TCP that the *urgent* field indicates the byte position in the data stream of data that should be processed before other data in the
  message. We will discuss how this works when we discuss the *urgent* field.

- ACK

  Acknowledges the correct receipt of data up to and including the relative byte
  number found in the *acknowledgement* field. This bit is set most of the time,
  since most TCP messages contain a valid *acknowledgement* field.

- PSH

  Indicates that a received message should be sent to the process associated with
  the connection immediately. In normal operation, a receiving TCP will place
  all received data in a queue and only send it to the receiving process after the
  number of bytes in the queue has reached a threshold value. When this bit is
  set, the receiving process can read the data stream immediately. An interactive
  process uses the PSH bit to send data to the receiving process immediately. For
  example, the TELNET protocol sets the PSH bit when transmitting user input.
  Accordingly, the receiving TELNET daemon is sent the character immediately,
  so it may echo the character back to the sender when using TELNET in full
  duplex mode.

- RST

  Indicates that the connection should be reset due to a software or hardware failure. For example, a server process that terminates prematurely due to, say, its
  host crashing, leaves a client of the server waiting for the server to respond,
  since TCP has no notion of connection timeout. When the server is subsequently restarted, TCP may see a message from the old client. The server will
  send a response with the RST bit set, thus asking the client to reset the connection. For most applications, the client simply terminates; however, by using
  this feature, the server and the client could use a more sophisticated recovery
  mechanisms.

- SYN

  Used during the initial connection setup as part of the connection negotiation
  and the exchange of initial sequence numbers. Its purpose is to synchronize the
  connection.

- FIN

  Indicates that the sender has no more data to relay. When a FIN is sent, the
  connection state is half-closed in that the receiver of the FIN can continue to
  send data but will not receive any more data from the sender. Only when the
  receiver sends a FIN is the connection completely closed.

- *window*

  The number of data bytes the sender of the message is willing to accept. TCP
  uses this field for flow control and buffer management, which is very important
  in an internetwork with links of varying speed. We further discuss using the
  window field later in this section.

- *checksum*

  The 16-bit 1's complement sum of each 16 bits in the header and data portion of the message. The checksum also covers a 12-byte pseudo-header, that is not carried as part of the actual TCP message. We will discuss the purpose of the pseudo-header after we finish discussing the rest of the fields in a TCP message.

- *urgent*

  The byte position of data in the message that should be processed first. An interactive protocol such as TELNET can use the *urgent* field to process output flow control or to process interrupt characters before a long stream of data is processed by a receiver. The value in this field is only used when the URG bit is set.

- *options*

  Various TCP options of various lengths, ranging from security to the maximum segment size a receiving TCP can handle, that can be added to the header.

- *pad*

  When necessary, pads the TCP header out to a multiple of 4 bytes.

- *data*

  The user data that composes the rest of the TCP message.

TCP Pseudo-Header. The TCP pseudo-header is a 12 byte structure shown in Fig. 4.2. It is called a pseudo-header because it is not carried as a part of the TCP message; you could say it is a skeleton IP header. It contains the IP source and destination addresses, the transport protocol being used (TCP = 6), and the length in bytes of the TCP message. The pseudo-header information is passed to IP and is carried in the IP header of the packet in which the TCP message is encapsulated. Note that the *length* field in the pseudo-header is not carried directly in the IP header. Rather, IP uses this value to compute the total packet length that is carried in the IP header. When IP receives a packet with an encapsulated TCP message, the pseudo-header is regenerated and the TCP input routine carries out the checksum operation on the TCP message plus the pseudo-header. The checksum is computed with the checksum field set to 0, and if the message contains an odd

---

Figure 4.2 TCP Pseudo Header.

0   3 4   7 8   15 16   23 24   31
source IP
destination IP

protocol	length

number of bytes, a final 8 bits of 0 is assumed at the end of the message but not included as part of the message.

Use of the pseudo-header means TCP is closely coupled to IP addressing. The IP addresses in the pseudo-header are needed because they (along with the *source port* and *destination port* fields) help uniquely identify the processes associated with the connection. (The port number fields are not sufficient in themselves as identifiers because they can be used for more than a single connection.)

Initiating and Closing Connections. TCP uses a three-way handshake to initiate a connection and a two-way handshake to close a connection. The three-way handshake sets the initial sequence numbers for each end of the connection. A connection request is always initiated by a client process, which sends a message with the SYN flag set and the client's initial sequence number. This initial sequence number is a 4-byte unsigned number that is incremented each time a new connection is requested. The number is incremented modulo 2^{32}, so it wraps around to 0 after reaching its maximum value.

Each end of a TCP connection has a new starting sequence number. This number is usually a function of the time-of-day clock and is incremented over time. Because a TCP connection with the same port numbers and IP addresses can be reused many times, changing the initial sequence number prevents each connection from using stale data that is still in transit from an old connection and that has the same connection address.

When the receiving TCP (the server) sees the initial SYN message, it sends a SYN message with its own initial sequence number and the ACK flag set. The message also contains the client's sequence number in the *acknowledgement* field, thus indicating that the server received the client's initial sequence number. The client in turn ACKs the server's SYN message with a final ACK message. In this manner, the client and the server reliably exchange their initial sequence numbers and can start communicating. Note that none of the three messages contain any data; all information passed is conveyed in the TCP header.

Connection close is handled by a two-way handshake. When one side of a connection has finished sending data, it sends a message with the FIN flag set. Because the connection is full duplex, the other side can continue to send data until it sends a message also with the FIN flag set. The close algorithm is complicated because both sides of the connection can send their FIN at the same time. Also, the full duplex nature of the connection differs from normal UNIX I/O descriptor semantics. Normally, when a close is done on a UNIX descriptor, no more communication is possible on that descriptor. TCP on the other hand allows reception to continue until the other side of the connection sends a FIN message.

Sliding Windows and Flow Control

IP is unreliable and can randomly drop packets because of transient buffer space shortages. The simplest method to ensure end-to-end reliability is to run a **lock-step** protocol. This kind of protocol provides that the sender transmit a single message and wait for the receiver to acknowledge receipt of that message. If an acknowledgement is not received within a certain period of time, the message is presumed lost and the sender retransmits the message. Obviously, the wait time must be at least the round-trip time of the path between the two endpoints. However, in a network with long transmission delays or very high bandwidth, this protocol is very inefficient.

For example, suppose a TCP sends 1000-byte messages over a network with a 100 millisecond round-trip time. Suppose also that the overall network bandwidth is 100,000 bytes per second. It takes the sender about 10 milliseconds to transmit the message. The sender then must wait another 50 milliseconds for the receiver to receive the message and another 50 milliseconds to receive the acknowledgement before it can send the next message (we assume the time to send the ACK is negligible). The overall throughput of the network is $1000 \div 0.110 = 9.09$ messages per second. This is a 9.09% utilization of the existing network bandwidth.

To make a connection reliable and improve performance, TCP uses a **sliding window** protocol with timers. Using this protocol improves bandwidth utilization by allowing the sender to send several TCP messages before an acknowledgement is received for any of the messages. The receiving TCP sends an acknowledgement for multiple messages by ACKing the highest byte received successfully. The number of messages allowed in flight is negotiated dynamically using the window field in the TCP header. This field tells the sending TCP how many bytes can be in-flight before the sender must see an acknowledgement from the receiver. This arrangement provides for much better utilization of the available network bandwidth and allows transmissions to be sent down a long delay pipe more efficiently.

When TCP receives a message or a series of messages, it sends an acknowledgement of the highest byte received. It does this by setting the ACK bit and setting the acknowledgement field to the number of the highest byte plus 1, received from the remote TCP. Each TCP message contains the relative byte number of the first byte in the message in the *sequence* field, so it is easy to determine the relative byte of the last byte received in the message. If messages are being sent bidirectionally, TCP piggybacks the acknowledgement by setting the ACK bit on a message it is sending back and correctly fills in the acknowledgement field.

Figure 4.3 shows an example TCP exchange that demonstrates the acknowledgement strategy. In this example, System A sends messages with 10-bytes of data one after the other. The sender will transmit messages as long as the window size is greater than the total number of unacknowledged bytes. The receiver, System B, collects the messages and acknowledges all of them with a single ACK because, in this case, System B is processing the data fast enough to allow several TCP messages to be sent before an ACK is required.

Optimally, the receiver sends the ACK just before the sender's window closes. In this example, System A has just sent the 50th byte and the receive window is now closed. But just as it gets ready to send the next message, it receives an ACK from System B and the window is again reopened to 50 bytes. System A can then continue to send more messages. System B can dynamically control the flow-rate on the connection by adjusting the window size sent in each ACK reply. It then updates its sending window accordingly.

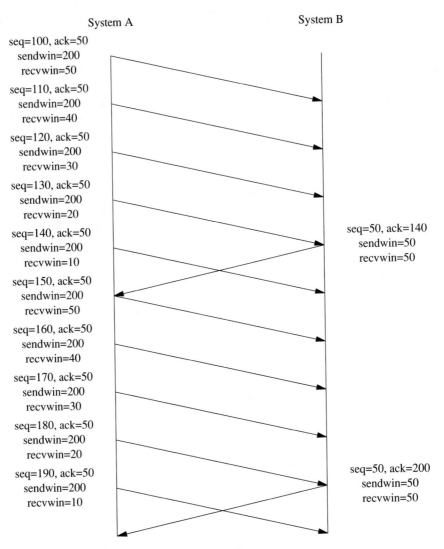

Figure 4.3 Example TCP Acknowledgement Strategy.

Using the parameters of the previous example — 100 millisecond round-trip time and 100,000 bytes per second transmission speed — we can use the sliding window protocol to dramatically improve network utilization. In this case, the receiver sets its window size to 11,000 bytes. The sending TCP begins sending 11 1,000-byte messages back-to-back, which takes 100 milliseconds. The receiver in the meantime has received the first message and already sent an ACK for it. This ACK is received by the sending TCP after 110 milliseconds or when the sender has just finished sending the 11th message and is just about to stop sending (there are 11,000 bytes in flight). This ACK leaves the window size at 11,000 bytes;

thus, because the window has opened by 1,000 bytes, the sender starts to send the next message, Then, after another 10 milliseconds, the sender receives another ACK for the second message and the window again opens by 1,000 bytes. This pattern repeats itself until all data has been sent and received. As you can see, using the sliding window protocol increases network utilization to nearly 100%.

In a network with minimal frame loss, a low frame error rate, and a low variance round-trip time, this algorithm works extremely well. However, in a network that experiences high frame loss or errors, the receiving TCP might not receive one or more outstanding messages. These messages will remain unacknowledged. Eventually, after the sending TCP's retransmission time for those messages expires, that TCP will retransmit the unacknowledged messages, that is, all bytes queued from the last byte for which it received an acknowledgement.

On a network that experiences high frame loss, using a large window size can result in excessive retransmission. Suppose a sender's relative byte 100,000 is acknowledged and the window size is 4 kilobytes. The sending TCP sends 2,000 more data bytes in two equal-sized messages. If the first message is lost but the second is received successfully, then both must be retransmitted, since the highest byte acknowledged will still be 100,000.

Another potential inefficiency in TCP involves a situation in which a high-speed network is connected to a low-speed network using a router. In such as situation, a host sending data packets on the high-speed network to a host on the low-speed network can cause poor bandwidth utilization and packet loss. This occurs when the host on the high-speed network sends packets to the router, which meters the packets out on the low-speed link. Eventually, however, the router will run out of buffer space and because it cannot transmit incoming packets fast enough on the low-speed link, it starts to drop packets. In response, the router will send a *source quench* ICMP message to tell the sending TCP on the high-speed link to stop sending so much data. The receiving TCP, meanwhile, will set a large window size, since it is receiving packets at a much slower rate and can accommodate more data. Consequently, the sending TCP will again start sending packets at a high speed, and the cycle will start all over again. Because the sending TCP retransmits packets the router has dropped, the effective throughput rate is much lower than it would be if the TCP smoothly transmitted packets at a rate that matched the bandwidth of the low-speed network. An algorithm called **TCP slow start** provides a remedy to this problem. It uses a smoothing function to slowly increase a sender's transmission rate until packets start to be lost, and then it backs off transmitting until the rate is below the packet loss threshold. This algorithm is so successful, it is part of most TCP implementations.

4.3   User Datagram Protocol

The **User Datagram Protocol (UDP)** [Postel 1980] is like TCP in several ways. Each UDP message is encapsulated in an IP packet and UDP has the byte stream abstraction of TCP. UDP also has the same notion of ports as TCP, and the

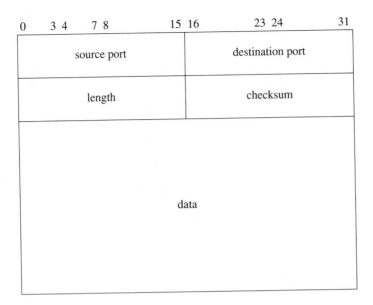

Figure 4.4 UDP Message Format.

destination port and *source port* fields serve the same purpose as they do for TCP. Further, it does a checksum of the entire UDP header and message that is carried in the *checksum* field.

Unlike TCP, however, UDP is a packet-oriented protocol. An application using UDP sees discrete messages that are exactly the size of the UDP payload. It has no acknowledgement strategy or guarantee of reliable delivery; UDP adds only port numbers to the basic IP best effort delivery paradigm, so a UDP message, shown in Fig. 4.4, has a much smaller header than TCP.

UDP is an unreliable protocol. Messages can be lost or arrive out of sequence, and it becomes the job of the application using UDP as a transport protocol to handle these situations. Keep in mind, however, that over most networks, 99% of UDP messages are delivered, and for those services that don't need 100% reliability, UDP works quite well and is more efficient than TCP. If a service needs 100% guaranteed delivery, TCP is the better protocol. However, UDP can be used effectively where the application takes care of the reliability issues. For example, most implementations of NFS use UDP; its less than 100% reliability is overcome by adding reliability within the NFS protocol itself. UDP also is often used to disseminate routing information, for instance, by RIP. It is the principal transport protocol of the Domain Name System (DNS) (see Chapter 5), where 100% reliability is not essential. In DNS, as with NFS, the application retransmits lost UDP messages. Voice or video UDP applications may not even retransmit.

UDP does not have a standard connection setup procedure. Because sequence numbers and window sizes need not be exchanged, neither the initial three-way handshake nor the closing two-way handshake are needed. In fact UDP itself has no notion of a connection. Rather, a server process using UDP can receive messages from any client that sends the message to the server's port address. A UDP based server's ability to receive UDP messages from any number of clients contrasts sharply with the TCP paradigm of having each server only receive messages from a single client.

An application using UDP also can take advantage of simultaneous broadcasting of messages to many destinations. RIP uses this feature, as do the Sun RPC services when they want to find application servers on the network.

4.4   Packet Multiplexing

Packet multiplexing enables packets received by IP to be sent to the correct host process. IP can receive packets destined for many different local processes. Looking at the value of the *protocol* field in the IP header, it sorts the packets by transport protocol. Figure 4.5 shows a packet stream and the division by protocol that occurs as IP processes the packets. IP sends each packet to the input routine for each protocol type. Note in the figure the further subdivision by each of the transport protocols.

At this point, the *source port* and *destination port* fields, along with the source and destination IP addresses, uniquely identify the process to send the message. Ports are uniquely assigned to each client process running on a single host; therefore no two clients on the same host use the same port address for either a TCP or UDP connection. Client port assignments are enforced by the host operating system.

Because ports are defined by protocol, a TCP connection can use, without conflict, the same port number as can a UDP connection. Figure 4.5 shows two

Figure 4.5 IP Packet Stream.

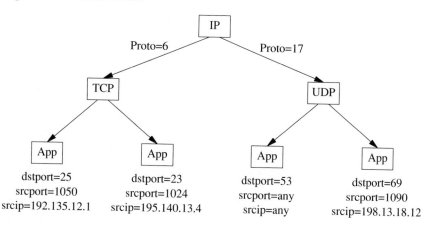

processes using TCP and two using UDP. The TCP processes are connected to a remote endpoint identified by the *srcport* and *srcip* values. Another TCP connection to the same destination port using a different source port could be established from one of the same remote IP addresses. Or a TCP connection could use the same source and destination port numbers but be from a different IP address. UDP, since it is connectionless, can use wildcards for the source port or the source IP address. Note that in the figure, any UDP message bound for port 53 from any remote destination using any port is handed to the process. However, a process using UDP also can be specific regarding from where messages can be received, as shown in the other UDP connection in the figure.

Well-known ports are assigned to server processes depending on the service. For example, an SMTP server uses TCP port 25 and a TELNET server uses TCP port 23, while an FTP server uses TCP port 21 for the interactive session and TCP port 20 for the data connection. Because client port assignments are unique for each host and servers use well-known ports, a unique address for each connection is the concatenation of the server IP address, the server port, the client IP address, the client port, and the transport protocol.

To illustrate, suppose a TELNET server listens on port 23 on a host with IP address 129.12.34.5 using TCP. A client on a host with IP address 130.12.13.4 wants to establish a connection with this server and so obtains a unique and unused port number (say, 1234) for its end of the connection. It then initiates a connection to port 23 with IP address 129.12.34.5. When the connection is established, it is identified by the unique tuple <129.12.34.5, 23, 130.12.13.4, 1234, TCP>, which is often written with each IP address and the port number concatenated together, that is, <129.12.34.5.23, 130.12.13.4.1234, TCP>. Also the tuple is written with the local system IP address and port first. Therefore on the client, the tuple is <130.12.13.4.1234, 129.12.34.5.23, TCP>, which is a unique identifier for the processes on both the client and server side of the connection.

Normally, a service using TCP allows more than one connection to a well-known port. The TELNET server forks a copy of itself to handle the current connection and the original process goes back to listening on port 23. No conflicts exist because all TCP messages destined for the first connection are uniquely identified by the tuple connection address that is contained in every message sent. If the TELNET server in the example establishes another TELNET connection from host 130.12.13.4, then that connection will have a different client port number (recall that port assignments are unique for each client on a host). Therefore messages destined for that connection will have a different connection address.

4.5   Programming Interfaces

It would be inconvenient for every application to have to deal directly with TCP or UDP, and indeed, the construction of TCP messages, as well as the details of TCP flow control, need not and should not be a part of every application. To facilitate dealings with TCP and UDP, a generalized **interprocess communications**

facility (IPC) works with different transport protocols. Two popular IPC interfaces are BSD Sockets [Leffler *et al.* 1989] and TLI [USL 1990]; see also PII in Chapter 1. They are rather similar; TLI is more general than the BSD socket interface because it is designed to support other protocol families, notably OSI; however, a great deal of UNIX TCP/IP software uses the BSD socket interface.

BSD Socket Interface

BSD socket interfaces give the application writer a set of system calls to interface to a set of network protocols; The basic communications abstraction is the **socket.** A socket is a communication end-point not unlike a UNIX file descriptor. In fact, under UNIX, a socket is associated with a UNIX descriptor when the operating system creates it, and the programmer can manipulate a socket descriptor in almost the same way as a file descriptor. The closest analogy to a socket is one end of a UNIX pipe, except that data can be both read and written on a socket. When two sockets are logically connected by an underlying transport mechanism like a network protocol family, then data can pass from one socket over the network to the other socket.

Before data is passed in this manner, an association must be established between the two. In the case of a client/server using TCP as the transport protocol, Fig. 4.6 shows the server code. BSD sockets follow the TCP connection model very closely. The server first must get a socket from the operating system. The *socket()* call then returns a socket of the right type; in this case, the correct type is SOCK_STREAM, which implies a socket that can handle a two-way byte stream. The address family is the TCP/IP family (AF_INET) and the transport protocol used is TCP.

The *bind()* call assigns an address to the socket. For the server, the local address is the concatenation of the host's IP address with the service's well-known port number. The *getservbyname()* call is a support routine that maps the service name to a well-known port. (The service mapping is obtained from the /etc/services file or from an NIS map.) The INADDR_ANY is used as the IP address of the connection. Binding the socket to INADDR_ANY allows the server to accept messages sent to any of its IP addresses, including the loopback address — a convenient shorthand.

The *listen()* call sets a queue length on incoming connections. If a connection is in process when another connection request arrives, the second request is held on a backlog queue; if the backlog queue is full, that request is dropped. The *accept()* call blocks indefinitely until a client requests a connection. When a client request is fielded, the *accept()* call takes the bound socket descriptor as an argument and returns a new socket descriptor. This new socket descriptor is identical to the original one but is associated with the accepted connection; that is, the remote socket number and remote IP address are now known and the connection address is the five-tuple of <local_port, local_ip, remote_port, remote_ip, protocol>. Returning a different socket for each connection allows multiple connections to the same well-known port.

```
/* server code stub */
int s;
int status;
struct servent *serv;
struct sockaddr_in addr;

s = socket(AF_INET, SOCK_STREAM, TCP);
serv = getservbyname("telnet", "tcp");
addr.sin_family = AF_INET;
addr.sin_port = serv->s_port;
addr.sin_addr = INADDR_ANY;
addrlen = sizeof(addr);
bind(s, &addr, addrlen);
listen(s, backlog);
for (;;) {
    snew = accept(s, clientaddr, clientaddrlen);
    /* child code - a new connection */
    if ((fork() == 0) {
        close(s);
        doit(snew);
        exit(0);
    }
    /* parent */
    close(snew);
    wait3(&status, WNOHANG);
}
```

Figure 4.6 Socket Server Code.

At this point, a child process is forked and the connection is handed off to the programmer-supplied *doit()* routine. The parent process loops back and waits for other connections by using the original socket descriptor. The parent also reaps child processes as they exit by using the *wait3()* system call, which picks up child processes that have exited.

The client side code, shown in Fig. 4.7 is fairly simple. The client gets a socket and binds the address to its local address using the same mechanism as the server does. The only nonzero field is the address family. Because no port address is specified, the socket port number is selected by the operating system. After binding the local socket, the client does a *connect()* using the IP address of the server and the well-known port of the service offered. When the connect call returns successfully, the client socket is associated with the full connection address. The client now can use the socket descriptor to read and write data from the network connection. Used in this way, the socket descriptor behaves just like an ordinary UNIX file descriptor.

For a UDP client/server, the overall code is very similar to that of a TCP client/server. Figure 4.8 shows the code used for a server and Fig. 4.9 shows the client code. In this example, a client writes a message to a server and waits for a response. The primary difference between the UDP and TCP server code, is the

```
/* client code segment */
struct servent *serv;
struct hostent *servhost;
int s;
struct sockaddr_in addr;

s = socket(AF_INET, SOCK_STREAM, TCP);
serv = getservbyname("telnet", "tcp");
servhost = gethostbyname("akasha.tic.com");
bzero(addr, sizeof(struct sockaddr_in));
addr.sin_family = AF_INET;
addrlen = sizeof(struct sockaddr_in);
bind(s, &addr);
addr.sin_port = serv->s_port;
addr.sin_addr = servhost->h_addrlist[0];
connect(s, &addr, addrlen) == -1)

/* start reading and writing from the socket descriptor */
```

Figure 4.7 Socket Client Code Stub.

---

that UDP server simply reads and writes to its socket, whereas the TCP server must explicitly accept each connection and fork a new process to handle each connection. The remote address of the client is filled in as an argument to the *sendto()* system call, and the *recvfrom()* system call returns the remote address of the client writing to the server. There are no *accept()* or *connect()* calls required. A UDP

Figure 4.8 UDP Server Code Stub.

```
/* server code stub */
struct sockaddr_in addr, from;
int s, fromlen, err, n;
char buf[BUFSIZ];

s = socket(AF_INET, SOCK_DGRAM, IPPROTO_UDP);
addr.sin_family = AF_INET;
addr.sin_port = htons(2000);
addr.sin_addr.s_addr = INADDR_ANY;
err = bind(s, &addr, sizeof(addr));
fromlen = sizeof(from);
n = recvfrom(s, buf, BUFSIZ, 0, &from, &fromlen);
fprintf(stderr, "%s0, buf);
strcpy(buf, "hello");
n = strlen(buf) + 1;
sendto(s, buf, n, 0, &from, fromlen);
```

```
/* client code stub */
struct sockaddr_in addr, serv;
int s, servlen, err, n;
char buf[BUFSIZ];

s = socket(AF_INET, SOCK_DGRAM, IPPROTO_UDP);
addr.sin_family = AF_INET;
addr.sin_port = 0;
addr.sin_addr.s_addr = INADDR_ANY;
bind(s, &addr, sizeof(addr));
serv.sin_family = AF_INET;
serv.sin_port = htons(2000);
serv.sin_addr.s_addr = inet_addr("127.0.0.1");
strcpy(buf, "hi there");
n = strlen(buf) + 1;
n = sendto(s, buf, n, 0, &serv, sizeof(serv));
servlen = sizeof(serv);
n = recvfrom(s, buf, BUFSIZ, 0, &serv, &servlen);
fprintf(stderr, "%s0, buf);
```

Figure 4.9 UDP Client Code Stub.

---

server uses a socket type of SOCK_DGRAM which implies a datagram oriented service in which a message is sent or received with its message boundary preserved.

It is up to the server code to multiplex the connection from each client. It is possible to associate a UDP socket with a specific client, in which case all data sent and received on the socket can be sent to and received from only that specific client. In practice, this is seldom done because most UDP-based servers are interested in sending and receiving data from more than one client.

TLI Interface

TLI, found on System V UNIX variants, is an alternate user interface that provides much the same functionality as the BSD socket interface does. In Figs. 4.10 and 4.11, a TCP server and client use the TLI interface. Many of the TLI routines have names similar to those of socket routines. A transport endpoint is created using the *t_open()* function, which uses a pseudo-device name describing the type of endpoint desired. In this case, a TCP endpoint is created using the device */dev/tcp*, and the *t_bind()* routine binds an address to the endpoint. The user can either specify an address or let the underlying protocol select it. Unlike the socket *bind()* call, *t_bind()* also sets the connection queue, an action that in the socket case is performed by *listen()*. The *t_listen()* call waits for a new connection and returns the remote connection address. The connection at this point is idle. Using TLI, a server can listen for several connections without accepting them. A connection is not ready to be used until it is accepted using the *t_accept()* call. Because TLI's *t_accept()* does not open a new descriptor explicitly, a new

```
/* server code stub */
int fd, new;
struct sockaddr_in addr;
struct servent *serv;
struct t_bind bind_request;
struct t_call *call;

fd = t_open("/dev/tcp", O_RDWR, NULL);
serv = getservbyname("telnet", "tcp");
addr.sin_family = AF_INET;
addr.sin_port = serv->s_port;
addr.sin_addr = INADDR_ANY;
bind_request.addr..maxlen = sizeof(addr);
bind_request.addr.len = sizeof(addr);
bind_request.addr.buf = (char *) &addr;
bind_request.qlen = 3;
t_bind(fd, &bind_request, NULL);
call = t_alloc(fd, T_CALL, T_ADDR);
for (;;) {
    t_listen(fd, call);
    new = t_open("/dev/tcp", O_RDWR, NULL);
    t_bind(new, NULL, NULL, 0);
    t_accept(fd, new, call);
    if ((fork() == 0) { /* child code - a new connection */
        close(s);
        doit(new);
        exit(0);
    }
    /* parent */
    close(new);
    wait3();
}
```

Figure 4.10 TLI TCP Server Code Stub.

---

descriptor must be created using *t_open()* and an address must be bound to the new descriptor using *t_bind*. In this case, any address will do. *t_accept* accepts the new connection, which is now associated with the *new* descriptor. Just as in the socket case, a new process is forked to handle the connection and the server loops back and fields any new connections.

The client code is very similar to that in the socket case. An endpoint is created and an address bound to it. The remote address and port numbers are filled in, and then a *t_connect()* call is made to connect to the remote server. Note in both the server and client cases the use of explicit buffers, which must be allocated for the protocol structures. These structures are allocated using the *t_alloc()* routine. The UDP code using TLI is not shown, but is very similar to the BSD socket code.

Some TCP/IP services are written using TLI, but most services are implemented using the BSD socket interface which is quite adequate for use with both

```
/* client code segment */
struct servent *serv;
struct hostent *servhost;
int fd;
struct sockaddr_in addr;

fd = t_open("/dev/tcp", O_RDWR, NULL);
t_bind(fd, NULL, NULL);
serv = getservbyname("telnet", "tcp");
servhost = gethostbyname("akasha.tic.com");
bzero(addr, sizeof(struct sockaddr_in));
addr.sin_family = AF_INET;
addr.sin_port = serv->s_port;
addr.sin_addr = servhost->h_addrlist[0];
call = (struct t_call *) t_alloc(fd, T_CALL, T_ADDR);
call->addr.maxlen = sizeof(addr);
call->addr.len = sizeof(addr);
call->addr.buf = (char *) &addr;
call->opt = 0;
call->udata.len = 0;
t_connect(fd, call, NULL);

/* start reading and writing from the socket descriptor */
```

Figure 4.11 TLI TCP Client Code Stub.

TCP and UDP transport. The TLI code is somewhat longer than the equivalent socket code, primarily because the TLI interface is more general. An excellent reference for programming using both BSD sockets and TLI is [Stevens 1990].

References

Leffler et al. 1989.   Leffler, Samuel J., McKusick, Marshall Kirk, Karels, Michael J., & Quarterman, John S., *The Design and Implementation of the 4.3BSD UNIX Operating System,* Addison-Wesley, Reading, MA (1989).

Postel 1980.   Postel, John B., *User datagram Protocol (RFC768),* August 1980.

Postel 1981.   Postel, John B., *Transmission Control Protocol (RFC793),* September 1981.

Stevens 1990.   Stevens, W. Richard, *UNIX Network Programming,* Prentice-Hall, Englewood Cliffs, NJ (1990).

USL 1990.   USL, *UNIX System V Release 4 Programmer's Guide: Networking Interfaces,* Prentice Hall, Englewood Cliffs, NJ (1990).

CHAPTER 5

Naming Hosts and Other Objects

The lower layers of the TCP/IP stack work exclusively with numbers. Application protocols, however, typically allow a user to type mnemonic names to identify network objects. Mnemonic names are easier for users to remember. Obviously, it is simpler to type

```
telnet akasha.tic.com
```

than the harder-to-remember, but equivalent

```
telnet 192.135.128.129
```

when using the TELNET protocol to remotely log on to a machine. In this example, the TELNET client software calls on a nameservice to map the name *akasha.tic.com* into the IP address 192.135.128.129.

This very useful network service hides the nitty-gritty details of how the lower-layer network protocols work. An application called a **nameserver** uses a well-defined programmatic interface to translate, or **map,** a name into a network object that is usable by the lower-layer protocols. This naming interface, which could be a simple table lookup or a distributed database, hides the details of how the name is looked up and mapped. The network object is then passed as a parameter to the transport protocol interface. A nameservice is a very important application because it is used by most other applications. As it turns out, the principal naming system used by TCP/IP based applications is itself implemented as a network application.

Naming evolved along with the other protocols. Vestiges of earlier systems, still with us today, have resulted in confusion about naming and nameservices. We hope this chapter will clear up some of this confusion and clarify how naming is handled on a UNIX systems that use TCP/IP.

5.1   History of Naming

The predecessor to the Internet was the ARPANET. The most important network resource in that network was the IP address. The ARPANET used a simple manual protocol to give meaningful names to IP addresses. A single naming authority assigned names and their corresponding IP addresses to network interfaces on an as-needed basis. Because most hosts on the ARPANET had a single network interface, these interface names became synonymous with host names. A host name, or **hostname,** was a simple identifier, such as *ut-sally* or *sri-nic*. A common convention in those early days was to use a sitename prefix followed by a unique machine name. So the name *ut-sally* was the name of a host at the University of Texas called *sally*. The name *sri-nic* was the name of a host at SRI International called *nic*.

A central registry maintained these names and their corresponding IP addresses in a machine readable file [Harrenstien *et al.* 1985a]. A site administrator wanting to name a new host would submit to the central registry the name along with the IP address of the host. The administrator knew what IP network number to use, since it was assigned to the site when the network was established. If the hostname was not already assigned, the registrar would add the name along with the IP address to the central host file; if the name was already assigned, the registrar would reject the name and ask the administrator to supply another one.

Periodically, site administrators would copy the central host file from a well-known location to each site's local machines using a simple protocol [Harrenstien *et al.* 1985b]. The information on each host contained in this file was used by a simple lookup function to map a hostname to an IP address. On UNIX systems the */etc/hosts* file became the standard place to hold the hostname to IP address mappings. Two library routines, *gethostbyname()* and *gethostbyaddr()* were used to look up entries in this file in a standard way. Other operating systems used a similar programmatic interface. When the ARPANET comprised only a few hundred hosts, this system worked fairly well. Additions to the central registry were relatively infrequent and the size of the table was reasonably small. Further, propagating updates was straightforward — every site simply copied the central file.

The early Internet inherited this centralized naming system from the ARPANET. As the Internet grew beyond a few hundred hosts, central administration of hostnames became impractical. One reason for this was the large size of the central host table and the exponential growth in the number of sites. With just a few sites, copying a small host file was not a problem; with a thousand sites copying a much larger file, a significant load was placed on the central registry's server and personnel.

Another problem was that all machine names had to be unique across the entire Internet. As the Internet grew, name conflicts became more frequent. It was also cumbersome for a system administrator to notify the central registry every time a name was added. So Internet researchers invented the **Domain Name System (DNS)** to replace the central registry and allow automatic distribution of naming authority [Mockapetris 1987a].

5.2   Domain Name System

The Domain Name System is the Internet's official naming system and is designed to name various network resources, the most common of which is the IP address. DNS is a **distributed naming system,** that is, the database that translates names to objects is scattered across many thousands of hosts. As a true distributed resource, it is maintained by many organizations; no single organization controls or owns this database but rather each manages only a small piece of it. We describe how this is accomplished shortly. Note that DNS defines both the resources named and the protocols used to communicate between the nameservers that maintain the database.

Adoption of DNS by the Internet community improved the naming procedure by allowing the following:

• Delegation
Naming could be delegated, leaving the central registry to register only naming authorities rather than having to name every host. Doing this reduced the registry's workload considerably.

• Dynamic Distribution
Name lookups were dynamically distributed, so site administrators no longer needed to copy a large central host file from one remote host.

• Redundancy
The lookup algorithms were redundant, that is, a name could be found on more than one server, thus distributing the load across several servers. Also, reliability was improved because a name lookup no longer depended on a single server.

• Extensibility
Resources in addition to IP addresses could be defined in the system and distributed as IP addresses are.

We discuss all but redundancy next.

Delegation: Domain Names and Naming Authorities

DNS defines a name space that is a tree structure with a single root node. Each node is owned by a naming authority. The owner of a node can create any number of child nodes. Each child node of a parent must have a unique name. Figure 5.1 shows part of the DNS naming tree.

A **domain** is any node and all of its descendant nodes. A **domain name** uniquely identifies a single node within a domain. Names are written by combining node names and separating each node name with a period. For example, the node *akasha* in the figure has the domain name *akasha.tic.com.*. This name, which uniquely identifies that node, is derived by following the path from node *akasha* to node *tic* to node *com* to the root node. Note that the root node is unnamed and is designated by a single period. A domain name is very similar to a

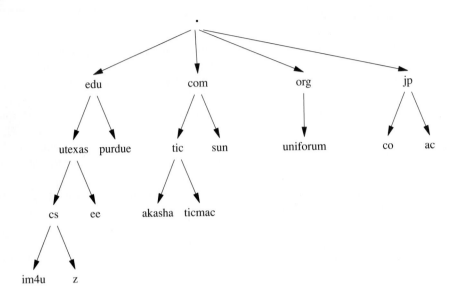

Figure 5.1 Part of the DNS Naming Tree.

UNIX pathname, except that a domain name traverses the naming tree from the target node to the root (instead of from the root to the filename as in a UNIX pathname and the separator character is a period rather than a slash.

The children of the root node are called **top-level domains.** In Fig. 5.1 the top-level domains shown are *edu, com, org,* and *jp* (the real tree has many more). These domains split the tree both geographically and by type of organization. For example, the top-level domain, represented by node *com,* stands for "Commercial"; commercial for-profit organization are assigned names under this node. The assigned names are usually the names or initials of the organization. For example, *tic.com.* is the domain name assigned to Texas Internet Consulting. Similarly, the children of the top-level domain *edu* are the names of educational institutions. In this case, the domain name *utexas.edu.* stands for the University of Texas at Austin.

You will notice an anomaly in the top-level domains. Every country in the world, including the United States, has a top level domain that is identified by a two-letter country code. However, most organizations in the U.S. register a domain under one of the other top-level domains. Country codes as a geographical partitioning of the top-level domains make more sense, but the original assignment of top-level domains defined an *organizational* partitioning at a time when almost all Internet hosts were in the United States. So educational institutions ended up under *edu,* commercial companies under *com,* and nonprofit organizations under *org.* Most foreign country registries mirror the top-level domain structure. For example, the domain *co.jp.* is the domain name for commercial companies in Japan, while *ac.jp.* is the domain for academic institutions in Japan.

A domain name that traverses the path from a node to the root is called a **fully qualified domain name (FQDN).** A domain name that traverses only part of the path to the root is a **relative domain name** because it is relative to the parent of the node where the traversal ends. Relative domains are a convenient shorthand when you know the context in which the domain name is used.

An FQDN should always end with a period — the period that represents the root node — to distinguish it from a relative domain name. In practice, it is common to drop the final period since it's usually clear from the context when a domain is fully qualified. Most applications that use DNS names don't require the final period on domain names and some applications — for example, electronic mail — don't allow a final period to be appended to a domain name even if it is fully qualified.

This inconsistency can cause considerable confusion. For example, is the name *cs.edu* fully qualified or is it a relative domain name under some other domain? How do you tell the difference? A good rule of thumb is to avoid relative domain names that end with one of the top-level domain names. For university computer science departments, however, this can be a problem: The common abbreviation for the department *cs* is also the top-level domain name for the country Czechoslovakia! In the remainder of this book, we will generally drop the final period on fully qualified domain names except when they are absolutely required, and we'll make it clear when a domain name is relative.

Dynamic Distribution: Naming Authority Distribution

The naming authority for any domain can delegate naming authority to any of its children. Descendants of a domain are called **subdomains.** For example our company, Texas Internet Consulting, has authority for all the names under the domain *tic.com*. The naming authority for the top-level domain *com* granted that authority. The grant of authority is given when the new subdomain is registered with the registry that owns the parent node. The registration procedure is under the complete control of the parent authority.

A naming authority can assign subdomain names arbitrarily, as long as each child node is unique. However, several common naming conventions exist. An authority can organize subdomains by department or division. Or it can organize them geographically by country, state, or city. Some may choose to do both at the same time. All are allowed within the DNS naming framework.

Each naming authority can delegate authority for any of its own subdomains. For example, we may chose to delegate authority to the subdomain *austin.tic.com,* which is for an office in Austin, Texas. Later, we might delegate authority to *la.tic.com,* which is for an office in Los Angeles, California. In turn, each subdomain's authority can delegate authority for any of its own subdomains and so forth down to any level in the DNS hierarchy. In practice, however, four to five levels of hierarchy appear to be sufficient. The DNS tree is in fact much broader than it is deep. (It appears that a domain name with more than five levels is too much for most people to remember.)

Extensibility: Resources with Names

A name gives a resource a convenient reference. The name is then mapped to the resource. The original ARPANET central naming authority dealt primarily with mapping names to IP addresses. Most DNS lookups apply the same name to IP address mapping. However, you can map a DNS name to other resources besides IP addresses. DNS uses a typed **resource record** to identify the resource being named. You can associate one or more resource records with a single node in the DNS tree.

A resource record is a five-tuple:

<domain_name ttl IN *resource_type resource_value>*

This five-tuple is broken down into the following fields:

• *domain_name*
The FQDN for the resource that is the key to identifying that resource. These appear in a resource record with the trailing period. For clarity in the text, we will drop the final period, since the context is understood.

• *ttl*
The time in seconds that the resource record can be cached by a nonauthoritative server before the record is discarded, that is, a nameserver that has retrieved a resource record from another server can cache the resource record for the number of seconds shown in the *ttl* field. This field is decremented every second; when it reaches 0, the resource record is discarded. This algorithm lets cached values timeout after a specific period of time so that updates can be propagated over time. This field generally is set to a default value. For clarity, we will omit this optional field when we define the various resource records later in this chapter.

• IN
Identifies this resource record as belonging to the TCP/IP or INternet protocol family. Because this is really the only protocol family in wide use within DNS, we will, for clarity, omit this field in the following sections.

• *resource_type*
A unique identifier for the type of resource named. During a lookup, the *resource_type* is used to distinguish between resource records mapped to the same domain name.

• *resource_value*
The value of the resource. This field can be either a single value, such as an IP address, or a record with several fields.

DNS defines a set of standard resource record types. We describe the most common types next.

IP Addresses. IP addresses or "A records" are the most commonly named resource within DNS. Each of these records maps the domain name to an IP address. The format of an A the record is:

domain_name A *ip_address*

For example, the resource record

```
ticmac.tic.com. A 192.135.128.131
```

maps the domain name *ticmac.tic.com* to the IP address 192.135.128.131. We show the IP address in dotted-decimal notation; however, in practice, it is stored by DNS as a 4-byte integer. As with all resource records, the resource type, A, is encoded as an integer number. This record means the host with the name *tic-mac.tic.com* has a network interface with the address 192.135.128.131.

A multi-homed host or router has an A record for each network interface as follows:

```
router.tic.com. A 192.135.128.1
router.tic.com. A 193.1.1.1
```

This example illustrates the mapping of the name *router.tic.com* to two IP addresses, thus identifying a machine with two network interfaces.

Host Information. An HINFO record identifies the hardware and operating system of the host with the given domain name. The format of this record type is:

domain_name HINFO *hardware os*

For example, the HINFO record

```
akasha.tic.com HINFO Sun SunOS
```

says that the host *akasha.tic.com* is a Sun running the SunOS operating system.

Aliases. A CNAME record associates a domain name with another domain name. Its format is:

domain_name CNAME *canonical_name*
```
For example,
```

the CNAME record

```
mac.tic.com. CNAME ticmac.tic.com.
```

indicates the name *mac.tic.com* is an alias for the name *ticmac.tic.com*. A lookup for a resource record under the name *mac.tic.com* will immediately continue the search under the domain name *ticmac.tic.com*. A CNAME record can be the only resource record at a given node in the domain tree. This is because once a CNAME record is encountered, resource record lookup continues at the aliased domain name.

Mail Related Resource Records. Several resource records aid in the delivery of electronic mail. Except for the MX record type, most are experimental and rarely used and, in fact, most UNIX mail software does not support their functionality. For completeness, we include them here:

• Mail Exchanger. An MX record identifies the location of a SMTP server that will accept mail for the target domain. The format of this record type is:

domain_name MX *priority server_name*

priority is an integer number. *server_name* is the domain name of the SMTP server. You may define more than one MX record for a given target domain. Servers with a lower priority will be used before servers with a higher priority. This arrangement lets redundant mail servers for a given domain exist simultaneously. MX records also are very useful for gatewaying mail to non-Internet hosts. We discuss MX record usage at length in Chapter 8.

• Mailbox. An MB record identifies the name of a host that contains the given mailbox name. An MB record's format is:

domain_name MB *mail_host*

MB records enables the location of a user's mailbox to be decoupled from the user's domain mail address. For example, the MB record

```
smoot.tic.com. MB ticmac.tic.com.
```

indicates that mail addressed to *smoot@tic.com* is forwarded to the host *ticmac.tic.com,* which is where the mailbox for the user *smoot* exists. An MB record treats the mail address as a domain name, with the "@" in the mail address replaced with a period. Much of the functionality of MB records can be obtained by using aliases, as we show in Chapter 8.

• Mail Renaming. An MR record allows a mailbox to be renamed. Its format is:

domain_name MR *mailbox_rename*

It is similar to the CNAME record but is used for mailbox names. For example, the MR record

```
fred.tic.com. MR fj.tic.com.
```

indicates that mail to *fred@tic.com* should be sent to the mailbox *fj@tic.com*.

• Mailing Group. The MG record allows a mailing group to be established. The format of this type of record is:

domain_name MG *member_mailbox*

The *domain_name* is the group mailbox and the *member_mailbox* is the mailbox of a group member. For example, the MG record

```
group.tic.com. MG sally.tic.com.
group.tic.com. MG fred.tic.com.
```

indicates mail to *group@tic.com* is sent to *sally@tic.com* and *fred@tic.com*. These records are functionally equivalent to mail address aliasing that we discuss in Chapter 8.

• Mail Information. The MINFO record allows the mailbox of a mailing group's administrator to be specified. A mailbox for error messages can also specified. Its format is:

domain_name MINFO *owner_mailbox* *error_mailbox*

Adding this record type results in better control over maintenance of mailing lists built from MG records. For example, the MINFO record

```
group.tic.com. MINFO jill.tic.com. group-error.tic.com.
```

indicates the owner of the *group@tic.com* mailing list is *jill@tic.com*. Error messages are sent to *group-error@tic.com*. By convention, a mail message sent to *group-request@tic.com* will be sent to *jill@tic.com*.

Well-known Services. The WKS record indicates the services available on a given host. The format of this record type is:

domain_name WKS *protocol services*

protocol is the transport protocol used by the service, either TCP or UDP. *services* is a set of well-known service names found in the file */etc/services*. For example, the WKS record

```
ticmac.tic.com. WKS TCP daytime smtp telnet ftp
```

indicates that the host *ticmac.tic.com* supports the *daytime*, *smtp*, *telnet*, and *ftp* services. WKS records are not essential, but when they are present, an application can use them to determine if the service is available on the remote host.

Pointer. The PTR record lets one domain point to another domain within the naming tree. Its format is:

domain_name PTR *domain_name*

A PTR record is semantically different than a CNAME record. A CNAME record, unlike a PTR, always causes the lookup for a specific resource record to continue with the mapped domain name. A PTR record simply returns the domain name found as the value of the record. The purpose of a PTR record is embedded in the semantics of the DNS namespace. Most commonly, PTR records map an IP address back to a domain. We explain how this works when we talk later about the special *in-addr.arpa* domain.

Nameservers. An NS record identifies the locations of the authoritative name-servers for the given domain. Its format is:

domain_name NS *server_name*

server_name is the domain name of the host that maintains an authoritative set of resource records or database for the domain. This host is not required to be within the domain for which it is an authority. The domain name system requires at least two authoritative servers, preferably at different geographic locations for purposes of redundancy and reliability. These servers also should have identical copies of the database for the domain.

Naming Authority. An SOA record indicates the start of a naming authority. The format of an SOA record is:

domain_name SOA *host_name mailbox serial refresh retry expire minimum*

It is the first resource record found in a nameserver database. *host_name* is the host in which the database resides. *mailbox* identifies the person responsible for the domain. *serial* is the serial number of the database. The remaining parameters are times in seconds. *refresh, retry,* and *expire* are used by a secondary server to control how frequently it should refresh its copy of the database obtained from an authoritative server. We will have more to say about how these parameters are used when we discuss the NS database.

DNS Operational Architecture

The general DNS architecture is shown in Fig. 5.2. DNS is implemented using a set of distributed nameservers. Each nameserver maintains a set of resource records. Servers read queries sent to them by listening on the TCP and UDP well-known port 53. Most queries to a nameserver use the UDP port; TCP is used only when an entire zone is to be transferred from one server to another server. If a server cannot answer a query directly, it can forward a query to another name-server or send a response to the sender that contains the IP address of a better nameserver for the sender to use.

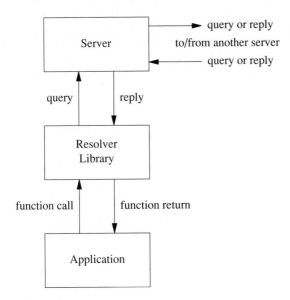

Figure 5.2 DNS Architecture.

A query and a response use the same message format, as shown in Fig. 5.3. The format breaks down as follows:

• *query header*
Includes various flags that control the query processing.

Figure 5.3 DNS Query Format.

header
question
answer
authority
additional

• *question*

Completed by the DNS client. This section contains the target domain name and the **type** and **class** of the query. The type of a query either matches a resource record type or may be wildcarded to ask for any resource record. The class of a query is always the code for the IN class for TCP/IP queries.

• *answer*

Completed by the nameserver that replies to the query. The nameserver fills in the resource record asked for and returns it to the client.

• *authority*

Filled in by the nameserver, at its option, with NS and SOA resource records for authoritative servers. This is used when a nameserver cannot answer a query, but does have information about the location of nameservers that can be used to help answer the query. For example, a query for the A record for *akasha.tic.com* to a server with no information about *akasha.tic.com* may return the NS records for the authoritative servers for the *tic.com* domain, if the server has them cached.

• *additional*

Completed by the nameserver, at its option, with useful information to aid the client in answering the query or give the client information needed for subsequent queries. For example, a nameserver that answers an MX query might send the A records of the SMTP servers returned with each MX record since it is highly likely the client will need them when attempting an SMTP connection.

An application sends a DNS query to a nameserver and waits for a response. To do this, the application uses a standard set of query interface routines that implement a **DNS resolver.** The resolver not only generates the query and transmits it to a nameserver; it also handles responses and retransmits a query request (perhaps to an alternate nameserver) if a response is not received within a specified time. Query processing is described more fully in [Mockapetris 1987b].

Applications that support DNS usually wrap the standard UNIX hostname lookup routines, *gethostbyname()* and *gethostbyaddr()*, around the DNS specific routines. The application calls the standard library routines, which in turn call the DNS library routines that query DNS nameservers.

The DNS domain tree is divided into zones. A **zone** is a subtree for which naming authority has been delegated. It includes the node for which naming authority has been delegated and all children of that node for which naming authority has not been further delegated. Figure 5.4 shows an example DNS tree divided into zones. The dashed lines show the zone boundaries. So in this example, the root node is in a separate zone. The domains *edu, com, org,* and *jp* are each separate zones. The domain *utexas.edu* and its subdomain *ee* are a single zone, while the subdomain *cs* is in a separate zone. Each zone has an associated **zone database** that contains the resource records for that zone. A **primary nameserver** for each zone maintains an up-to-date copy of the zone database. Copies of this zone database also are maintained on alternate, or **secondary**

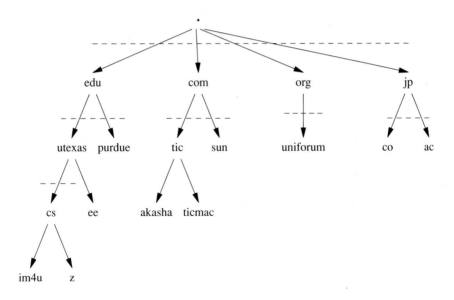

Figure 5.4 DNS Zones.

nameservers, that periodically poll the primary server for updates to the database. At least one secondary server must exist for each zone. Using secondary servers increases the reliability of the system.

A zone's parent zone database has copies of the zone's NS records as well as copies of the A records for each nameserver for the zone. The NS records "glue" the DNS tree together. Each server also maintains a cache of recently used resource records that is initially "hotwired" with the names and IP addresses of the root servers. (A server needs the location of the root servers to acquire the location of other servers outside of its own zone.)

Resource records are cached in response to queries from a resolver. A resolver usually asks a nearby server for the answer to a query. It usually also indicates that if a server can't answer the query, the server should pass it on to a more authoritative server that can. Eventually, the original server receives the answer, which it caches and then passes on to the resolver. By caching the answer, the server will be able to answer directly any other requests for the same information.

Answers also contain additional resource records. Usually these records are the names and IP addresses of the server that finally answered the query and are referred to when additional queries for the same domain are received. The server can query the remote server directly rather than going through a root server to find the server for a remote domain.

Cached records speed query processing by reducing network traffic and delays for frequently asked queries. Each cached record's *ttl* field is decremented over time. When the *ttl* reaches 0, the record is purged from the cache. This timing-out of cache entries allows updates to be propagated around the network. Because most DNS resources change slowly over time, data inconsistency is less of a problem than in a more volatile database. The cache method is sufficient to ensure that reasonably up-to-date information is available. However, applications that need absolutely up-to-date information can set a resolver flag so that queries can be answered only by an authoritative server for a zone.

Figure 5.5 illustrates a typical query sequence, including how the NS glues records and how the cache works to optimize query processing. The zone *com* holds NS records for the nameservers for the *tic.com* and the *widget.com* zones. It also has copies of A records for each nameserver that is authoritative for each of its child zones.

Suppose the following scenario occurs:

1. A query from the machine *able.widget.com* is sent to the nameserver on *ns.widget.com* (step 1 in the figure) for the IP address (an A resource record) for the domain name *baker.austin.tic.com*.

2. *ns.widget.com* has no cached resource records for *baker.austin.tic.com*, so the nameserver tries to find an NS record for the parent domain *austin.tic.com*.

3. Finding no cached records for that domain, it attempts to find an NS record for the *tic.com* domain. Finding no records for that domain, it tries for the *com* domain without success. Finding no cached resource records, it forwards the original query to one of the root nameservers (step 2 in the figure).

4. The root nameserver repeats the above algorithm. However, it finds an NS record for the *com* server and passes the query to that server (step 3 in the figure).

5. The nameserver for the *com* domain, once again, repeats the above algorithm and finds NS records and associated A records for the domain *tic.com* and

Figure 5.5 Query Example.

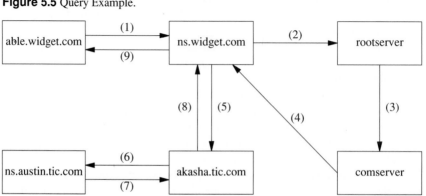

returns this information to the nameserver on *ns.widget.com* (step 4 in the figure). Note that the nameserver for the *com* domain could have answered the entire query, but chose instead to respond with an answer for a server closer to the target domain.

6. At this point, the nameserver on *ns.widget.com* caches the NS and A records and sends the original query to a server for the *tic.com* domain (step 5). If that server fails to respond within a specified time, *ns.widget.com* tries another server for that domain.

7. The server for *tic.com* that receives the query forwards it to a server for the *austin.tic.com* domain (step 6 in the figure).

8. That server has the answer desired by *baker.austin.tic.com* and so returns the answer to the server for *tic.com* (step 7), which then sends the answer to *ns.widget.com* (step 8), which in turn returns the answer to *able.widget.com* (step 9). *ns.widget.com* caches the answer for later use.

When another query comes in for *baker.austin.tic.com,* the answer will be found in the cache on *ns.widget.com,* so no query forwarding will occur. A query for *sam.austin.tic.com* will be forwarded directly to the nameserver for the *austin.tic.com* domain, since the NS and A records for that domain are returned as a part of the answer to the original query.

Using caching, most nameservers are able to answer many queries locally. Host usage patterns also make this possible because most hosts on the Internet communicate with relatively few remote hosts. When a nameserver first starts up, all remote queries go at first through one of the root nameservers. As the server caches NS and A records, the number of root requests declines and most requests go directly to the appropriate remote nameserver.

The DNS Database

For each domain, DNS resource records are assembled into zone database files. A nameserver reads these database files and creates a memory image of the zone database optimized for query processing. The database format gives you a standard way of writing down information contained in a DNS domain, a method that can be used by different nameserver implementations. This lets you move zone files from one nameserver implementation to another without changing the database format.

Figure 5.6 shows an example database file for the domain *aci.com*. Text after a ";" is a comment. The database format defines several metacommands, which are introduced with a "$" in column one; the $ORIGIN meta-command defines the default domain. All domain names that don't end in a period are assumed to be relative to this domain. This convention enables you to abbreviate domain names with a common suffix. Be very careful using this convention, however. Every domain name, including those that are a part of a resource value that do not end in a period, will have the default domain appended.

```
; database for fictitious aci.com domain
$ORIGIN aci.com.
@ SOA big hostmaster ( 10 86400 3600 3600000 604800 )
        IN NS big.aci.com.
        IN NS y.bigu.edu.
        IN MX 10 twinky
        IN MX 5 big
big     IN A 132.145.10.1
big     IN HINFO SUN4 SUNOS
twinky IN A 132.145.10.2
        IN A 132.145.2.1
twinky IN HINFO DECSTATION ULTRIX
```

Figure 5.6 Example Domain Database.

The next line is an SOA record. Every zone database begins with an SOA record. The "@" at the beginning of the line is another notational convenience and indicates that the domain name for this SOA record is the current origin, that is, *aci.com*. The first parameter after the SOA is the name of the authoritative host, followed by the mail address of the domain administrator. The mail address is a domain name that uses periods as delimiters. To convert this address to a standard mail address, change the first period to an "@" and omit any final period. Note that usually this standard mail address should be a well-known alias such as *hostmaster.aci.com (hostmaster@aci.com)*.

The next five parameters, set out within parentheses, are used to configure the operation of the zone database and are described as follows:

1. *serial*. Uses by the nameserver to determine whether an update to the database has occurred and consequently, if the nameserver should reread the database file. This number should be incremented each time the domain is updated. This parameter also is used when a secondary nameserver requests a zone transfer. In this case, a secondary nameserver sends a transfer request to a primary server. The primary returns the current serial number of the database, while the secondary checks the primary's serial number against the one in its copy of the database. If the serial number has changed, then the secondary asks the primary for a copy of the new zone database.

2. *refresh*. Lets you define the refresh interval for a zone transfer. For example, a secondary server requests a zone transfer in order to obtain a copy of the database. The refresh interval indicates the time the next transfer should be requested. It helps ensure the copy of the database is at most this amount of time in seconds old. Usually, on a fast network, it is set to 5 minutes (300 seconds) or so. On slower links, a time period of several hours or even days may be acceptable, particularly if the zone database changes infrequently.

3. *retry.* Enables you to set the retry interval, that is, the time to retry a zone transfer if the first transfer fails because of a communications failure.

4. *minimum.* Lets you establish defaults for expiration times. It sets the default *ttl* for any resource record without an explicit *ttl*.

5. *expire.* The time in seconds before a secondary copy of the zone database becomes unauthoritative. Queries to a secondary server within this time interval are considered authoritative, that is, the zone information is considered to be a current copy of the primary server's database. An application that wants only authoritative answers can set a query flag, thus requiring that answers come from a primary server or from a secondary server with an up-to-date copy of the zone database. Also, a secondary server can conceivably lose connectivity with a primary server for a long period of time. In this case, the *expire* field sets a reasonable time interval after which the zone database is considered nonauthoritative. Queries can still be answered against the database, but the answers will be flagged as nonauthoritative. The timeout interval is reset each time a successful zone transfer from a primary server is completed.

Following the SOA record are NS records that are the names of the authoritative servers for this zone. In this case, the *aci.com* domain has two authoritative servers: *big.aci.com* and *y.bigu.edu.* A server does not have to be in the same domain for which it is authoritative. Whitespace (spaces or tabs) at the beginning of a line means the domain name for this resource record is the same as the domain name of the previous resource record. The NS records could have been written as follows:

```
aci.com. IN NS big.aci.com.
aci.com. IN NS y.bigu.edu.
```

The trailing periods after the resource values are very important. If you omit them, *.aci.com.* (the value specified in the $ORIGIN meta-command) will be appended to each domain name, which would change the meaning of each record substantially. With the default domain being *aci.com* and the SOA record being associated with the *aci.com,* these two lines could have also been written as

```
        IN NS big
        IN NS y.bigu.edu.
```

or alternatively as

```
@       IN NS big
        IN NS y.bigu.edu.
```

When in doubt, use fully qualified domains and end them with a period. (Zone files are one of the few cases in which FQDNs with trailing periods are used.)

Next are all the resource records for the domain. MX records point to mail gateways for the *aci.com* domain. The domain *twinky.aci.com* (presumably the name of a host) has two IP addresses — 132.145.10.2 and 128.21.2.1. HINFO records are used to define the hardware type and the operating system used by this host. While the order of records within a zone file is immaterial (except that the SOA record must be the first record), it is convenient to place together all the records associated with a single domain name. Doing this enables you to use the leading whitespace convention and cuts down on typing.

Authoritative Subdomains. Suppose you establish an authoritative zone for *eng.aci.com.*. This domains database file is shown in Fig. 5.7. The domain has an SOA record. The $ORIGIN shorthand is used with the domain as *eng.aci.com*. The NS records point to two authoritative nameservers: *big.eng.aci.com* and *backup.aci.com*.

Because *eng.aci.com* is a subdomain of *aci.com*, the following additional lines are placed in the *aci.com* domain database:

```
eng.aci.com.      IN NS big.eng.aci.com.
                  IN NS backup.aci.com.
big.eng.aci.com. IN A 134.123.4.2
```

or, using the whitespace shorthand:

```
eng           IN NS big.eng
              IN NS backup
big.eng       IN A 134.123.4.2
```

The two NS lines are copies of the NS lines in the *eng.aci.com* zone database file. These lines provide the "glue" that indicates the location of the *eng.aci.com* nameservers. The A record for *big.eng.aci.com* is needed to hotwire the address of one of the *eng.aci.com* primary servers that is otherwise unknown to the *aci.com* zone. This takes care of a bootstrapping problem. Without this A record, the *aci.com* nameserver does not know the address of one of the nameservers for *eng.aci.com*. When a nameserver gets a request for, say, *plot.eng.aci.com*, it will find the NS entry for *eng.aci.com* and, consequently, will attempt to forward the query to that nameserver. Because it doesn't know the address of the server that is *big.eng.aci.com*, it will attempt to look up the server's address. It can't find it because the server itself is within the *eng.aci.com* domain. Although it could use the alternate server, which knows the address, that server might be unavailable. Therefore it adds an A record to the zone database for *big.eng.aci.com*, thus enabling the server to know how to get to a server for the *eng.aci.com* zone.

Conceptually, the NS records are pointers to the authoritative database for the *eng.aci.com* domain. If that domain is not delegated, its database file without the SOA record can simply replace the NS records in the *aci.com* zone database. Then, when a query for a resource record in the *eng.aci.com* zone is received by the *aci.com* zone server, the NS records will tell the server where to forward the query.

```
; database for fictitious eng.aci.com domain
$ORIGIN eng.aci.com.
@ SOA big hostmaster ( 10 86400 3600 3600000 604800 )
        IN NS big.eng.aci.com.
        IN NS backup.aci.com.
big     IN A 132.145.20.1
big     IN HINFO HP9000 HPUX
eng1    IN A 132.145.20.2
eng2    IN A 132.145.20.3
```

Figure 5.7 Example Domain Glue.

Reverse Mapping of IP Addresses to Domain Names

DNS is optimized to answer queries for resource records associated with a domain name; this process is called a **forward query.** Sometimes querying for a domain when the resource record value is known also is needed; this process is called an **inverse query.** Generally an inverse query works only when you are querying a single zone file; it will not work on the entire set of distributed zone database files because it is too expensive to process an inverse query over more than one zone file. To do so would potentially require a complete linear scan of every zone file.

The inverse mapping of IP addresses (A records) to domain names is a special case of an inverse query; this process is called a **reverse query.** Reverse queries are so useful, the DNS architecture made a special provision to allow them. *rlogin* and *rsh* use reverse queries for address authentication. *sendmail* uses it to look up the domain name of an SMTP client to authenticate the client's name. The *netstat* utility uses it to get the domain names for connection and routing table addresses.

So that reverse queries consume only a reasonable amount of resources and complete in a reasonable amount of time, a form of indexing is needed. Reverse queries use a special domain, *in-addr.arpa,* which uses PTR records to map every IP address back to its associated domain. (The name of the top-level domain *arpa* is an historical anomaly.) *in-addr.arpa* exploits the dotted decimal notation of writing IP addresses to create the reverse lookup map. For example, the domain *1.12.30.141.in-addr.arpa* contains a PTR record that is the domain name with an A record with a value of 141.30.12.1. The IP address is written backwards, thus allowing delegation of entire network numbers.

Lookups in this special domain are for pointer records that point back to the domain associated with the IP address. The semantics of the pointer records are bound implicitly to the special *in-addr.arpa* domain. Extensions to this scheme have been proposed for encoding of network numbers and other numeric values that need to be mapped to a specific domain, but those extensions are not yet widely implemented [Mockapetris 1989].

Figure 5.8 shows an example DNS reverse tree with the *in-addr.arpa* domain and the reverse mapping for *aci.com.* The solid lines indicate the pointer records

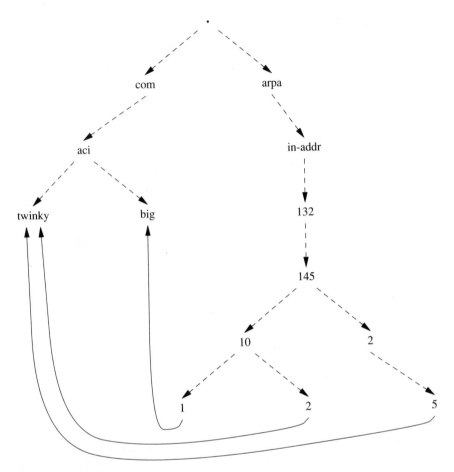

Figure 5.8 DNS Reverse Tree.

that exist at each node in the reverse map and that point back to the domain name associated with that IP address.

Figure 5.9 shows a reverse domain database file. This file is similar in structure to a forward domain database file. It starts with an SOA record and has NS records that point to the authoritative nameservers. Following the NS records are PTR records that point to domains. An $ORIGIN metacommand can be used to establish a base domain, so domain names can be abbreviated. This example also shows how authority for a portion of the name space can be delegated in the same way as for a forward domain. You use the same "glue" NS records and "hotwired" A record for the delegated server as for a forward domain.

Keeping a reverse domain map for IP addresses is an essential part of DNS maintenance. Every IP network registered with the central naming authority must have a reverse map created. Generally, because a domain is usually associated

```
; reverse database for network 132.145.0.0
$ORIGIN 145.132.in-addr.arpa.
@ SOA big.aci.com. hostmaster.aci.com (
            10 86400 3600 3600000 604800 )

        IN NS big.aci.com.
        IN NS y.bigu.edu.
10.1    IN PTR big.aci.com.
10.2    IN PTR twinky.aci.com.
2.5     IN PTR twinky.aci.com.
```

Figure 5.9 DNS Reverse Domain Database.

---

with a single IP network, a forward domain database is often associated on a one-to-one basis with a reverse domain. This is not always true, however. Organizations with multiple IP networks will have more than one reverse address database. Similarly, an IP network can have multiple domains associated with it, for example, the common case of when you delegate naming authority to one of your sub-domains.

Maintaining two sets of host information can easily result in excessive errors. Fortunately, as we see in Chapter 6, you can generate both the forward and reverse maps from a common set of host information. Creating reverse maps is very similar to creating an index in a database system, except that the index is across a distributed set of information.

There is a distinct drawback to using the dotted decimal notation for delegation boundaries in a reverse domain: subnets that use non-byte boundaries are difficult to delegate. At worst, several subnets must be grouped together and given a common naming authority. This is one reason that byte boundary subnets are preferable. Using this type of subnet means delegation is simpler and more natural, given the DNS scheme of delegating the reverse domains.

Often when you create a subdomain, you will also delegate a subnet number for address assignments to that domain. In such cases, a one-to-one mapping of forward domains to reverse domains exists. However, whenever you name a new host, you also must map an IP address to that hostname. For example, you might have only a single physical network to manage using a Class C network number, but you could divide the hosts into separate subdomains for naming convenience. The forward domain database is kept as a single file with subdomains established but not delegated. This file can be mapped to the reverse address table in a one-to-one fashion. If naming for one of the subdomains is delegated, then if you add a new host in that subdomain, you must also add a reverse entry in the single reverse address database. Because adding a host involves creating both a domain name and allocating an IP address, you should set up the functions under a common administration.

```
tcpmux       1/tcp
echo         7/tcp
echo         7/udp
discard      9/tcp       sink null
discard      9/udp       sink null
systat       11/tcp      users
daytime      13/tcp
daytime      13/udp
netstat      15/tcp
chargen      19/tcp      ttytst source
chargen      19/udp      ttytst source
ftp-data     20/tcp
ftp          21/tcp
telnet       23/tcp
smtp         25/tcp      mail
              .
              .
              .
```

Figure 5.10 /etc/services.

5.3   Services and Port Naming

TCP and UDP ports used for well-known services are assigned unique names. For example, TCP port 25 is associated with an SMTP server. An SMTP server will always listen on this port for requests from clients. However, rather than your having to remember the port numbers, names are assigned to these well-known ports. For example, an application uses a library function to look up a port number by its associated name. On UNIX systems, the name-to-port mapping is given in the /etc/services file. If you add additional services, you might want to do this. Figure 5.10 shows an example /etc/services file. Unfortunately, service and port names are not a part of the DNS. On a UNIX system, port mappings either are looked up directly in the local /etc/services file or that file is used to build a Sun NIS database that is queried by all hosts that support NIS.

5.4   The Nameserver Confusion

Most systems give you a combination of methods for looking up resource names. Which you use depends on your system configuration and your lookup requirements. However, UNIX systems provide no single standard way to do it. This can create serious problems. All UNIX network applications use a set of library routines to do the name-to-resource mapping. How you configure this set of routines determines which type of name lookup takes place. Three distinct methods exist — static tables, Sun's NIS, and DNS servers. We show next how each works and the strengths and weaknesses of each.

Static Tables

Static tables maintained on each host system are the old way of doing resource mapping. For service and port names, this method is still widely used. For host-name-to-IP address mapping, it is common to use a static table for bootstrapping and follow with a more dynamic host-to-address mapping method. Some systems, however, still use static tables exclusively for host-to-address mapping. For networks of fewer than a several hundred hosts that don't have Internet access, static tables work fairly well. UNIX systems keep static host-to-address mappings in the file /etc/hosts. An example /etc/hosts file is shown in Fig. 5.11. Note that each line in the file starts with an IP address. Following the IP address is the canonical or official name of the host, after which are any number of alias names for the host.

The static host table has no notion of domain names. If you want to use domain names, you must enter the FQDN of each host as the canonical hostname. Also, unlike DNS, static tables have no notion of multi-homed hosts. If a host has more than one network interface, more than one line must be placed in /etc/hosts, with a unique name attached to every IP address.

Sun Network Information Service (NIS)

NIS is a system for distributing resource lookup across a network without copying static tables to every host. In its simplest form, NIS relies upon a single server that does all resource mapping for all other hosts on the network. It uses Sun RPC, which does the resource library calls across the network rather than on just a single host. Although reasonably flexible, NIS doesn't have the richness or flexibility of DNS in its server architecture. Redundant servers can be established for reliability. Delegation of naming authority is more difficult and the host namespace cannot be divided and shared easily. NIS is useful for distributing relatively static information, such as that in the /etc/services file. It also is commonly used to distribute user and group name information found in the /etc/passwd and /etc/group files.

Figure 5.11 /etc/hosts.

```
127.0.0.1 localhost localhost.tic.com loopback
192.135.128.129 akasha.tic.com akasha
192.135.128.133 spike.tic.com spike mailhost.tic.com mailhost
192.135.128.131 ticmac.tic.com ticmac
```

DNS Server

A DNS server supports the DNS architecture. You must run a DNS server if you have Internet connectivity. The most common UNIX DNS server is the Berkeley Internet Name Daemon (BIND), which is part of most UNIX systems. BIND implements the full DNS architecture and allows all the flexibility of DNS naming and delegation of naming authority.

Which Resource Naming Method to Use

Each naming method has its strengths and weaknesses. Static tables are the easiest to configure and the table syntax is simple. Adding a new mapping is straightforward. They also are easy to debug, since all lookups are made through a set of lookup routines that are themselves very simple. However, static tables don't work well in large networks. Also, if you want to access remote services on the remote hosts without remembering IP addresses, static tables require you to add remote hosts in all the local tables. Further, if you have Internet access, static tables are totally inadequate. Finally, in a network of any size, static tables quickly become cumbersome to maintain and to keep up to date on every host system.

NIS extends the static table paradigm to local networks. NIS maps are really network accessible static tables, but they don't need to be distributed on all hosts to be accessible. Consequently, on large networks, the information is easier to update than are static tables. However, configuring NIS is harder than configuring static tables; debugging also is more difficult. As currently implemented, NIS does not scale well and makes it impossible to distribute naming authority to sub-domains.

A DNS server is really the only system flexible enough to support resource naming in a network of any reasonable size. If you expect your network to grow beyond a few hundred hosts and you expect that naming delegation will be required either now or in the future, set up your network with a DNS server. On the downside, however, DNS is much harder to configure correctly that either of the two other methods. Also, in a heterogeneous network with hosts from different vendors, the resource lookup defaults are sufficiently different to cause some unexpected problems.

Regardless of the method you select for resource lookup, use domain names for your hosts. Get a registered domain and adopt a naming convention and then stick with the convention. Eventually you will get Internet access, and you will find that adding a DNS server is much easier if you are already using legal domain names.

References

Harrenstien et al. 1985a.   Harrenstien, K., Stahl, M. K., & Feinler, E. J., *DoD Internet Host Table Specification (RFC952)*, October 1985.

Harrenstien et al. 1985b.   Harrenstien, K., Stahl, M. K., & Feinler, E. J., *Hostname Server (RFC953)*, October 1985.

Mockapetris 1987a.   Mockapetris, Paul V., *Domain Names — Concepts and Facilities (RFC1034)*, November 1987.

Mockapetris 1987b.   Mockapetris, Paul V., *Domain Names — Implementation and Specification (RFC1035)*, November 1987.

Mockapetris 1989.   Mockapetris, Paul V., *DNS Encoding of Network Names and Other Types (RFC1101)*, April 1989.

PART 2

Practice

CHAPTER 6

Setting Up Basic Network Services

TCP/IP networks are complex, multilayered hardware and software systems. Figure 6.1 shows schematically the hardware and software layering. The system is divided as follows:

• *network hardware*
At this level lies the physical wiring, the network interface hardware, and the electronic equipment that transmits the bits on the wire. This equipment includes dedicated network controllers, such as bridges, repeaters, and routers.

• *operating system services*
These services control the transmission and reception of data between the physical devices and host-based network applications. This layer is almost exclusively embedded in the host operating system.

Figure 6.1 Network System Layering.

End-user Applications
User-level System Services
Operating System Services
Network Hardware

• *user-level system services*
These services include resource naming services and routing daemons implemented as user-level processes.

• *end-user applications*
These applications include mail, remote login, and remote file access. End-user applications use as support functions both the user-level system services as well as the operating system services.

This layering model differs somewhat from the traditional ISO-OSI seven-layer version. (See Chapter 1 for a discussion of the ISO-OSI model.) It offers a good picture of how a modern TCP/IP network system is actually implemented. Note that both end-user applications and user-level system services use operating system calls and the basic TCP/IP communication services. However, these two levels differ in that an end-user application depends on the user-level system services in order to function properly, while user-level system services depend only on the functionality of the underlying operating system services.

To ensure reliable and efficient operation, network systems rely on all their components working together as a cohesive whole. If the physical wiring is of poor quality, the entire system will be adversely impacted. Or if system software is badly designed, the network will not function reliably. Each network layer must be properly planned and installed in order to build a system that is reliable, efficient, and maintainable.

In this chapter, we show you how to properly configure the essential hardware and system services that applications depend on for their operation. Once you have set up the basic system services, you can configure other applications that use those services. We divide this chapter into four basic sections as follows:

1. The types of hardware that can be used to build a TCP/IP network.

2. The active network devices — such as bridges or routers, how they fit into the overall system, and where each type can be used effectively.

3. How to create an IP address assignment scheme that anticipates future growth and network changes.

4. The fundamentals of setting up the resource naming system, a critical support service.

6.1   Physical and Datalink Protocols

Because TCP/IP is independent of any specific datalink protocol, it works on top of a wide variety of network media. You can select and intermix different types of media by interconnecting them using routers and bridges. This interoperability across a wide variety of network media is one of TCP/IP's key strengths. It enables a single virtual network to span a large geographic area using appropriate lower-layer technologies: LANs can use Ethernet, Token Ring, or FDDI, while WANs can use point-to-point leased lines or other common carrier services, such as Frame Relay. You also can employ low-speed serial links for low bandwidth applications or where cost is a significant factor. Further, you can integrate all of these different types of media into a single virtual network where any host can communicate with any other host no matter the type of network connection the latter host has.

Having a variety of media available is helpful when you configure a TCP/IP network, but you must select wisely. Media chosen haphazardly can result in a confusing and hard-to-manage network. Also, when confronted with choosing between several options, you might find it difficult to cut through the inevitable sales hype and make a rational choice. While in this book we emphasize software configuration, we also feel it is important that when you design your network, you are aware of the different types of network media available.

Network media are generally classified as suitable either for LANs or WANs. How do the two differ? The distinction is fuzzy at best (and getting fuzzier), but following are some general rules of thumb:

- A LAN covers a relatively small geographic area — say, a few floors of a building or maybe a small campus. All hosts connect directly to the LAN wiring and share equal access to the LAN using a low-level access protocol. This type of network usually allows hosts to use broadcasting to send data to every other host on the network.

- A WAN, on the other hand, spans a large geographic area such as a city, a state, a country, or even an entire continent. WANs predominantly comprise a collection of dedicated routers connected by point-to-point links. The links are usually leased from a common carrier and dedicated to data communication. Host systems don't usually connect directly to a WAN, but are interconnected by an intervening router or other dedicated network switch.

Some networks fall between a LAN and a WAN; for example, a **metropolitan area network (MAN)** covers a large urbanized area. A MAN is a WAN but might have more of the speed and topological characteristics of a LAN. You could think of a MAN as a very large LAN.

LAN and WAN Speeds

When state-of-the art technologies for WANs and LANs are compared, LANs typically operate at much higher data rates than WANs do. And although speeds are increasing for all network media as technology advances, the relative speed differences between the comparable technologies remain fairly constant.

When the ARPANET was first installed in 1969, WAN link speeds of 56 kb/sec were considered state of the art. Today speeds of over 1 mb/sec are common, with speeds of up to 45 mb/sec deployed on some larger, faster networks. Further, WAN speeds of one gigabit/sec already exist in several experimental laboratories. In the area of LAN technology, Ethernet at 10 mb/sec is very popular, while the FDDI is pushing LAN speeds to 100 mb/sec and beyond. LAN speeds are expected to continue to rise, eventually reaching the gigabit/sec range.

LAN Topologies

Most LANs connect a relatively large number of hosts to a single medium, with all hosts having equal access to the network. Figure 6.2 shows the following three typical LAN topologies:

• A **bus** configuration connects hosts at many points along a single cable or a set of cables in the shape of a tree. Only one physical path exists between individual hosts on the network.

Figure 6.2 LAN Topologies.

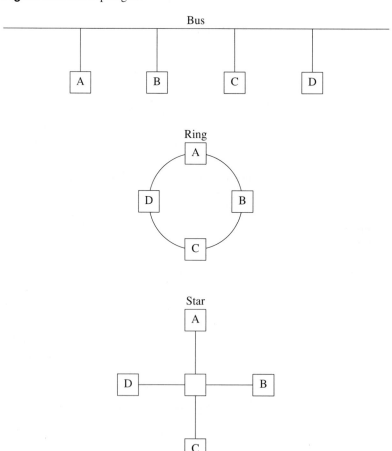

- A **ring** configuration connects all hosts to a set of wires configured as a circle. Signals on the ring pass from one host to another in only one direction around the ring. Each host interface reads each signal and regenerates it to pass it on to the next host.

- A **star** configuration connects each host to a central hub. The hub arbitrates between all the hosts and ensures signals reach the right host.

With few exceptions, LANs are electrically either a bus or a ring that often are wired in a physical star configuration. This type of configuration is for management convenience, since with a star all the wiring comes together at a central point, thus enabling you more easily to reconfigure and service the network. Typically the wiring is connected to a patch panel and from there to an active hub. You can physically patch individual wires into and out of the hub, in which case, the hub could simply repeat the signal from one cable segment to another. More sophisticated active hubs can activate and deactivate cable segments electrically and provide network monitoring tools as aids to cable management. Two of the most popular LAN types, twisted-pair Ethernets and Token Ring, are always configured as a physical star. But electrically, the Ethernet is still a bus and the Token Ring is still a ring.

WAN Topologies

WANs generally use point-to-point links. These links are interconnected by routers, with possibly redundant data paths between the routing nodes. Hosts are rarely connected directly to WANs; rather a host system is connected to a LAN, which in turn is connected to a WAN using a router with connectivity to both the LAN and the WAN. Figure 6.3 shows a typical WAN topology.

Some WANs have unusual configurations. An Ethernet can be used over a wide area by using hardware that forwards Ethernet frames from one remote Ethernet to another across a dedicated high-speed point-to-point link. This is called a **wide-area Ethernet** or an **extended Ethernet.** These configurations work but are more susceptible to broadcast storms and network congestion problems (we describe these problems in detail in Chapter 12).

Figure 6.3 A Typical WAN Topology.

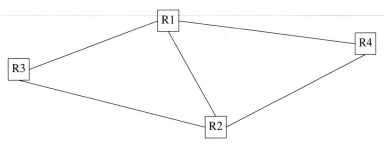

LAN Media

Ethernet. Because of its low cost, wide availability, and technical maturity, Ethernet is by far the most popular medium for LANs. Ethernet and TCP/IP grew up together; Ethernet was the first LAN technology to use TCP/IP. This specification defines an access method and a framing protocol. Each host is attached to an Ethernet by a **transceiver** that is connected to the host's network controller by a separate cable. It transmits and receives electrical signals to and from the physical medium and turns the signal into its digital equivalent for use by the network interface card. In many cases, the transceiver is built in to the network interface card.

Ethernet is electrically a bus and works much like a telephone party line. When a host is ready to send a frame, the transceiver checks to see if any other host is transmitting. If not, the transceiver sends the frame, while simultaneously monitoring the signal on the cable to see if any other host started to transmit at the same time.

If another host was also transmitting, a **collision** results. A collision is not a disastrous event. Rather, it garbles the signal on the cable, just as if two people on a party line picked up the phone and started talking at the same time. When a collision is detected, the transceiver notifies the network interface, which invokes a back-off algorithm. This causes the transceiver to retry the transmission. The retry is performed at a later, random time interval, thus ensuring the two host transmissions that collided before don't do so again. This access strategy is called **carrier sense multiple access/collision detection (CSMA/CD)**. The process of collision detection, backoff, and retry takes only a few microseconds and is transparent to the host system.

Intuitively, you might think that collisions would occur frequently on an Ethernet and would therefore degrade network performance. In practice, this is not the case. Most Ethernets run with long-term average traffic loads of less than 10% of the available bandwidth, with short, intermittent bursts of higher loads that sometimes reach 100% of available bandwidth. On a well-configured Ethernet, collisions under these circumstances should be fewer than 1% of total frames transmitted. Also, collisions happen over very short microsecond time intervals, so high collision rates usually indicate a network configuration problem, although very heavy and continuous traffic loads also can cause collision rates to soar.

Baseband bus topology networks, of which Ethernet is the predominant type, come in several different but related specifications. The original Ethernet specification, **Ethernet I,** with a speed of 3 mb/sec is rarely seen today. However, it's upgrade, **Ethernet II,** with a speed of 10 mb/sec, is widely deployed. The **IEEE 802.3** specification for baseband networks is closely related to Ethernet, as we saw in Chapter 3. They differ in the way they frame and encapsulate higher-layer messages. Both Ethernet and 802.3 encapsulation can be used on the same physical network, but two hosts that do not share the same encapsulation method can't interoperate except through a router or host that supports both encapsulation methods.

Ethernet supports a variety of cabling types. You can intermix different cabling types by using the appropriate interconnection hardware, since the fundamental media access control protocol is the same regardless of the cable used.

• *thickwire*

The original Ethernet specification uses 50-ohm coax cable called, because of its size, **thickwire** Ethernet cable. This cable is used most often for backbone cabling between building floors or within a computer room. The maximum length of a single thickwire cable segment is 500 meters. The cable is terminated with 50-ohm resistors on each end.

The thickwire Ethernet cabling specification is called **10Base5,** that is, 10 mb/sec using baseband signalling with a maximum single cable run of 500 meters. Special tools are required both to splice and tap a thick Ethernet cable. You connect transceivers to the cable by either cutting the cable and splicing in a transceiver using barrel connectors or by tapping the cable and connecting a transceiver using pins that make electrical connections with the center conductor and the shield.

• *thinwire*

You also can use a smaller-diameter, 50-ohm cable called **thinwire** Ethernet cable or, because the cable is much thinner and cheaper than thick cable is, **cheapernet.** This cable also is called **10Base2,** that is, 10 mb/sec using baseband signalling with a maximum cable run of about 200 meters. Other than the distance limitation, the specifications are identical to thickwire Ethernet cable. This cable is similar to that used to hook up color video monitors. It uses bayonet type BNC connectors, which make it very simple to install. You also can purchase Ethernet boards that have built-in thinwire transceivers, which eliminate the need for a separate transceiver and drop cable. You hook up the thinwire cable directly to the board using a BNC tee connection.

Because of its low cost, thinwire Ethernet cable is commonly seen in small networks. You also can use it with an active hub for wiring workgroups or office floors in a star configuration. In this case, the active hub supports a large number of thinwire cables, each of which goes to separate offices and supports one or more host connections. The hub repeats the signals between the cable segments.

• *twisted-pair*

This system, also called **10BaseT,** is a very popular medium. It is used to transmit and receive the Ethernet signal from each transceiver. Each twisted-pair wire is connected to an active hub that repeats the signal between each wire. Maximum wire runs from the active hub are 100 meters, although actual distance depends on the wire quality. However, unlike with a thinwire hub, only one host can be attached to a single twisted-pair wire. You can use it to wire entire office floors and even whole buildings. It is much cheaper than either thickwire or thinwire and its installation is no more difficult than that involved with regular phone wiring. You also can bring all the separate wires together to a centralized patch panel, where the network can easily be reconfigured or even subdivided into separate physical networks. There is one disadvantage to twisted-pair wiring: The active hub to which it is connected has a single point of failure (although with the current reliability of electronic equipment, this is less of a problem than it used to be).

It is not uncommon to see all three types of Ethernet cabling in a single installation. Figure 6.4 shows an Ethernet installation in a large building. Because of the long cable runs required between building floors, thickwire is common as a backbone cable. Thinwire and twisted-pair are used to wire separate workgroups or within an office floor. In this figure, the backbone cabling between floors is thickwire, although if the distances were short enough, thinwire could be used. On the third floor, a router interconnects two twisted-pair hubs. Hosts are connected to the hubs through a patch panel. The patch panel enables you to reconfigure the network if, say, a machine moves from one office to another or the traffic patterns

---

Figure 6.4 Building Wiring Layout.

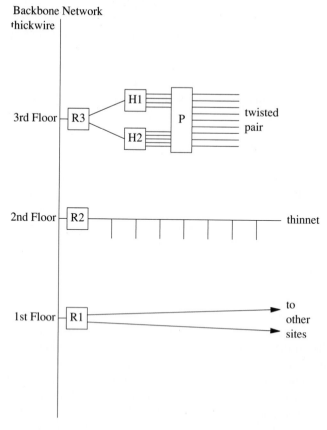

dictate a change in the configuration. On the second floor, a router connects the backbone to a thinwire network. Then on the first floor, a router interconnects the building's LAN-to-WAN links. The routers also could be interconnected using fiber optic cabling, which supports longer cable lengths than even 10Base5 wiring does.

Token Ring Networks. A **Token Ring** network uses an entirely different access method than the Ethernet does. It arbitrates network access by passing a known signal, called a **token,** in a round robin from one host to the next on the network. The standard for Token Ring networks is the **IEEE 802.5** specification. Figure 6.5 shows a diagram of a Token Ring network. In this type of network, if a host has a frame to transmit, it waits for the token, removes the token from the network, and places a frame on the network. Each receiving host in the ring checks the frame destination address against its own address, and if the two addresses match, the host copies the frame to a buffer for use by any higher-level protocol. It also copies the frame onto the network and sets a frame status bit that indicates the frame has been successfully received. After the frame has made a complete circuit of the ring, the original sending host removes the frame, sees that the receiving host got the frame, and places the token back on the ring. Because no two hosts may have the token at the same time, access to the network is serialized; thus collisions never occur. To begin transmitting, all a host need do is wait until it has the token. A host holding the token is guaranteed that no other host can transmit at that same time.

Access serialization using a Token Ring is very elegant. Network access is deterministic and the access delay depends only on the circumference of the ring.

Figure 6.5 Token Ring.

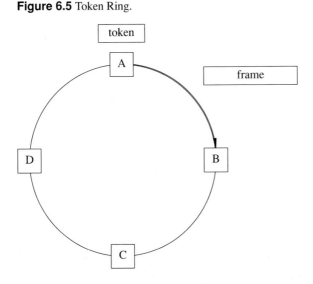

However, the hardware logic of the ring is more complicated than Ethernet's, since the logic must deal with lost tokens and the bypassing of nodes in case of failure.

A Token Ring network can handle higher bandwidths than an Ethernet can. Further, unlike an Ethernet network, a Token Ring potentially can be very large — a primary advantage over Ethernet, although a large ring has the disadvantage of increasing the time between each host access (in practice, however, this is not a significant problem).

Token Rings are not wired as a physical ring but rather as a physical star, as shown in Fig. 6.6. As you can see, all cabling to each workstation is wired from a central point. Each workstation connection has a mechanism that bypasses the node if the workstation is unplugged or powered down. This wiring system is much easier to maintain and install than a true physical ring.

A Token Ring can consist of any of three different wiring systems, as follows:

• The original Type 1 wiring uses a cable with two shielded twisted pairs.

• Type 2 wiring also uses two shielded twisted pairs except that four unshielded pairs for voice or lower-speed data service are also included in the wire.

• Type 3 wiring has four unshielded twisted pairs.

Token Rings, like Ethernets, also can be interconnected using bridges or routers. Since Token Rings encapsulate IP packets using the same encapsulation method as an 802.3 network, you can bridge a Token Ring to an 802.3 network. Further, the

Figure 6.6 Star Token Ring Topology.

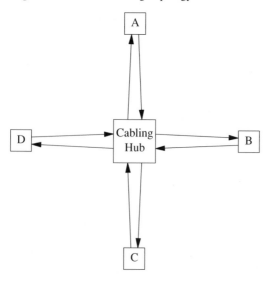

Token Ring and Ethernet frame addresses are sufficiently similar; therefore you can bridge a Token Ring with an Ethernet, although these networks are more commonly interconnected using routers.

Fiber Distributed Digital Interface Networks. The **Fiber Distributed Digital Interface (FDDI)** network is a high-speed, fiber optic network standard. Supporting speeds up to and beyond 100 mb/sec, FDDI is considered an eventual replacement for Ethernets and Token Rings when much higher bandwidths are required. As with Token Rings, this type of network uses token passing, but it has its own framing and access protocols that differ from the 802.5 Token Ring standard. You can configure an FDDI ring that has a circumference of several hundred kilometers, so a great deal of fault tolerance is built into its design, given the potentially dispersed connection points. FDDI includes elaborate algorithms for detecting and bypassing faulty devices. For redundancy, the architecture includes a dual-ring topology whereby two separate fiber optic cables are employed. Under this system, if a segment of one ring fails, the two rings are automatically "wrapped" into a single ring. Refer to Fig. 6.7. A host can be either dual-attached or single-attached; in this figure, Host D is a single-attached node. Failure of the ring around Host D will cause D to lose connectivity. The other hosts take advantage of their dual attachment to maintain connectivity with the wrapped ring.

FDDI is only now starting to be widely deployed. It often is seen as a higher bandwidth backbone network that interconnects several Ethernets or 802.5 Token Rings. As of this writing, FDDI is seldom seen wired directly to a host system because of the much higher cost of the interface hardware. This cost is expected to drop, however, and these networks then probably will be deployed with direct host connectivity where high bandwidths are required. In addition, because of its large maximum ring size and high capacity, FDDI also is seen in MANs.

A related standard called **Copper Distributed Digital Interface (CDDI)** defines a standard for running the FDDI protocol over unshielded twisted-pair wiring. CDDI networks can use the same wiring plant that existing Ethernet or Token Ring networks do but they operate at much higher bandwidths.

Broadband Networks. A **broadband** network uses 75-ohm coax wire to carry data. Unlike Ethernet or Token Ring cabling, broadband cabling uses purely analog signaling technology. Sometimes employed as a campus or site backbone network, it provides a great deal of flexibility when simultaneous voice, video, and data traffic is required. Traffic is frequency multiplexed on the cable in much the same way that home cable television systems send many stations simultaneously. For data one key difference from a cable television system is the requirement for any station to transmit, as well as receive. Generally this is accomplished by sending transmissions using one frequency and receiving using another. Access to a broadband cable is via high-speed modems. Broadband networks can be configured to behave much like an Ethernet and can even use Ethernet framing, thereby connecting widely separated sites into a very large Ethernet. Given the ever lower cost of fiber optics cable, broadband systems are not seen very often in new installation. For data communication, it is very likely they eventually will be replaced in favor of FDDI systems.

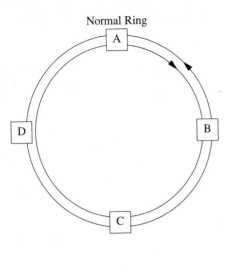

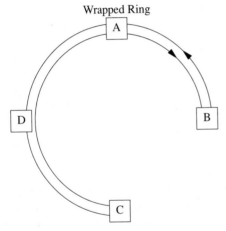

Figure 6.7 FDDI Topology.

Point-to-point Links

Point-to-point links are used most often in WANs. They are either dedicated or switched and vary from very low-speed switched circuits to high-speed dedicated links. Usually these links employ a simple datalink encapsulation method, such as the **High-level Data Link Control (HDLC)** protocol. Unlike Ethernet or Token Ring, however, they don't have any real datalink addressing. Rather, each end of the link is associated with an IP address. Because on a point-to-point link there is only one place to send a packet, no ARP is needed. Typically each point-to-point connection is treated as a separate and distinct IP network. Some routers also support point-to-point links that are not associated with any IP address; two routers connected using this type of link will appear as a single routing node.

High-speed WAN Links. Usually high-speed WAN links are leased from a common telecommunications carrier on a flat-fee basis. Typical network speeds are 64 kb/sec **Digital Signal Level 0 (DS0)**, 1.544 mb/sec **Digital Signal Level 1 (DS1)**, and 44.736 mb/sec **Digital Signal Level 3 (DS3)**. The framing used on the higher-speed links is called **T-carrier;** for example, a DS1 circuit is called a T-1 channel and a DS3 circuit is called a T-3 channel. T-1 consists of 24 DS0 circuits that are time-division multiplexed using the T-carrier protocol, while a T-3 consists of 28 DS1 circuits or 672 DS0 circuits. High-speed links are interconnected with routers using a **data service unit/channel service unit (DSU/CSU).** In this case, the router is connected to the DSU and the serial line is connected to the CSU. The DSU offers a digital interface to the router via a serial port.

Also, Ethernets and Token Rings can be connected to each other with high-speed point-to-point links using bridges that transmit the Ethernet or Token Ring frames over the long-haul connection. Figure 6.8 shows two Ethernets connected to each other using a wide area point-to-point link. To a host on either Ethernet, the two appear as a single network. The figure shows the wide area Ethernet as a stub network with only a single router attached to each end. The routers are in turn connected to other LAN and WAN media. The stub network in this case is a WAN that uses Ethernet framing.

Emerging network technologies such as **frame relay** are common carrier replacements for dedicated point-to-point links. A frame relay network consists of a set of interconnected switches that are shared by many customers. Each site is connected to the frame relay network using a single dedicated circuit. The frame relay provider assigns each customer a set of virtual circuits between each of the customer's sites. Thus using Frame Relay, you can build a virtual network that appears to have many connections to the network but which in fact has only one.

Low-speed SLIP and PPP Links. Low-speed links are usually carried over switched telephone circuits that are connected directly to a host or router via a modem. Switched circuits can support speeds of up to 56 kb/sec using various signalling and compression techniques. Low-speed IP links use either **Serial Line**

Figure 6.8 Wide Area Stub Ethernet.

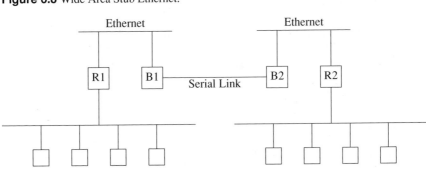

IP (SLIP) or the **Point-to-Point Protocol (PPP)** encapsulation method, both of which usually use low-speed (RS232) serial ports. SLIP or PPP links are very useful for either low bandwidth or intermittent connectivity. They also provide a low-cost entry-level means of connecting to the Internet itself.

6.2   Routers and Bridges

Routers and bridges connect separate network segments. A router and a bridge differ in how and when data is transferred from one network segment to another. A **bridge** forwards datalink layer *frames* unchanged from one network segment to another; a **router** forwards network layer *packets* unchanged from one network segment to another, except for possible fragmentation or reassembly of the packets.

IP sees two networks segments connected by a bridge as a datalink network. In other words, to IP, the bridge is transparent. On the other hand, IP sees two network segments connected by a router as two distinct IP networks that therefore must have different IP network or subnetwork numbers. IP knows about the router and each of the router's interfaces has an IP address. Note that whether you use a router or a bridge significantly influences how IP addresses are assigned.

We can illustrate the differences between a bridge and a router with the following simple example. Suppose you connect two Ethernet segments using a bridge. When Host A on segment 1 sends an Ethernet frame to Host B on segment 2 (see Fig. 6.9), the bridge passes the frame intact byte for byte from one network segment to the other; nothing is changed in the frame. Because Ethernet addresses are unique, the bridge can, at its option, scan the source Ethernet

Figure 6.9 Two Ethernets Connected by A Bridge.

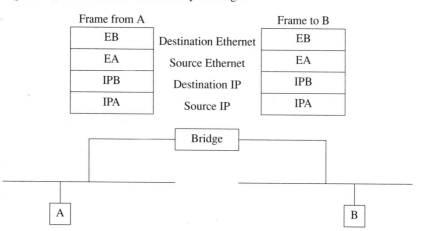

address and learn to which segment the source of the frame is attached. The bridge next builds a table noting from which segment each source address came. Then when the bridge receives a frame, it looks up the destination address in the table and sees the segment to which the host is attached. If the segment is the same as that from which the frame was received, the bridge discards the frame, since the frame is already seen by the destination host on that segment; otherwise the bridge forwards the frame to the other segment. The result is that the two Ethernet segments connected by the bridge look like a single, albeit larger, Ethernet. The forwarding or discarding of frames by the bridge is transparent to IP.

This type of bridge is called a **filtering bridge.** Filtering bridges are quite common and the types of filtering can go beyond the simple destination filtering used in the above example. Since this type of bridge already examines each frame's source address, it is simple to extend it to examine other fields in the frame or even fields in the encapsulated IP packet.

A bridge must always forward broadcast frames, so that a service using Ethernet broadcasting will work on a bridged Ethernet. So ARP, which uses broadcasting to send requests, works on a bridged Ethernet. Because of this, an IP packet from one host destined for another host anywhere on the bridged network is simply encapsulated in an Ethernet frame and sent directly to its destination; no routing is required.

In our example, suppose you use an IP router instead of a bridge to connect the two Ethernet segments. In this case, a frame encapsulating an IP packet can't be sent directly from Host A to Host B. Rather the frame must be received by the router and reencapsulated in a different frame (see Fig. 6.10). For this to work, Host A and Host B must have separate IP network or subnetwork addresses with proper routing table entries. Assuming this is the case, Host A explicitly sends the IP packet to the router, which reframes it. The router then forwards the new frame

Figure 6.10 Two Ethernets Connected by a Router.

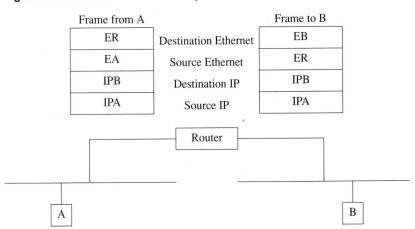

to Host B. The IP routing paradigm is followed at each step. A destination host with the same IP network or subnetwork number receives IP packets directly; that is, a packet is encapsulated within an Ethernet frame whose destination Ethernet address is the Ethernet address of the host with the destination IP address. A packet sent to a host on a separate IP network is encapsulated in an frame whose destination address is the address of the next router on the path to the ultimate destination. In this latter case, each frame is received by the router, which examines the encapsulated IP packet, looks up the destination IP address in its routing table, and determines the next hop destination for the packet. It then reencapsulates the packet in a new frame and sends it to its final destination.

In this scenario, the router is not transparent to IP. IP must know about the router and forwards to it the IP packets that are addressed to IP networks reachable from the router.

Connecting two network segments using a bridge is a simple plug-and-play operation; connecting them using a router, however, is much more complicated — the IP network numbers must be planned for each Ethernet segment and proper routing must be established. So why use a router instead of a bridge? The key reason is broadcast isolation. A bridge is transparent to broadcast frames; otherwise, broadcasting would not work properly. A router, on the other hand, acts as a "firewall" against broadcast frames. We explain this further next.

On a large bridged network with many thousands of machines connected to a large number of bridged network segments, a single broadcast frame on one network segment must be forwarded to every network segment. Because of this, a few misconfigured hosts can quickly slow the network down to a crawl by incessantly sending broadcast frames. One source of these broadcast frames is ARP. As we saw in Chapter 3, IP uses ARP to determine how to map IP addresses to datalink addresses on networks that support datalink broadcasting. An ARP request packet is encapsulated in a datalink layer broadcast frame and is subsequently received by all hosts on the bridged network. On a large bridged network, hosts can generate a large amount of ARP traffic that can adversely impact every

Figure 6.11 An Example Enterprise Internetwork.

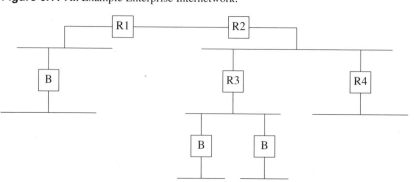

network segment. Routers, on the other hand, isolate broadcast frames in a large network. One errant host that chatters broadcast frames in a large bridged network can cause disastrous performance degradation over the entire network. (We examine this issue at length in Chapter 12.) But this same errant host, isolated by a router, impacts only the segment the host is attached to. Because the router forwards packets, not frames, it blocks the broadcast frame. In this way, the router acts as a firewall against the frames.

You should use bridges only to link together network segments into logical network groupings. You should use routers to insulate logical network groups from each other. Figure 6.11 shows an example enterprise internetwork using bridges and routers. In this example, bridges are used only within local workgroups and never over a wide area. R1 connects a satellite site to a bigger site via router R2. The site behind R1 uses a simple bridged network, while the larger site uses bridges and routers internally. Routers R3 and R4 isolate workgroups from the main network. The workgroup behind R3 uses several bridged networks.

Setting Up Routing

Almost all UNIX systems come with the *routed* program that implements the **Routing Information Protocol (RIP).** *routed* keeps track of RIP routing updates and passes any changes to the kernel. Another program called *route* adds manual routes directly to the UNIX kernel routing tables. For a simple network with a single outside gateway adding a single default routing table entry at startup is all that is required. The following example uses *route* to add a single default route to a host system.

```
route add net 0 193.1.1.1 1
```

This command says to add a route to network 0 (by definition the default route) that points at a router with address 193.1.1.1 that is one hop away. You use this in a topology where the single router connecting your network to all other networks has an address on our network of 193.1.1.1.

For more complicated topologies where multiple routers are exchanging routing information using RIP, you can run the *routed* process in passive mode. This is done simply by adding the following line to the startup script on each host system.

```
routed -q
```

Note that any RIP routing update messages broadcast on your network by an active router will be added to the host's routing tables by *routed*. When in passive mode, *routed* simply listens for routing updates and does not broadcast any of its own routes. Note that most (but not all), UNIX systems will run *routed* in passive mode if the host has a single network interface. The *-q* flag makes this behavior explicit.

A UNIX system may also act as a router when it has more than a single network interface. In this case, the *routed* process is run in active mode and broadcasts its routes to other systems on the locally attached networks. Again most *routed* implementations detect when multiple network interfaces are active and run in active mode. You can force this behavior by starting *routed* with the *-s* flag as follows:

```
routed -s
```

While a UNIX host can be used as a router and actively participate in RIP message exchanges, it is generally better to use a dedicated router for this purpose, except in very small installations.

Multiple Network Protocol Support

You might hear the argument in favor of bridges that they can transparently support multiple network protocols, while a router may not support routing of all network protocols in use. Because a bridge makes several networks appear to be a single network at the datalink layer, routing — which is a principal function of a network layer protocol, is not required and the routing handled by the network layer is never used. However, most routers on the market today support the routing of multiple network protocols; for example, IP routing is supported alongside Appletalk routing and DECNet routing. Some protocols still require the transparency of a bridge, but you can support these protocols using a **brouter.** A brouter combines the functionality of a router and a bridge in a single piece of hardware. It can route some protocols and be configured to bridge the remainder. And for the major network protocols in use today, it also possesses both the flexibility of a bridge and the firewall protection of a router.

Building a reliable network that supports multiple protocols is complicated and detailed discussion of how to do it is beyond the scope of this book. However, we can say that you can support multiple protocols by using a technique called **protocol tunnelling.** This technique enables you to arrange for other network protocol packets to be encapsulated in IP packets or for IP packets to be encapsulated inside other network protocol packets. Even "virtual" IP networks can be constructed by encapsulating IP packets within other IP packets. Other possible combinations exist as well.

6.3   IP Address Assignment

The first axiom of network administration is that a network will grow beyond its current size and will grow in complexity beyond what you can reasonably anticipate at a given time. Since IP addresses are a scarce resource and becoming even more so, proper IP addresses assignment is critical for a successful network; it helps ensure that unanticipated changes in the network do not create the need for massive address reassignments at a later date. Many administrators err by not planning a coherent address assignment policy before having the first machine installed. However, by ensuring early on that IP addresses are assigned in an orderly manner, you can avoid many future headaches.

IP addressing is fairly flexible, and you can assign IP addresses in a variety of ways. Interestingly though, one strength of TCP/IP addressing is also one of its weaknesses: IP addresses of all network interfaces on the same physical network must have the same IP network or subnetwork address. This restriction greatly simplifies the IP routing algorithm, but it also means that when you split a single network into two or more networks, you must change the IP address of all hosts on the new networks. Further, TCP/IP doesn't have any standard method for dynamically assigning network interface addresses. On a simple network, you can do this with RARP or BOOTP, and some vendors support the use of these protocols for querying a server for a host's interface address. In any case, it's obviously to your advantage to avoid redoing a host's IP address when possible. As this is not always going to be possible, you should plan in advance for situations in which address reassignment is needed, for instance, when a bridge is replaced by a router and suddenly one Ethernet becomes two separate networks. Judicious assignment policies can help you avoid network "flag days" when you must reassign all your host IP addresses. While you can easily change the IP addresses for a few hosts, changing them for several hundred hosts is very time consuming. On a network with thousands of hosts, you will find address reassignment to be nearly impossible to complete in any reasonable amount of time.

Subnets

IP subnets are a powerful and flexible tool for building complex network topologies. They allow you to plan for future growth by enabling you to subdivide the host part of an IP address into separate subnet addresses. When a network is initially installed, it might have only a few hosts on a single physical network. Eventually the network might grow to the point where you would want to divide it into several subnets. Advance planning of the layout and use of subnets can help you avoid unnecessary host address reassignments.

Class B network addresses are most commonly subnetted. Class A addresses are also frequently subnetted, but because they number only 126, they are hard to get. Class C addresses, too, can be subnetted, but with only 8 bits to split into subnet and host parts, it often is not worth the effort except on very small, topologically complex networks.

A Class B network address should be split into an 8-bit subnet field and an 8-bit host field. Dividing the address along the byte boundary has two advantages: You can easily identify the subnet number using the standard dotted decimal notation for IP addresses, and you can easily delegate addressing authority for the *in-addr.arpa* domain to each subnet. Using the third byte for the subnet number may not always be optimal, but you will find it is the easiest to administer.

Even if your network is not yet subnetted, it is prudent policy to allocate addresses as if it were. For example, you should assign IP addresses on a bridged network with two segments as if the two segments were separate subnets, as

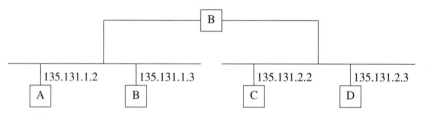

Figure 6.12 Bridged Ethernet Address IP Assignments.

shown in Fig. 6.12. By doing this, if you later replace the bridge with a router, the IP addresses can be used without change. In Fig. 6.12, the Class B network number, 135.131.0.0, is used. Segment A has IP addresses in the range 135.131.1.1 to 135.131.1.254 and segment B has addresses in the range 135.131.2.1 to 135.131.2.254. If the bridge subsequently is replaced with a router and if you use an 8-bit subnet, then the IP addresses can stay the same; you would need to change only the subnet mask on each host. You also could run Proxy ARP on the router and leave the subnet masks on all hosts, the result of which would be as if the two networks were unsubnetted.

If you are unsure about which size subnet mask you will need for future growth, then assign subnet numbers from the high end of the subnet part of the address and host numbers from the low end. Doing this lets subnet numbers and host numbers fill in the address space from either end of the address range and leaves bits in the middle of the range within which the subnet mask can float. Using this algorithm, you assign host numbers in a natural ascending order and subnet numbers in a reverse bit order, as illustrated in Table 6.1.

You can gain additional flexibility in address assignment by using the OSPF routing protocol, which permits variable-length subnet masks. However, you

Table 6.1 High End Subnet Address Assignment.

Subnet Numbers			
Decimal	Binary	Decimal	Binary
128	10000000	144	100100000
64	01000000	80	010100000
192	11000000	208	110100000
32	00100000	48	001100000
160	10100000	176	101100000
96	01100000	112	011100000
224	11100000	240	111100000
16	00010000		

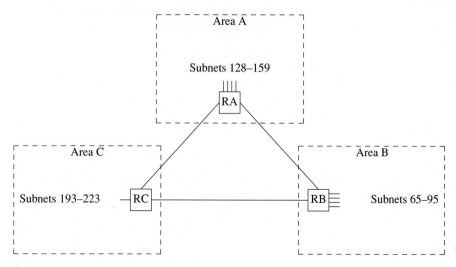

Figure 6.13 OSPF Subnet Assignments.

---

must take care to ensure that, for flexibility, addresses are still grouped logically. For example, using OSPF routing you would assign subnet numbers that have the same high-order bits set to subnetworks that share a common router. Figure 6.13 shows a large network divided into geographic areas. Each area has several sub-netted networks that use 8-bit subnet masks. The high-order 3 bits of the subnet mask determine in which area each host is physically located. The areas exchange IP packets through a set of core routers. Routers using OSPF have a single rout-ing table entry for each area. Area A's subnet numbers are in the range 128–159 and its routing table entry is to IP address 135.131.128.0 with a subnet mask of 255.255.224 (224 = 0xe0 = 11100000). In this figure, each subnet in area A has the first 3 bits of its subnet set to 100 binary, each subnet in area B has its first 3 bits set to 010 binary, and each subnet in area C has its first 3 bits set to 110 binary. Area A and area B have several subnets that use 8-bit subnet masks, while area C has a single LAN that uses a 3-bit subnet mask. The routing table entry for area C is 135.131.196.0, also with a subnet mask of 255.255.224. If you divide area C into two LANs, you change the subnet mask within area C to accommodate the size of the subnets without changing the subnets in area A or B. You can define six areas using 3 bits and 14 with 4 bits.

OSPF reduces the size of routing tables when IP addresses are divided into large group areas. You can use this methodology during a transition to OSPF routing to minimize IP address changes as the network grows. With it, IP address-ing authority can be delegated along the natural byte division of the IP address within each area. Also, tracking down routing problems is simplified, since you can determine the location of hosts by area.

6.4   Naming Hosts and Other Resources

Several methods exist for maintaining and looking up names and mapping them to system resources. Fortunately, the application interface to this mapping service is fairly uniform across all UNIX platforms. A UNIX application uses the *gethostbyname()* and the *gethostbyaddr()* library routines to map a hostname to an IP address and an IP address to a hostname, respectively. The specific lookup method is embedded in the library functions.

gethostbyname() takes a hostname or alias as an argument and returns a pointer to a structure that includes the host's IP address, the canonical hostname, and any alias names for the host. This routine usually is used to map a hostname to an IP address for use by the transport protocols during the process of establishing communication with a remote host. For example, a TELNET client program, uses the lookup to determine the IP address of a remote TELNET server.

gethostbyaddr() takes an IP address and returns the same information that *gethostbyname* does. It looks up the information about a host based on the host's IP address. A TELNET server, for example uses this function to get the name of a remote client, which is then displayed as a part of the *who* program. *rlogin* and *rsh* use this function to authenticate the name of a remote host.

Both of these lookup functions can use any of the nameservices — static host table, NIS or the DNS. In some cases, you can configure which nameservice to use; for example, DEC Ultrix lets you set a nameservice preference globally in the file */etc/svcorder*. You also can list more than one lookup method in order of preference so that if one nameservice method fails, the next ones are tried in order until one is reached that works. IBM AIX systems, for example, use DNS if the file */etc/resolv.conf* exists. However, if *ypbind* is running on the host, the system will use NIS; otherwise, AIX will use the static file */etc/hosts*. Sun workstations use NIS if *ypbind* is running, but an NIS server will forward NIS queries to a DNS server, provided the NIS server is configured for DNS forwarding. (We discuss *ypbind* later on in this section.

Other operating systems require you to change the *gethostbyname()* and the *gethostbyaddr* library routines in order to change the lookup method. On systems with static libraries, you must reload all the programs that use the host lookup library calls. On systems with shared libraries, you must build and install a new shared library; for example, when you want to change a Sun system so that it uses pure DNS lookups and bypasses NIS completely.

The seemingly myriad ways of mapping hostnames to and from IP addresses can be very confusing, particularly in a heterogeneous environment. When possible, try to stay with a consistent method when setting up networked hosts. However, as this is not always possible, you might have to support several different methods on the same network. We will show you later in this section how to set up a consistent naming system, even when different naming methods are used in your environment. Doing this can greatly simplify naming system maintenance and avoid inconsistencies between host systems.

The Bootstrap Problem

A host cannot use a dynamic host to address a lookup mechanism such as DNS or NIS when a machine is first bootstrapped. A bootstrapping machine doesn't even know its own hostname or IP addresses; you normally set these values as a part of the bootstrap startup scripts. UNIX systems vary widely in how their startup scripts work. Most use the *hostname* command to set the hostname of the system being bootstrapped. Sometimes the hostname is set to the host's simple name but without its domain suffix; for example, a host with a domain name *felix.tic.com* can set its own hostname with the following line in the bootstrap script:

```
hostname felix
```

If you are not careful, however, doing this can lead to peculiar problems when using DNS and even NIS. A better practice is to set the hostname to the machine's full domain name. For most machines, you can set this directly in the startup script. Some systems use indirection and read the hostname from a well-known file; others set a shell variable in one of the startup scripts. In the case of a diskless machine that uses RARP or BOOTP to determine its own IP address and later uses TFTP to load its operating system from the server, you must ensure that if full domain names are used, they are used consistently throughout.

Hosts that use NIS set their NIS domain name using the *domainname* command. A NIS domain is not the same as a DNS domain, although in most cases you should set it to the same string for administrative convenience; for example, the machine *felix.tic.com,* which uses NIS, sets its hostname to *felix.tic.com* and its NIS domain to *tic.com.* Note that unlike in DNS, the periods in the NIS domain name have no real meaning; the name is simply a string of characters.

You set interface addresses with the *ifconfig* command. This command sets the IP address and associated parameters for each active network interface. Some systems read these parameters from a configuration file, in which case, *ifconfig* usually is set to use static lookup of hostnames in */etc/hosts* in order to find its interface address. DNS or NIS are not running when the initial interface address is established. Some systems set the broadcast address and network masks after the interface address is set and after NIS is started. The real broadcast and subnet mask can be set later using NIS. How can the broadcast address and subnet mask be looked up by NIS when NIS itself relies on the broadcast address? A simple example shows how this can be done. Suppose you configure an interface with the following command:

```
ifconfig le0 131.135.5.1
```

This sets the interface address of *le0* to 131.135.5.1, the broadcast address defaults to 131.135.255.255, and the subnet mask defaults to 255.255.0.0. If your system sets the broadcast address to 131.135.0.0, no harm is done since all reasonable TCP/IP implementations recognize that address as a broadcast address even though it is wrong (see Chapter 12 for why this is wrong). So NIS starts up and uses the broadcast address 131.135.255.255 to find an NIS server. If an NIS server is up and running, it will respond even if the real subnet mask is 255.255.255.0 and the broadcast address is 131.135.5.255. Later the mask is set to 255.255.255.0 and the broadcast address also is changed to the correct value.

Before you try this, ensure your system supports NIS lookup of the subnet mask and that the broadcast address changes dynamically when the mask is changed. Sun, for example, supports this method. However, it supports only NIS lookup of the subnet mask; the broadcast address defaults to all 0's in the host part, which won't work for systems that use as the broadcast address all 1's in the host part of the address.

To be absolutely sure you have set the interface parameters correctly, you should set them all in a single place in the startup script. For example, the following *ifconfig* command will establish the correct broadcast address and subnet masks using explicit parameters:

```
ifconfig le0 `hostname` subnet mask 255.255.255.0 \
          broadcast 131.135.5.255
```

The *hostname* command returns the name of the host. *ifconfig* then looks up the IP address of the host in */etc/hosts*. If you use DNS or NIS, */etc/hosts* should have only an entry for the loopback interface and the name of the local host.

For machines with multiple interfaces, set the address of the second and subsequent interfaces explicitly or add a name for the secondary interface in the */etc/hosts* file. Once the interfaces are configured correctly, then DNS or NIS can run properly.

DNS Setup Using BIND

As we explained in Chapter 5, DNS is a functional distributed naming service and the standard resource lookup protocol in the Internet community. It consists of two major components: a resolver and a server. The resolver composes and sends queries to a server; the server answers queries and returns the answers to the resolver.

On UNIX systems, the predominant nameserver is the **Berkeley Internet Name Daemon (BIND)** that implements the full DNS specification. The DNS resolver is a set of library functions called by applications that need DNS services, and the server is a separate process that listens for DNS requests on the well-known UDP and TCP nameservice port 53.

Four different types of host DNS configurations can be set up: one that just a resolver and three that are different types of nameservers. We explain each of these configurations in the next four sections.

Resolver-only Host. All hosts on a network must be configured to use the DNS resolver. You can configure a host to run only a resolver. A resolver-only host uses the resolver library routines to access one or more remote nameservers. You place resolver configuration data in the file */etc/resolv.conf*, as shown in the following example file:

```
domain tic.com
nameserver 135.131.1.1
nameserver 192.35.82.2
```

This file is read by the resolver library routines. Each line is a keyword/value pair that uses one of the following keywords:

1. *domain*

    The name of the default domain. The resolver appends this name to each name-server requests, thus allowing you to enter shorthand names for hosts in your local domain.

2. *nameserver*

    The IP address (not name) of a nameserver to which queries are sent. You must enter an IP address and not a name since the resolver does not keep any infor-mation about hostname-to-IP address mappings. (If a name is used, there is no way to map the name to an address.) This is another bootstrapping problem. You can have multiple *nameserver* keywords. Each server at each address is queried by the resolver in a round-robin fashion starting with the first address.

In this example, the resolver will append the default domain *tic.com* to a simple name such as *ajax*, as directed by the first line of the file. Queries are sent to the nameserver port on host with IP address 135.131.1.1; if no answer is received, queries are sent using the address 192.35.82.2. All hosts that use DNS must have an */etc/resolv.conf* file. If a host does not run a nameserver, then the addresses of remote nameservers must be listed in the */etc/resolv.conf* file. Doing this results in every nameserver query being answered by a remote server and every query gen-erating network traffic because the resolver cannot cache any answers, since it is implemented as a run-time library.

Primary Nameserver. A primary nameserver stores the definitive DNS database for one or more domains. There is one primary nameserver per dele-gated domain, but a primary nameserver may be authoritative for more than one domain. The DNS database is periodically copied to secondary nameservers and answers to single queries are cached by other remote nameservers. The primary nameserver also caches answers from remote nameservers. Also, all queries for nonlocal domains can be directed through the primary nameserver, where they are cached. Subsequent queries for the same domain will be answered by the primary nameserver, thus minimizing traffic outside the local domain's networks.

Secondary Nameserver. A secondary nameserver has an exact duplicate of a primary nameserver's DNS database. The server automatically and periodically updates the copy by polling the primary server. Secondary nameservers have two functions: They are redundant backups for the primary nameserver, and they are used to distribute the DNS query load among several nameservers.

Slave Nameserver. A slave nameserver runs a minimal DNS server that caches answers received from other more knowledgeable nameservers. This type of nameserver is initialized with very little authoritative information; most queries received by the server are forwarded to a secondary or primary nameserver. The */etc/resolv.conf* file for a slave nameserver host has a single nameserver line that points at the host's loopback interface address. A slave nameserver's database has information only about the loopback interface.

A slave nameserver is similar to a resolver-only host in that all domain queries, except for the loopback interface name, are directed to a remote server. However, unlike a resolver-only host, the slave nameserver can cache and save answers from remote nameservers. This is an important difference. Because most hosts communicate with only a few remote systems, a slave nameserver will quickly cache answers for these systems. All queries thereafter will be answered locally, thus generating no additional network traffic. A resolver-only system does no caching, so if its remote nameservers fail it has no way to perform lookups. In a similar situation, a slave nameserver can continue to answer queries for the cached answers.

A Reliable DNS Architecture

Figure 6.14 illustrates a reliable DNS server architecture for an enterprise network that uses a combination of slave nameservers, secondary nameservers, and one primary nameserver. Solid arrows show the query flow and dashed arrows show the flow of zone transfers. With this architecture, you configure and run a DNS nameserver on all host systems. No resolver-only systems are configured. All */etc/resolv.conf* files are identical and have a domain line for the default domain and a nameserver line that points at the loopback interface address. This file contains the following two lines:

```
domain tic.com
nameserver 127.0.0.1
```

Having all these files identical simplifies administration because every new machine has the exact same file, which can simply be made a part of a standard configuration process.

The primary nameserver located on one major backbone network loads the authoritative database files for the domain. If the primary is unavailable, one secondary server in a separate administration serves as the principal and official backup for the domain. The addresses of the primary and official secondary servers are registered with the parent domain registry. You configure other unregistered secondaries within the local enterprise network to distribute the query load across a number of servers and provide additional redundancy for the primary server. All other hosts are configured to run slave nameservers that forward queries to the secondary or primary nameserver on the same local network or, as an overall backup and as a last resort, to the local primary nameserver. These slave nameservers also cache answers obtained from the primary or any secondary nameservers.

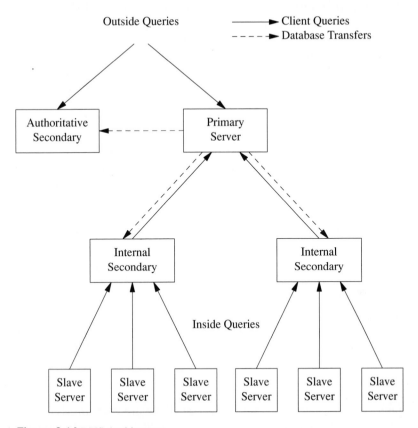

Figure 6.14 DNS Architecture.

If you delegate a subdomain that has its own naming authority, the subdomain architecture mirrors the parent domain architecture. This subdomain has its own primary nameserver plus an advertised secondary for backup purposes. Other secondary nameservers exist to handle local queries. The rest of the hosts in the subdomain run slave nameservers. Domain name requests are handled hierarchically, that is, a request is sent first to a slave nameserver. If the slave can't answer the query, it sends the request to a secondary or primary nameserver within the default domain. If neither of those servers can answer the query, the slave then sends the query to the parent domain nameserver. If the parent cannot answer the query, it sends the request to one of the root servers that returns pointers to the correct domain server. Answers returned from outside the domain are cached for later use on the primary and secondary nameservers.

A hierarchical structure with redundancy makes the nameservice system more reliable. It also eliminates the need for any server except the main domain's primary nameserver to query any root servers, an important consideration when most name-to-address translations are within the local domain.

Configuration Files. The DNS configuration should be kept in a well-known directory. A good choice is */etc/named*. Also, because the nameservice is initialized early in the bootstrap process, ensure the configuration files are on an already-mounted filesystem and that the file */etc/services* has the proper port configuration entries as follows:

```
domain       53/tcp      nameserver
domain       53/udp      nameserver
```

The DNS bootstrap file, */etc/named.boot*, contains all the configuration information needed to boot the nameserver daemon, including the location of DNS database files and how they are used, as well as other generic configuration information. The nameserver daemon itself is called *in.named*, or sometimes just *named*, and is usually kept in */usr/etc*.

Storing the DNS database files in the */etc/named* directory keeps everything in one well-known location on all machines and simplifies administration. Similarly, keeping copies of all the bootstrap files for primary, secondary, and slave servers in */etc/named* simplifies nameserver maintenance. You then can simply make a symbolic link to the correct bootstrap file for that host; for example, you could name the bootstrap files *boot.prm, boot.sec,* and *boot.slv*.

If you want to make a machine a slave server, create a symbolic link */etc/named.boot* that points to the correct bootstrap file as follows:

```
ln -s /etc/named/boot.slv /etc/named.boot
```

Further, storing all the bootstrap scripts on all the machines enables you to keep a generic set of bootstrap files that configure all three types of nameservers, which in turn lets you easily change a host from a slave to a secondary nameserver; all you need to do is change the symbolic link and restart the server.

Common DNS Files. Applications occasionally use the loopback interface, 127.0.0.1, commonly called *localhost,* with aliases of *loopback* and *loghost*. The names are considered top-level, special-case names; that is, the FQDN for this interface is simply *localhost.* — note the trailing period. Generally, every DNS server is authoritative for its own loopback interface. The two standard loopback DNS database files are shown in Fig. 6.15. These two files are the same regardless of the server type; they simply name the loopback interface, as given above. They are referred to in the bootstrap files and loaded by the server at startup.

The DNS cache file, shown in Fig. 6.16, is used to hot-wire the names and addresses of the root DNS servers. The cache is required on every type of server. Root servers generally remain constant over long periods of time; an updated list of them is available via anonymous FTP from the host *nic.ddn.mil*.

Slave Nameserver Configuration. Most hosts run as a DNS slave server. The bootstrap file for a slave server is shown in Fig. 6.17 and breaks down as follows:

```
; localhost
$ORIGIN localhost.
@ SOA localhost. root.tic.com. ( 1 86400 3600 3600000 604800 )
@ IN NS localhost.
@ IN A 127.0.0.1


; f.127
$ORIGIN 127.in-addr.arpa.
@ SOA localhost. root.tic.com. ( 1 86400 3600 3600000 604800 )
@ IN NS localhost.
localhost. IN A 127.0.0.1
0.0.1 IN PTR localhost.
```

Figure 6.15 localhost and f.127 DNS Files.

- *directory* line
  Indicates the directory in which the nameserver database files reside — in this configuration, */etc/named*.

- *domain* line
  Sets the default domain for this server. This domain should be the parent of the host. In this example, it is *tic.com*.

- *primary* line
  Indicate that the nameserver is authoritative for the loopback interface and its reverse map. The files used are the generic files described in the last section.

- *forwarders* line
  Gives the IP addresses of one or more nameservers to which all requests are forwarded for resolution. More than a single forwarder can be listed. In this example, the forwarders are the addresses of the primary nameserver and a secondary nameserver on the same physical network. Without the *forwarders* line, the nameserver would attempt to forward an unresolved query to one of the root nameservers or to a cached NS entry for the domain of interest. If the query was for the current domain, the root nameserver would bounce the query back to the primary nameserver for the domain. However, the *forwarder* line will short circuit the path and forward the query directly to one of the nameservers listed. If the query is for another domain, the nameserver to which the query was forwarded caches the answer, which can be used by other slave nameservers when they make the same query.

- *cache* line
  Names the file that contains bootstrap information about root nameservers. This data is necessary for the orderly startup of the nameserver.

```
;
; Full cache of all known root domain servers
;
   .          99999999        IN      NS         C.NYSER.NET.
              99999999        IN      NS         TERP.UMD.EDU.
              99999999        IN      NS         NS.NASA.GOV.
              99999999        IN      NS         NIC.DDN.MIL.
              99999999        IN      NS         A.ISI.EDU.
              99999999        IN      NS         GUNTER-ADAM.AF.MIL.
              99999999        IN      NS         AOS.BRL.MIL.
;
NS.NIC.DDN.MIL.        99999999     IN    A      192.112.36.4
A.ISI.EDU.             99999999     IN    A      26.3.0.103
A.ISI.EDU.             99999999     IN    A      128.9.0.107
AOS.BRL.MIL.           99999999     IN    A      128.20.1.2
AOS.BRL.MIL.           99999999     IN    A      192.5.25.82
C.NYSER.NET.           99999999     IN    A      192.33.4.12
GUNTER-ADAM.AF.MIL.    99999999     IN    A      26.1.0.13
NS.NASA.GOV.           99999999     IN    A      128.102.16.10
NS.NASA.GOV.           99999999     IN    A      192.52.195.10
TERP.UMD.EDU.          99999999     IN    A      128.8.10.90
```

Figure 6.16 DNS Cache.

• *slave* line
  Permits the nameserver to forward queries only to one of the nameservers found
  in the *forwarders* line and not to any arbitrary server. This means a nameserver
  that is a slave must have a list of forwarders for proper operation. Otherwise the
  server has no information about where to send any queries it cannot answer
  itself.

Figure 6.17 DNS Slave Nameserver Bootstrap File.

```
directory      /etc/named
domain         lgc.com
primary        127.in-addr.arpa      f.127
primary        localhost             localhost
cache          .                     cache
forwarders     135.131.1.1
slave
```

```
directory       /etc/named
domain          tic.com
secondary       tic.com                   135.131.1.1 tic.com
secondary       131.135.in-addr.arpa      135.131.1.1 f.135.131
primary         localhost                 localhost
primary         127.in-addr.arpa          f.127
cache           .                         cache
forwarders      135.131.1.1
```

Figure 6.18 Secondary Nameserver Bootstrap File.

Secondary Nameserver Configuration. Figure 6.18 shows an example secondary nameserver configuration file. The first few lines are very similar to a slave nameserver's configuration file. The major difference is in the *secondary* lines for each domain and its reverse map. These lines identify the domain for which this host is a secondary nameserver. The last two arguments identify the IP address of the primary nameserver for this domain and the name of a backup file, respectively. This example use the convention whereby the name of the domain is the name of the backup file. The reverse domain's backup filename is the dotted quad network number preceded by an "f.". When the secondary nameserver initially boots, it tries to copy the primary nameserver's database file. If the secondary can't communicate with the primary, it uses the local copy found in the backup file instead. Periodically, the secondary nameserver queries the primary to see if any updates have modified the domain database. If so, then the secondary replaces its existing database for that domain with the updated version. It also updates the local backup copy of the database. In this manner, current copies of the database are generally always available, except when communication with the primary nameserver is interrupted for a long period of time.

The *forwarder* line points at the primary nameserver. All queries for domains outside the current domain are routed through the primary nameserver. This keeps the secondary nameserver from having to directly access other nameservers. For this to work properly, the primary must be very reliable. If the primary goes down, then queries for outside domains will fail, except for those that the secondary nameserver has already cached. You might want to remove the *forwarder* line. Then the secondary nameserver will go directly to outside servers for outside domain requests. Note that secondary nameservers also require the *cache* line to initiate the cache at startup.

A secondary nameserver provides a redundant backup for instances when the primary server is unavailable. There should be at least one secondary nameserver for each physical network. For a large network, you should set up several secondaries on each physical network. All slave nameservers on the same network should forward requests to the secondary nameservers on that network.

```
directory       /etc/named
domain          tic.com
primary         tic.com                     tic.com
primary         131.135.in-addr.arpa        f.135.131
primary         localhost                   localhost
primary         127.in-addr.arpa            f.127
cache           .                           cache
```

Figure 6.19 Primary Nameserver Bootstrap File.

Primary Nameserver Configuration. The primary nameserver is the most important DNS component, for it retains the authoritative database of host information. Figure 6.19 shows an example bootstrap file for a primary nameserver. Notice that the primary's configuration is very similar to a secondary nameserver's. The nameserver is primary for the forward domain and the reverse map. When the primary server starts up, it reads the DNS database files and loads them into memory. When DNS files are updated, you should increment the serial field in the SOA record so that all secondary servers will receiver a new copy of the database.

Subdomain Setup. Suppose in our example that a separate subdomain is created for *eng.tic.com* on a separate subnet 135.131.64.0. All hosts with domain names under *eng.tic.com* are assigned network addresses with a subnet of

Figure 6.20 Primary Domain Database with Delegated Subdomain.

```
$ORIGIN tic.com.
@   IN SOA tic.com. root ( 100 86400 3600 3600000 21600 )
@   IN NS akasha
    IN NS ns2.psi.net.
eng IN NS primary.eng
eng IN NS alternate

akasha          IN A 135.131.1.1
ns2.psi.net.    IN A 192.35.82.2
primary.eng     IN A 135.131.64.1
alternate       IN A 135.131.1.6
    .
    .
    .
```

135.131.64.0. In this example, the subnet mask is 8 bits. The *tic.com* database file is modified by adding nameserver records and an address record for the DNS nameservers in the subdomain. The head of the *tic.com* DNS database file is shown in Fig. 6.20. The NS records delegate authority for this subdomain to two nameservers — the primary nameserver *server.eng.tic.com* and the secondary nameserver *alternate.tic.com* (you could select other nameservers instead). The address record is required because the *tic.com* domain needs to know the address of *server.eng.tic.com* in order to forward queries to that nameserver for its subdomain, *alternate.tic.com,* because its parent domain is *tic.com,* already has an address record in the *tic.com* DNS file.

The head of the DNS database for *eng.tic.com* is shown in Fig. 6.21. Note the addition of the addresses for the *tic.com* nameservers. These records are not essential; however, they enable you to reach the parent domain more efficiently because the nameserver doesn't need to query the root nameserver to get the A record of the nameserver for the *tic.com* domain. The reverse map files for *131.135.in-addr.arpa* and *128.131.135.in-addr.arpa* are similarly modified and shown in Fig. 6.22 and Fig. 6.23. The reverse map subdomain does not contain address records for the parent or child nameservers, since these can be found in the forward database file for the subdomain.

The subdomain's primary nameserver has the bootstrap file shown in Fig. 6.24. This file is identical to the parent domain's, except that the domain name is changed to the name of the subdomain. The bootstrap file for the nameservers for the *tic.com* domain remain the same.

Figure 6.21 eng.tic.com Database File.

```
$ORIGIN eng.tic.com.
@ IN SOA eng.tic.com. root ( 2 86400 3600 3600000 21600 )

  IN NS primary
  IN NS alternate.tic.com.

primary             IN A 135.131.64.1
alternate.tic.com.  IN A 135.131.128.5

tic.com.               IN NS akasha.tic.com.
                       IN NS ns2.psi.net

akasha.tic.com.     IN A 135.131.1.1
ns2.psi.net.        IN A 192.35.82.2
   .
   .
   .
```

```
$ORIGIN 131.135.in-addr.arpa.
@ IN SOA 131.135.in-addr.arpa. root.tic.com.\
                          ( 1 86400 3600 3600000 21600 )
@       IN NS akasha.tic.com.
        IN NS ns2.psi.net
64      IN NS primary.eng.tic.com.
64      IN NS alternate.tic.com.

    .
    .
    .
```

Figure 6.22 Reverse Map for Network 135.131.0.0.

A DNS nameserver can act as a server for multiple domains. We have already seen this for the loopback network interface data that are maintained as a separate domain under each nameserver. The primary nameserver for *tic.com* also can be the secondary for *eng.tic.com* as well as for the reverse domain map. For this to occur, you need to add two *secondary* lines to the modified primary boot-strap file. Figure 6.25 illustrates these changes. In the same way, the primary nameserver for *eng.tic.com* can become a secondary for *tic.com,* as shown in Fig. 6.26. These new secondary nameservers are hidden unless nameserver records are added to the authoritative databases. Letting the primary nameserver for a domain be a secondary backup for its delegated subdomains is usually a good idea because it ensures the primary domain always has a recent copy of the

Figure 6.23 Reverse Map for Subnetwork 135.131.64.0.

```
$ORIGIN 64.131.135.in-addr.arpa.
@ IN SOA tic.com. root.eng.tic.com.\
                          ( 2 86400 3600 3600000 21600 )

64      IN NS primary.eng.tic.com.
64      IN NS alternate.tic.com.

131.135.in-addr.arpa. IN NS akasha.tic.com.
131.135.in-addr.arpa. IN NS ns2.psi.net.
    .
    .
    .
```

```
directory       /etc/named
domain          eng.tic.com
primary         eng.tic.com              eng.tic.com
primary         64.131.135.in-addr.arpa  f.135.131.64
primary         localhost                localhost
primary         127.in-addr.arpa         f.127
cache           .                        cache
```

Figure 6.24 Domain eng.tic.com Bootstrap File.

subdomain's database even if network communication between the two nameservers is disrupted. Also, if the delegated subdomain is separated from its parent by a slow network connection, mutual secondary nameservers reduce the amount of network traffic on the connection.

A Stand-alone Network Using DNS. You can use DNS in an isolated network that has no Internet connectivity. Because a DNS nameserver requires the location of the root nameservers before proper operation can begin, a stand-alone network must have a "fake" root nameserver. You create this fake root nameserver by building a fake root database that has only an entry for your domain. You then would add an entry to this fake server in the nameserver cache database and remove the entries for the real root nameservers. Figure 6.27 shows an example fake root database. This file mimics the activity of a real root server, that is, it lists the location and addresses of nameservers for valid domains. The root database file simply has an NS record that points to the nameserver for the only real domain under this fake root. Only name lookups for the existing domain will work; all others will fail even though the other domains really exist. This has some implications for mail delivery that we discuss in Chapter 8.

Figure 6.25 Primary Server for tic.com with secondary for eng.tic.com.

```
directory       /etc/named
domain          tic.com
primary         tic.com                  tic.com
primary         131.135.in-addr.arpa     f.135.131
secondary       eng.tic.com              135.131.64.1 eng.tic.com
secondary       64.131.135.in-addr.arpa  135.131.64.1 f.135.131.64
primary         localhost                localhost
primary         127.in-addr.arpa         f.127
cache           .                        cache
```

```
directory       /etc/named
domain          eng.tic.com
primary         eng.tic.com              eng.tic.com
primary         64.131.135.in-addr.arpa  f.135.131.64
secondary       tic.com                  135.131.1.1 tic.com
secondary       131.135.in-addr.arpa     135.131.1.1  f.135.131
primary         localhost                localhost
primary         127.in-addr.arpa         f.127
cache           .                        cache
```

Figure 6.26 eng.tic.com boot with secondary authority.

If you set up this fake nameserver and later connect to the Internet, be sure to eliminate the fake root nameserver and its database. DNS, currently, has no authentication mechanism for messages from nameservers. If some host queries your fake root nameserver and caches an answer, then the bogus information can cause the whole DNS distributed database to be perturbed with the invalid information.

Static Tables

Static tables should be used only when you are bootstrapping a system. In this case, the only entries in the /etc/hosts file should be for the loopback interface and the local host. However, if static tables must be used for general host to IP address mapping, then use domain based names instead of simple ones. Sooner or later you will establish Internet connectivity and transitioning from simple names to domain names can be a huge undertaking. Static table entries should use the full domain name as the canonical name of the host (the first entry in the table).

Figure 6.27 Fake Root Server.

```
$ORIGIN .
@   IN SOA . root.tic.com. ( 4 300 150 3600000 21600 )
@   IN NS akasha.tic.com.
tic.com                 IN NS akasha.tic.com.
131.135.in-addr.arpa IN NS akasha.tic.com.
akasha.tic.com.         IN A 135.131.1.1
    .
    .
    .
```

```
127.0.0.1 localhost  .
135.131.1.1 akasha.tic.com akasha
135.131.1.2 beast.tic.com beast
135.131.1.3 ticmac.tic.com ticmac
   .
   .
   .
```

Figure 6.28 Static Host Table.

The hostname without the parent domain can be used as an alias. Doing this mimics the way DNS uses the default domain and allows you to use simple, unqualified hostnames. An example static host table is shown in Fig. 6.28.

Static tables must be distributed to all machines, a time-consuming and error-prone task that usually is feasible only on small networks. (another reason for not using static tables). Usually you can do this by writing some simple shell scripts or by using a remote distribution utility such as *rdist*. To avoid inconsistencies between host tables from developing, establish a single host as a master for all host names and distribute this file to all other hosts on the network.

Sun NIS

NIS is an alternative to DNS for hostname-to-address mapping. A single host system serves as an NIS master server, and NIS information is distributed to NIS slave servers that have copies of the NIS tables. Other hosts query a master or slave server and are called clients. NIS automates the lookup of such resources as hostnames across the network. However, it doesn't have the same notion of hierarchical domain names as DNS does. Instead, each host is configured at boot time into a single NIS domain and all lookups are performed within that domain. The major advantage NIS has over static tables is that you do not need to manually copy the host table to every machine. Also, NIS is a generalized lookup service and can handle information in addition to hostname-to-address mapping.

NIS Architecture. NIS has two major components: an NIS domain binder — *ypbind* — and an NIS database server — *ypserv*. Ypbind must be run on all hosts that use NIS; Ypserv is run only on machines that have a copy of the NIS database files. Each database file is also called an **NIS map,** which is simply a hashed file created with the NIS utility, *makedbm*. Both ypserv and ypbind use Sun RPC to communicate with remote clients. When they startup, they register a UDP and TCP port with the local RPC portmapper. We discuss more about RPC and the portmapper in Chapter 9. Initial queries from clients are directed at the portmapper, since a client does not know the ypbind or ypserv port numbers, which are assigned dynamically.

```
% rpcinfo -p
   program vers proto    port
    100000    2   tcp     111   portmapper
    100000    2   udp     111   portmapper
    100004    2   udp     662   ypserv
    100004    2   tcp     663   ypserv
    100004    1   udp     662   ypserv
    100007    2   tcp    1024   ypbind
    100007    2   udp    1027   ypbind
    100004    1   tcp     663   ypserv
    100007    1   tcp    1024   ypbind
    100007    1   udp    1027   ypbind
         .
         .
         .
```

Figure 6.29 Using rpcinfo.

There are two versions of NIS — 1 and 2. Both ypbind and ypserv will accept queries from clients that support either version. You can see the port numbers associated with ypbind and ypserv by running the *rpcinfo* command with the *-p* option, as shown in Fig. 6.29.

ypbind. Ypbind determines the location of a server for a given NIS domain. Once a server is located, its IP address and port number are remembered by ypbind and the client machine is bound to that server for queries for its NIS domain. A client machine can bind to only one server at a time, although multiple redundant servers may be present on the network. The *ypwhich* command displays the current binding, as follows:

```
% ypwhich
akasha.tic.com
```

If the client is unbound (that is, it is unable to locate a server), then a message is displayed to that effect as follows:

```
% ypwhich
domain tic.com is unbound
```

The manner in which ypwhich gets the binding from ypbind is a good illustration how NIS works. Ypwhich makes an RPC call to the local ypbind process and asks ypbind for the name of the server to which it is bound. Because the client process does not know the port ypbind is listening on, the client really makes this call indirectly by asking the portmapper (which is listening on a well-known port) to make the call to ypbind.

Some systems let ypbind put the current binding in a well-known file in the */var/yp/binding* directory. The filename consists of the domain and the version of NIS being used; for example, the file */var/yp/binding/tic.com.2* contains the binding information for version 2 of NIS for domain *tic.com*. The binding file contains the port number of the ypbind process, as well as the IP address and port of the remote ypserv process that is the current binding. An NIS client simply looks up the binding in the correct file and makes the call directly to ypbind or ypserv. This procedure speeds up query processing significantly.

An application using NIS makes an RPC call on the bound server using the information provided by the local ypbind process. It does this either by querying ypbind or indirectly by reading the information from one of the well-know binding files. If the request times out, then the domain is said to be unbound and ypbind will attempt to rebind the domain to an operational server.

At system startup and when attempting to rebind an unbound domain, ypbind sends a UDP broadcast message to all portmappers on the same physical network. This message asks the portmapper to call its local ypserv, if one has registered, and respond if it serves the NIS domain of the client. The first server to respond will be the one the client binds to. The reply contains the port number of the remote ypserv process, and the UDP packet contains the IP address of the server. With this information, the client becomes bound to that server. If no server responds, then the client is not bound to any domain and all NIS queries will hang indefinitely.

Ypserv. Ypserv looks up key-value information in an NIS map, accepts queries from clients, then processes and returns the answers to the queries. Queries against an NIS map can be random by key using a simple hashing scheme or sequentially through an entire map. Sequential access is not guaranteed to be in any lexical order, but it is guaranteed to return every record in the map. Because a client's binding could change in the middle of a sequential access, a client handles the access by creating a TCP connection to the server.

NIS Map Organization. Maps on a server are organized as a set of *dbm* files. You create the *dbm* files from text input files using the *makedbm* program. The files are kept in the well-known directory */var/yp/<domain>*, where *<domain>* is the name of the domain for which the server is authoritative. Maps are organized by the type of information they contain and by their index key. For example, the map *hosts.byname* shown in Fig. 6.30 is a map of all entries in */etc/host* indexed by the canonical hostname and all the host aliases, while *hosts.byaddr,* shown in Fig. 6.31, is a map of the same entries indexed by IP address.

You might at first find some of the entries confusing. The first entry of each line is the key; the rest of the line is the value the key is indexing. All hostnames and aliases are used as indices. There are also some special key-value pairs in every map, as follows:

- YP_LAST_MODIFIED
  The last time, in seconds, that the map was modified since midnight on December 31, 1969.

```
localhost 127.0.0.1
YP_LAST_MODIFIED 0694842879
ticmac.tic.com 135.131.1.3 ticmac.tic.com ticmac
akasha.tic.com 135.131.1.1 akasha.tic.com akasha
beast.tic.com 135.131.1.2 beast.tic.com beast
akasha 135.131.1.1 akasha.tic.com akasha
YP_MASTER_NAME akasha.tic.com
YP_INTERDOMAIN
beast 135.131.1.2 beast.tic.com beast
ticmac 135.131.1.3 ticmac.tic.com ticmac
```

Figure 6.30 NIS hosts.byname Map.

• YP_MASTER_NAME

Gives the name of the NIS server that is a master for this map.

• YP_INTERDOMAIN

Tells ypserv that it is to query a DNS server if a hostname is not found.

These special keys are always in all uppercase and are used not as search keys but rather internally by the protocol.

The *ypinit* command performs the initial map creation. Ypinit is a shell script that creates the default set of maps. It also takes care of creating the special *ypserver* map that gives the names of the master and slave NIS servers. The command assumes that a single machine will be the master for all the maps in the domain. This is a reasonable choice, but nothing in the protocol requires it. Each map can have its own master. However, if you organize each NIS map with a separate server, NIS administration becomes more complicated. Ypinit also has an option to create the necessary files and copy maps from the master server in order to set up a slave NIS server.

Figure 6.31 NIS hosts.byaddr Map.

```
YP_LAST_MODIFIED 0694842880
135.131.1.3 135.131.1.2 beast.tic.com beast
135.131.1.2 135.131.1.3 ticmac.tic.com ticmac
135.131.1.1 135.131.1.1 akasha.tic.com akasha
YP_MASTER_NAME akasha.tic.com
YP_INTERDOMAIN
127.0.0.1 127.0.0.1 localhost
```

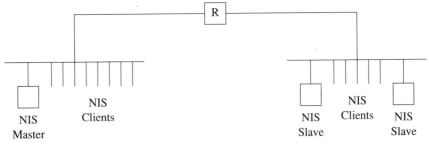

Figure 6.32 NIS Architecture.

NIS Organization. An NIS system should be structured much like a DNS system. Establish a single master server to keep all the NIS maps and set up redundant slave servers with at least one slave per physical network. You can configure all the other hosts as NIS clients that run only ypbind. Figure 6.32 shows NIS running on a network with multiple physical LANs. An NIS master runs on one of the networks; the other network runs two NIS slaves, each of which is updated simultaneously with the master server. Each slave server and the master server field requests from the NIS clients.

The NIS Master. The NIS master runs both ypserv and ypbind. The directory */var/yp/<domain>* exists on this host and is used by the startup scripts to determine whether to run ypserv. Note, ypserv must start up before ypbind does. Also the portmapper must be initialized before either of the programs are started. The *domainname* command sets the domain, usually by reading the default domain from a file. The system startup scripts determine if the domain name has been set and if so, sets up NIS properly. The order of events at startup is shown in Fig. 6.33.

A master server is set up using the ypinit shell script with the *-m* option. This procedure will invoke the default *Makefile* in the directory */var/yp* and set up all the default maps. You should edit the Makefile and delete maps that are not used,

Figure 6.33 NIS startup order.

```
determine NIS domain name and set it if one exists
if NIS domain name is set then
    if the directory /var/yp/<domain> exists then
        startup ypserv
    end if
    start ypbind
end if
```

then add maps that are local to your system. The Makefile uses ASCII files as input to makedbm to create each NIS map. A careful reading of this Makefile shows the organization of each map. Makedbm also adds the special map entries found in each map.

Generally, the ASCII input files are found in /etc on the master server. You generate the host table maps — *hosts.byaddr* and *hosts.byname* — from the /etc/hosts file on this server. You can edit the Makefile to use an alternate input file. The Makefile generates all the NIS maps except *ypservers,* which is generated by the ypinit script. If you use domain addressing, be sure hostnames are fully qualified in the input file.

When you add or delete a slave server, you must modify the *ypserver* map. There is really not a good command to do this. However, the scripts shown in Fig. 6.34 and Fig. 6.35 perform these functions. To add a new slave server use the

---

Figure 6.34 Adding a New NIS Slave Server.

```
#!/bin/sh
# add a NIS slave to server list
# arguments are slave servers to add

PATH=/usr/etc/yp:/usr/etc:/bin:/usr/bin:
PROGNAME=add_server
YPDIR=/var/yp/`domainname`

if [ $# -eq 0 ]; then
    echo usage: $PROGNAME host ...
    exit 1
fi

if [ ! -d ${YPDIR} ]; then
    echo ${PROGNAME}: directory ${YPDIR} does not exist
    exit 1
fi

cd ${YPDIR}
tmp=/tmp/${PROGNAME}.$$

ypcat ypservers >$tmp
(cat $tmp; rm $tmp; for i do
    echo $i
done) | sort | uniq |\
awk '{ print $0, $0 }' | makedbm - ypservers
```

add_server script. The script uses *ypcat* to make a list of the current master and slave servers found in the ypservers map. It then adds the new server names to the list and creates a new ypservers map by using makedbm. To delete a server from the master list, use *delete_servers* script. This script takes a list of server names to delete and rebuilds the *ypservers* map by removing the named hosts. It also ensures the master server is never removed from the list of servers.

NIS Slave Server. An NIS slave server duplicates the master server's map tables. Its startup sequence is identical to the master's. Because ypbind uses UDP broadcast messages when it binds to a server, an NIS slave or master must be present on each physical network. Broadcasts are not heard through routers, so a client on a network segment without a master or slave server will never bind to the domain.

A well-configured NIS architecture has more than one slave server per network segment. NIS clients will bind to the first server that responds to a binding requests. Usually, this will be the server with the least load. Also, if one server crashes, a second server acts as a backup; clients subsequently will rebind to the second server as requests for NIS services time-out.

An NIS slave server runs both ypserv and ypbind. Operationally it looks and feels like an NIS master server. The only difference is a slave is notified by the master server when a map has been updated. The slave then retrieves a copy of the updated map. An NIS master that has updated one or more of its maps does a *yppush* to the servers listed in the *ypservers* NIS map. Yppush notifies the slave server to request an update from the master server. The last update time for the pushed map is read from the master and compared with that in the slave's map. If the master's update time is more recent, the slave sets up a TCP connection with the master and copies its map. The slave server then uses the updated map for query processing.

With only a few slave servers on the network, this method works reasonably well. When the number of servers exceeds a few, it's better to have the slaves use the *ypxfr* utility to schedule periodic updates from the master.

You can organize map updates by frequency of updates and build appropriate shell scripts to accommodate the transfers. Figure 6.36 shows a generic shell script for executing ypxfr commands on a remote host. The arguments to the script are the NIS maps to be updated. If the master's map is not newer than the slave's, ypxfr won't copy the master's map to the slave. So checking for a map update consumes few resources on the master, that is, until the map is actually updated. Note, you also can run the *ypxfr_script* out of *cron*.

NIS Clients. An NIS client runs only ypbind; all queries are handled by a remote NIS server, either the master or a slave. When bootstrapped, an NIS client sends UDP broadcast messages to the local network looking for a response from a slave or master NIS server. When the client receives a response, it will bind to the server and send all NIS requests to the bound server. If an NIS client is on a network that doesn't have a slave or master or is on a network that doesn't support broadcasting, the client will have to bind explicitly to a known server on another

```
#!/bin/sh
# delete a NIS slave server
# arguments are slave servers to delete

PATH=/usr/etc/yp:/usr/etc:/bin:/usr/bin:
PROGNAME=add_server
YPDIR=/var/yp/`domainname`


if [ $# -eq 0 ]; then
    echo usage: $PROGNAME host ...
    exit 1
fi

if [ ! -d  ${YPDIR} ]; then
    echo ${PROGNAME}: directory ${YPDIR} does not exist
    exit 1
fi

cd ${YPDIR}
tmp1=/tmp/${PROGNAME}.$$.1
tmp2=/tmp/${PROGNAME}.$$.2

master=`makedbm -u ypservers | awk '/YP_MASTER/ { print $2 }'`
ypcat ypservers | sort >$tmp1
for i do
    if [ $i = $master ];  then
        continue
    fi
    echo $i
done | sort >$tmp2
comm -23 $tmp1 $tmp2 |\
awk '{ print $0, $0 }' | makedbm - ypservers

rm $tmp1 $tmp2
```

Figure 6.35 Deleting an NIS Slave Server.

physical network. This is done with the *ypset* command. For example, suppose you attach a workstation to the network via a serial line, as shown in Fig. 6.37. The workstation needs NIS services, so its ypbind will attempt to locate an NIS server. It will fail, however, because the workstation is not on a broadcast network. ypset solves this problem. The single argument to ypset is the IP address

```
#!/bin/sh
# check for and update NIS maps
# arguments - names of NIS maps

if [ $# -eq 0 ]; then
    echo usage: ypxfr_script map ...
    exit 1
fi

for m do
    /usr/etc/yp/ypxfr $m
done
```

Figure 6.36 ypxfr shell script.

of the remote NIS server to which the host is to be bound. So the bootstrap sequence

```
ypbind
ypset 135.131.10.5
```

binds the workstation to the NIS server on host 135.131.10.5.

The ypset program sends a request to the ypbind process requesting that it change the binding of its NIS server. This is potentially dangerous, since any user can send a ypset request to a client's ypbind process. If ypbind were then to honor the request, then a machine could be taken over by binding it to a bogus NIS server with, say, an alternate password file. To prevent this, some versions of ypbind will not honor a ypset request unless the *-ypsetme* flag is set at startup. Doing this allows only a ypset that runs on the same host to change the binding.

Figure 6.37 Workstation Attached to a Serial Line Using NIS.

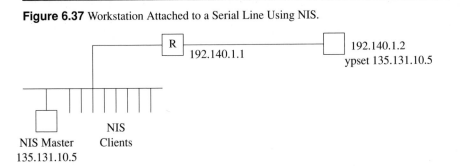

Combination Nameservers

Occasionally you might want to combine different nameserver methods. Some hosts might not support DNS and therefore will require nameservice support using NIS. Others might have only DNS support or might support only static host tables. It is possible to run the different nameservice methods side by side. However, simultaneously maintaining a separate static host file, NIS maps, and a DNS database is very difficult to do without inconsistencies cropping up. Because all three methods track the same data, you will find it convenient to maintain only one set of files and have the DNS database files, the NIS maps, and the static host table generated from a common database.

A Common Host Database

You can construct a common host information database and maintain it using shell scripts. The example we discuss next organizes the host information as a set of text files that are themselves organized as a set of tables. This structure is very similar to that used in a relational database system. Shell scripts are used to generate the static host tables, the NIS maps, and the DNS database files. This system also demonstrates the ease of building a simple but useful system using available UNIX tools. You change and add to the host information in the common database. After you enter the updates, the static host table, the NIS maps, and the DNS database files are generated and the DNS and NIS servers are updated. If you use this methodology, then all changes to host information are made in one place, which guarantees consistency between host lookup methods.

The host database is organized as a set of flat files, each containing information about host systems and each consisting of a set of fields separated by blanks or tabs. The value of each field is considered to be simply a string of characters. A field value can be surrounded by double quotes or characters can be escaped with a backslash to be included literally in the field value. Comments begin with a "#" in the first column. The "#FIELDS" special comment line names each of the fields in a file. Each field has a name that can also have keywords associated with it; for example, the *suffix=* and the *prefix=* keywords let a default suffix or prefix be added to a field value when the field is extracted. This is a notational convenience designed to reduce typing. And the *no=* keyword followed by a single character overrides the inclusion of the prefix or the suffix value when the character is prefixed or appended to a field value.

The host files are as follows:

• *hosts.main*

• *hosts.cname*

• *hosts.ns*

• *host.soa*

- *hosts.wks*

- *hosts.mx*

Each is discussed in detail next.

hosts.main. Each line of this file contains information about a host. See Fig. 6.38. The fields are as follows:

- *host:* the hostname.

- *ip:* the IP address of the host.

- *datalink:* the hardware address of the host.

- *hard:* the hardware type.

- *os:* the host operating system.

- *contact:* the contact person for this host.

Notice the use of the *prefix=* and *suffix=* keywords to reduce the amount of text in the file. Also note that additional information not used by DNS, such as the datalink address and the contact person name, is kept for each host. This information could be used by other applications or as a way of keeping pertinent information about each host in one place.

hosts.cname. This file keeps host aliases, as shown in Fig. 6.39. It has two fields as follows:

- *host:* the real name of the host.

- *alias:* an alternate or alias name for the host. A host with multiple aliases lists each alias separately, one per line.

Figure 6.38 hosts.main.

```
#FIELDS host suffix=.tic.com no=@ ip prefix=135.131. no=@\
        datalink hard os contact
#host      ip            datalink            hard      os      contact
#==================================================================
akasha     1.1           8:0:20:d:c:a:13     SUN4      SUNOS   smoot
beast      1.2           7:10:2:c:d:a        RS6000    AIX     smoot
ticmac     1.3           0:0:94:1:36:4c      MAC       MACOS   smoot
localhost@ @127.0.0.1    X                   X         X       X
```

```
#FIELDS host suffix=.tic.com no=@ alias suffix=.tic.com no=@
#=============================================================
#host               alias
akasha              mailhost
beast               printserver
```

Figure 6.39 hosts.cname.

---

hosts.ns. This file contains the names of the authoritative servers for each domain. See Fig. 6.40. It has two fields as follows:

• *domain:* the domain name for which the server is authoritative.

• *server:* the domain name of the nameserver.

host.soa. This file contains the SOA parameters for each domain for which this server is authoritative. See Fig. 6.41. It contains seven fields as follows:

• *domain:* the name of the domain that starts the SOA record.

• *server:* the name of the authoritative server.

• *contact:* the mail contact address.

• *refresh:* the refresh interval.

• *retry:* the retry interval.

• *expire:* the expiration time for the zone.

• *min:* the minimum TTL value.

Figure 6.40 hosts.ns.

```
#FIELDS domain server suffix=.tic.com no=@
#domain                  server
#========================================
tic.com                  akasha
tic.com                  ns2.psi.net@
131.135.in-addr.arpa     akasha
131.135.in-addr.arpa     ns2.psi.net@
localhost                localhost@
127.in-addr.arpa         localhost@
```

```
#FIELDS domain server suffix=.tic.com no=@ contact suffix=.tic.com\
       refresh retry expire min
#domain                    server      contact refresh retry  expire   min
#=========================================================================
tic.com                    akasha      root    86400   3600   3600000 604800
localhost                  localhost@  root    86400   3600   3600000 604800
131.135.in-addr.arpa akasha           root    86400   3600   3600000 604800
127.in-addr.arpa           localhost@  root    86400   3600   3600000 604800
```

Figure 6.41 hosts.soa.

The SOA *serial* parameter is not included, but is generated by the script that updates the DNS files.

hosts.wks. This file contains the well-known services advertised by each host. See Fig. 6.42. It has four fields as follows:

• *host:* the host's domain name.

• *ip:* the IP address of the interface advertising the service.

• *proto:* the transport protocol the service uses.

Figure 6.42 hosts.wks File.

```
#FIELDS host suffix=.tic.com no=@ ip prefix=135.131. no=@ proto wks
#host          ip            proto     wks
#=================================================================
akasha         1             tcp       smtp
akasha         1             tcp       telnet
akasha         1             tcp       ftp
akasha         1             tcp       domain
akasha         1             udp       domain
beast          2             tcp       telnet
beast          2             tcp       domain
beast          2             udp       domain
ticmac         3             tcp       telnet
localhost@     @127.0.0.1    tcp       smtp
localhost@     @127.0.0.1    tcp       telnet
localhost@     @127.0.0.1    tcp       ftp
localhost@     @127.0.0.1    tcp       domain
localhost@     @127.0.0.1    udp       domain
```

```
#FIELDS domain priority host suffix=.tic.com no=@
#domain         priority      host
#================================================
tic.com         10            akasha
```

Figure 6.43 hosts.mx.

• *wks:* the name of the service.

hosts.mx. This file contains the MX information for each domain that needs an MX record. See Fig. 6.43. It has three fields as follows:

• *domain:* the domain name of this MX record.

• *priority:* the priority for this record.

• *host:* the domain name of the MX forwarder.

Shell and Awk Scripts for Information Retrieval. We have written several shell and awk scripts to retrieve information from the aforementioned database files (see Appendix B). From that information, we can build the static host table and the DNS database files. A brief description of each script follows:

• *readinfo*
Extracts a set of fields from each file. Its arguments are the names of the fields to extract and only the fields listed are extracted. Fields are separated on the output by tab characters. The script obtains the field information from the *#FIELDS* line found in the file. Readinfo is implemented using two *awk* scripts, as follows:

  • The first script places each line of the file into a canonical form. It separates all fields with a tab character and handles quoted fields and escaped characters.

  • The second script extracts the enumerated fields.

Readinfo reads the file information from *stdin* and places the extracted field information on *stdout*. This script is a "poorperson's" database system. Nothing prevents the host files described here from being implemented as part of any modern relational database system as the format and layout of the files would drop right into such a system.

• *updatehosts*
Updates the various host files. Its arguments are the names of the files you want to edit. Updatehosts uses SCCS to maintain the host files and update the DNS serial parameter for each zone. In this implementation, the serial field is incremented each time a host file is updated. After you edit a file, updatehosts calls on two scripts — *genstatic* and *gendns* — to build the static host file and the

DNS database files, respectively. It uses the *serial* file to store the latest serial number that is attached as a comment to each updated file.

- *genstatic*

Transforms the host database files into the standard UNIX */etc/hosts* format. This script uses readinfo to read the *hosts.main* and the *hosts.cname* files and constructs the static host table from the extracted information. It assumes the canonical host names are in domain name format, and for each domain name, it automatically creates an alias that is the host's simple name. It also adds all the aliases found in *hosts.cname* to the generated */etc/hosts* file.

- *gendns*

Builds the DNS database zone files for each zone listed in the *hosts.soa* file. This script is a bit more complicated than the others. Both the forward and reverse (*in-addr.arpa*) zones must be included in *hosts.soa* file in order for either zone to be generated. The script first reads *hosts.soa* and for each zone determines if it is a forward or reverse domain. The script identifies the reverse domains by the presence of an *in-addr.arpa* in the domain name. The forward domains are identified by the absence of an *in-addr.arpa* in the domain name. The script builds forward domains using the *makeforw* shell function, and builds reverse domains using the *makerev* shell function. Before these functions are called, several shell variables are defined, as follows:

- *servers*

A list of all nameservers for the zone being built.

- *escape_domain*

A search pattern for the domain name. This variable is needed because, to *grep*, a period in a search pattern is a special character. *escape_domain* has all the periods in the domain name escaped.

- *unreverse*

For a reverse zone, holds the unreversed domain name, less the *in-addr.arpa* for matching IP addresses.

- *filename*

Names the zone output file. Forward domain databases are output to files with names that are the same as the domain name. Reverse domain databases are output to files that begin with an "f." followed by the contents of the *unreverse* shell variable. Thus, the name of the database file for the reverse domain *128.135.192.in-addr.arpa* is *f.192.135.128*.

The SOA header information for each domain is output first using the information in the *hosts.soa* file. The serial field is filled in with the contents of the *dateserial* shell variable. This puts the current date, in *yymmdd* format, into the serial field of the SOA header for each zone (assuming the zone files are updated at most once per day). Other conventions could be used here, but this one is convenient and makes the serial field easy to interpret.

Next, depending on the domain, the script calls the *makeforw* or *makerev* function. Makeforw builds the forward DNS zone file, as follows:

1. It reads the *hosts.main* file using readinfo. If the host is a nameserver for this domain, an NS record, A record, and HINFO record for the host are output. If the host is only in the domain, an A record and HINFO record are output.

2. The *hosts.cname* file is read and CNAME records are added for aliases that are a part of the current domain.

3. The *hosts.mx* and the *host.wks* files are read and the appropriate MX and WKS records are inserted in the output.

Makerev builds the reverse zone files, as follows:

1. It reads the *hosts.main* file and constructs the reverse zone file. If the host is a nameserver for this domain, it outputs an NS record and an A record for the nameserver. The A record is not entirely necessary, but it speeds searches.

2. For hosts with IP addresses within this domain (that is, hosts with IP addresses that match *unreverse*), a PTR record is created.

The final step in the script is using an *sed* script to eliminate the extraneous domain information in each file. While this step is not essential, it reduces the size of the zone files and makes them more readable.

This set of scripts builds all the DNS zone files. If the information for the loopback interface is included in *hosts.main* and an entry is include in *hosts.soa,* then the forward and reverse loopback zones also will be built. The command *poke_ns* at the end of updatehosts informs the nameserver that the zone file has been updated. This program is run setuid to *root* and is executable by the group of users able to update the DNS database; execute permission is turned off for all others. Poke_ns uses the */etc/named.pid* file, which contains the nameserver process id, and sends the correct, and easily forgettable, signals that perform various nameserver housekeeping functions. To update NIS maps, updatehosts copies the new host table to */etc/hosts* and invokes the NIS make script to update the maps.

Naming Revisited

As we have seen, naming is a very important TCP/IP service because it helps make network services easy to use. Unfortunately, no single naming protocol convention exists in the real world of TCP/IP networks. We have shown the overall architecture of a good naming system and outlined the software that is available for setting such a system. We also demonstrated a way of organizing the naming system so it is coherent and easy to manage and troubleshoot. And, as it turns out, with UNIX you can build some relatively simple tools to help you out with the management task.

CHAPTER 7

Electronic Mail

Many TCP/IP networks are initially justified and funded based on the network's cost-effectiveness regarding shared access to scarce resources such as expensive supercomputers. Often, however, the most widely used TCP/IP network service turns out to be **electronic mail.** More commonly called **e-mail,** or simply **mail,** electronic mail enables network users to send and receive correspondence over the network.

UNIX systems with TCP/IP support provide for building robust and extensible mail systems. To transport and present mail, TCP/IP defines several protocols, including the following:

- **Simple Mail Transfer Protocol (SMTP)**
  SMTP is the standard TCP/IP application protocol for transporting mail between systems that have full TCP/IP support [Postel 1982]. As the name suggests, SMTP is fairly simple. It uses TCP as its underlying transport protocol, thus ensuring reliable message delivery.

- **RFC-822 message format**
  This important mail protocol is a standard format for presenting mail messages [Crocker 1982]. Although originally designed solely for use in the Internet community, it now can be used to extend mail delivery beyond the Internet. You can send and receive messages that conform to RFC822 format using any transport protocol that supports 7-bit ASCII. Doing this enables you to send and receive mail from the UUCP mail network or from BITNET, FidoNet, and almost any PC-based Bulletin Board System.

Mail's extensibility beyond the Internet is perhaps its greatest strength. However, because the mail system architecture can quickly become very complex, this quality of extensibility also can lead to a great deal of confusion. Further complications arise because UNIX and TCP/IP mail configurations rely on traditions and folklore that are poorly documented. In this chapter, we explain the mail maze and offers ideas and pointers on how to build robust mail configurations using TCP/IP and UNIX.

7.1   A General Mail System Architecture

A mail system typically consists of two parts: UAs and MTAs. A **user agent (UA),** is a program that interacts directly with end users. While an **message transfer agent (MTA),** routes and transfers mail from the user system to the destination system. Figure 7.1 shows a general architecture for a mail system. The terms UA and MTA are borrowed from the X.400 MHS. specification which is an international standard for electronic message systems. Although UNIX and TCP/IP-based mail systems don't conform completely with the X.400 specification, X.400 is a good conceptual framework for describing such systems.

UAs typically have facilities for users to compose, edit, and send mail messages; reply to incoming messages; and store messages for later perusal. When you send a mail message, the UA relays it to the local MTA, which in turn routes the message to the next MTA. That MTA then routes the message to the next

Figure 7.1 Mail System Architecture.

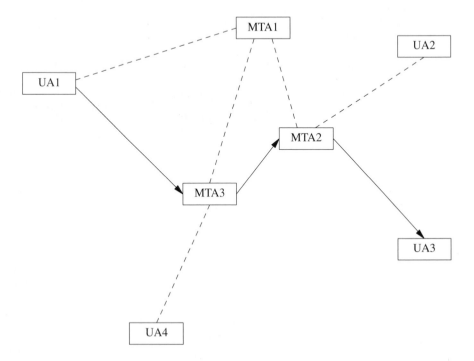

MTA, and so forth until the message reaches the MTA on the destination system. Incoming mail messages are stored by the destination MTA in the recipient's **mailbox.** A mailbox is usually just an ordinary file. A mailbox is a convenient method for storing incoming mail messages until a user runs a UA to read the messages.

Generally, a UA runs on the same host where the mailbox is located. However, the **Post Office Protocol (POP)** enables you to read a mailbox on a remote system. This facility is useful when you prefer to read your mail on a workstation or PC that might not be running or be connected to the network all the time. In this case, mail is collected by a more reliable system and then downloaded by POP to the workstation when you want to read your mail. We discuss POP in detail in Chapter 8.

The mail system general architecture is depicted in Fig. 7.1. The dashed lines show possible communication paths between the MTAs and UAs. The solid arrows shows how a mail message might be routed from UA1 to UA3. UA1 sends the message to MTA3 where it is forwarded to MTA2. MTA2 stores the incoming mail message in a mailbox. Finally a user running UA3 reads the message. This architecture permits different UAs and MTAs to coexist within a single networked mail system, provided all the software agrees on the standard RFC822 message format. Also the MTAs must agree on some common protocols and conventions; that is, for any two MTAs to communicate they must both support the same mail transport protocol, whether that protocol is SMTP, the UUCP *rmail* remote execution convention, or some other protocol. However, an MTA can support multiple mail transport protocols and use each to send a message to a specific set of remote MTAs. For example, an MTA can use SMTP to send a message to another MTA, which in turn can use UUCP to send the message to another MTA. The UAs and the MTAs that store mail messages in a user's mailbox also must agree on a common file locking protocol in order to serialize access to the mailbox. For example in the figure, MTA2 passes mail messages to UA3 by storing them in a user's mailbox. If the MTA is adding a message to the mailbox at the same time the UA is removing messages, then it is possible the mailbox contents could be garbled. Access to the mailbox must be serialized to avoid this problem. Thus, the UA and MTA must agree on a common file locking protocol. On a UNIXsystem, this is usually achieved by using the *flock()* or *lockf()* system calls. Or, a locking file that depends on the atomic nature of the *link()* system call could be used by the UA and the MTA.

The division of a mail system into UAs and MTAs has several advantages. UAs can focus on the user interface for sending and receiving mail; their primary job is to make composing and reading mail messages easy. MTAs can focus on validating mail addresses and routing mail; validation is particularly important in mixed environments that have more than one mail-address standard. In a very practical sense, mail demonstrates the power and success of the layered protocol model. You can send and receive mail that complies with RFC822 message format using several different underlying transport protocols. Systems that interchange mail either can share a common mail address space or take advantage of well-defined gateways that translate one address space to another. So a mail system can span several different networks using different transport protocols and yet, as far as the end user is concerned, look like a single coherent system.

Messages and Envelopes

A mail message comprises two parts: an envelope and its contents. The distinction between the two is important and sometimes confusing. Each distinct message has an envelope that is used to route and deliver the message. The envelope includes a return address so the mail system can return undelivered mail and error messages to the original sender. The return address also makes it convenient for a mail recipient to reply to a mail message. To route the message, the delivery system — that is, the MTAs — uses only the envelope information and not the message contents.

Inside the envelope, the mail contents are divided into a header followed by a message body. Following RFC822 convention, the header and message body are separated by a blank line. The header usually includes the following lines:

- *To:*
  The address of the message recipient.

- *From:*
  The address of the sender of the message.

- *Subject:*
  A brief description of the contents.

- *Date:*
  The date and time the message was sent.

- *Received:*
  Electronic postmarks added by the MTAs the message passed through.

- *Cc:*
  Addresses of "carbon copy" recipients.

All RFC822 header lines are keywords, followed by a colon (":"), followed by a formatted string that is the header line's value. A header line may be extended over more than a single line by prefacing the continuation lines with either ASCII space or tab characters. UAs use header lines to display and organize messages; for example, a UA could sort messages by sender or by date received, by examining the *From:* line or the *Date:* line, respectively.

The message envelope information is located in several places depending on which transport mechanism is used. This lack of consistent placement can result in considerable confusion. The inconsistency emerged from a set of informal conventions; for example, SMTP puts the recipient addresses of each mail message in the SMTP dialogue while UUCP mail transport includes recipient addresses in the arguments of the *rmail* command, which is remotely executed after the message is

```
From: sally@widget.com
To: george@tic.com
Subject: Party Invitation
Cc: jane@tic.com, opus!jill

Hi,

You are invited to a party at 5:00 PM after work
at the office.  Bring a friend.

Sally
```

Figure 7.2 Example Message.

received by the remote system. SMTP sender addresses, like recipient addresses, are placed in the SMTP dialogue, whereas the UUCP sender address is attached to the beginning of the message header, as a part of the UUCP *From* line (we describe how both SMTP and UUCP envelope addresses work in detail in Section 7.3).

The UUCP *From* line — note the missing colon (:) — differs from the RFC822 *From:* line and serves an entirely different purpose than the RFC822 line does. The UUCP *From* line is the return address on the outside of the envelope, while the RFC822 *From:* line is part of the message contents. UUCP's *From* line serves two other purposes: First, it timestamps the message to indicate when it was delivered. This serves much the same purpose as the RFC822 *Received:* lines. Second, it is recognized by almost all UNIX UAs as a message separator that marks the beginning of a new message in a mailbox. This is an old UNIX convention. Some UAs use different message separation conventions. However, all UAs that read the same mailbox must agree on the message separator convention used.

To help you distinguish between an envelope and a message, consider the case of a single message you send to many recipients. Each copy of the message has the same message header and message body, but each envelope has a different address. Suppose, for example, the mail message shown in Fig. 7.2 is sent by Sally. The message is sent to George, Jane, and Jill. The message, header and all, is copied and placed in three distinct envelopes, one for each recipient. The first has a recipient address of *george@tic.com;* the next, a recipient address of *jane@tic.com;* and the third, a recipient address of *opus!jill.* The sender envelope address is always *sally@acme.com.* Although each envelope has a separate destination address, the message header inside informs each recipient that all recipients were sent the party invitation.

As each message is processed by MTAs along the delivery route, the MTAs may add header lines, such as *Received:* postmarks. The message received by

```
From sally@widget.com Mon Aug 19 15:31:31 1991
Received: from mailgateway.widget.com
    by tic.com (5.64/1.90) via SMTP
    id AA20317; Mon, 19 Aug 91 15:30:55 -0600
Received: by mailgateway.widget.com (4.22/acme.1.2)
    id AA10817; Mon, 19 Aug 91 13:05:05 cst
Posted-Date: 19 Aug 91 13:05:05 CDT
From: sally@widget.com
To: george@tic.com
Subject: Party Invitation
Cc: jane@tic.com, opus!jill
Message-Id: <9108190851.AA10817@widget.com>

Hi,

You are invited to a party at 5:00 PM after work
at the office.  Bring a friend.

Sally
```

Figure 7.3 Message Received by George.

George therefore could appear as in Fig. 7.3. Here, the analogy to an actual paper mail delivery breaks down somewhat. RFC822 lets MTAs add *Received:* postmarks and other lines to headers; post offices, on the other hand, don't open envelopes and put postmarks on the mail inside. MTAs ignore message bodies but can and do manipulate headers. In our example, note the *Received:* lines added by each MTA, the *Posted-Date:* line added by the MTA at *mailgateway.widget.com* when the message was sent, and the *Message-Id:* line added by the same MTA to give a unique identifier for the original message.

In contrast, Jill's invitation appears as in Fig. 7.4. Note the *From* and the *>From* lines added by the UUCP MTAs. (The ">" is added in front of each line beginning with *From* to avoid confusion with the mailbox message separator lines) A more intelligent MTA would collapse these lines into the single line

```
From acme!sally Mon Aug 19 13:30:23 1991.
```

This particular message was sent via UUCP from *widget* to *opus*. The key point is that although the message contents are identical, each copy of an original message is unique and has a unique envelope.

```
From uucp Mon Aug 19 13:30:23 1991
>From sally Mon Aug 19 13:10:31 1991 remote from acme
Posted-Date: 19 Aug 91 13:05:05 CDT
From: sally@widget.com
To: george@tic.com
Subject: Party Invitation
Cc: jane@tic.com, opus!jill
Message-Id: <9108190851.AA10817@widget.com>

Hi,


You are invited to a party at 5:00 PM after work
at the office.  Bring a friend.

Sally
```

Figure 7.4 Message Received by Jill.

7.2   UNIX Mail System Architecture

Figure 7.5 shows a UNIX mail system on a networked host. The center of the system is the MTA (1). incoming mail comes into the system from three directions:

1. via UUCP transport using the *rmail* (2) remote execution facility of UUCP,

2. via SMTP transport (3) from another TCP/IP host, and

3. locally using a UA (4) interface to the MTA.

Mail is forwarded as follows:

1. To remote systems by UUCP transport through the *uux* (5) remote execution facility of UUCP. To remote systems via SMTP (6) to a remote host that supports TCP/IP.

3. Locally into a users mailbox (7) using the */bin/mail* (8) program, which supports the required mailbox file locking protocol, or the */bin/bellmail* program. */bin/mail* is used for final delivery on most BSD-based UNIX systems; */bin/bellmail* is used on System 5 machines. The important point here is final local delivery is handled by a program that understands the local mailbox file locking protocol.

The message queue (9) is a temporary message repository for mail messages before they are finally delivered. The aliases database (10) is a list of aliases for mail recipients. This lets you, for example, send a message to a single address and

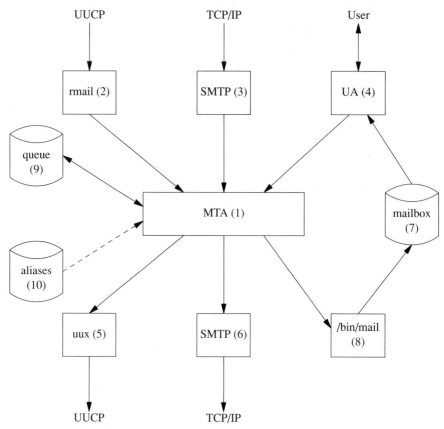

Figure 7.5 UNIX Mail System Architecture.

have it sent to a list of addresses. We will say more about aliases later on in this section.

Mail Delivery Procedure

The local MTA that delivers the mail runs as *root,* which means it can append mail messages to any user's mailbox. UNIX usually keeps a user's mailbox in a well-known mailbox directory, generally */usr/spool/mail* or */usr/mail*. When a well-known directory is used, its "sticky-bit" is turned on so that only the owners of the files in the directory can delete messages. Although you can reconfigure UAs and MTAs to read and write to a mailbox in, say, a user's home directory instead of a well-known mailbox directory, all UAs and MTAs must agree on the common convention for mailbox names and locations. The mailbox typically has the same name as the user's username; for example, a user with username *jill* will have her mail appended to a file by the same name in the well-known mailbox directory. This file is owned by *jill* and file protections on the file are set so that only *jill* can write to or read from the file.

Usually when a UA reads mail, it copies the user's mailbox to a temporary file and releases the file lock on the mailbox, so the local MTA has access to the real mailbox for further message delivery. When the user finishes reading messages, any unread messages are filed in an alternate file or returned to the user's mailbox, marked for future reading. Some UAs do things a little differently, however; for example, MH, a common UNIX UA, reads a user's mailbox, places each received message in a separate file, and then immediately deletes the messages from the mailbox.

UAs generally pass composed mail messages to the MTA for routing and delivery through a pipe or socket interprocess communications facilities. The UA forks a copy of itself, sets up a pipe to its parent, and calls the MTA program. The MTA then reads the message from the pipe. Mail envelope recipient addresses are passed as program arguments, and the MTA places the incoming message in the queue. Queuing the message promotes reliability; if the system crashes before the message is delivered, it can be recovered from the queue. Also a message that can't be delivered immediately can be delivered later.

The MTA checks its real UNIX userid to determine who sent the message and puts the corresponding username in a *From:* header. It also adds other necessary headers, such as a *Received:* date stamp, to indicate when the MTA received the message. Next, it looks up how to deliver the message. The MTA determines the delivery method solely by looking at the envelope's recipient address. It can deliver mail immediately or queue it for later delivery. Determining the delivery method and the route the mail will be sent are core MTA functions.

This basic UNIX mail system architecture can configure delivery mechanisms and routing strategies dynamically, which makes it adaptable to a wide variety of network configurations and administrative policies. Mail can be delivered to individual workstations directly from outside systems, or, for security reasons, it can be funneled through a mail gateway and distributed internally. The choice of delivery strategies is entirely up to each organization.

Local Mail Delivery

When an MTA determines a mail message is to be delivered locally, it first checks the local address against an alias database. Each entry in the alias database is a local mail address followed by an address list. If the message recipient address matches the local address, the MTA scans the address list and determines the delivery method for every address. If on of the new addresses is also to be delivered locally, it too is checked against the alias file. The alias expansion of local addresses continues recursively in this manner. To prevent alias loops, only a certain number of alias expansions are allowed before the MTA finally rejects the recipient address. Once all alias expansion is completed, the original message is sent to every address in the list. A unique envelope is created for every message, but the message contents remain the same for every recipient.

Aliases are a powerful feature. They let a short, easily remembered name replace the names of a large group of mail recipients and thereby reduce the amount of typing a user must do to send a mail message to the group. They also

are a useful administrative tool. You can set up well-known mail addresses that
are aliased to specific, but possibly changeable addresses. Then when the target of
the alias changes, you need change only the alias. Aliases also allow for the creation of **mailing lists,** enabling many users with a common interest to correspond
with each other simply by sending messages to the list name.

If a local address is not an alias, the MTA assumes the address is the name of
a local user. The MTA checks whether the local user has a valid password file
entry and find's the mailbox for that user by following whatever the mailbox naming convention is. If a mailbox with that name exists, the MTA locks the mailbox
file, appends the incoming message to the end of the mailbox, and then unlocks
the mailbox so that a UA is free to read any new messages. The MTA will create
the mailbox, if it does not exist. If the user does not have a valid account, the
MTA uses the envelope return address to return the message, along with an error
message, to the sender.

7.3   Mail Addressing, Routing, and Transport

Types of Addressing

Mail addressing is complex because no single standard address format exists. Fortunately, you can configure a UNIX mail system to understand most common
address formats. The two formats used most often are **domain-based addresses**
and **UUCP addresses.** These two types can be combined into **mixed-mode
addresses.** There are also other miscellaneous address format.

Domain Mail Addresses. Domain mail addresses define *absolute* destinations,
that is, they hide the routing of mail from the user. Consequently, they are easy to
use, for the user is not required to know and specify the exact route the message
will take. The form of a domain mail address is *local_part@domain_part.*

Domain_part is a FQDN without the trailing period. It identifies an organization or a location within which the local_part is known. For example, the mail
address *george@tic.com* directs the MTA to send a mail message to a host that can
route mail to anyone in the *tic.com* domain. That host will in turn deliver the mail
to a mailbox called *george*. Mailbox names are assigned by the mail administrator
and are subject only to local conventions.

An MTA only uses the local_part when doing final local delivery. That is, the
address is considered to be a local address. This part can be any string of print-
able ASCII characters. In most cases it is the name of a user's mailbox.
Local_part also can be an alias that is mapped to a real mailbox name when the
mail reaches its final destination. Aliasing conventions, too, are a local matter.
Some systems have no standard for login names, but provide an additional, uniform alias for each user — for example, the user's full name — so that senders
can "guess" a legitimate address for any recipient.

You also can give the local-part a more complicated syntax. Some simple
conventions for doing this have been widely adopted. For example, the percent

sign ("%") is often used to signal that mail must undergo additional processing or be sent to another machine by a mail gateway. This convention, though widely used, is still a local matter and not a standard. To the extent possible, you should hide local addressing conventions from outside users; doing so simplifies addressing, as we demonstrate next in an example.

The mail address *fred%freds_machine@widget.com* is generally interpreted to mean "send mail to the mail gateway for *widget.com,* where it is forwarded to a machine called *freds_machine,* which delivers the mail to a mailbox called *fred.*" This format, however, doesn't hide the internal mail routing within the *widget.com* domain. A better option is to let the internal routing be handled by the mail gateway for *widget.com.* Fred's address could be *fred_smith@widget.com* in this case. The mail gateway for *widget.com* then would handle the internal mail routing for it knows that mail to *fred_smith* is to be delivered to the mailbox *fred* on machine *freds_machine.*

UUCP Addresses. UUCP addresses, also are used for mail. An example UUCP mail address is *opus!onyx!sally.* Each UUCP address is a **relative address;** that is, it specifies the exact route — a chain of named UUCP hosts that link the sender and receiver — the message will take. Relative addresses are longer, harder to type, and more error prone. Because they are relative to the origin of the message, they also are harder to use than absolute addresses; tightly coupling mail addressing to the route the mail will take requires users to know and remember routing details for everyone to whom they want to send mail. By analogy, if you were handling paper mail you would have to specify on the envelope every post office a message passes through to its destination. In the example *opus!onyx!sally,* mail is sent to *opus,* which forwards it to *onyx,* which in turn delivers the message to the mailbox *sally.* A message to the same mailbox from *opus* would be addressed to *onyx!sally.* Although UUCP relative addressing is still around, there are ways to avoid it entirely while still using UUCP transport, as we explain in Chapter 8.

The UUCP name space differs in other ways from the domain name space. UUCP hostnames must be eight characters or fewer, and hostnames can be duplicated, that is, more than one host can use the same name. The name-length limit is likely to persist, but UUCP sites now can register their names and DNS MX records allow such sites to have valid domain names. Because registered names must be unique, name duplication should soon disappear.

Mixed-mode Addressing. You can intermix UUCP and domain addresses in mixed-mode addresses. For example, a site several hops off of the Internet can use a mixed-mode address to send mail: UUCP addresses to route mail from that site to the nearest Internet site and domain addresses to get the mail to its final destination. Using these addresses requires great care in order to avoid ambiguity. Does the address *onyx!sam@bigcorp.com* mean send the mail via UUCP to *onyx* and then on to the mail gateway for *bigcorp.com,* with finally delivery to *sam*? Or does it mean send the mail to *bigcorp.com* and then on to *onyx* using UUCP transport, with final delivery to *sam*? Are we dealing with a domain address with a

UUCP local part or a UUCP address with a valid domain address as its final component? Without more information or some standard convention, it's impossible to tell.

We advise you to avoid mixed-mode addresses. Instead, encourage your UUCP neighbors to register a domain name. If you are a UUCP-only site, register a domain name and get an Internet host to act as a mail relay gateway for you. If this isn't possible, then simplify and clarify addresses with a UUCP format, where the two interpretations are syntactically unique, as follows:

```
bigcorp.com!onyx!sam
```

or

```
onyx!bigcorp.com!sam
```

All major Internet mail relays understand this syntax, which is described in [Horton 1986], and can handle mail addressed in this way. Such a relay will automatically interpret acme.com!fred as fred@acme.com.

Other Addresses. UNIX mail supports other types of mail addresses, usually as extensions of domain addresses. Mail to DECMail sites includes the DECMail gateway in the domain part of the address and uses DECMail syntax in the local part; for example, the address

```
host::user@gateway.com
```

X.400 addresses are handled similarly, as in

```
(S=/PRMD=somewhere/ORG=bigcorp@x400relay.org
```

which lets Internet users reach a number of commercial X.400 providers.

Mail Routing

Mail routing is always performed by MTAs, not UAs. An MTA determines the next hop the message will take on its way to its final destination. They support mail routing in a heterogeneous environment by using a number of different methodologies. UUCP addresses always explicitly show the route the mail will take to its final destination. Within the Internet, on the other hand, the DNS helps to direct mail to its destination via its MX records. Originally, a domain address like *george@tic.com* indicated that mail to the user *george* was sent via SMTP to a host named *tic.com*; now the meaning of the address is more general. An MTA sends mail to a host that understands how to forward mail to the final destination. From the forwarder host, mail might be sent to its final destination via SMTP transport or by some other means, such as UUCP from the relay host. Or it could simply be delivered locally on the relay host.

```
(1)  220 cs.utexas.edu Sendmail 5.64/1.129 ready \
          at Thu, 7 May 92 16:08:02 -0500
(2)  HELO akasha.tic.com
(3)  250 cs.utexas.edu Hello akasha.tic.com
(4)  MAIL FROM:<smoot@tic.com>
(5)  250 <smoot@tic.com>... Sender ok
(6)  RCPT TO:<fred@cs.utexas.edu>
(7)  250 <fred@cs.utexas.edu>... Recipient ok
(8)  RCPT TO:<sally@bigcorp.com>
(9)  250 <sally@bigcorp.com>... Recipient ok
(10) DATA
(11) 354 Enter mail, end with "." on a line by itself
(12) { message header }
          .
          .
          .

     { message body }
     .
(13) 250 Mail accepted
(14) QUIT
(15) 221 cs.utexas.edu closing connection
```

Figure 7.6 SMTP Dialogue.

Mail Transport Protocols

SMTP. SMTP is the TCP/IP standard protocol for transferring mail from one host to another. It is a simple lockstep protocol that uses TCP as its underlying transport mechanism. Figure 7.6 shows an example SMTP dialogue. Each line of the dialogue is terminated with an ASCII <CR><LF>. The dialogue runs as follows:

• Line 1
The server starts the dialogue by displaying a greeting message that states the server's name and information about the software version being used and the time the connection was accepted.

• Line 2
The client identifies itself using the HELO command followed by its own domain name.

• Line 3
The server acknowledges the client using a simple three-digit code followed by an informative message. The three-digit code is used to direct the actions of the

client. Without going into a lot of detail about the specific return codes, we can say that an SMTP server returns a code of 250 when a client request has been successfully accepted and understood. A return code of 354 means a client command has been accepted but more input is required to complete the request. A return code in the range 400-599 indicates an error has occurred. Return codes are documented in the SMTP specification found in [Postel 1982].

- Line 4 – 5
After the initial handshaking, the client identifies who the mail is from using the MAIL FROM command. This is the message envelope sender address.

- Line 6 – 9
The name of the recipient is entered using the RCPT TO command. This is the message envelope recipient address. If there is more than one recipient, the SMTP client sends each on a separate line and each is individually acknowledged by the remote SMTP server.

- Line 10
The client uses the DATA command to tell the server a message is to follow.

- Line 11
The server acknowledges that it is ready to receive the message.

- Line 12
The client sends the message terminated with a line containing a single period. (Note: The client sends the entire message contents — both header and body.)

- Line 13
The server acknowledges receipt of the message.

- Line 14 – 15
The client is then free to start a dialogue with someone new or, as in this example, use the QUIT command to tell the server to terminate the connection.

SMTP is very simple and straightforward but does have some restrictions. Only 7-bit ASCII is supported, so it's not possible to send binary files unless they are encoded in ASCII. As of this writing, a number of extensions to the basic SMTP protocol are under consideration. They include facilities for encryption of mail messages as well as for the ability to send and receive binary information in a standard format [Linn 1989; Kent 1993; Balenson 1993; Kaliski 1993; Borenstein & Freed 1992]. Once these extensions are widely deployed, it will be possible for the existing SMTP transport infrastructure to send both encrypted and multimedia messages that can be decoded by a UA.

UUCP. While UUCP is not a part of TCP/IP, it is so ubiquitous in UNIX mail systems, a discussion of how it works is essential. UUCP was developed as a stop-gap until "real" networking was developed. Like many stop-gaps, it continues to be widely used. The reasons for this are simple: UUCP comes with virtually every UNIX based operating system. Further, it is very inexpensive; to implement UUCP network connection requires only a serial port, a phone line, and a modem.

A mail message is transported via UUCP using the protocol's remote execution feature. By convention, for sending mail to a remote system, the *rmail* command is the command to be executed on the remote system. On some systems, rmail is a simple front-end to a real MTA. Or it might be an MTA in its own right. Message recipients are passed as arguments to the rmail command.

For example, to send a message to *jane* on system *opus,* the *uux* command to create the appropriate UUCP files is:

```
uux - opus!rmail (jane)
```

The "-" says to take input from stdin, where the mail message is read from. The parentheses around *jane* tell *uux* to take the argument literally rather than interpreting the argument as a filename. The *uux* command creates three files shown in Fig. 7.7, and is explained next.

- *command*
  The command file lists the names of the files needed to execute the remote command.

- *message*
  The message file contains the mail message header and body.

- *execution* The execution file contains the script to be executed remotely by the *uuxqt* utility.

In the command file, each line is composed of seven fields as follows:

1. command letter – either an S or an R. An S indicates the file should be sent to the remote system. An R means the file will be received from the remote system. For mail delivery the first field is always an S.

2. local filename – the name of the local file to be sent. If it is a relative pathname, then it is relative to the UUCP spool directory. This is almost always the case for mail transfer.

3. remote filename – the name of the file on the remote system. Again a relative name is relative to the UUCP spool directory.

4. file owner – owner of the file on the local system. Always *uucp* for mail transfer.

5. options – options for this transfer. For mail this is almost always just a "-" which indicates no options were specified.

6. spool filename – the name of the file on the local system in the UUCP spool directory. UUCP always copies or links the files it sends to its own spool directory. UUCP uses the spool file to perform the actual transfer.

The command file: `C.opusA01rn`

```
S D.widgetb01rq D.widgetb01rq uucp - D.widgetb01rq 0666
S D.widgetX01ro X.widgetX01ro uucp - D.widgetX01ro 0666
```

The message file: `D.widgetb01rq`

```
From tom Mon Aug 19 13:10:31 1991 remote from widget
Posted-Date: 19 Aug 91 13:05:05 CDT
From: tom@widget.com
To: opus!jane
Subject: Meeting
Message-Id: <9108190851.AA10817@widget.com>

There will be a staff meeting in my office at
3:00 PM.

Thanks,

Tom
```

The execution file: `D.widgetX01ro`

```
U uucp widget
F D.widgetb01rq
I D.widgetb01rq
C rmail jane
```

Figure 7.7 UUCP Example Transfer Files.

7. permissions – access permission to give the file on the remote system.

Each line in the command file describes a single file to transfer to the remote system. The first line describes the the message file; the second the remote execution file. Note that the filenames are internally generated by the UUCP system and are therefore rather cryptic. A few of the naming conventions are illustrated by this example. The command file name is *C.opusb01n*. This indicates it is a command file (the leading C.) and the remote system to send the files listed in the command file is called *opus*. The single character after the system name is the grade of the file that can be used to prioritize transfers. The last four characters are internally generated by UUCP to make the filename unique.

This example sends the message file and the remote execution file to the remote system. In the command file, the first file listed is the message file that is sent to the remote system with the same name – D.widgetb01rq. The next line is the remote execution file. Its name is changed on the remote system to *X.widgetX01ro*. The leading X in the name tells the remote UUCP system to interpret and execute the contents of the file.

The remote execution file is described as follows:

• Line 1
Indicates this command file is from user *uucp* on remote system *widget*. It is used to validate what commands can be run on the remote system by this user.

• Line 2
Tells *uuxqt* that this file must be present to execute this script. This is the name of the message file.

• Line 3
Indicates the named file (the message file) is to used as stdin.

• Line 4
Represents the command to execute. In this case, the rmail command is executed on the remote system with the single argument *jane*

The remote system executes the command file giving rmail the message file as input. rmail delivers the message locally to user *jane*.

In the above example, the mail message is sent to a direct UUCP neighbor. That is the remote system is directly connected to the sending system. The UUCP mail transport mechanism allows mail to be sent to a system that is not directly connected to the sending system. For example, can be sent to *opus* and then forwarded to another remote host for final delivery. The command

```
rmail opus!oxnar!sally
```

executed on *widget,* generates the command

```
uux - opus!rmail (oxnar!sally)
```

This in turn generates the command on *opus*

```
uux - oxnar!rmail sally
```

which forwards the mail message to *oxnar* for final delivery.

This simple store and forward mechanism allows the message to be sent through many intermediate hosts before the final destination. The rmail command on most UNIX systems simply passes the message to a remote MTA, which then routes the message to its final destinations. All UUCP MTAs that do mail transport follow this convention.

The UUCP transport protocol usually is used with UUCP addresses. This isn't required, however; UUCP's remote execution facility, which lets any command be executed on the remote system, enables UUCP to handle domain-based addresses. To forward the messages with such addresses, the remote system needs only a variant of rmail that understands domain-based addresses. We describe in Chapter 8 such an rmail variant.

7.4   Mail Forwarding Using DNS Support

DNS includes facilities to support mail routing and delivery. The most widely supported is the MX record type. MX records identify one or more hosts to which to forward mail for a particular domain. The algorithm for using MX records is simple. Rather than looking up a host address for the domain part of an mail address, the MTA asks for the set of MX records for that domain name. Each record identifies a host that can receive mail for the domain. An SMTP connection is then made to one of the identified hosts. An example of how this works is shown in Fig. 7.8. In this figure, mail with a domain part *tic.com* is sent to the host *akasha.tic.com* or to the host *backup.tic.com*. MX records are tried in order of numeric preference, lowest number to highest; in this case, the record

```
IN MX 10 akasha.tic.com.
```

will be tried before the record

```
IN MX 20 backup.tic.com.
```

MX records are very powerful tools. With multiple MX records, you can establish redundant mail gateways for a domain. Also, by using MX records in this fashion, you can easily hide the details of where mail is finally delivered within the domain or by what means. This lets you change delivery methods and mailbox locations without impacting mail addresses.

In Fig. 7.9, an MX record for the domain *offnet.com* points at the host *relay.acme.com,* which is not even in the same domain as *offnet.com*. This is permissible. When the mail message for *fred@offnet.com* arrives at *relay.acme.com,* the MTA forwards the message using UUCP transport to the UUCP host *offnet,* which then delivers the message to the user *fred*. The *offnet* site simply registers a domain and finds an Internet site to be a mail gateway. This ability of *MX* records for a domain to point to host that is not part of that domain is a very powerful feature for it allows domain names to be used by hosts without SMTP transport. This extends domain addressed mail messages to hosts without direct SMTP connectivity. Thus, it allows the mail system to extend far beyond the Internet proper using a uniform addressing convention.

MX Records for domain tic.com:
tic.com. IN MX 10 akasha.tic.com.
tic.com. IN MX 20 backup.tic.com.

Message Sender/Recipient:
From:sam@remote.com
To: smoot@tic.com

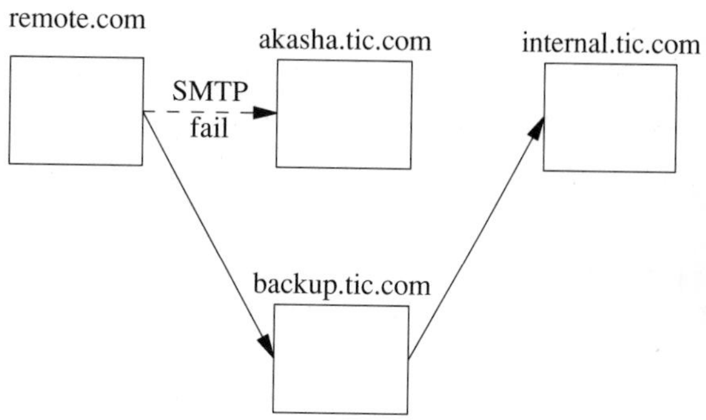

remote.com

akasha.tic.com

internal.tic.com

SMTP
fail

backup.tic.com

Figure 7.8 MX Forwarding within the Internet.

7.5   Mail Transfer Agent Selection

Three principal MTAs are available for use by TCP/IP UNIX hosts: *sendmail, smail,* and *MMDF.* All operate similarly, support SMTP, and can interface to the UUCP transport system. Further, all three are publicly available. Of the three, however, the most widely deployed is sendmail. Also available are several other lesser-known MTAs. The *zmailer* MTA was designed as a one-to-one replacement for sendmail with a cleaner implementation. Finally, *pp* is a fully functional X.400 MTA for UNIX systems. It can be used as a gateway between RFC822-based mail and X.400 systems.

A system can run only one MTA at a time. Choosing among them can be difficult as any can do the job under most circumstances. The deciding factors are most likely to be the complexity and specific requirements of your mail system

Figure 7.9 MX Forwarding beyond the Internet.

MX Records for domain offnet.com:
offnet.com. IN MX 10 relay.acme.com.

Message Sender/Recipient:
From:sam@cs.utexas.edu
To: fred@offnet.com

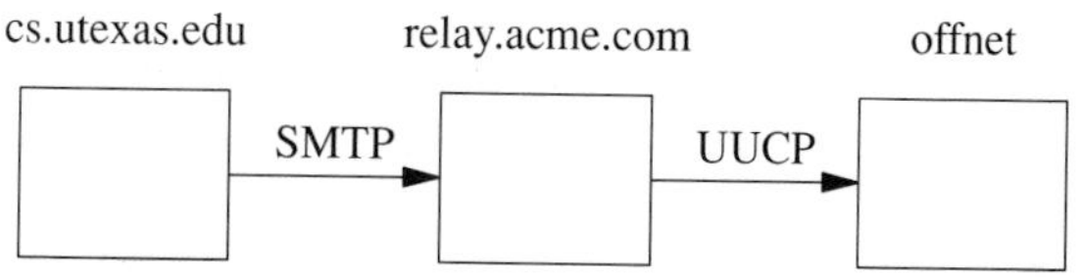

cs.utexas.edu

relay.acme.com

offnet

SMTP

UUCP

and whether the MTA is supported by your operating system vendor. In many respects, the choice is driven by familiarity and availability. Sendmail is probably the clear winner when it comes to availability because it is included in nearly every UNIX operating system. It does have a significant disadvantage, however: its cryptic configuration syntax. (We describe in the next chapter how to configure and manage a mail system using sendmail.) If you use another MTA besides sendmail, many of the configuration principles we discuss in the next chapter are the same.

References

Balenson 1993.   Balenson, D., *Privacy Enhancement for Internet Electronic Mail: Part III: Algorithms, Modes, and Identifiers (RFC1423)*, February 1993.

Borenstein & Freed 1992.   Borenstein, N., & Freed, N., *MIME (Multipurpose Internet Mail Extensions) Mechanisms for Specifying and Describing the Format of Internet Message Bodies (RFC1341)*, June 1992.

Crocker 1982.   Crocker, David, *Standard for the format of ARPA Internet text messages (RFC822)*, August 1982.

Horton 1986.   Horton, Mark R., *UUCP Mail Interchange Format Standard (RFC976)*, February 1986.

Kaliski 1993.   Kaliski, B., *Privacy Enhancement for Internet Electronic Mail: Part IV: Key Certification and Related Services (RFC1424)*, February 1993.

Kent 1993.   Kent, S., *Privacy Enhancement for Internet Electronic Mail: Part II: Certificate Based Key Management (RFC1422)*, February 1993.

Linn 1989.   Linn, J., *Privacy Enhancement for Internet Electronic Mail: Part I: Message Encipherment and Authentication Procedure (RFC1113)*, August 1989.

Postel 1982.   Postel, John B., *Simple Mail Transfer Protocol (RFC822)*, August 1982.

CHAPTER 8

Sendmail Architecture
and Configuration

8.1 Sendmail Architecture

Sendmail follows fairly closely the general mail architecture we described in Chapter 7. It performs two major tasks: mail routing and mail address rewriting. Routing is the obvious and most important MTA function. Through address rewriting, sendmail acts as a gateway between mail systems that use different addressing formats and conventions. Rewriting enables the MTA to ensure all mail addresses are unambiguous and are independent of the context in which the message was sent.

The sendmail configuration file describes how the MTA treats each message. The file uses a seemingly simple, fixed-format language. Unfortunately, the language is actually very cryptic and at first glance difficult to understand.

The general format is simple. Commands are single letters placed in column 1 of each line and perform the following functions:

- Define one-letter name macros.

- Specify the format of mail headers.

- Set options.

- Define mailers.

- Rewrite addresses.

- Route mail.

Sendmail also supports aliasing and the queuing of mail messages for later delivery when delivery initially fails due to a communications error. Configuration commands control these functions. Before describing sendmail configuration in detail, let's first discuss the basic pattern-matching language used by the system.

Pattern Matching

At the heart of sendmail is a pattern-matching language; both mail routing and address rewriting use it. This language defines a finite-state machine that transforms an input string of characters into a possibly different output string of characters. The basic language construct, the **rule,** does this transformation. A **ruleset** is a sequence of rules. By analogy, a rule is a single line of code in a function and a ruleset is the entire function definition. A ruleset takes an initial input string, manipulates it, and returns another string. We discuss rules and rulesets in greater depth later in this section. But first let's look at a smaller piece of the picture, the token.

Tokens. Before a string is transformed by any ruleset, a lexical analyzer breaks it into pieces called **tokens.** You might recall that we dealt with tokens in Chapter 6. There the term means a known bit-pattern and tokens are part of a Token Ring Network. Used when discussing sendmail, however, the term means something else. Here a token is either a single **operator character** or any string of non-operator characters that are delimited by operator characters.

The lexical analyzer is driven by the set of operator characters that are treated as single character tokens. The normal set of sendmail operator characters follows:

```
. : % @ ! ^ = / [ ] |
```

You can change the set of operator characters. However, it is unwise to do so because some of the internal heuristics used by the lexical analyzer rely on most of the above characters being defined as operators. Generally the set of operator characters doesn't need to be changed when sendmail is used in a typical UNIX mail environment.

Rules. A rule is a pattern-matching element followed by a pattern-transformation element. These elements are often referred to as the **left-hand side** and **right-hand side** of a rule, respectively, because the pattern-matching element is written first and the pattern-transformation element is written second. The left-hand side describes a pattern match on a tokenized string. If the input string matches the pattern, it is then transformed by the right-hand side, which uses a set of replacement tokens. The transformed string is again tested against the left-hand side pattern and transformed until the string does not match the pattern. At that point, the string is passed as input to the next rule in the ruleset. If there are no more rules, the transformed string is returned as the value of the ruleset.

A left-hand side pattern is composed of **literal tokens** and **indefinite patterns.** A literal token is either an operator character or any sequence of non-operator characters. An indefinite pattern starts with a "$" and matches one or more tokens in the input string, depending on what characters follow. Figure 8.1 shows the possible indefinite patterns. The last two patterns — "$=" and "$~" — compare the input against a **class.**

```
$+ - one or more tokens
$- - exactly one token
$* - zero or more tokens
$=class_name - matches one of the class values
$~class_name - does not match any class values
```

Figure 8.1 Sendmail Indefinite Patterns.

A class consists of one or more tokens. The name of the class follows the "=" or the "~" character and is any uppercase or lowercase alphabetic character, resulting in a potential 52 classes. Sendmail reserves most lowercase class names for specific purposes; therefore 26 classes are available for your use. A class definition like

```
CA alpha beta gamma
```

defines a class named "A" that contains the tokens "alpha," "beta," and "gamma." With this class definition, the indefinite pattern

```
$=A
```

will match any of the literal strings "alpha," "beta," or "gamma" found at that position in the input string.

An example pattern and a few of the possible strings it can match are shown in Fig. 8.2. Left-hand-side patterns are similar to **regular expression** patterns used by most of the UNIX text manipulation programs, such as *ed, sed,* or *grep.* A key difference between the two types of patterns is that the patterns used by sendmail match a set of tokenized strings, while regular expression patterns match untokenized text strings. Remember that an input string to a sendmail rule is tokenized before being passed to the rule and remains tokenized throughout the transformation process. Also, the pattern matcher of sendmail is not case-sensitive.

The right-hand-side pattern describes the transformation to be performed on a tokenized string that matches a left-hand-side pattern. The right-hand-side syntax is shown in Fig. 8.3. The "$:" and "$@" tokens optionally control rule evaluation. If you use either of them, it must appear as the first token of the right-hand side. The "$@" acts as a *return* from the entire ruleset, that is, the input string is transformed by the right-hand-side exactly once and then returned as the final result of the ruleset. The "$:" lets only a single transformation occur and after which, requires that the rewritten string be passed on to the next ruleset for evaluation. This prevents infinite loops when a transformed string would otherwise always match the left-hand side. It also is commonly used when a ruleset calls another ruleset. The fifth transformation takes whatever tokens are between the brackets and does a hostname lookup and replaces the tokens with the canonical

The pattern

```
$+<@$=A.$+>
```

will match the following strings

```
user<@alpha.com>
```

```
sally<@gamma.edu>
```

```
fred<@beta.org>
```

and many others

Figure 8.2 Example Pattern.

___

hostname. This is used to insure that all mail addresses use the true hostname and not any aliases.

Sendmail uses the last three tokens — "$#", "$@", and "$:" — for mail routing. (See the last three lines of Fig. 8.3) These always appear together on the right-hand side and in the following order:

1. $#

   The pattern that follows it is the name of the mailer to use for the current message.

___

Figure 8.3 Pattern Transformations.

num – the n'th left-hand side pattern
$@$ – transform the string and return from the ruleset
$:$ – transform the string exactly once
$>rule$ – call a ruleset using the transformed string as input
$[\ \ldots\ $]$ – return the canonical hostname of the tokens between the two brackets

In ruleset 0 only

$#mailer$ – the name of the mailer
$@host$– the name of the domain or host to send the message
$:user$ – the name of the user to send the message

2. $@

The pattern that follows is the host or domain to send the message to.

3. $:

The pattern that follows is the user name of the message recipient.

These three special tokens and their arguments provide all the information sendmail needs to route a message. Taken together they return a *<mailer, host, user>*
triple that tells sendmail by what means the message will be sent, where it needs
to be sent, and who to send it to. Note that if the message is to be delivered
locally, the host part of the triple must be empty. You probably have noted that the
host and user tokens use the same syntax as two other right-hand-side tokens of
the pattern. This unfortunate duplication can create confusion. Just remember
that the host and user tokens cannot appear *first* on the right-hand side.

Rulesets. A simple ruleset is shown in Fig. 8.4 and explained as follows:

- Line 1

The ruleset is introduced by the "S" command, followed immediately by the
number of the ruleset, in this case, 31. This number must be unique and between
0 and 31. The maximum number of allowable rulesets is a constant defined
when sendmail is compiled and can be changed only if you have access to the
source code. The relatively small number of allowable rulesets is usually more
than adequate.

- Lines 2 – 3

Each rule in a ruleset is introduced by an "R" in column 1. Immediately following the "R" is the left-hand side. Note that spaces are significant and are treated
as part of the left-hand-side pattern. The right-hand side is separated from the
left-hand side by at least one tab character (not a space). Anything after a tab
following the right-hand side is considered a comment. A ruleset is terminated
by any other sendmail command in the first column.

The ruleset in Fig. 8.4 rewrites a domain-style address into its equivalent UUCP
syntax. This ruleset could be used to help rewrite addresses on a host that

---

Figure 8.4 Example Ruleset.

```
S31

R$+<@$+.uucp>        $2!$1              u@h.uucp => h!u
R$+!$+<@$-.$+>        $3.$4!$1!$2        h!u@h.dom => h.dom!h!u
```

forwards mail messages between UUCP systems and Internet connected systems. For example, the following input string

```
user<@host.uucp>
```

will match the left-hand side of the first rule — R$+<@$+.uucp>. The above string will be transformed by the right-hand side of the first rule — $2!$1 — into the string

```
host!user
```

The string

```
h!user<@acme.com>
```

does not match the first rule's left-hand side, but does match the second rule's left-hand side — R$+!$+<@$-.$+> — and is transformed by the right-hand side — $3.$4!$1!$ — into

```
acme.com!h!host
```

The example input to this ruleset is not in strict domain syntax, but rather in a common canonical format used by most sendmail configurations. The angle-brackets "<>" around the domain part of the address (including the "@") make the address easier to parse. We will see how this is done when the intricacies of some of the standard rulesets is explained in Section 8.2.

Routing and Address Rewriting

Sendmail uses its pattern matching language to route mail and rewrite sender and recipient addresses. The pattern language transforms only mail addresses. Sendmail assumes that a message is in substantially RFC822 format. It takes sender and recipient addresses in the message envelope and header and applies specific transformation rules to each address depending on where it occurs. Because sendmail knows about RFC822 headers, it can distinguish between sender and recipient addresses.

If a message is received via SMTP transport, sendmail takes the envelope addresses directly from the SMTP dialogue. The sender address is the argument to the SMTP MAIL FROM command; the recipient address is the argument to the SMTP RCPT TO command. If the message is input to sendmail without SMTP support, sendmail takes the recipient addresses from the argument list when sendmail is executed. In this case, it considers any argument not preceded by a minus sign ("-") to be a recipient address. You can, however, explicitly give the sender address as an argument after an -f flag. Absent the -f flag, sendmail considers the sender to be the local user who invoked the sendmail command and therefore uses the user's username as the sender address.

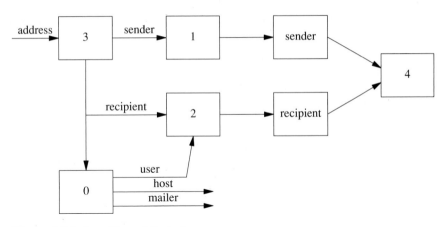

Figure 8.5 Ruleset Flow of Control.

Sendmail takes all envelope addresses, tokenizes them, and passes the tokenized address as input to the set of rulesets shown in Fig. 8.5. It sends all envelope addresses first through Ruleset 3. This ruleset puts each address into a canonical format, which is easy for subsequent rulesets to parse. Sendmail then sends each envelope address through Ruleset 0, which returns a <*mailer, host, user*> triple using the special right-hand-side tokens "$#," "$@," and "$:." Every envelope address, whether that of the sender or a recipient, has an associated triple of this form. For a sender address, sendmail uses this information to send error replies back to the originator of the message, while for a recipient address, sendmail uses the information to determine which mailer to use to forward the message, what host to forward the message to, and what the recipient envelope address is for this message.

Mailers. A **mailer** is a user-defined program that transports mail either locally or to another MTA. Sendmail uses the mailer name in the <*mailer, host, user*> triple to find the appropriate mailer for each message. You define each mailer in the configuration file. (We describe the syntax of the mailer definition in more detail in Section 8.2.) Associated with each mailer definition is the pathname of the program to which to pass the mail message, plus data on how arguments are passed to this program. Each mailer expects a mail message to be sent to it on its standard input. For each recipient address, sendmail invokes a mailer. A mailer can interpolate the *host* and *user* values returned in Ruleset 0 as arguments to the mailer. The internal macro h is set to the host name in the <*mailer, host, user*> triple and the internal macro u is set to the user name in the triple. Also associated with each mailer is a sender rewriting rule and a recipient rewriting rule. These rules, along with some other rulesets, are used to rewrite envelope and header addresses. The *host* value of the <mailer, host, user> triple is used as evaluated; the *user* part is rewritten first by Ruleset 2, then by the recipient rewriting ruleset specified in the mailer, and finally by Ruleset. If SMTP is the delivery method, *user* is interpolated into the RCPT TO part of the SMTP dialogue and *host* is used as the name of the host system to which to establish an SMTP connection. On versions of sendmail that support MX lookups, *host* is used as the domain name under which MX records are searched.

For non-SMTP delivery, sendmail pipes a mail message to the mailer's standard input. For SMTP, the message is transmitted after the DATA command in the SMTP dialogue. Any sender address found in the message header is transformed under the control of first Ruleset 3, then Ruleset 1, then the sender rewriting rule specified in the mailer definition, and finally Ruleset 4 Also the sender address used as an argument to the SMTP MAIL FROM is rewritten by the same sequence of rulesets. Each recipient address found in the message header is rewritten first by Ruleset 3, then by Ruleset 2, then by the recipient rewriting rule specified in the mailer, and finally by Ruleset 4 (see Fig. 8.5 for the ruleflow).

Message Queuing

In addition to mail routing and address rewriting, sendmail also supports message queuing. Queuing is a useful function, especially when communication to a remote system is unreliable. The mail message can be placed in a queue and saved and a queuing daemon invoked at regular intervals to attempt to deliver messages in the queue. Sendmail places messages in a queue directory specified in the configuration file.

8.2   Configuring Sendmail

Sendmail is a very flexible MTA, but its configuration syntax is cryptic and confusing to those unfamiliar with it. Most implementations of sendmail as distributed by UNIX vendors come with some simple configuration files. These files might meet your site needs as is. More often, however, you must customize them to work well in your environment. The best documentation on sendmail is still the original BSD system documentation [Allman 1983a; Allman 1983b]. Many versions of sendmail have various features and extensions to the basic system. All the examples used in this chapter make no assumption about these extensions, except that the system supports DNS MX records.

Configuration Maintenance

Maintaining different sendmail configuration files can quickly become a nightmare. Because much of the configuration information is identical, if configurations are maintained in completely separate files, common information can quickly diverge. A good administrative technique is to divide sendmail configurations into logical pieces that can be brought back together when the real configuration file is generated.

The UNIX *m4* macro processor is a convenient configuration maintenance tool that can be used to great advantage to maintain configuration files. For example, a great deal of information in the typical sendmail configuration file is "boilerplate," that is, it rarely changes from one configuration to the next. You can keep most of this boilerplate information in a single common file. You also can keep each mailer definition and its associated header rewriting rulesets in separate files. Then you can pick and choose the mailer definitions needed for each configuration.

Table 8.1 shows a logical division of a sendmail configuration file. Each piece shown there can be brought together into an overall configuration file. In Fig. 8.6, we've given you a configuration for a machine that uses SMTP (the *tcp* mailer, the local mailer, and the UUCP mailer. You can automatically generate each configuration by using m4 and the UNIX *make* facility. Note the use of the m4 *include* directives, which adds the appropriate file to the particular configuration. Each of these pieces will be explained in the next section. The resulting configuration file is far more understandable and maintainable than a huge, cumbersome file would be.

Configuration Philosophy

To avoid repetition and inconsistency, you should compartmentalize as much specific local information as possible in your configuration files. Doing this makes updating the files easier since you need change only the local data in one place. We advise you to avoid using explicit hostnames in a configuration file and to try instead to find a more general way of accomplishing the same goal. For example, some configurations include lists of local hosts that signal the use of a special mailer for mail delivery. Avoid listing hosts explicitly; if a new host is added to the network then the sendmail configuration must be regenerated. A better approach in this case is to use a heuristic — say, a common domain name suffix — that identifies all the local hosts in a more general way.

You also should try to isolate special cases. For example, give an alias name to a well-known mail relay host and use the alias name in place of the real hostname in the configuration. Using the alias enables you to change the mail relay to another host by changing only the alias hostname rather than every sendmail configuration. This procedure can be a real time saver in a large network. It also is

---

Table 8.1 Logical Division of Sendmail Files.

File Name	Purpose
general.m4	boilerplate information (headers, file locations, etc)
local.m4	local mailer specs and rewriting rules
rules.m4	global rules (S1, S2, S3, S4, etc)
tcp.m4	TCP mailer specs and rewriting rules
uucp.m4	UUCP mailer and rewriting rules
zeropre.m4	Common prefix to S0

```
DVrelay.1.17
Oc
OC10
Dj$w
DDtic.com
DUakasha
DMtcp

include(general.m4)
include(rules.m4)
include(local.m4)
include(uucp.m4)
include(tcp.m4)
include(zeropre.m4)

R<@$-.uucp>:$+    $#uucp $@$1 $:$2 $.
R$+<@$-.uucp>     $#uucp $@$2 $:$1 $.
R$*<@$-.$D>$*     $#tcp $@ $2.$D $:$1<@$2.$D)>$3
R$*<@$*.$+>$*     $#$M $@$ $2.$3 $:$1<@$2.$3>$4
R$+%$+            $@$>29$1@$2
R$+              $#local $:$1
```

Figure 8.6 Sample Configuration File.

possible to exploit the DNS MX records to avoid hardwiring relay host names in configuration files.

When possible, use the same configuration on multiple hosts and avoid hard-coding the specific hostname into each sendmail configuration. Instead, always try to obtain the hostname dynamically using the sendmail *w* macro and class. Be aware that the *w* macro should return the canonical hostname, which should be the FQDN. This usually will present no particular problem; remember, however, to match the canonical hostname using the *w* macro and not the *w* class. Note that some versions of sendmail return only the unqualified hostname in both the *w* macro and class; in this case, be sure to append the domain where you want the fully qualified hostname.

Boilerplate Configuration Data

Every sendmail configuration contains considerable boilerplate information that does not change from one configuration to another. A sample boilerplate file is shown in Fig. 8.7 and described in the follow four subsections. The m4 name of this file is *general.m4*.

```
(1)   # macros
(2)   De$j Sendmail $v/$V ready at $b
(3)   DlFrom $g  $d
(4)   DnMailer-Daemon
(5)   Do.:%@!^=/[]|
(6)   Dq$g$?x ($x)$.

(7)   # options
(8)   OA/usr/local/lib/aliases
(9)   OF660
(10)  OH/usr/lib/sendmail.hf
(11)  OL9
(12)  OQ/usr/spool/mqueue
(13)  OS/etc/sendmail.st
(14)  OT14d
(15)  Odbackground
(16)  Og1
(17)  Oo
(18)  Or15m
(19)  Os
(20)  Ou1

(21)  Pfirst-class=0
(22)  Pspecial-delivery=100
(23)  Pjunk=-100
(24)  T root daemon uucp

(25)  # header definition
(26)  H?P?Return-Path: <$g>
(27)  HReceived: $?sfrom $s $.by $j ($v/$V)
(28)     id $i; $b
(29)  H?D?Resent-Date: $a
(30)  H?D?Date: $a
(31)  H?F?Resent-From: $q
(32)  H?F?From: $q
(33)  H?x?Full-Name: $x
(34)  HSubject:
(35)  H?M?Resent-Message-Id: <$t.$i@$j>
(36)  H?M?Message-Id: <$t.$i@$j>
(37)  HErrors-To:
```

Figure 8.7 Boilerplate (general.m4).

Part 1 of the Boilerplate Information . Lines 1 – 6 define various macros used by sendmail. A macro definition is introduced by a "D" in column 1 in the configuration file (see line 2). The next character is the name of the macro. The string following the name up to the first whitespace character (either a space, tab or newline) is the value of the macro, in this case $j. A macro is interpolated with its current value by introducing its name preceded by a "$".

All macros in the figure have lowercase names and have specific uses. Note that redefining lowercase macros generated by sendmail itself should be done with care. The macros are defined as follows:

- *e* (line 2)
Defines the format of the SMTP banner message that is sent to an SMTP client when the connection is first established. As part of its definition, this macro uses the value of the *b, v* and *V* macros.

- *l* (line 3)
Defines the syntax of a UNIX *From* line. The *From* line may be prepended to the message before delivery, depending on the configuration of the specific mailer used to deliver the message. This macro uses the values of the *g* and *d* macros, where the *g* macro is the fully-qualified sender address and the *d* macro is the current date and time. Sendmail internally generates these macros each time it processes a new message.

- *n* (line 4)
Defines the address of the mail system itself. This address is used when the system encounters an error in delivering a message. In this case, the mail system address is used as the sender address in error messages returned to the sender. The *n* macro is required to be defined for proper error message generation.

- *o* (line 5)
Defines the operator or delimiter characters used by the address parser.

- *q* (line 6)
Defines the syntax of a complete mail address as found in the message header. This address should be RFC822 compliant. Two alternatives can be specified. You can place the fullname of the user (the *x* macro) in parentheses, as shown in the figure. The *x* macro is filled in by sendmail with the fullname of the local user that is sending the message. On UNIX systems this is normally obtained from the GCOS field of the password file. An example of this style of address is:

```
george@tic.com (George Smith)
```

Or you can enclose the mail address in angle brackets, preceded by the user's full-name. An example of this style address is:

```
George Smith <george@tic.com>
```

The macro for this address style is as follows.

```
Dq?x $x$. <$g>
```

Either alternative is acceptable and conforms to RFC822 syntax.

Notice the conditional syntax used to generate the preceding macro definition that can be used anywhere in the configuration file. The "if" construct — $?x — tests whether the *x* macro (note the letter following the "$?") exists (see line 6). A "$?" followed by a letter means that if the macro is defined, then interpolate into the input data that follows the letter and precedes the "$.". 'If then Else" constructs are also possible by starting the else part with a "$|."

Part 2 of the Boilerplate Information. Lines 7 – 20 of the boilerplate configuration file set various sendmail options. A sendmail option is introduced by the "O" character in column one of the configuration file. As with macros and classes, there are 52 option letters available. The option letter is always in column two of the configuration file. Most options set an internally used switch, define the location of a file that sendmail uses, or define an operating mode. All 52 option letters are not used and some sendmail versions define specific options unavailable or not defined in other versions. The options defined in this boilerplate file are:

• *A* (line 8)

Defines the name of the alias database. The alias file is a text file that defines global aliases used by sendmail. It usually is hashed for faster access using the *dbm* library functions The hashed dbm files are placed in the same directory as the alias file and use the same name as the alias file, one with a ".dir" suffix and one with a ".pag" suffix.

• *F* (line 9)

Defines the default file creation mode used by sendmail. This should be set to disallow access by any user. The file access mode shown (660) is usually a good choice. All sendmail files are created in the *sendmail* queue directory.

• *H* (line 10)

Defines the location of the SMTP help file, which is displayed using the SMTP HELP command.

• *L* (line 11)

Sets the default log output level for *syslog* output generated by sendmail. Generally a value of 9 logs sufficient information for most operations while a value above 11 starts logging debugging information that can be used for detailed problem determination but which is not appropriate for day-to-day operation. We will have more to say about *syslog* in Chapter 9.

• *Q* (line 12)

Gives the location of the mail queue directory, which is where intermediate queue files are stored before they are delivered. The first action sendmail takes after reading its configuration file is to change directories to the mail queue directory. This directory should not be confused with the /usr/spool/mail or the /usr/mail directories. Only the *root* user needs to be able to read or write to the mail queue directory, and generally the average user should not be able to do either.

- *S* (line 13)

Gives the location of the sendmail status file. The status file contains statistics on message delivery, which are displayed by the auxiliary program *mailstats*.

- *T* (line 14)

Provides that any undelivered mail in the queue is returned to the originator after a certain time period. The time period can be specified in days, hours, or minutes by appending the number with a "d," "h," or "m," respectively. Combinations of days, hours, and minutes also can be specified by combining the three forms.

- *d* (line 15)

Defines the delivery mode. The value "i" tells sendmail to deliver mail in the foreground synchronously. The value "q" tells sendmail to queue all mail being sent and deliver it later during a queue run. The value "b" tells sendmail to deliver mail in the background. Note that setting "b" or "q" frees up the user to do other tasks. Background delivery is usually a good compromise between foreground and queuing delivery. You also can set the delivery mode on a per mailer basis.

- *g* (line 16)

Defines the default groupid used when sendmail delivers a mail message that is not from a local user. Before delivering mail from a local user, sendmail sets the groupid to the principal groupid of the sender of the mail. For mail delivered from an SMTP connection, where there is no local sender, the groupid is set to the value of the *g* macro before delivery.

- *o* (line 17)

Sets the messages headers to old style where spaces can delimit addresses. RFC822 specifies all addresses should be separated by commas only. Leaving this option active does not hurt anything, since it really invokes an adaptive heuristic. If commas are found in an address list, it is assumed they delimit the addresses. Absent commas, spaces will delimit addresses.

- *r* (line 18)

Defines the read timeout interval for an SMTP connection. If an SMTP server hangs for this interval, it's probably best to assume either that the server crashed or that a route to the server is unusable and therefore you should try again later. Because mail can always be queued, it does no real harm to timeout connections.

- *s* (line 19)

Tells sendmail always to create a queue file for any message being sent. Always set this value so that if delivery fails for any reason, otherwise the mail message will be lost. It can be retried later using the queue file.

- *u* (line 20)
  Sets the default userid to the given value when the message is not from a local user. Doing this ensures the UNIX *From* line is generated correctly for a message from a remote source that is to be delivered locally. Setting it to the value 1 (the daemon userid) allows the final local delivery method to use the "trusted user" notion to properly generate a sender address. Otherwise the sender address would be *daemon*. (See the next section for further information about trusted users.)

Part 3 of the Boilerplate Information. Lines 21 – 23 define various message precedences. If a *Precedence:* field is found in the mail header, the precedence value is set according to the value of the field. Higher values mean higher precedence, with the default being 0. More than one precedence can be defined. A message that includes a negative precedence and that sendmail fails to deliver won't return an error message to the originator. This feature is seldom used.

The fourth line of this section (line 24) defines the usernames of **trusted users.** A trusted user can override the sender address by using the *-f* flag when sendmail is invoked. The usual trusted users are *root, daemon,* and *uucp.* The *-f* flag is followed by the "real" sender address of the message. This procedure typically is used when incoming UUCP mail is sent to sendmail for delivery. When mail is received via UUCP, the *rmail* command is invoked to read the message. On a system with sendmail support, the rmail passes the message to sendmail. Since rmail is running under the *uucp* userid, the message will appear to be from the user *uucp.* However, rmail inserts an *-f* flag with the real address of the sender. Since the *uucp* username is in the trusted list, the mail message will be seen correctly as coming from the real sender. This is also used when a message is received via SMTP. In that case the userid is set to *daemon* that is in the trusted user list. If the message is delivered locally, the sender address is the argument of the MAIL FROM command in the SMTP dialogue.

Part 4 of the Boilerplate Information. In this section (lines 25-37), the formats of the mail header fields are defined. The "H" letter starts each defined header, The rest of the line defines the format of each header line. The cryptic syntax "?x?" where the "x" is replaced with a single letter are header line keys. These header line keys are "F," "D," "x," "M," and "P." If the header line key starts the header definition, then the syntax of the particular header is defined by the rest of the line. A mailer will include a particular header if a defined letter appears as mailer flag. If the header line is already present, then the line is retained in the message header regardless of the presence or absence of a flag. Each header definition can interpolate other macro values and also use the conditional "$? ... $| ... $." syntax. Multiple headers can be defined for each option letter. Header lines also can be defined unconditionally without an option letter. These may also be included in outgoing mail.

Mailer Definitions

Sendmail does not perform final delivery of mail. Rather, a mailer defines how a program is invoked to deliver mail or to forward mail closer to its final destination. Mailers make sendmail an extensible system. New mailers can easily be defined to meet new circumstances.

Sendmail in most circumstances forks the mailer program and sends mail message to the mailer via a pipe connected to the mailer's standard input. In this method, the message envelope is usually carried as arguments when the mailer program is invoked. As an option, bidirectional pipes can be set up between sendmail and the mailer program and the SMTP protocol used to send the message envelope and contents. An SMTP dialogue also can be established using the [IPC] built-in mailer. This mailer establishes a TCP connection to a remote mailer and uses the SMTP protocol to transmit the envelope and contents. A mailer definition also defines how sender and recipient addresses found both in the envelope and header lines should be rewritten.

Each mailer definition should be placed in a separate file. Generally a site that uses SMTP and UUCP mail transport has six or fewer defined mailers. Sender and recipient address rewriting should be minimized for each mailer. It is generally a good idea to display all mail addresses in canonical form using domain style addressing. Even if you are a UUCP-only site, registering a domain name and using domain-style addressing avoids many of the UUCP address syntax pitfalls.

A mailer definition, as shown in Fig. 8.8. is denoted by an "M" as the first character of a line in the configuration file. Following the "M" is the mailer's name, which can be any string of alphanumeric characters. A mailer definition may extend across multiple lines by simply starting each subsequent line with a tab character. Next is a comma-separated list of *<keyletter=value>* pairs. The keyletters are as follows:

Figure 8.8 Example Mailer.

```
Mwidget,P=/usr/local/bin/widgm, F=msDFMhu, S=28, R=29, E=\c\r
    A=widgm $u

R28
    { sender address rewriting ruleset }

R29
    { recipient address rewriting ruleset }
```

- *P*

The pathname of the program to invoke as the mailer program.

- *F*

A list of one-character mailer flags. Mailer flags are used to tailor the message format for the specific mailer.

- *S*

The ruleset to use to rewrite sender addresses when the specified mailer is invoked.

- *R*

The ruleset to use to rewrite recipient addresses when the specified mailer is invoked.

- *A*

The list of arguments to pass to the mailer program.

- *E*

The line terminator sequence. These are the characters to add to the end of each line in the message. By default a line is terminated with a <LF>; however, some mailers require each line be terminated with a different sequence, such as a carriage return <CR> followed by a linefeed <LF>.

Local and Program Mailers. There are two required mailers: *local* and *prog*. These mailers must be present for sendmail to function properly. Also, *local* is special because only messages that are delivered using this mailer will have their recipient address looked up as a possible alias. The basic definitions for both mailers are shown in Fig. 8.9.

The example *local* and *prog* mailer definitions are very simple. Neither rewrites addresses; note the empty Rulesets 10 and 20. Generally, this setup is prudent because the basic address canonicalization is handled using other rulesets; no further processing of addresses is really needed. Some administrators like to strip off the domain part of an address to make it more readable when delivered locally. It is generally better, however, to leave fully qualified addresses alone.

Figure 8.9 Local and Program Mailers.

```
Mlocal,   P=/bin/mail, F=rlsDFMmnP, S=10, R=20, A=mail -d $u
Mprog, P=/bin/sh,    F=lsDFMeuP,  S=10, R=20, A=sh -c $u

S10

S20
```

Local Mailer. The local mailer performs final local delivery only after all alias expansion is completed. An address that is initially parsed as a local address by ruleset 0 is checked by sendmail to see if it is an alias for other addresses. If it is, each element of the alias list is parsed and resolved to a mailer. If the address is once again local, the aliasing process is invoked again. This procedure continues until all aliases are expanded to their components. Each final address that is local is handled by the *local* mailer.

Local mail delivery from sendmail is handled by the program defined in the *local* mailer definition. In Fig. 8.9 that program is */bin/mail*. (Another command often used for local delivery is the */bin/bellmail* program, which is found on System V UNIX systems, as well as on IBM's AIX.) Sendmail forks */bin/mail* using the arguments found after the "A" keyletter. In this figure, */bin/mail* is called (see line 1) with the arguments

```
mail -d recipient
```

Here the *u* macro is interpolated from the *user* part of the *<mailer,host,user>* triple that was resolved in Ruleset 0 for this address. The *-d* argument specifies that instead of the program using sendmail to perform delivery, the mail is to be delivered directly to the local user's mailbox This prevents an endless loop where */bin/mail* calls on sendmail which then calls on */bin/mail* again.

Mailer flags for the local mailer alter the way sendmail interacts with the specified program. For example, the *r* flag says to add a *-r sender* to the invoked mailer, where *sender* is the mail address of the real sender of the message.. The result is that the name of the real sender is added as an argument to the mailer invocation. So this mailer calls */bin/mail* with the arguments:

```
mail -d -r sender recipient
```

The *sender* name is the value of the *g* macro and is derived when the message is initially parsed. Other flags that affect how this local mailer is called include the following:

- *l*

  Indicates to sendmail that the mailer will perform final delivery. Sendmail uses this flag to allow the generation of a return receipt when the message is finally delivered. If a message is simply being forwarded to another MTA, then a return receipt should not be generated and this flag should not be used.

- *s*

  Indicates that quote characters are to be stripped off the addresses before the mailer is called. For local delivery, this procedure is prudent because the local mailer program might not understand quotes in addresses (*/bin/mail* doesn't, for example).

• *DFM*

As needed, "D" adds a *Date:* header line into the mail message, "F" adds a *From:* header line, and "M" adds a *Message-Id:* header line.

• *m*

Indicates that the mailer can send to multiple recipients. Although */bin/mail* rarely does this, it does support sending to multiple recipients on the same host.

• *n* flag

/bin/mail itself inserts a UNIX-style *From* line when it performs final delivery. The *n* flag is used here, so that sendmail does not place one before the message. The sendmail default is to add a UNIX style *From* line in front of the message.

• *P* flag

Indicates that sendmail is to add a *Return-Path:* header to the message. When mail is received via SMTP, the value of the *Return-Path:* header is the argument to the MAIL FROM command in the SMTP dialogue. Otherwise it is the address of the sender, as passed as an argument to sendmail.

Program Mailer. The *prog* mailer invokes the shell to deliver mail. A special case for delivering mail to an arbitrary program, it's used when the final mail destination starts with the shell pipe ("|") symbol. Note that this convention is hard-wired into sendmail. So ordinary user names should never begin with the shell pipe symbol. Its use is legal only in the system alias file or in a recipient's *.forward* file (note the leading period in the filename).

A user cannot directly send to a program. To allow this would enable a user to easily forge mail and invoke any arbitrary program — a serious security hole. Expansion of an alias to a program allows some useful functions to be performed by the mail system. For example a message sent via mail can be forwarded to a USENET newsgroup automatically using this feature. Or a user can do their own post-processing of messages.

The flags to the *prog* mailer resemble those of the *local* mailer flags, with the following exceptions:

• The *r, m,* and *n* flags aren't specified. First, arbitrary programs are unlikely to know the specific semantics of the *r* flag. Second, multiple recipients (the *m* flag) might not be supported by all programs that are invoked by this mailer. And third, for consistency a UNIX-style *From* line should be inserted in front of the message; the *n* flag calls for its deletion.

• This mailer definition includes two additional flags — *e* and *u*. *e* signifies the mailer is expensive to run and should be invoked only during a queue run, thus saving host resources. On a lightly loaded host, this economy is probably unnecessary, so the flag could be removed. Note, this flag can appear in any mailer. *u* says that for this mailer, uppercase in usernames should be preserved. This is required because the *u* macro is the name of the program to invoke and UNIX programs are case sensitive. The leading "|" is stripped from the *u* macro before the program is invoked. The program name must be an absolute pathname.

```
Mtcp, P=[IPC], F=msDFMuX, S=22, R=22, A=IPC $h, E=\r\n

S22
R$*<@$+>$*        $@$1<@$2>$3
R$+               $@$1<@$D>
```

Figure 8.10 SMTP Mailer.

SMTP Mailer. A single mailer definition usually suffices for mail sent via SMTP whether the mail is sent on your own local network or to a distant host on the Internet. Figure 8.10 shows the definition of a mailer that uses SMTP transport. Sendmail configuration files packaged with most UNIX system usually call this mailer *tcp*. We will abide by this old, if somewhat misleading name. As SMTP is built in to sendmail, the mailer invoked is a special situation. In this case, the program is [IPC], which says to connect to a remote host using SMTP. Some sendmail implementations also support the string [TCP], which is equivalent to [IPC].

For [IPC], the second argument that follow the A keyletter specify the domain to which to connect (the first argument is the name of the mailer). It is almost always the *h* macro, which is the *host* part of the <*mailer,host,user*> triple. This host is not necessarily the SMTP server host that will be connected to; the value is used to look up MX records for the specified domain, which in turn give the real hostnames to try. Some implementations of sendmail, however, don't support MX records and so use this value as the name of the SMTP server. The value of one additional keyletter — E — specifies that each line sent is terminated with a <CR><LF> in accordance with the SMTP specifications. (The sendmail default is to terminate each line with just a <LF>, which violates the SMTP standard.)

The *tcp* mailer flags differ somewhat from those of a local mailer, due to the nature of SMTP delivery. These specific flags are as follows:

- *m*
  Is included because multiple users can be sent in a single SMTP dialogue.

- *s*
  Calls for quote characters to be stripped from addresses.

- *DFM*
  Note, this is the same as in the *local* mailer definition and is included here only for reference.

- *u*
  Preserves case in usernames.

- *X*
  Enables the mailer to use the RFC822 "hidden dot" algorithm. This algorithm provides that a line with only a single dot has an extra dot added which is

stripped off by the receiving SMTP server. Using this algorithm prevents a message with a dot as the only character of a line from prematurely terminating a message that is sent via SMTP.

The *tcp* mailer uses one rewriting ruleset for both sender and recipient addresses. The first rewriting rule of the ruleset returns any address with a domainname without change.

The second rewriting rule adds the local domainname (the value of the D macro) onto an unqualified address; for example, the address *sue* becomes *sue@domainname*. It is assumed that any address that did not match the first rule is an unqualified address.

UUCP Mailer. A generic UUCP mailer is shown in Fig. 8.11. In the figure, Ruleset 5 (see line 1) converts the canonical representation of a UUCP address used by sendmail back to the real UUCP format. The internal canonical form is

```
h!h1!user<@host.UUCP>
```

The first rule (see line 2) of this ruleset converts addresses of this form back into the familiar UUCP route addresses. The second rule (see line 3) converts a

---

Figure 8.11 UUCP Mailer.

```
(1)   S5
(2)   R$+<@$+.uucp>    $@ $2!$1
(3)   R$+<@$*>         $@ $2!$1
(4)   R<@$+>$*         $@ @$1$2
(5)   R$*<$*>$*        $@ $1$2$3

(6)   Muucp,  P=/usr/bin/uux, F=msDFMhuU, S=13, R=23,
(7)      A=uux - -r $h!rmail ($u)

(8)   S13
(9)   R$+            $:$>5$1
(10)  R$w!$+         $1
(11)  R$U!$+         $1
(12)  R$*$D!$+       $2
(13)  R$+            $:$U!$1

(14)  S23
(15)  R$+            $:$>5$1
(16)  R$*$D!$+       $2
```

standard domain address into its UUCP form in accordance with RFC976. The last two rules (lines 4 and 5) handle SMTP style route addresses that are rarely seen, plus any other syntax that gets by the earlier rules.

The UUCP mailer (lines 6-7) uses the *uux* program to send each message. The arguments to uux say to read the message from stdin (the - flag) and don't generate a UUCP status message when the commands are executed successfully on the remote system (the -*r* flag). The rmail command is run on the remote system, with the argument being the username of the recipient. Given this format for the basic uux program, the *user* part of the triple *<mailer,host,user>* resolved by Ruleset 0 must be the simple name of the user on the remote system or the rest of the UUCP address path after the first "!" in the address. So mail to *h1!h2!user* should resolve to *<uucp,h1,user<@h2.uucp>>*. The uux command executes as

```
uux - -r h1!rmail (h2!user).
```

The *user* part of the triple is sent through the recipient rewriting ruleset (ruleset 23), which convert it back into normal UUCP syntax.

The mailer flags for the UUCP mailer resemble those of other mailers already described, with several additions.

• *h*

Preserves case in the hostname. Doing this is required because UUCP host names are case sensitive. For example, site *Xyz* is different from site *xyz*.

• *U*

Adds an "Ugly UUCP" *From* line of the form

```
From user date remote from h1
```

where *date* is the current date and time. This flag is required, unfortunately, because of the way UUCP mail handles recipient addresses. As the message is sent from one UUCP host to the next, each time the message is forwarded, one of these lines must be added to the front of the message. A return path can be generated from these lines, but RFC822 superseded these lines with the *Received:* header lines. UUCP mail still requires these rather nonconforming and ugly *From* lines.

Following the mailer definition are the two rewriting rulesets. The sender rewriting Ruleset 13 (lines 8-13) takes each sender address and attaches to its beginning the UUCP hostname of this site followed by a "!". The ruleset does this by converting the address to UUCP format and then stripping off either the canonical domainname of the sending host, the UUCP name, or possibly just the domain name. The UUCP name of this host (the U macro) is then attached to the beginning of the address.

For UUCP mail delivery, these conversions are correct. The transformations are done on every sender address in the header; for example, a sender address like *u@xyz.widget.com* is transformed into *sitename!xyz.widget.com!u.* For domain style names, however, you might not want to convert them at all, since the receiving site might understand them directly without conversion. Whether you do this or not depends on your overall mail configuration and the ability of neighboring UUCP sites to handle domain style addresses.

Recipient addresses are converted similarly by Ruleset 23 (lines 14-16), except only the local domain name is stripped off the address. In this case, the recipient address will be only the simple username for the UUCP recipient. For recipient addresses in the the *To* or *Bcc* fields, only the site domain is stripped.

General Rulesets

Some general all-purpose rulesets used by most sendmail configurations are shown in Fig. 8.12.

- Rulesets 1 and 2 (lines 1 – 2)
  The prerewriting rules used to rewrite canonical sender and recipient addresses. In the figure they are empty and in most cases they aren't needed.

- Ruleset 3 (lines 3 – 18)
  Places addresses into an internal standard or canonical form. This ruleset is called on every address before any other ruleset is called. Some of the techniques for canonicalizing an address are a bit baroque, but the general idea is to put all addresses into an easily parseable syntax. In general, this syntax can be chosen arbitrarily. The one most sendmail configurations use closely resembles domain address syntax. The only difference between the two is that the domain part of the address is delimited by angle brackets. This delimiting lets the domain part of an address be found easily for later pattern matching.

    A brief aside about the internal parsing mechanism used by sendmail is in order here. Sendmail address parsing is designed to be very general. However, the internal parser does have extensive knowledge of RFC822 syntax. In particular, the parser knows how to pick addresses out of headers and whether the address is a sender or recipient address. It also knows about various header formats. For example, it can pick out the address of a *From:* header line and ignore the parts of the address that are comments. In a *From:* header like

```
fred@acme.com (Fred Jones)
```

sendmail's lexical analyzer will only pass the string *fred@acme.com* to the rewriting rewriting rulesets. On the other hand an address like

```
Fred Jones <fred@acme.com>
```

is passed as is to the rulesets. The lexical analyzer has no way of knowing that the fullname should be ignored. This is handled by the rewriting rulesets.

```
(1)   S1

(2)   S2


(3)   S3
(4)   R<>                        $@@
(5)   R$*<$+>$*                  $2


(6)   R@$+,$+:$+                 @$1:$2:$3
(7)   R@$+:$+                    $@<@$[$1$]>:$2
(8)   R$+:$*;@$+                 $@$1:$2;@$3


(9)   R$+@$+                     $:$1<@$2>
(10)  R$+<$+@$+>                 $1$2<@$3>
(11)  R$+<@$*.$=Z>               $@$1<@$2.$3>
(12)  R$+<@$+>                   $@$1<@$[$2$]>


(13)  R$-!$+                     $@$2<@$1.uucp>
(14)  R$-.$+!$+                  $@$3<@$1.$2>
(15)  R$+%$+                     $@$>3$1@$2


(16)  S4
(17)  R$+<@$+.uucp>              $2!$1
(18)  R$+                        $: $>9 $1
(19)  R$*<$+>$*                  $1$2$3


(20)  S9
(21)  R@                         $@$n
(22)  R<@$+>$*:$+:$+             <@$1>$2,$3:$4


(23)  S29
(24)  R$*                        $: $>3 $1
(25)  R$*                        $@ $>0 $1


(26)  CZ uucp bitnet
```

Figure 8.12 General Rules.

We now describe the parts of ruleset 3.

1. An address of the form "<>" is turned into an "@" (line 4), which in turn is expanded to "Mailer-Daemon" in Ruleset 0 and Ruleset 9.

2. An address that already includes angle brackets is focused on just what is inside the brackets (line 5). Essentially any fullname in the address is stripped

out of the address by this rule. The assumption is that any address which already contains angle brackets is in the *fullname <address>* format.

3. Next handle rarely seen but still legal route syntax (lines 6 – 8). This is done by changing all the commas to colons in the list syntax (line 6). This is undone later in Ruleset 4 to put the syntax back into its correct form. Angle brackets are then placed around the first element in the list, which is then canonicalized (line 7). The modified list syntax is considered to be in canonical form and returned (line 8).

4. Next comes the parsing of *user@domain* addresses (line 9 – 12). In the first two steps (line 9 – 10) angle brackets are placed around the domain part of the address and focused on the right-most "@". Note, this step also will parse illegal addresses. For example, the address

```
u@host@domain
```

will be rewritten as

```
u@host<@domain>
```

Sendmail does not strictly enforce the style of addresses, since it was designed to work with a variety of address formats. Next the fake top-level domains listed in the Z class (line 26) are exempted from being fully-qualified and are returned unchanged. A common convention when sending BITNET or UUCP mail is to append the string *.bitnet* or *.uucp* onto the end of the address. The address is strictly speaking not a valid address, but the convention is very widespread. Since the domain name constructed is not valid, there is no need to canonicalize it. For other addresses the domain part of the address is then canonicalized in conformance with RFC822 standards that all domain names in a mail header must be fully qualified (line 12) and returned.

5. The last three lines of the ruleset (13 – 15) convert some old-style addresses into pseudo-canonical format. UUCP path addresses are converted to domain format (line 13) by taking the first path element as the hostname; the rest of the path elements (with the "!" delimiters) as the user name; and appending a *.uucp* to the end of the address. Line 14 takes a UUCP path address with a domain name as its first element and converts it to domain syntax. Line 15 turns a "%" found in an address without a domain part and converts it to an "@". The rule then calls on Ruleset 3 to canonicalize the resulting address.

• Ruleset 4 (lines 16 – 19)
Converts an address in internal canonical form back to its legal format. It also removes the angle brackets from all addresses. UUCP addresses are converted back to their original form (line 17). Line 18 uses Ruleset 9 to do some additional cleanup. Finally the angle brackets added on in Ruleset 3 are removed (line 19).

- Ruleset 9 (lines 20 – 22)

  Used by Ruleset 4 and Ruleset 0 to convert the special token "@" to whatever the *n* macro is defined to be, usually "Mailer-Daemon" (line 21). It also converts the routing syntax back to its real format (line 22).

- Ruleset 29 (lines 23 – 25)

  Calls first Ruleset 3 and then Ruleset 0. This is used by Ruleset 0 to call itself recursively. You might think that Ruleset 0 could just call itself recursively without going through Ruleset 29. This is not the case, since all addresses must go through Ruleset 3 first. When Ruleset 0 is initially called from within sendmail itself, sendmail has arranged to call Ruleset 3 before Ruleset 0. So to call Ruleset 0 recursively, Ruleset 3 must be called first. Ruleset 29 makes this possible.

Prefix to Ruleset 0

The first part of Ruleset 0 is common to all configurations. Generally, this part handles some special cases and eliminates redundant information in addresses. Figure 8.13 shows the ruleset's prefix rules and is described as follows:

- Line 2

  Ensures proper delivery of error messages to the mail system itself. An address of "<>" is transformed into the pseudo-address "@" in Ruleset 3. It marks a message that needs to be delivered to the user name that is the value of the *n* macro, usually "Mailer-Daemon." In this line the mail is delivered locally if the

---

Figure 8.13 Prefix to Ruleset 0.

```
(1)   S0
(2)   R@                    $?R $#$M $@$R $:$n $|#local $:$n $.
(3)   R<@[$+]>:$*           $:$>9 <@[$1]>:$2
(4)   R<@[$+]>:$*           $#$M $@[$1] $:$2
(5)   R<@[$+]>,$*           $#$M $@[$1] $:$2
(6)   R$*<@[$+]>            $#$M $@[$2] $:$1
(7)   R$*<@$j>$*            $1<@>$2
(8)   R$*<@$=U.uucp>$*      $1<@>$3
(9)   R$*<@$D>$*            $1<@>$2
(10)  R$*<$*.>$*            $1<$2>$3
(11)  R<@>:$*               $@$>29$1
(12)  R$*<@>                $@$>29$1
(13)  R$*<@$j>              $@$>29$1
(14)  R<@$j>:$+             $@$>29$1
(15)  R$*                   $:$>9 $1
```

R macro is not defined. We see how the value of this macro is used when we construct configuration files for various configurations. If the R macro is defined, the message is delivered to the address "Mailer-Daemon" on the remote host, whose name is the value of the R macro.

- Lines 3 – 6
Resolves addresses that use IP addresses instead of hostnames. A legal though seldom used syntax replaces the domain part of a mail address with an IP address. Examples of these types of addresses are:

```
sam@[129.12.23.1]
 @[129.12.23.1]:sam
 @[129.12.23.1],sally.utexas.edu:sam
```

are valid mail address. Although seldom used, they need to be handled properly. Within this group, line 4 converts a route address with an IP address as an element from its legal form; for ease of parsing, all commas in the route address are converted to colons. Lines 4 – 6 calls on the mailer defined in the M macro to deliver the message. The value of the M macro is usually the *tcp* mailer, but it can be a different mailer depending on the configuration.

- Lines 7 – 9
Detect whether the address is a local address and if so, reduce the domain part of the address to a single "@." The rules check if the values of the following macros appear as the domain name of the address. The value of the j macro is this hosts' full domain name. The value of the U macro is this host's UUCP name. The value of the D macro is this host's parent domain. For these configurations, mail addressed to the domain the host is in is considered local.

- Lines 10 – 14
Handle recursively calling Ruleset 0 after the local domain name is stripped. These rules all call Ruleset 29, which calls Ruleset 3 and then Ruleset 0 again. Doing this handles addresses of the form *sam%machine@this_domain*. If *this_domain* is stripped by an earlier rule because it was the local domain or the name of this machine, then the part of the address before the "@" sign is run back through Rulesets 3 and 0 again to be resolved.

- Line 15
Calls Ruleset 9, which does some cleanup on the mailer address and ensures route addresses are put back into their correct format before the rest of Ruleset 0 is invoked.

Address Aliases

Sendmail uses a simple ASCII file for alias definition. Figure 8.14 shows an excerpt from an alias file. The file's location is defined in the *sendmail.cf* file. As the figure illustrates, an alias entry consists of an alias name followed by a colon, which is in turn followed by a comma-separated list of replacement addresses.

```
(1)   root: smoot, jsq
(2)   news: smoot

(3)   postmaster: smoot

(4)   Mailer-Daemon: postmaster

(5)   S.Carl-Mitchell:smoot

(6)   scm: smoot

(7)   fred: fred@acme.com

(8)   staff: smoot, jsq, linda, sally, george,
(9)       fred, james

(10)  accounting: :include:/export/home/acct/members

(11)  owner-accounting: george

(12)  rnews:|"/usr/local/uurec"

(13)  archive:/usr/local/lib/archive
```

Figure 8.14 Aliases.

The replacement addresses can be local or non-local. Each local address can itself be another alias that is recursively replaced by a new set of replacement addresses. The alias file is referenced for every locally resolved address. To speed access, the alias file is transformed into a *dbm* database file.

Aliases are handy for redirecting mail to common user addresses. The example Fig. 8.14 the following aliases are defined:

• Lines 1 – 2
The *root* alias redirects mail for user *root* to the addresses of the system administrators *smoot* and *jsq*. Likewise, mail sent to the user *news* is redirected to the user *smoot*. Note that in both the cases, no mail messages will ever get delivered to the local mailbox for either the user *root* or *news*.

• Line 3
Aliases also can redirect mail from required addresses to a real user. In this case mail addressed to *postmaster* is sent to the user *smoot*. Note that there is no local user *postmaster*.

- Line 4

This example demonstrates recursive alias expansion. In this case mail addressed to *Mailer_Daemon* will end up in *smoot's* mailbox, since *Mailer-Daemon* is aliased to *postmaster* which in turn is aliased to *smoot*. A reasonable level of recursive expansion is supported; however, beyond 10 levels of expansion an error is generated, which prevents a loop in the alias file from aliasing an address forever.

- Line 5

Aliases also can be used to set up standard or easily remembered mailing addresses. This shows a popular convention with an alias that consists of a user's first initial followed by the user's full last name. For example, mail sent to *S.Carl-Mitchell* is actually relayed to the user *smoot*.

- Line 6

Alternate or common user names also can be supported; for example, mail sent to *scm* is also sent to the user *smoot*.

- Line 7

An alias must be a local address, but the target of an alias can be nonlocal. Mail sent to *fred* is sent to *fred@acme.com*.

- Line 8

Aliases also can be used to maintain mailing lists, as shown in the figure where mail sent to *staff* is redirected to usernames that are presumably the addresses of the system staff.

- Line 9

Extremely long replacement address lists are continued across multiple lines with the beginning of each subsequent line marked by whitespace (either one or more spaces or tab characters). This line is a continuation of the *staff* alias.

- Line 10

This line used the *:include:* construct which lets you maintain the replacement address list in a separate file. Note that following *:include:* is the pathname of the file containing the replacement addresses. With this procedure, the system administrator can limit access to the primary alias database while still allowing separate maintenance of specific alias lists. The address *accounting* is aliased to the address list found in the file */export/home/acct/members* and shown Fig. 8.15. The format of this file is a list of addresses separated by commas. If the

---

Figure 8.15 Accounting Alias include File.

```
sue@acct.tic.com, bob@acct.tic.com,
george@acct.tic.com, sarah@acct.tic.com
```

list continues across multiple lines, no whitespace is required on the continuation lines because the names are assumed to be the expansion of a single alias. The members of the *:include:* file list might also include other *:include:* files or other alias names. This nesting of *:include:* specifications is not recommended, however, because confusion could result. The *:include:* specification also allows authority over aliases to be distributed. Doing this enables different groups to administer different parts of the alias database without interference.

- Line 11

An alias prefixed with the string *owner-* is treated by *sendmail* in a special manner. In this case any error messages generated by sending to the address list *accounting* while be sent to the user *george,* rather than back to the original sender. This is a convention that eases the maintenance of large mailing lists.

- Line 12

Aliases further can be used to redirect mail directly into a file or pipe the mail message through a program. In this example, the address *rnews* is aliased to a string that begins with the shell pipe symbol, "|". The string following the pipe symbol is considered to be a shell command that reads the mail message from its stdin. The shell used is taken from the *prog* mailer definition. The program can manipulate the message in any fashion it likes. In the figure, the *uurec* program is called, which transforms the mail message into a USENET news article and delivers it into the USENET news system. Note the quotes around the command. These are not essential, but serve to delimit the command that is called to deliver the message.

- Line 13

An alias that starts with a "/" is interpreted as a filename. The mail message is appended to the target file. This technique is handy for creating archive records of mail messages. In the figure, mail sent to the address *archive* is appended to the file */usr/local/lib/archive*. Security when mailing to files is enforced by running sendmail with the userid and groupid of the user that invoked sendmail. If the setuid bit is set in the target file and the target is not executable, then sendmail delivers the mail with its userid set to the file's owner. This convention allows any user to mail to a specific file without needing write permission on that file; without the *setuid* bit set, a user must have write permission on the file before being able to send mail to the file.

Sendmail allows a user to send a message to a program or a file only if the targeted program or file is an alias expansion. Without this restriction, system security could be compromised. A malicious user could invoke any program at will and send a mail message to that program or append a message to the end of any file. If the invoked program were a shell, the user could do just about anything. Sendmail protects against this by running the target program using its default userid (the value of the *u* option), which is usually userid 1 (the *daemon* user). or the userid of the user that invoked sendmail locally.

1. Forward to another host:

```
smoot@acme.com
```

2. Retain a local copy:

```
smoot, smoot@acme.com
```

3. Archive in a file and deliver locally

```
smoot, /export/home/smoot/mailarchive
```

4. Mail to a program:

|"/export/home/smoot/bin/massage"

Figure 8.16 .forward File.

The .forward File

Sendmail further allows aliases in an individual user's **.forward** file. A *forward* file serves as a local alias for the individual user. Located in the user's home directory, it is commonly used to forward mail to another machine. However, arbitrary replacement addresses and even lists can be placed in this file, thus enabling an individual user to create an alias list for that user's own mail address. If alising a local name fails, then each local name is looked up in the */etc/passwd* file to see if it matches a local username. A match results in the user's home directory being examined for the *forward* file. If the file is found, the file contents are considered an alias expansion of the local user. Note that for security purposes, the *forward* file must be owned and readable by the local user.

Figure 8.16 shows four examples of how a *forward* file can be used. The first example illustrates mail forwarding to a remote system. The second results in mail sent both to a local address —*smoot* — and to a remote address. The third example shows delivery to a local address and to a file. In this example, the file's pathname, as in the system-wide alias file, must be absolute and the file must either be writable by the sender or have the setuid bit set and be owned by the receiver of the mail. The last example shows how to pipe mail through a program. The program can do anything it wants with the message. Conceivably it could parse the mail headers and deliver the messages to alternate mailboxes or even parse the message contents and throw away junk mail. If you write the incoming message to a file, relative file pathnames should not be used, since the working directory where sendmail runs the command is the mail spool directory that is generally not readable or writable by normal users.

Sendmail in a Networked Environment

Sendmail is a very flexible MTA and for any particular environment, it can be configured in many different ways. However, reasonable choices generally fall into just a few categories. Given the palette of boilerplate information, general rulesets, mailers, and the sendmail alias facility described earlier, it is fairly easy to build a set of coherent and easy to maintain configuration file. We assume that the system running sendmail has a registered domain, although it might or might not be connected to the Internet. We also assume that DNS is being run. When naming and assigning values to sendmail macros and classes, a few conventions are followed, as explained next.

The conventions consist of the lists of user-defined macros and classes, along with their uses, shown in Fig. 8.17. By employing them consistently, you will find it easy to change the configuration.

- *D* macro

The domain this host belongs to.

- *E* macro

The parent of the domain the host belongs to. We will see this macro used to forward messages to a parent domain from a machine within a subdomain for further processing.

- *M* macro

The mailer that is the major relay mailer. For Internet connected hosts, this will be the *tcp* mailer. For hosts connected via UUCP, the mailer usually will be the *uucp* mailer or some variant that relays mail outside the local system to an Internet connected host.

Figure 8.17 Macros and Classes.

```
Macros
D - the domain the system is in
E - parent domain of the system is in
M - major mailer to get to remote hosts
O - name of relay outside our domain
R - name of major relay within our own domain
U - UUCP name of this host

Classes
P - list of peer domains
S - list of subdomains within this domain
X - hosts directly reachable using UUCP
```

- *O* macro
  The name of the relay machine to send mail which is to be delivered outside the host's domain. This macro is used only for networks not directly connected to the Internet.

- *R* macro
  The name of the mail relay machine within the host's domain. This relay machine acts a "smart" mail gateway for host's with simpler and easier to maintain configurations.

- *U* macro
  The host's UUCP hostname. This name usually differs from the host's domain name and is defined only for hosts with UUCP connectivity.

- *P* class
  Peer (domains a the same level of the domain tree) domains that this system wants to send messages to directly.

- *S* calls
  The list of legal subdomains within this systems domain. This lets the system determine which subdomains must have mail forwarded to them.

- *X* class
  The names of hosts directly reachable by a UUCP connection. Other UUCP addresses are sent to the relay host.

A Single Host with Internet Connection. A single host system has one host that sends and receives all network mail. Figure 8.18 features an example of such a system. All user mailboxes reside on this one system, and all aliasing is performed on the single mail host. Here the host has both UUCP and Internet connectivity. Users wishing to read mail must log in to the host and read mail on that host.

Administratively, a single host system is fairly easy to manage and configure, since their is no internal forwarding of mail messages required. The only mail routing issues are gatewaying mail between the Internet and the UUCP hosts. You may wish to disallow this or at least not advertise the fact that it is possible.

Figure 8.18 Single Host.

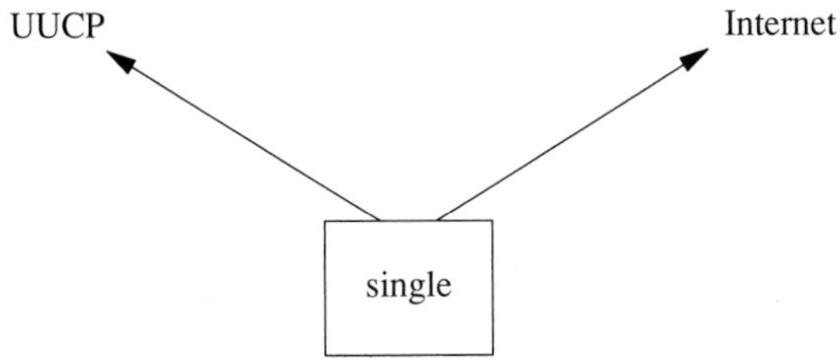

```
(1)   DVsingle.1.1
(2)   DDtic.com
(3)   Dj$w
(4)   DUsingle
(5)   CX bull lester
(6)   DO outside.com
(7)   DMtcp

(8)   include(general.m4)
(9)   include(rules.m4)
(10)  include(local.m4)
(11)  include(uucp.m4)
(12)  include(tcp.m4)
(13)  include(zeropre.m4)

(14)  R$+<@$=X.uucp>   $#uucp $@$2 $:$1<@$2.uucp>
(15)  R$+<@$-.uucp>    $#$M $@$O $:$1<@$2.uucp>
(16)  R$*<@$+>$*       $#$M $@$2 $:$1<@$2>$3
(17)  R$+%$+           $@$>29$1@$2
(18)  R$+              $#local $:$1
```

Figure 8.19 Single Host with Internet and UUCP Connectivity.

Figure 8.19 shows an example configuration file for a single host system. The file is explained in part as follows:

- Line 1 The version number of this configuration displayed in the SMTP server banner message.

- Line 2
  The domain is set to *tic.com*.

- Line 3
  The *j* macro is set to the value of the *w* macro. Some versions of sendmail set *w* to the unqualified hostname. In this case, *j* should be set to *$w.$D*.

- Line 4
  The UUCP hostname is set to *single*.

- Line 5
  Directly connected UUCP hosts are added to the *X* class. Adding UUCP hosts to the "X" class also can be done by directly reading the names from the UUCP *L.sys.* file. You would replace the fifth line in the example with a line like:

```
FX /usr/lib/uucp/L.sys %s
```

In this line, the *F* means take the class values from a file rather than including them in the configuration file itself. A *scanf( )* format string follows the filename and is used to parse each line in the file for a single class value. The class values are assumed to be one per line in the file.

- Line 7
The major relay mailer used is the *tcp* mailer, since the host has Internet connectivity.

- Lines 8 – 13
The previously described configuration *include* files are added at this point.

- Line 14
Sends mail to all directly connected UUCP hosts.

- Line 15
Sends all other UUCP mail to the outside relay.

- Line 16
Sends all non-local domain-addressed mail directly to the destination using the *tcp* relay mailer.

- Line 17
Rewrites and retries any address of the form *user%host*. Presumably these addresses are internal routing addresses. Ruleset 29 changes the "%" to an "@" and then calls Ruleset 3 to canonicalize the address and to call Ruleset 0 again. Addresses of this form are resolved by calling Ruleset 0, so this ruleset is called exactly once by prefixing the right-hand side with "$@."

- Line 18
Assumes any address not matching a previous rule is a local address. Note that if the username is not a valid local user or alias, sendmail still generates an error reply, since the local delivery will fail.

A Cluster of Machines with Mail Relay. In Fig. 8.20, a cluster of machines uses a single mail gateway. The gateway machine does all the mail forwarding to the Internet and to any UUCP hosts, and all the client machines send all mail to and receive all mail from the gateway. The mail routing topology does not necessarily reflect the physical topology of the underlying network, but it is a logical one for mail transport. SMTP is used to move mail between the gateway and a client. Using this architecture, only two configuration files are required — one each for a gateway configuration and a client configuration.

It's possible to configure all clustered machines to send mail directly to remote Internet machines using SMTP; however, managing this type of setup can be difficult. For security reasons, it might not be desirable to have all machines directly reachable from outside systems. It also is important to have mail addressing be independent of any specific machine names because machines come and go and people change where their mail is delivered.

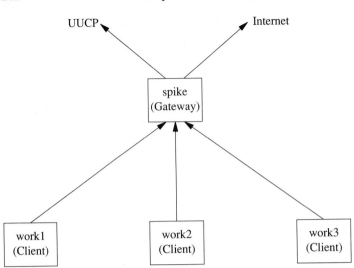

Figure 8.20 Machine Cluster with UUCP and Internet Connectivity.

Having a consistent mail addressing scheme is prudent policy. The mail address *george@acme.com* is much better than *george@work1.acme.com*. The first address, unlike the second, is independent of the mailbox's real location. It allows a user to change the internal location of the user's mailbox without requiring everyone who receives mail from that user to change the mail address on their end. Although changing a mail address can be simplified by using aliases, it's much better to pick an address that is less likely to change over time.

Aliasing in a clustered architecture is intended to hide the location of individual mailboxes. Hostnames are eliminated from mail addresses; that is, a specific hostname appears in the envelope address but is used only by SMTP and is never seen in the messages. The alias database in effect becomes a mechanism to redirect mail to the correct host on which the user's mailbox is located. As the example cluster configuration shows, it's simple to set up a mail system that hides machine names internal to the domain. All mail addresses within this domain take the form *user@acme.com*. The gateway machine, *spike.acme.com,* maintains the alias file for the entire cluster. For example, when a message addressed to *harry@acme.com* is received by the gateway, the sendmail configuration on the gateway strips the domain part from the address and considers the resulting address *harry* to be local. Sendmail then looks up an alias for *harry*. For example, suppose the alias for *harry* is *harry@work1.acme.com*. The address — *harry@work1.acme.com* — appears only in the SMTP envelope. The visible recipient address in the message header — *harry@acme.com* — remains unchanged. The gateway forwards the message to *work1.acme.com,* which treats the address as local and delivers it to the mailbox named *harry*.

Because mail sent from one client to another is directed through the mail gateway, the gateway can handle all address aliasing. Consequently only a single copy of the alias database needs to be maintained. Conversely, if the client machines sent mail directly between each other then in order to properly deliver mail, all machines would need access to the global alias database.

Figure 8.21 shows the configuration file for the cluster gateway machine, *spike.acme.com* in the previous example, explained as follows:

- Lines 1 – 7
  Same general configuration parameters as in the single host configuration. The only changes are the version name of the configuration and a change in the domain name for this example, as well as changes to the specific UUCP hosts that are directly connected.

- Lines 8 – 13
  Same template configuration files as in the single host example.

- Lines 14 – 15
  Handle UUCP mail in exactly the same way as in the single host configuration.

Figure 8.21 Cluster Gateway.

```
(1)   DVrelay.1.17
(2)   DDacme.com
(3)   Dj$w
(4)   DUspike
(5)   CX alice moby
(6)   DO outside.com
(7)   DMtcp

(8)   include(general.m4)
(9)   include(rules.m4)
(10)  include(local.m4)
(11)  include(uucp.m4)
(12)  include(tcp.m4)
(13)  include(zeropre.m4)

(14)  R$+<@$=X.uucp>   $#uucp $@$2 $:$1<@$2.uucp>
(15)  R$+<@$-.uucp>    $#uucp $@$O $:$1<@$2.uucp>
(16)  R$*<@$-.$D>$*    $#$M $@ $2.$D $:$1<@$2.$D>$3
(17)  R$*<@$+>$*       $#$M $@$2 $:$1<@$2>$3
(18)  R$+%$+           $@$>29$1@$2
(19)  R$+              $#local $:$1
```

- Line 16
Directs mail to the correct host when mail is forwarded to one of the client machines. Most alias expansions will resolve to this ruleset. Note that the left-hand side will match a domain name of the form

```
host.acme.com
```

The message will be sent to this host with an envelope address of the form

```
user@host.acme.com                                    .
```

We will see shortly how the client handles this address.

- Line 17
Sends mail that is outside the *acme.com* domain directly to the mail gateway for that domain.

- Lines 18 – 19
Does internal routing and local address resolution that is the same as the single host configuration.

Let's consider an example of how mail addressed to *harry@acme.com* is handled. The gateway receives this message and examines the recipient's address. In this case, the address has its domain part stripped in the *zeropre.m4* part of Ruleset 0. The address *harry* resolves to the *local* mailer, and an alias lookup for *harry* is tried. Let's assume the alias for *harry* is *harry@work1.acme.com*. This address is then sent through Rulesets 3 and 0. This time the address matches line 16 in the configuration file and the message is sent to *work1.acme.com* using the *tcp* mailer.

The configuration file for all other machines within the cluster is shown in Fig. 8.22. There are a few changes. In line 3 the list of local users known to this machine is kept in the *L* class. A client machine forwards all mail messages except those that are in the *L* class, which in this configuration is maintained in the file */etc/local_names*. For a single user workstation, maintenance of the *local_addresses* file is trivial. Only a user whose mailbox is on the local system is listed in this file. Also included in this file is any alias that expands locally (non-local aliases are expanded on the gateway). The *R* macro is set to the value *mail_relay.acme.com,* which is a host alias name for the gateway machine *spike.acme.com* (see line 6). Lines 7 – 11 include the required template files. Since this host does not have any UUCP connections, the file *uucp.m4* is not included.

The end of Ruleset 0 consists of only three lines, as follows:

- Line 12
Identifies mail addresses that match the list found in */etc/local_names*. Messages associated with these mail addresses are delivered locally.

```
(1)   DVsub.1.6
(2)   DDacme.com
(3)   FL/etc/local_names
(4)   Dj$w
(5)   DMtcp
(6)   DRmail_relay.$D

(7)   include(general.m4)
(8)   include(rules.m4)
(9)   include(local.m4)
(10)  include(tcp.m4)
(11)  include(zeropre.m4)

(12) R$=L              $#local $:$1
(13) R$+               $#$M $@$R $:$1
```

Figure 8.22 Cluster Clients.

• Line 13
  Forwards all other addresses to the gateway machine.

We complete the previous example where a message with the recipient address *harry@work1.acme.com* is sent to *work1.acme.com.* On the workstation, the domain part of the address is stripped, and the address *harry* matches the only value in the *L* class. When the match is found, the mail is delivered to the local user *harry.* All other addresses are forwarded to the gateway machine. This includes addresses without a domain suffix. For example the address *sally* is sent to the gateway, where an alias for *sally* directs the message to the machine on which Sally reads her mail.

   A valid criticism of this architecture is the dependence on a single mail gateway. If the gateway is down, all mail traffic, both local and remote, is disabled. However, if DNS is used for host lookup, redundant gateways can be configured by exploiting DNS MX records. Rather than your creating an alias CNAME record for *mail_relay.acme.com,* you would create R records that point to one or more mail gateway machines. Note that for this to be possible, sendmail must support MX lookups. Therefore if machine *lee.acme.com* is a redundant gateway, the following MX records are found in the DNS database:

```
mail_relay.acme.com. IN MX 10 spike.acme.com.
mail_relay.acme.com. IN MX 20 lee.acme.com.
```

Mail is sent to the relay through *spike.acme.com.* If *spike* is unavailable, delivery is attempted through *lee.acme.com.* Host *lee* is configured as a mirror copy of *spike*, therefore if both *lee* and *spike* relay external mail then the following MX records are added:

```
acme.com.  IN MX 10  spike.acme.com.
acme.com.  IN MX 20  lee.acme.com.
```

This assumes that all mail addresses are of the form *user@acme.com*. Any subdomain addresses will need additional MX records.

For this to work, both *lee* and *spike* must be configured identically and both must have the same UUCP and Internet connectivity. If only *spike* has UUCP and Internet connectivity, then UUCP and Internet mail must be relayed from *lee* to *spike*. If this is the case, *lee*'s configuration file requires minor modification, as shown in Fig. 8.23. Comparing Fig. 8.21 which shows the original gateway configuration file with Fig. 8.23, note that the *CX* and the *DU* lines have been removed (line 7 – 8 in Fig. 8.20) and the outside relay for *lee* changed to *spike.acme.com* (line 4 in Fig. 8.23). Also the rule in Ruleset 0 that does direct UUCP connections was removed (line 14 in Fig. 8.20) and all mail with an outside domain destination address forwarded to *spike* (line 14 in Fig. 8.23). With these changes made, *lee* then forwards all UUCP and Internet mail to *spike*.

Figure 8.23 Secondary Cluster Gateway.

```
(1)    DVrelay.1.17
(2)    DDacme.com
(3)    Dj$w
(4)    DO spike.$D
(5)    DMtcp

(6)    include(general.m4)
(7)    include(rules.m4)
(8)    include(local.m4)
(9)    include(uucp.m4)
(10)   include(tcp.m4)
(11)   include(zeropre.m4)

(12)   R$+<@$-.uucp>     $#$M $@$O $:$1<@$2.uucp>
(13)   R$*<@$-.$D>$*     $#$M $@$2.$D $:$1<@$2.$D>$3
(14)   R$*<@$+>$*        $#$M $@$O $:$1<@$2>$3
(15)   R$+%$+            $@$>29$1@$2
(16)   R$+               $#local $:$1
```

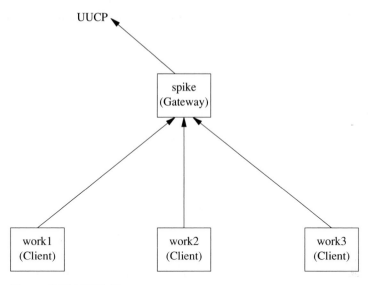

Figure 8.24 UUCP Cluster.

A Cluster with UUCP Connectivity Only. The cluster configuration described in the previous section assumes direct TCP/IP connectivity to the Internet. If only UUCP mail access is available to an Internet host, you need to modify the configuration, as shown in Fig. 8.24. The major configuration change concerns how mail is· forwarded to and from an Internet mail gateway. A simple UUCP connection can be configured and mail can be sent to and from your internal network using UUCP-style addresses. However, this configuration is very ugly and requires mixing UUCP and domain-style addresses. For example, if the name of the Internet relay is still *outside.com,* mail sent to an Internet host will have return addresses of the form *acme!Iharry@outside.com.* This is not very descriptive addressing. Mail sent to your network from an Internet host will have return addresses like *outside!bigu.edu!sally* (assuming *outside* is the UUCP host name of the relay). The address translation is necessary because the address must be transformed into UUCP syntax. It's better to send mail using domain-based addresses like *sally@bigu.edu* and receive mail with domain-based addresses like *harry@acme.com.* To use domain addressing, you must do the following:

• Register a domain name for your site. See Appendix A for how to do that.

• Find a site that will maintain an MX record for your domain.

• Find a neighbor with Internet connectivity that will act as your Internet mail forwarder using UUCP dialup access to your site. This site might be the same one that maintains your MX record or a different one. In either case, the only DNS record in your domain will be an MX record that identifies your forwarder.

Consider for example that the registered domain *acme.com* gets registered and the mail forwarder is *relay.outside.com*. In this situation, the single MX record therefore is

```
acme.com. IN MX 10 relay.outside.com.
```

This record directs all mail with a domain part of *acme.com* to the Internet host *relay.outside.com*. For this to occur, the mail configuration on *relay.outside.com* must be able to forward to your gateway machine, using UUCP, the mail messages that are bound for the *acme.com* domain.

The configuration is very similar to the cluster configuration with direct TCP/IP connectivity. The cluster configuration with only UUCP access is shown in Fig. 8.25. It differs from the cluster configuration with TCP/IP access in the method used to exchange mail with the Internet gateway. Here mail to the Internet uses the *tcprmaild* mailer. All mail bound for any domain outside of your own is carried over UUCP transport to *relay.outside.com,* where it then is forwarded to the proper site. Mail incoming for *acme.com* is received by *relay.outside.com* and sent to *spike.acme.com* via UUCP transport.

Figure 8.25 Cluster UUCP Configuration.

```
DVrelay.1.17
DDacme.com
Dj$w
DUspike
CX alice moby
DO relay.outside.com
DMtcprmaild

include(general.m4)
include(rules.m4)
include(local.m4)
include(uucp.m4)
include(tcp.m4)
include(zeropre.m4)

R$+<@$=X.uucp>     $#uucp $@$2 $:$1<@$2.uucp>
R$+<@$-.uucp>      $#uucp $@$O $:$1<@$2.uucp>
R$+<@$-.$D>$*      $#tcp $@$2.$D $:$1<@$2.$D>$3
R$+<@$+>$*         $#$M $@$O $:$1<@$2>$3
R$+%$+             $@$>29$1@$2
R$+               $#local $:$1
```

The *trcprmaild* mailer transports domain-addressed mail over UUCP transport, thus eliminating the need for UUCP-style addressing in the message envelope. As described in Chapter 7, standard UUCP mail uses a different syntax for mail addresses and encodes the envelope sender address as a part of the ugly UUCP *From ... remote from ...* lines. Most UUCP implementations require these lines as part of the mail header; they are the UUCP equivalent of the *Received* header in RFC822 mail. Also, for much the same reason, the recipient header address is usually in UUCP format The following example demonstrates the problem connected with using UUCP transport to send a fully-compliant RFC822 mail message.

Suppose *judy@acme.com* sends a message to *sam@bigcorp.com*. When the message is sent by *spike.acme.com*, the envelope addresses are rewritten as follows using the *uucp* mailer:

```
judy@acme.com   →  spike!judy
sam@bigcorp.com → bigcorp.com!sam
```

The code in sendmail that adds the UUCP *From .. remote from ..* header takes the sender address and splits it at the "!" so the UUCP *From* line becomes:

```
From judy date remote from spike
```

The uux command executed to send the message is:

```
uux - outside!rmail (bigcorp.com!sam)
```

Where *outside* is the UUCP name for the Internet relay. When the message is received by the relay, the leading *From* line is parsed and a return address — *spike!judy* — is created from it. The mail is forwarded to *sam@bigcorp.com* with this return address. Also because most Internet mail relays add their own domain name to any address without a domain suffix, the resulting return address is *spike!judy@relay.outside.com*, which is very ugly.

If pure domain addresses are used for the sender and recipient addresses, sendmail can't find a "!" in the sender address and so can't construct the UUCP-style *From* line. The result is sendmail fails to send the message. The problem is created in the first place by mixing two mail addressing and transport standards. SMTP transport explicitly sends the envelope recipient and sender address as part of the SMTP dialogue. UUCP on the other hand has a different way of handling the recipient and sender envelope addresses. The sender envelope address is encoded in the *From ... remote from* lines inserted at the beginning of the message. Sendmail deals with these lines as best it can but really doesn't handle the situation well at all. This is one reason mixed-mode addresses should be avoided when possible.

One possible solution to this dilemma might be to send the message using UUCP transport, but leave off the ugly *From ... remote from* header line. Doing this means pure domain names can be used for addresses. However, this method fails when the standard UUCP mailer is used; the *rmail* program running on receiving system expects to see at least one *From* line in the message header. Therefore this is no solution.

One way to solve this problem is to handle the sender envelope address as an explicit argument to the remotely executed rmail command. It turns out that this is easily done, provided the remote system is running sendmail or its MTA has a way of receiving sender envelope addresses as an argument. Rmail on a UNIX system that supports sendmail is nothing more than a simple front-end to sendmail itself. In this case, rmail parses the *From ... remote from* lines in the message and creates a sender address that it passes to sendmail as the sender address using the *-f* flag. The *From ... remote from* lines are simply stripped from the message. Figure 8.26 shows an rmail command and a message with *From ... remote from* header lines and the resulting sendmail invocation. In this figure, the message is relayed from the UUCP host *tutor* to the UUCP host *acme*. Each relay operation adds a *From ... remote from* line; this is the standard way UUCP mail operates.

When rmail runs on a site with sendmail support, each *From ... remote from* line is read in turn and a UUCP address created from it. In this case, the UUCP sender address is *acme!tutor!fred,* which is passed to sendmail using the *-f* flag. The other argument to sendmail is simply the recipient envelope address, that is,

---

Figure 8.26 rmail Invocation with sendmail Support.

rmail command:

```
rmail george
```

Message text read by rmail:

```
From uucp  Tue May 19 13:42:37 1992 remote from acme
From fred  Tue May 19 13:42:37 1992 remote from tutor
Date: Tue, 19 May 92 13:42:37 -0500
From: tutor!fred
Message-Id: <9205191842.AA17495@aahsa.tic.com>
To: bigu!george
Subject: hello

Hello
```

sendmail command:

```
/usr/lib/sendmail -facme!tutor!fred george
```

```
Mtcprmaild,  P=/usr/bin/uux, F=DFMuCLR, S=22, R=22,
      A=uux - -z -r $h!sendmail (-f$g) ($u)
```

Figure 8.27 SMTP Mail Over UUCP Transport Mailer Using Sendmail Directly.

the original rmail argument. The two leading *From ... remote from* lines are removed from the message before they are passed to sendmail.

It's possible to create a mailer that uses UUCP transport and executes sendmail directly on the remote system. This mailer would use domain addresses and have the mailer definition shown in Fig. 8.27. The sender address, which is conveniently placed in the *g* macro, is simply inserted as a command line argument. The recipient address too is handled as an argument. Also the *U* mailer flag is eliminated. No *From ... remote from* lines are attached to the beginning of the message; the remote system passes the complete message directly to sendmail and all the remote system need do is add the sendmail command as a valid command for a remote UUCP to execute. Address rewriting is handled by the same rewriting rule (Ruleset 22) as used by the *tcp* mailer, since the addresses are expected to be in domain-style syntax.

While this solution allows transport of domain addresses over UUCP transport, the remote system will have made sendmail itself executable by remote UUCP systems. This is probably not wise. sendmail runs setuid to *root;* allowing any remote UUCP user to access it directly permits that user to do anything with sendmail that a local user can do. Moreover, running via UUCP executes sendmail under the *uucp* userid, which is trusted to allow certain actions. Letting any remote user have direct and unlimited access to sendmail in this manner is not a good idea.

You can alleviate this problem by using a simple front-end to sendmail called *rmaild*. Using rmaild the mailer definition for the *tcprmaild* mailer is shown in Fig. 8.28 and the rmaild program itself is shown in Fig. 8.29. This front-end checks arguments and limits the type of arguments passed to sendmail. The only valid arguments are the *-f* flag and sender envelope address and a list of recipient addresses. The program determines whether its first argument is a *-f* and whether all subsequent arguments are simply addresses and not any other options to sendmail. For valid arguments, sendmail is simply called using the value of the rmaild *-f* flag as the value of its own *-f* flag. Sendmail then reads the message from its standard input.

Figure 8.28 SMTP Mail Over UUCP Transport Mailer Using Rmaild.

```
Mtcprmaild,  P=/usr/bin/uux, F=DFMuCLR, S=22, R=22,
      A=uux - -z -r $h!rmaild (-f$g) ($u)
```

```
#include <stdio.h>

static char *usage = "rmaild -f<sender> recipient...";

main(argc, argv)
int argc;
char **argv;
{
    char *fromarg;
    int i;

    if (argc < 3) {
        fprintf(stderr, "%s0, usage);
        exit(1);
    }
    if (strncmp(argv[1], "-f", 2) != 0) {
        fprintf(stderr, "%s0, usage);
        exit(2);
    }
    /* check remainder of arguments
     * to be sure they are just plain names */
    for (i=2; i<argc; i++) {
        if (argv[i][0] == '-') {
            fprintf(stderr, "%s0, usage);
            exit(3);
        }
    }
    /* now just exec sendmail */
    execv("/usr/lib/sendmail", argv);
    /* NOTREACHED */
}
```

Figure 8.29 Rmaild Program.

The remote system adds the rmaild command to the list of valid UUCP commands. Having the *tcprmaild* mailer and a cooperative remote system, sendmail can pass domain-style addresses back and forth using UUCP transport. No UUCP style addresses ever appear in the message, and the message is treated as if it were transported using SMTP. Using the same mechanism, the gateway can receive domain addresses via a UUCP link. A site using this mail transport mechanism looks for all intents and purposes as if it has SMTP mail connectivity to the Internet.

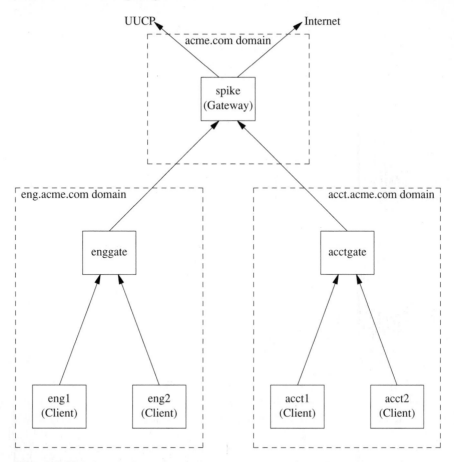

Figure 8.30 Gateway with Subdomains.

Subdomain Addressing

For relatively small organizations, single-level domain addressing is usually sufficient. As an organization's mail system grows, subdomain addresses can be added
to distribute administrative authority and to clarify mail addresses. Subdomains
are supported by changing the basic sendmail cluster configurations described earlier in this section. As Figure 8.30 shows, a mail system with subdomain
addresses assumes that the administrative authority for addresses is divided into
discrete subdomains. In this figure, the authority for the *acme.com* domain creates
an *eng* subdomain for the Engineering Department and an *acct* subdomain for the
Accounting Department. Mail to Sam in the Engineering Department is addressed
as *sam@eng.acme.com*. The *eng* subdomain keeps its own alias list. Within that
subdomain, one or more mail gateways and clients are configured using the identical cluster configuration described earlier.

```
(1)   DVrelay.1.17
(2)   DDeng.acme.com
(3)   Dj$w
(4)   DO mail_relay.acme.com
(5)   DMtcp

(6)   include(general.m4)
(7)   include(rules.m4)
(8)   include(local.m4)
(9)   include(uucp.m4)
(10)  include(tcp.m4)
(11)  include(zeropre.m4)

(12) R$+<@$-.uucp>    $#$M $@$O $:$1<@$2.uucp>
(13) R$*<@$-.$D>$*    $#$M $@$2.$D $:$1<@$2.$D>$3
(14) R$*<@$+>$*       $#$M $@$O $:$1<@$2>$3
(15) R$+%$+           $@$>29$1@$2
(16) R$+              $#local $:$1
```

Figure 8.31 Engineering Subdomain Gateway.

Figure 8.31 shows the *eng* gateway configuration. Exchanging mail external to the *eng* subdomain requires some minor changes to the gateway configuration for the *eng* domain, as follows. All UUCP mail is relayed through *mail_relay.acme.com* (line 12). Mail addressed outside the domain is also relayed through *mail_relay.acme.com* (line 13). Mail within the domain *eng.acme.com* is sent to the machine within the domain (line 14). The assumption is that mail outside the domain is sent to the next higher level relay where it is forwarded to its final destination. Also if *mail_relay.acme.com* (which is an MX record for *spike.acme.com*) is the only machine allowed access to the Internet or it just has a UUCP gateway to the outside world, then it makes sense to relay mail to that host.

The sendmail configuration on *spike* also requires a few changes to work properly. This is particularly true if the gateway, in this case *spike,* is the only machine accessible from the Internet. If this is the case, then for each subdomain MX records that point to *spike* need to be created. For the *eng* and *acct* subdomains, these MX records are the following:

```
eng.acme.com.   IN MX 10 spike.acme.com.
acct.acme.com.  IN MX 10 spike.acme.com.
```

If multiple Internet gateways exist, then additional MX records should be created for each gateway. All mail with a domain address part of *eng.acme.com* is first forwarded to *spike.acme.com*. The gateway mailer then must relay the mail to the correct internal gateway.

```
(1)   DVrelay.1.17
(2)   DDacme.com
(3)   Dj$w
(4)   DUspike
(5)   CX alice moby
(6)   DO outside.com
(7)   DMtcp
(8)   CS eng acct

(9)   include(general.m4)
(10)  include(rules.m4)
(11)  include(local.m4)
(12)  include(uucp.m4)
(13)  include(tcp.m4)
(14)  include(zeropre.m4)

(15)  R$+<@$=X.uucp>  $#uucp $@$2 $:$1<@$2.uucp>
(16)  R$+<@$-.uucp>   $#uucp $@$O $:$1<@$2.uucp>
(17)  R$*<@$=S.$D>$*  $#$M $@mail_relay.$2.$D $:$1<@$2.$D>$3
(18)  R$*<@$-.$D>$*   $#$M $@$2.$D $:$1<@$2.$D>$3
(19)  R$*<@$+>$*      $#$M $@$2 $:$1<@$2>$3
(20)  R$+%$+          $@$>29$1@$2
(21)  R$+            $#local $:$1
```

Figure 8.32 Cluster Gateway Modified for Subdomains.

The configuration file for *spike* needs to recognize each internal subdomain and forwards mail to the correct gateway. For convenience and naming independence, each internal gateway has an MX record for *mail_relay.domain*. This arrangement enables the internal gateways to change names or move without affecting the major gateway configuration. Accordingly, the following MX record that points at *enggate* is created:

```
mail_relay.eng.acme.com. IN MX 10 enggate.eng.acme.com
```

Figure 8.32 shows *spike's* revised configuration file. The *S* class (line 8), which lists all the delegated subdomains, is added. In this case, only *eng* and *acct* are delegated. A new rule is added to Ruleset 0 (line 17), just after the UUCP mail relaying is resolved. This rule matches on a domain part, which is one of the valid delegated subdomains, and the mail message consequently is forwarded to the gateway for that subdomain.

This architecture routes mail between peer subdomains by passing the message to the next higher-level gateway. Messages can be relayed directly between

```
(1)   DVrelay.1.17
(2)   DDeng.acme.com
(3)   DEacme.com
(4)   Dj$w
(5)   DO mail_relay.acme.com
(6)   DMtcp
(7)   CP acct

(8)   include(general.m4)
(9)   include(rules.m4)
(10)  include(local.m4)
(11)  include(uucp.m4)
(12)  include(tcp.m4)
(13)  include(zeropre.m4)

(14)  R$+<@$-.uucp>     $#$M $@$O $:$1<@$2.uucp>
(15)  R$*<@$=P.$E>$*    $#$M $@mail_relay.$2.$D $:$1<@$2.$D>$3
(16)  R$*<@$-.$D>$*     $#$M $@$2.$D $:$1<@$2.$D>$3
(17)  R$*<@$+>$*        $#$M $@$O $:$1<@$2>$3
(18)  R$+%$+            $@$>29$1@$2
(19)  R$+              $#local $:$1
```

Figure 8.33 Subdomain Gateway with Direct Peer Connection.

---

subdomain gateways by having each gateway know about the other subdomains and so send mail bound for that subdomain directly to the gateway for that subdomain. This is done by adding the known subdomains explicitly to the S class and sending the message directly to the peer domains gateway. For two subdomains that exchange a lot of mail traffic, this arrangement can benefit performance. Any subset of the subdomains can be logically connected in this manner. Figure 8.33 shows the Engineering Department gateway modified to send mail directly to the Accounting Department. The modifications include adding the following lines to the configuration file:

• Line 3

Add an E macro that is the name of the parent domain.

• Line 7

Add the *acct* subdomain to the P class.

• Line 15

Add a rule that sends mail directly to the domain mail gateway for any subdomain in the P class.

Post Office Protocol

In a case in which a user always reads mail on a single workstation, delivering mail for that user to that workstation is a reasonable architecture. With the just described gateway configurations, mail flows in a hierarchical fashion from gateway machines to user mailboxes on workstations. All mail from outside the organization enters the domain through one or more gateways. The gateway then forwards the mail to the correct internal gateway, which in turn sends the mail to its final destination host. However, if users move from one workstation to another or share public computing facilities, it's better to deliver mail to a mailbox located on a server and have the user access the server mailbox from a workstation. This procedure also is useful when workstations are powered off at night and so can't receive mail. In this case, rather than queue mail and continuously retry delivery, the server deposits messages in the appropriate local mailboxes, which users can query when ready to read their queued up messages.

Having only a central maildrop requires fewer reliable and available servers. In a small organization, all mail can be delivered on a single server and the user can then retrieve mail from the server. The simplest way for the user to do this is to log in to the server and read the mail contained thereon. This method has several drawbacks, however. First, the user must have an account on the server and can use only the mail software found on that server. Second, remote login to a server can be cumbersome. Finally, the method poses a potential security risk because the server might hold other critical files. For security purposes, servers should be configured with as few regular user logins as possible.

Because UNIX systems use a common directory on which to store all mailboxes, the mailbox directory can be mounted remotely, using Sun NFS, from the server on a workstation. The workstation user, unaware the file is on a remote system, accesses the mailbox file as if it were local.

Note that care must be taken to ensure that mailbox locking works on the remote file system, or messages could become corrupted. This doesn't mean, however, that you should use NFS for remote mailbox access. Employing NFS to support remote mailbox access is overkill; it is designed as a general remote file access mechanism. A better and simpler approach is to use POP which is designed specifically to transfer mail messages from a remote server to client machines. There are two versions of POP: POP2 [Butler *et al.* 1985] and POP3 [Rose 1991]. Both have similar functionality, although POP3 has more features. POP3 is not upwardly compatible with POP2, either. Both can be run on the same system, where required, since they use different well-known ports. For our discussion, we will assume a POP3 client and server.

Figure 8.34 illustrates the interaction between a POP server and client. The user's mail is stored in a mailbox on the server. The user, who is the POP client, accesses the stored messages using POP. Replies or new mail messages generated by the client are sent to the server via SMTP. Mail sent from the client need not go to the server but can use another host to send mail through or send mail directly to the remote recipient. Under most circumstances, the POP server is also the mail relay for the clients. This simplifies administration of the system.

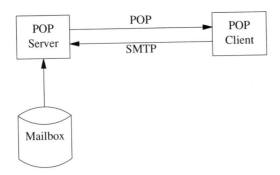

Figure 8.34 Post Office Protocol Client/Server.

POP is a simple lockstep protocol similar to SMTP. An example POP dialogue is shown in Fig. 8.35 and explained in part as follows:

• Line 1
The POP server displays a banner and invites the client to identify itself.

• Lines 2 – 5
The client then issues a USER and a PASS command and supplies a username and a password. The server responds with the an affirmative reply. An affirmative response always starts with a "+", while a negative response, indicating an error starts with a "-".

• Lines 6 – 7
The client then uses the STAT command to ask the status of the user's mailbox. The server replies with the number of messages in the mailbox (in this case, 1) and the total size (in bytes) (in this case, 246) of the messages in the mailbox.

• Lines 8 – 11
The client uses the LIST command to request a list of messages and their respective sizes. The server responds with an initial *+OK* response and then lists the ordinal number and size of each message. The server indicates the end of the dialogue with a line containing a single "." character.

• Lines 12 – 24
The client uses the RETR command to retrieve the first message. The message, including all headers, is sent to the user. The message is terminated with a line with a single "." character.

• Lines 25 – 26
The client uses the DELE command to request the server remove a message from the mailbox. The server deletes the message and returns an affirmative reply.

• Lines 27 – 28
The client uses the QUIT command to end the connection and the server issues a final sign-off message.

```
(1)   +OK akasha.tic.com POP server ready
(2)   USER poptest
(3)   +OK password required for poptest
(4)   PASS zzzzzzz
(5)   +OK maildrop has 1 message (246 octets)
(6)   STAT
(7)   +OK 1 246
(8)   LIST
(9)   +OK 1 message (246 octets)
(10)  1 246
(11)  .
(12)  RETR 1
(13)  +OK 246 octets
(14)  Received: by akasha.tic.com (5.65/akasha.m4.1.9)
(15)    id AA25658; Tue, 19 May 92 15:32:25 -0500
(16)  Message-Id: <9205192032.AA25658@akasha.tic.com>
(17)  To: poptest@tic.com
(18)  Subject: test
(19)  Date: Tue, 19 May 92 15:32:23 -0500
(20)  From: george@tic.com
(21)
(22)  Hi,
(23)  Are you coming to the office tomorrow?
(24)  .
(25)  DELE 1
(26)  +OK message 1 deleted (246 octets)
(27)  QUIT
(28)  +OK akasha.tic.com POP server signing off
```

Figure 8.35 POP Dialogue.

POP is a very simple, but effective, protocol designed to retrieve messages from a remote mailbox. While it's possible for an end user to use POP directly, the protocol is designed to be front-ended by a more user-friendly UA. The UA engages in the dialogue with the remote POP server and retrieves selected messages. The messages are transferred to the workstation and deleted on the server. The user can then read the messages without tying up any server resources.

MH POP Configuration. Sendmail does not directly support POP. Rather you must obtain POP server and client code and integrate it into your mail environment. A good POP server comes as part of the MH mail system [Rose & Romine 1985]. MH also supports a POP client for UNIX systems. See Appendix A for how to obtain a copy of the MH distribution. In MH the *inc* command reads a UNIX style mailbox and puts each message into a separate file. Other MH commands then manipulate the messages. The POP client extension is implemented as options to inc. Issuing the command

```
inc -host mailserver -user sally
```

tells *inc* to read a remote mailbox, found on host *mailserver*, rather than the local user's mailbox. Note that the name placed in the POP USER command will be *george*. If no *-user* argument is supplied, the remote user's name is the same as the local username.

MH POP also supports several authentication strategies. One strategy, which is the default, resembles R* authentication used by RLOGIN and RSH. We describe R* authentication in Chapter 9. It involves having the server maintains an access table of remote users. If the user is in the access table, the mailbox can be accessed without a password. An alternative strategy involves sending the password explicitly to the POP server. This process is enabled using the *-norpop* flag to the inc command. The inc program then prompts the user for a password, which is passed to the server as a part of the POP dialogue. Of the two, the default authentication is the better strategy because passwords are not sent over the network in cleartext.

The MH POP server keeps a separate set of mailboxes exclusively for use by a POP server. The POP mailboxes are kept in the directory */usr/spool/mail/pop* which should be the home directory of the *pop* user. The POP mailboxes are accessible only by the POP server and a special mailer, *spop,* that is used to direct incoming mail into each mailbox. The *spop* mailer runs setuid to *pop,* so it can write messages to each mailbox. The POP server runs as *root,* since it uses the POP well-known port.

An access file called *POP* also is kept in the POP mailbox directory. This file maps the names of a POP user to the name of each mailbox. It also maintains the set of remote access permissions. The file format is reminiscent of the */etc/passwd* file (fields are separated by colons), although the meaning of each field is different. Also, several fields are unused when this file is just used to authenticate remote POP access. Figure 8.36 shows an example of the access file, which is described as follows:

- Field 1
  The name of the POP user.

- Field 2
  Unused.

- Field 3
  The name of the mailbox in the */usr/spool/mail/pop* directory. Usually given the same name as the POP user.

- Field 4
  An encrypted access password. The password can only be changed by the POP administrator.

```
jill::jill:4JD0tJSy79Rxg::jill@jove.acct.acme.com::::0
fred::fred:8JD0sJSy89Rxg::fred@m1.eng.acme.com::::0
shirley::shirley:0jD0uJSy79Rxg::::::0
george::george:0JDisJfy79wxh::::::0
```

Figure 8.36 MH POP Access File.

- Field 5
  Unused.

- Field 6
  The names of valid remote users. Each remote user's names is written in domain
  syntax; if there is more than one user, their names are separated by commas. If a
  user is accessing the mailbox from a remote host and the name of the remote
  user and host both match, then access to the mailbox is granted without a password; otherwise a password that matches the encrypted password in the access
  file must be received from the POP client.

- Field 7 – 9
  Unused.

- Field 10
  A set of flags unused by POP and consequently set to 0.

A special sendmail mailer called *pop* is defined. The *pop* mailer places a mail
message in the proper POP mailbox. It is a very simple mailer; it's definition is
shown in Fig. 8.37. It performs no rewriting of mailer addresses. Rather, it simply takes a user argument, which is the POP user's name, and appends the message to the correct POP mailbox. The mailer program used to perform this task is
called *spop* which comes as part of the MH distribution.

  A sendmail gateway configuration file with POP support is shown in Fig.
8.38. Only a single line is changed from the the original gateway configuration
shown in Fig. 8.21. Mail with a pseudo-subdomain of *pop* is delivered using the

---

Figure 8.37 POP Mailer.

```
Mpop, P=/usr/local/lib/mh/spop, F=nsmFDM, S=17, R=27,
     A=spop $u
S17

S27
```

```
(1)   DVrelay.1.17
(2)   DDacme.com
(3)   Dj$w
(4)   DUspike
(5)   CX alice moby
(6)   DO outside.com
(7)   DMtcp

(8)   include(general.m4)
(9)   include(rules.m4)
(10)  include(local.m4)
(11)  include(uucp.m4)
(12)  include(tcp.m4)
(13)  include(zeropre.m4)

(14)  R$+<@$=X.uucp>  $#uucp   $@$2 $:$1<@$2.uucp>
(15)  R$+<@$-.uucp>   $#uucp   $@$O $:$1<@$2.uucp>
(16)  R$*<@pop.$D>$*  $#pop $@ pop $:$1
(17)  R$*<@$-.$D>$*   $#$M $@ $2.$D $:$1<@$2.$D>$3
(18)  R$*<@$*.$+>$*   $#$M $@ $2.$3   $: $1<@$2.$3>$4
(19)  R$+%$+          $@$>29$1@$2
(20)  R$+             $#local $:$1
```

Figure 8.38 Mail Gateway with POP Support.

---

pop mailer (line 16). For example with the POP access file shown in , mail to *jill@pop.acme.com* is delivered to the POP mailbox *jill*. Generally this address should not be used as a message address. A better address for general use is *jill@acme.com;* the alias database can be used to perform map this address to *jill@pop.acme.com*. The result is *jill@acme.com* resolves as the local address *jill,* and consequently an alias that maps *jill* to *jill@pop.acme.com* can be used to direct the mail to the POP mailbox. This procedure hides the delivery method, since the recipient mail address in the message header will simply be *jill@acme.com*. Note that each time a new POP user is added, the corresponding mapping must be added to the alias database. The alias file consequently becomes a mailer switch and the location of the valid list of POP users.

Figure 8.39 shows a client sendmail configuration when all mail is accessed using POP. Because there is no local mail delivery, all mail is sent to a relay host.

POP is a useful addition to any mail environment. It simplifies the mail administration and maintenance. A properly configured POP environment is transparent to the user. As we shall see in Chapter 10 when we discuss PC and Mac integration, it also is useful for integrating mail access to PCs and Macintoshes.

(1) DVsub.1.6
(2) DDacme.com
(3) Dj$w
(4) DMtcp
(5) DRmail_relay.$D

(6) include(general.m4)
(7) include(rules.m4)
(8) include(local.m4)
(9) include(tcp.m4)
(10) include(zeropre.m4)

(12) R$+ $#$M $@$R $:$1

Figure 8.39 POP Client.

Mailing Lists

A mailing list is a private redistribution list for mail messages. The list address receives a single copy of a message and then distributes copies to all members of the list, including the sender of the original message. A mailing list is usually set up so that a group of mail users who share a common interest can easily communicate.

Establishing a mailing list is relatively easy; the Internet has thousands of them. A few simple conventions apply, as follows:

1. The list itself should be given a mnemonic name and maintained on a single host. For example, a list about brushes, called *brushes,* could be established by the Acme Company. The list address therefore would be *brushes@acme.com*. This list name is entered in the alias database, as shown in Fig. 8.40, and each member of the list becomes a target of the alias. A message sent to

Figure 8.40 Mailing List Aliases.

brushes: sarah@acme.com, fred@acme.com, sarah@widget.com,
    bill@bigu.edu

owner-brushes: sarah@acme.com

brushes-request: sarah@acme.com

brushes@acme.com is distributed to the users in the *brushes* alias. For very large lists, using the *:include:* directive to place the list members in a separate file is prudent. The hashed alias file has a relatively small upper bound on the number of total characters that can be accommodated in an alias list.

2. As shown in the figure, several associated aliases also should be established, including one called *brushes-request*. Note that typically, the *brushes-request* alias would be used for list administration and usually points to the list maintainer. A user can request to be added or deleted from the mailing list by sending a message to this address, a convention that avoids administrative issues being sent to everyone on the list.

3. Another alias which should be created is *owner-brushes*. This is the owner of the list. Usually this alias would be aliased to the same mailbox as is the *brushes-request* alias. Any error messages generated by any user sending a message to the list is returned to *owner-brushes* and not to the user that sent the message. This return is sent to the *list owner* not to the originator of the message. This convention centralizes error message delivery to the person responsible for maintaining the list rather than to a list subscriber.

References

Allman 1983a.   Allman, Eric, *Sendmail — An Internetwork Mail Router*, 1983.

Allman 1983b.   Allman, Eric, *Sendmail Installation and Operations Guide*, 1983.

Butler et al. 1985.   Butler, M., Postel, John B., Chase, D., Goldberger, J., & Reynolds, Joyce, *Post Office Protocol: Version 2 (RFC937)*, February 1985.

Rose 1991.   Rose, Marshall T., *Post Office Protocol: Version 3 (RFC1225)*, May 1991.

Rose & Romine 1985.   Rose, Marshall T., & Romine, John L., *The Rand MH Message Handling System: User's Manual,* Department of Information and Computer Science, University of California, Irvine (November 1985).

CHAPTER 9

Other Network Services

In this chapter we discuss other useful services typically found on UNIX systems using TCP/IP. We first describe the two general service frameworks — inetd and Sun RPC — around which other services can run. Then we talk about specific services ranging from Sun's Network File System to distributed printing services. Finally, we discuss a server useful for allowing remote execution of selected UNIX commands with little authentication. Although by no means an exhaustive treatment of all these topics, the data in this chapter should give you enough information in order to set up the described services in a reasonable and reliable manner.

9.1 inetd — The Server's Server

The **Internet Daemon,** or **inetd,** is a superserver for other network servers. It multiplexes connection setup for a number of otherwise independent server processes. Before inetd was developed, each service had its own individual daemon process that created the server communication socket and listened for connection requests from clients. Most of the time a server simply waits for client requests; only when it accepts a request does a specific server code get invoked. However, a server process awaiting client requests still takes up process space, virtual memory, swap space, and other system resources. The resulting resource overhead can be considerable for even a small number of servers. Using inetd, a server needs to be running only when a client requests the specific service; thus the number of waiting servers is significantly reduced. Most traditional user-level client/server applications are configured to use inetd support.

Because much of the startup code is the same for every server, it makes a great deal of sense to have a single program handle all the common startup code and to invoke the specific server code when a client request is handled. This is what inetd does; that is, when a client requests a service, inetd determines which server the request is for and only then executes the appropriate server code.

Inetd also handles server housekeeping functions that otherwise must be coded as a part of every daemon. For example, detaching the server from its controlling *tty* and blocking signals are tedious and uninteresting details for UNIX network servers. Using inetd, however, each server's code is greatly simplified and it's a fairly simple matter to write a new server. Servers that run under inetd assume that the standard UNIX file descriptors — stdin, stdout, and stderr — are mapped to a single network socket connected to a remote client. In fact by using inetd, you can use many standard UNIX programs as simple servers.

How inetd Works

Inetd reads a list of services from its configuration file, which is usually */etc/inetd.conf,* an excerpt from which is shown in Fig. 9.1. Each line is divided into the following fields.

```
name type proto concur uid path params
```

• *name*
Gives the name of the service. The corresponding TCP or UDP port number is looked up in the */etc/services* file or via NIS.

• *type*
Indicates the type of connection desired. A two-way reliable byte stream is designated by the keyword *stream*. The *dgram* keyword in the last line indicates an unreliable packet- oriented service.

• *proto*
Gives the transport protocol — either *tcp* or *udp* used by the connection. The *type* field is always *stream* when TCP transport is used and *dgram* when UDP transport is used. Separating the type of connection from the the transport protocol allows for greater flexibility in the choice of protocols.

• *concur*
Flags whether concurrent connections are allowed for a specific service. If this

---

Figure 9.1 Example inetd.conf File.

```
ftp     stream tcp nowait root /usr/etc/in.ftpd in.ftpd
telnet  stream tcp nowait root /usr/etc/in.telnetd in.telnetd
login   stream tcp nowait root /usr/etc/in.rlogind in.rlogind
comsat  dgram  udp wait    root /usr/etc/in.comsat in.comsat
echo    stream tcp nowait root internal
echo    dgram  udp wait    root internal
```

field contains the *wait* keyword, then connections are handled one at a time. Further requests for the same service are blocked until the active connection has closed. The *wait* flag serializes access to a specific service. For example, a database transaction server could use it to ensure serialization of updates to an online database shared by many clients. The *nowait* keyword on the other hand allows multiple concurrent connections. In this case, inetd continues to field additional requests for the same service.

• *uid*

Gives the server's userid. Inetd runs as *root*. Most servers will fork and also run as *root,* although for security reasons some should run under another userid. For example, the *tftp* server is run usually as the unprivileged user *nobody* since it has no authentication and it would be an enormous security hole for it to run as *root*.

• *path*

Indicates the pathname of the server program. This must be an absolute pathname. The special name *internal* (see lines 5 and 6) means the request is handled by inetd itself. Internal services are simple services that require very little processing time, so executing a separate process to handle them would add unnecessary overhead. Internal services are hard-coded into inetd. Therefore unless you have the sources to inetd, you can't add any internal services.

• *params*

Shows the argument list passed to the server when it is executed. With this list, you can tailor the behavior of a given server.

In Fig. 9.2 we see how inetd works.

1. Inetd reads its configuration file.

2. Inetd creates a UDP or TCP socket for each service listed.

3. Inetd then binds the socket to the host's own interface address and to the service port number and for each stream socket, a service queue length is set with the *listen()* system call.

4. Inetd does a *select()* call on all the socket file descriptors. *select()* lets you synchronously multiplex several I/O descriptors. It blocks and waits for I/O activity on the descriptors, that is, either connection requests on the stream descriptors or UDP messages on the datagram descriptors. For a stream socket, inetd unblocks when a remote client makes a *connect()* call and the TCP initial handshake successfully completes. For a datagram socket, a remote client sending a datagram to the socket address will unblock the corresponding socket descriptor.

5. For each socket with I/O activity, inetd then determines the socket type.

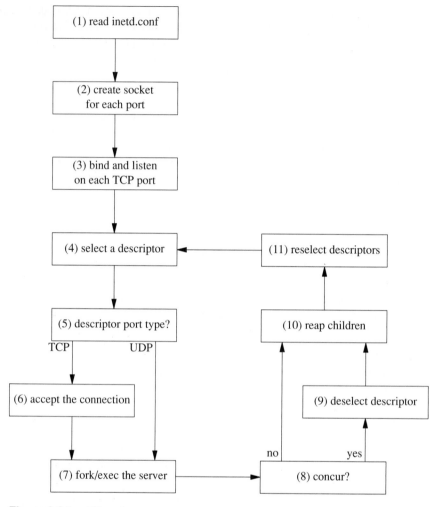

Figure 9.2 inetd Flowchart.

6. If the socket is a stream connection, inetd then does an *accept()* on the selected socket descriptor, which returns a socket descriptor for the newly established connection.

7. Inetd then forks and executes the real server for the service. Note that even if the service is internally handled by inetd, a copy of inetd is created to handle the service.

8. The *concur* parameter is examined for each selected socket descriptor.

9. If the parameter is *wait,* inetd deselects the socket descriptor from the *select()* list for that service, resulting in subsequent additional connections or UDP messages being rejected. If the parameter is *nowait,* the original socket is not

deselected and inetd continues to accept additional requests for the service from the original socket.

10. When a server completes, a SIGCLD signal is generated and inetd traps this signal and does a *wait( )* to collect the completed child processes.

11. Inetd then reselects the socket descriptors for any non-concurrent servers and returns to Step 4.

Inetd is a very useful framework for installing new services. Because much of the normal housekeeping code is handled by inetd itself, it's relatively easy to write new servers that run under inetd control, such as the Simple Client/Server we discuss later on in this chapter.

The following example shows how you can add the UNIX *date* command to run under inetd. Although running this command duplicates the functionality of the internal *daytime* service, we want to show how to add a simple server to inetd. First add the following line to the */etc/services* file:

```
unixdate   5001/tcp  # unix date command server
```

Now add the following line to the */etc/inetd.conf* file:

```
unixdate   stream  tcp  nowait nobody  /bin/date  date
```

Now send a hangup signal to the running superserver. Doing this causes inetd to reread */etc/inetd.conf* and reinitialize itself. To test the new service, connect to it as follows using the *telnet* program that has the port name of the new service as its second argument:

```
% telnet akasha.tic.com unixdate
Trying 192.135.128.129 ...
Connected to akasha.tic.com.
Escape character is '^]'.
Sat Jan 18 19:42:47 CST 1992
Connection closed by foreign host.
```

Obviously, using *telnet* as the client process is not ideal, but this example demonstrates the ease with which you can add new services using the inetd facility.

When to Use and Not Use inetd

Inetd is ideally suited for servers that field multiple independent client requests where each client is served by a separate copy of the server. For example, an FTP or TELNET server can run well under inetd control since each separate connection is independent of all other connections. However, servers that have significant initial startup costs are less ideally suited to run under inetd, since the startup overhead is excessive. In this case, it's probably better to run an independent server. The *sendmail* daemon is a good example of this type of service.

Servers that maintain state between connections won't work under inetd, unless the state changes are written out to a file and read back in by the next server invocation. For example, the DNS server shouldn't be run under inetd control because it caches remote resource records that otherwise would be lost by using inetd to start the server.

However, for most services inetd is an ideal framework. It's also a convenient management tool; a glance at the *inetd.conf* file gives you an excellent idea of the services currently active on your system.

9.2   Sun Remote Procedure Call

The Sun **remote procedure call (RPC)** protocol is a general way for programs to execute services found on a remote host. Unlike services run under inetd control, such as TELNET or FTP, an RPC server implements a programmatic functional interface [Sun 1991a]. Thus remote services can be imbedded as function calls within an application. From the client point of view, an RPC function is identical to a normal function, except the function is executed by a remote server. Hence RPC is a powerful and useful tool for it extends the notion of a service from being just a single monolithic program to being a set of related function calls. The NIS service discussed in Chapter 6 uses RPC as its underlying framework.

RPC Basics

Data Representation. RPC can use either UDP or TCP transport to pass function arguments and results between a server and a client. The server executes the function using the passed arguments as parameters and returns the function result to the client. Conceptually the idea is very simple. However, the client and server might be different machine types with different native representations for the parameters and result. To work properly in a heterogeneous environment, the client and server must agree upon a common representation for arguments and result. For example, in Fig. 9.3 an integer 1 is shown stored internally on both a DEC VAX and a Sun SPARC. Because each has a different native data

Figure 9.3 Byte Order.

Sun SPARC Integer = 1

00	00	00	01

VAX Integer = 1

01	00	00	00

representation, the VAX native integer representation passed unchanged to the SPARC is interpreted as 16,777,216! RPC avoids this problem by using a common **external data representation (XDR)** to represent a function's arguments and result. XDR defines a common format for integer numbers, character strings, floating point numbers, and other common data types. RPC converts all function parameters and results into this common format for transport over the network. For example, the format for a 32-bit integer using XDR happens to be the native Sun SPARC format, commonly called **big-endian.** Big-endian means the integer is stored from high-order to low-order byte in memory. A VAX on the other hand is a **little-endian** machine, that is, it stores an integer in memory from low-order to high-order byte. A VAX using RPC reads an integer off the network as a bytestream from high-order to low-order byte but reverses the byte order when it stores the bytestream as an integer number.

Table 9.1 shows the XDR representations for some common data types. XDR types are always multiples of 4 bytes. Standardizing this simplifies the encoding and decoding, although with some loss of storage efficiency. Complex types also can be encoded, as the example character string in Table 9.1 demonstrates. Here the encoding is a length field of 4 bytes followed by the character string padded to an even multiple of 4 bytes. The 0 byte at the end of the example is not a C string terminator but padding that is not interpreted by the receiving system. In a more complex example, also shown in Fig. 9.4, an entire C structure is encoded. To interpret a structure properly, the receiving system must know beforehand the structure type. To help with decoding complex structures, XDR routines to serialize pointers and encode them into their unique XDR representation are included as a part of almost all RPC packages.

Client/Server Communication. An RPC client calls a stub function like it would any other C function from within an application using the RPC service. This function transforms RPC arguments into the common XDR format and transmits the values to the RPC server. If a client uses TCP, retransmission of lost messages is unnecessary, although TCP does require state to be maintained for each client connection. Consequently a server crash in the middle of an RPC call while using TCP transport requires the connection to be reestablished when the server

---

Table 9.1 XDR Types.

Type	Length (bytes)	Example (hexadecimal)
boolean	4	1 = 00000001
integer	4	102 = 00000066
float	4	1.0 = 3f800000
char	4	'A' = 00000041
char *	variable	"abcdefg" = 0x00000007616263646566700

Structure Definition and Value:

```
struct tstruct {
    float x;
    int i;
    char *c;
};

struct tstruct z[3] = {
    1.0,  5,  "abc",
    5.1,  234,  "xyz",
    34.8,  23,  "hello"
};
```

XDR Encoding (hexadecimal)

```
00000003
 len

3f800000 00000005 00000003 61626300
 z[0].x   z[0].i           z[0].c

40a33333 000000ea 00000003 78797a00
 z[1].x   z[1].i           z[1].c

420b3333 00000017 00000005 68656c6c 6f000000
 z[2].x   z[2].i           z[2].c
```

Figure 9.4 Complex XDR Encoding.

---

comes back up. However, if a client uses UDP then lost messages must be handled by the client code. An RPC client using UDP transport can simply retransmit the request until the server responds. Because the server's response can be lost due to network failure, RPC functions that use UDP must be idempotent for correctness; that is, a function can be called repeatedly without changing the function value or without affecting the state of the server. For example, a function using RPC that updates a remote database entry — say by incrementing a value by 1 — is not idempotent because if the function call is repeated, the database entry is updated twice, which is incorrect. Generally most RPC functions using UDP are simple lookup functions that, called repeatedly, return the same value.

Service Identification. An RPC service is organized as a set of one or more function calls. Each service is assigned a unique service number. If you create a service that is to be used globally, then you must get a service number assigned from Sun Microsystems. On the other hand, if the service is only used locally, then the service number need only be unique within your organization. Each service also has a version number. This lets different versions of the same service run at the same time for backward compatibility. Each service function is assigned a unique function number. Thus a specific RPC function is completely identified by the triple *<service, version, function>*. An RPC client includes this triple in every call to an RPC server, whereupon the server executes the specific function within a specific service version for the client.

The Portmapper

Unlike other TCP/IP services, which advertise at a well-known-port, an RPC server dynamically binds itself to an unused UDP and/or TCP port. That port number is registered with the RPC **portmapper** on the host on which the service is offered. A portmapper is the server that acts as a clearinghouse for RPC services. It registers and keeps track of the ports associated with every RPC service and version running on the host system. Because it registers all RPC services, the portmapper is critical for RPC to function properly. The portmapper must be started up before any other RPC services. If the portmapper crashes, RPC services cease to function on that machine.

An RPC client that wants to use a particular RPC service on a particular host sends a request to the portmapper on that host asking for a port number for a service and version. (The portmapper always listens for requests on well-known port 111, so every client knows where to communicate with it.) The portmapper returns the port number of the port on which the specific RPC server is waiting for requests. The client then communicates directly with the RPC server using that port number. The portmapper also supports indirect RPC function calls. An indirect function call asks the portmapper to forward the request to the server instead of returning the server port number. The real server then answers the request, and the client picks up the server port number from the reply and uses that information for further communication with the server.

To list those services registered with the portmapper, use the *rpcinfo* command with the *-p* option. This also serves as a check to see that the portmapper is actually running. An example output from this command is shown in Fig. 9.5 and explained next.

- Columns 1
  The program number. Displayed in decimal for each service.

- Column 2
  Version number of the service.

- Column 3
  The protocol used by each service.

- Column 4
  The port number on which each service is listening for client requests. For most

```
% rpcinfo -p
   program vers proto    port
   100000   2   tcp      111   portmapper
   100000   2   udp      111   portmapper
   100003   2   udp     2049   nfs
   100005   1   udp      715   mountd
   100005   2   udp      715   mountd
   100005   1   tcp      718   mountd
   100005   2   tcp      718   mountd
   100001   2   udp     1041   rstatd
   100001   3   udp     1041   rstatd
   100001   4   udp     1041   rstatd
      .
      .
      .
```

Figure 9.5 rpcinfo Output.

services, both TCP and UDP are used. If so, each is listed in a separate line.

• Column 5
  The name of the service.

The rpcinfo command may also be used to check the status of a remote portmapper by adding a hostname as an argument to the command as in:

```
% rpcinfo -p beast.tic.com
```

You may also check to see if specific services have registered on a remote host, by issuing the following command:

```
% rpcinfo -u beast.tic.com ypbind 2
program 100007 version 2 ready and waiting
```

In this case the status of the *ypbind* service is checked. The service is called on a UDP port (the -u flag). For a TCP based service use a -t flag. The arguments to rpcinfo are the name of the remote host, the name of the service, and the version number. You may substitute IP addresses for host names and RPC program numbers for program names.
    You may also use rpcinfo to send a broadcast request, the result of which is a listing of all servers that respond. For example, to find all NIS servers on the local network, use the following command.

```
% rpcinfo -b ypserv 2
```

```
beast.tic.com 192.135.128.130
akasha.tic.com 192.135.128.129
```

This example lists the names and IP addresses of the responding NIS servers.

Some systems allow RPC servers to be started up using inetd. In this case, the service port registration also is handled by inetd. As with traditional servers, this procedure simplifies the RPC server code. In this case each line of the *inetd.conf* file is divided into the following fields:

```
prog/ver type proto concur uid path params
```

Here the syntax is similar to that involved with starting up a standard TCP/IP service. The parameters are as follows:

- *prog/ver*
  The name of the RPC service whose mapping to the service number is found in the file */etc/rpc*. The number after the "/" indicates the version number of the service to run. For compatibility, multiple version numbers can be run concurrently. A single server that supports multiple versions can be specified by a range of numbers separated with a dash.

- *type*
  The type of connection desired — either *stream or dgram*.

- *proto*
  The transport protocol to use. For RPC services, it's *rpc/* followed by either *udp* or *tcp*. The *rpc* keyword flags the entry as an RPC service.

The remaining parameters are identical to a normal inetd service entry.

9.3   Sun Network File System

The Sun **Network File System (NFS)** is a popular remote filesystem that is widely implemented and supported on most networked UNIX systems [Sun 1991b]. An NFS implementation usually is built into the UNIX kernel, although this is not an absolute requirement, and atop the Sun RPC/XDR protocols. The normal internal operating system functions to read and write filesystem blocks are mapped to RPC calls and sent to an NFS server, where the actual disk reads/writes are performed. This server then returns the filesystem blocks requested, as the result of the client RPC requests.

NFS is a **stateless** filesystem; that is, each read/write is considered an atomic operation and therefore not dependent on a previous NFS operation for consistency. This means that a read or write call can be repeated without causing filesystem corruption. It also means that a server can crash and reboot and yet continue to field NFS requests from where it left off before the crash. The client machine simply continues to make NFS requests and waits for the server to respond.

Because of NFS's statelessness, normal UNIX filesystem semantics are not completely implemented under NFS. For example, NFS doesn't support file locking, since locking a file means both the server and the client must remember the lock is in place. Also it doesn't support access to UNIX devices, since device access in general must also preserve some state.

NFS Mounting Service

Access to an NFS filesystem is handled by an extension to the normal UNIX filesystem mounting facility. An NFS filesystem can be mounted like any normal UNIX filesystem. An NFS server advertises local filesystems that it allows to be remotely mounted. These filesystems are listed in the file */etc/exports*. Unlike conventional UNIX filesystems, which are mapped one-to-one with physical disk partitions, the NFS server allows any arbitrary directory tree to be remotely mounted. This gives a much finer degree of control over what files are accessible from a remote client.

An example */etc/exports* file is shown in Fig. 9.6. As this file indicates, the server allows the directory tree under */usr/src, /export/home/src.local,* and */usr/spool/uucppublic* to be remotely mounted read/write (the *-rw* flag) on the remote host *beast.tic.com.* The directory */usr/share/lib* can be remotely mounted by any remote host but can be read only by a client (the *-ro* flag). Care must be taken to ensure that directory trees with sensitive data are not placed in */etc/exports* without some access limitations. Otherwise the directory tree can be accessed from any remote host.

The only export restriction is if a directory is exported then neither its parent directory nor any of its own subdirectories can also be exported, if those directories are a part of the same local filesystem. However, peer directories within the same filesystem may be exported.

On system startup, the *exportfs* command or its equivalent is run to update the internal export table kept in the file */etc/xtab,* which is similar to the */etc/mtab* file. Next the system starts the mount daemon (usually named *mountd* or *rpc.mountd*) and the NFS daemons (*biod* and *nfsd*). While biod runs on an NFS client and handles filesystem buffering, nfsd handles client filesystem requests that are run only

---

Figure 9.6 Example /etc/exports File.

```
/usr/src -rw=beast.tic.com
/export/home/src.local -rw=beast.tic.com
/usr/spool/uucppublic -rw=beast.tic.com
/usr/share/lib -ro
```

on NFS servers. Because more than one nfsd server is started, filesystem requests can be multiplexed. Four to eight daemons seem to be a good number for most systems; however, if your server is heavily loaded, starting more concurrent daemons might be called for.

An NFS client adds NFS filesystems to its own *etc/fstab* file and then mounts them using the normal UNIX mount request. An example *etc/fstab* file is shown in Fig. 9.7. For an NFS-mounted filesystem, the UNIX device name is replaced with a *host:pathname* pair that identifies the directory on the remote host to be mounted. Following this is the directory mount point on the local system. The next field tells the type of file system (nfs). Finally various mount options for the file are given. In this case, the mount is a hard mount and the file system is mounted read/write; however, a keyboard interrupt will terminate an NFS request that is hung because of a nonresponsive server. The final two fields indicate that backup schedules should be ignored and the filesystem should not be checked with the *fsck* utility before it is mounted (*fsck* is meaningless for an NFS filesystem).

The mount program includes options that provide for mounting only filesystems of a particular type. Usually, it's a good idea to mount all local filesystems and then mount NFS filesystems after other network services are set up. Note that naming services (either DNS or NIS) should be running before mounting remote filesystems.

NFS allows a filesystem to be mounted either *soft* or *hard*. A hard-mounted filesystem will retry requests indefinitely, while a soft-mounted filesystem terminates the request after retrying a specified number of times. Generally, any filesystem that is mounted read/write should be hard-mounted in order to avoid potential file corruption due to incomplete writes. Hard mounting ensures that a filesystem write request will eventually complete and that all write calls within an application complete in order.

The following example illustrates what can happen when a filesystem is soft-mounted read/write. Suppose an application is writing to a soft-mounted NFS filesystem and the server is intermittently dropping responses due to a faulty network connection. The application is writing sequential blocks to an open file on the soft-mounted partition. When the application does a *write()*, it blocks waiting for the NFS server to respond. When the server subsequently fails to respond after the client retries the write request, it returns a failure status and the *write()* call returns without writing to the file. Consequently if the application fails to

---

Figure 9.7 Example fstab.

```
/dev/sd0a   /       4.2 rw 1 1
/dev/sd0g   /usr    4.2 rw 1 2
/dev/sd1c   /export/home    4.2 rw 1 2
beast.tic.com:/u/srcstuff /usr/src nfs hard,intr,rw 0 0
```

check the return code of the *write()*, then it believes the write succeeded when in fact it did not. Believing the request succeeded, it goes on to write the next file block. Suppose this request succeeds and subsequent write requests fail or succeed intermittently. The remote file is left in a corrupted state, even though the application completed normally. This problem can be alleviated if the application checks each *write()* to ensure it completed properly. Unfortunately, few applications do this. The only way to avoid this problem is to hard-mount writeable NFS filesystems.

However, hard-mounted file systems are not without their problems. One is that NFS requests block until they succeed. If a server crashes, the request will be retried continually until the server comes back online. While doing this makes the filesystem very robust, it can be extremely annoying to a user who, when the server crashes, is simply displaying a remote file. All the user wants to do is terminate the display and go on to something else. Unfortunately, the display process is waiting for a read call to complete that is not interruptable. The only way out is either to kill the process from another terminal or window or to reboot the client. Fortunately, the NFS *intr* option allows keyboard interrupts to terminate the read or write request of a hard-mounted filesystem. This convenience allows the user to go on with some other work while the server reboots.

Filesystem Organization

NFS is very flexible because it imposes no restrictions on which directories can be mounted across the network. Filesystems can be cross-mounted between many machines, and a machine can be both an NFS server and client at the same time. As a result, you can easily create a tangled web of interdependent machines in which clients of one filesystem are servers for others. An NFS filesystem can even be mounted within another NFS filesystem. The only real restriction NFS imposes is that an NFS-mounted filesystem can access only files within the mounted subdirectory of the remote filesystem and those within the same remote filesystem; that is, an NFS mount won't cross a remote filesystem's mount points.

For example, suppose */usr* and */usr/src* are local filesystems on host *akasha.tic.com;* that is, */usr/src* is the local mount point for another physical filesystem. Now if */usr* is remotely mounted on host *beast.tic.com,* only the files physically stored within the /usr filesystem are accessible from *beast.tic.com.* The directory */usr/src* will appear as an empty directory; however, it's possible to mount *akasha:/usr/src* onto *beast.tic.com:/usr/src.* In this case, a reference to */usr/src* on *beast* will refer to *akasha:/usr/src.*

Heavily interconnected NFS-mounted filesystems can create administrative nightmares. Cross-mounted filesystems easily lead to deadlock situations in which servers freeze up and can't be rebooted. For example, suppose machine A NFS mounts *B:/u* as */b/u* and machine B mounts *A:/v* as */a/v.* The filesystems are both hard-mounted, which means mount requests will retry until they succeed. Now suppose the network interface on A fails. Subsequently a user on B tries to access */a/v/zzz*, but the request hangs. Thinking something is wrong with the machine the user reboots B. At first everything appears normal; however, the reboot hangs on the mount for /a/v. Further, machine B's reboot sequence has the NFS mount daemon start after it mounts all local and remote filesystems. Meanwhile machine A is fixed and rebooted. Now because the mount daemon is not running on B, machine A's attempt to reboot hangs while trying to mount /b/u. Consequently, both machines will wait indefinitely for the other machine to complete its reboot.

This example illustrates a classic deadlock. The only way to break it is to bring both machines down to single-user mode and then fix the startup scripts. The specific problem here arose because the local mount daemon was started after the remote filesystems were mounted; it should in fact be done just the opposite, that is, the local mount daemon should be started before remote filesystems are mounted. Another way to handle this problem is to have the filesystem mount requests handled in the background. The facility to do this can be added as an option to each /etc/fstab entry.

While most deadlock conditions can be identified and fixed, it nevertheless is administratively difficult to manage cross-mounted filesystems. Usually, it's best to mount NFS filesystems in a hierarchical manner. NFS works best and can be administered efficiently when filesystems are mounted from just a few servers onto many clients.

For example, if you want users to have access to their home directory from any workstation on the network, place the user filesystems on one or more server machines and NFS mount them on all workstations. If you have more than one server, you might want to cross-mount the user filesystems between the servers, taking care to avoid filesystem mount deadlocks. Each user workstation in this environment has minimal disk space for *swap,* the *root,* and *usr* filesystem. User files are not kept on the workstations at all. If a central password file is kept using NIS, then users can log in to any workstation and to their own files. The mounts are arranged so the view of the user filespace is identical regardless of the workstation the user logs into. This scheme is much better than having user directories placed on individual workstations and the various directories cross-mounted on all workstations. Also file system backup is easier to manage, since user files are on just a few systems. Its disadvantage is that if the server goes down, then users cannot access their files. Given the high reliability of modern hardware, this is usually a minor inconvenience unless your application demands near 100% reliability.

If each user always uses a single dedicated workstation, then user files can be kept on the individual workstations and the fileservers can be used to access common files only. However, if you still want a common view of the overall user filesystem, techniques such as automounting can be used when a user needs to access another user's files. Automounting, discussed later in this section, enables you to avoid having unused filesystems remotely mounted when not in use. Using automounting presents complications, however, since in a large user community the degree of cross-mounting can be considerable.

NFS in a WAN

NFS can be and is used in a WAN environment. When using NFS across a WAN, care must be taken to set the NFS retransmission timers appropriately. NFS is a stateless protocol and uses UDP transport to send and receive RPC requests and responses. However, UDP is unreliable; if no reply to a message is received within a set period of time. NFS itself handles message loss by retransmitting requests. The normal NFS timeout is 0.7 seconds. If on a WAN the mean packet round-trip time is greater than this value, then a client will end up needlessly retransmitting requests to the server. On a low bandwidth or high latency link, these unnecessary retransmissions can quickly lead to network congestion. This in turn leads to more delay and a subsequent further drop in performance. You can solve this problem by increasing the timeout parameter to a value that is more reasonable based on your network latency. By using the *ping* program, you can obtain a rough guess of the average round-trip time and then set the timeout value to be slightly above this amount for NFS. Note, setting the value too high also can lead to performance degradation. This occurs because when a client request is really dropped, the client will wait for the specified period of time before retransmitting the request. The result is equally slow performance, especially across a network that experiences frequent packet lossage.

Another problem with using NFS in a WAN environment is userid/groupid mapping consistency. Although NIS can be used to control userid/groupid mappings across a WAN environment, in many cases this is impractical. If the NFS filesystem is used by only a few users, you will need to ensure the userid/groupid mappings are consistent between the server and client machines.

Authentication and Security

Most NFS implementations have limited user authentication. The most commonly used authentication scheme validates access based upon UNIX groupids and userids. Each NFS request passes the userid and groupids of the end-user making the filesystem request. This emulates the standard UNIX filesystem call semantics. Note that this authentication scheme is very convenient, but very weak. Anybody with the ability to inject their own packets onto the network can easily spoof this scheme. However, in most environments, it is quite adequate.

Generally speaking, this authentication scheme means all systems that share files must use the same user and group ids. Otherwise user and group id mismatches can occur that can seriously compromise filesystem security. For example, suppose Sally on machine A has a userid of 200 and Bob on machine B also has userid 200. If some of Bob's files are mounted on machine A, then Sally can access those files using NFS. This is very likely not what is desired.

A good policy to adopt is always to share a common set of userids and groupids among a set of machines that share files using NFS. However, accomplishing this can be complicated because all systems don't use the same userid/groupid scheme as a default. As a result, you may need to locally modify every new system to conform to your userid/groupid scheme.

Automounting

NFS filesystems are most often mounted when a client machine is booted. This is appropriate for frequently used filesystems. For those used infrequently, the **automounter** enables mounts to be performed in a more dynamic manner. The automounter is a daemon process that to the local system looks like a remote NFS server. File requests are passed to the automounter daemon just like standard NFS file requests are. When the automounter intercepts the first file request, it then mounts the filesystem in a known location and creates symbolic links to the mounted filesystem. Additional requests for the file are handled using standard filesystem calls. After a period of filesystem inactivity (usually 5 minutes), the automounter unmounts the remote filesystem.

The automounter also allows the same filesystem to appear to be dynamically mounted in several places simultaneously. This is done using symbolic links. Suppose user A accesses a remote filesystem as */u/homea/remote* and user B accesses the same filesystem as */u/homeb/remote*. Note that the *remote* subdirectory is the mount point for the remote filesystem for both user A and B. When user A reads a file in the automounted directory */u/homea/remote,* the automounter daemon handles the request and mounts the filesystem as */tmp-mnt/remote*. A symbolic link */u/homea/remote* is created that points to */tmp-mnt/remote*. Then when user B accesses a file in */u/homeb/remote,* the automounter handles this request by simply creating another symbolic link /u/homeb/remote that points to */tmp-mnt/remote*. Note that the filesystem is only mounted once, which saves system resources.

The automounter also allows a limited form of filesystem load balancing. The target of an automounted filesystem might be on more than one remote host; the first host to respond has its remote filesystem mounted. This works only for read-only filesystems, however. In the event of a system crash, a mounted filesystem can't be unmounted and the alternative filesystem mounted in its place.

9.4   Line Printer System

Next to electronic mail, perhaps the most user-desired network service is the one that makes remote printers accessible on a network. UNIX systems fortunately have extensive remote print spooling support using either the BSD or System V print spoolers. The most common printer interface and a standard for the Internet community is the BSD line printer spooler. The line printer spooler protocol supports local and remote queuing of print job requests and automatic transfer of spooled jobs from a client system to a remote print server. The spooler is a peer-to-peer system and machines may share all printers on the network. We shall now describe in detail the BSD print spooling protocol and how to set it up to build a robust print-sharing environment.

BSD Print Spooler Protocol

The print spooler is a daemon process, */usr/lib/lpd*, that listens for print requests. For remote requests, it listens on TCP port 515; for local requests, it listens on a UNIX domain socket named */dev/printer.* A very simple lockstep protocol that is fully described in [McLaughlin 1990], the spooler is run on any machine that will accept printer requests. It's started up in one of the startup scripts. Note, however, that it can't be started using *inetd,* since it also listens on the local UNIX domain port and reads the */etc/printcap* printer description file. (We describe this file in the next subsection).

Every machine that wants to share local or remote printers must have a print spooler running. The spooler accepts local and remote requests and places them in a queue. Each request comprises two files — a control file and the actual printer input. The print spooler examines the control file of each queued print request and determines whether the destination printer is local or remote. If the printer is local, the job is sent directly to the local printer. The print file might also be sent through a filter program to do special formatting or to convert the data to the specific printer format (for example, for PostScript printers, from ASCII text to PostScript). If the printer is remote, the local spooler contacts the spooler on the remote system and transfers the print job to the remote host to which the printer is attached. Figure 9.8 shows the data flow in this system.

Print jobs are spooled both locally and remotely; therefore if a remote host is down, the job is preserved in the local queue. The spooler retries sending remote jobs on a periodic basis.

Figure 9.8 Remote Printing Data Flow.

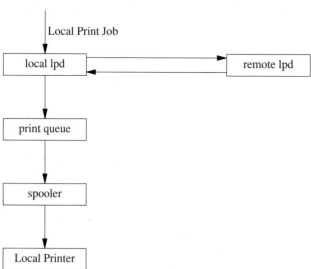

```
(1)    lp0|lp|0|lw|peaches|Apple Laserwriter:\
(2)         br#9600:\
(3)         lp=/dev/tty10:\
(4)         sd=/usr/spool/lp0:\
(5)         sh:\
(6)         tr=^D:\
(7)         lf=/usr/adm/lpd-errs:\
(8)         if=/usr/lib/lpdfilters/ttops:\
(9)         of=/usr/lib/lpdfilters/ttops:\
(10)        rw:\
(11)        fc#070:\
(12)        fs#0302:\
(13)        xc#0177777:\
(14)        xs:#040400
```

Figure 9.9 A Printcap Entry.

Printer Description Using Printcap

The */etc/printcap* file fully describes the printers attached to a particular host and the remote printers that are accessible from a particular host. A printcap entry describes a printer's configuration using a series of entries called **capabilities,** each of which is terminated by a colon (":"). The first capability is the name of the printer. Alternate names can be placed between vertical bars ("|"). Other capabilities are described using either keyletter=value pairs or a boolean switch that is true if the keyletter appears in the entry. Numeric values are prefixed with a pound sign ("#"). Continuation from one line to the next is handled by placing a backslash at the end of each line. Whitespace in a printcap entry is ignored. Figure 9.9 shows an example of a fully described printcap entry for a local printer, in this case an Apple Laserwriter.

- Line 1
  The name of the printer is "lp0" with alternative names "lp", "0", "lw", and "peaches". The string between the last "|" and the ":" is a description of the printer.

- Line 2
  The printer operates at 9600 bps.

- Line 3
  The printer device is */dev/tty10*.

- Line 4
  The printer spool directory is */usr/spool/lp0*.

• Line 5

The header page is suppressed when printing on this printer.

• Line 6

The final string to print when the queue is empty is an EOT character (CNTRL-D).

• Line 7

Errors are sent to the logfile */usr/adm/lpd-errs*.

• Line 8 – 9

The input and output filters that translate plain ASCII to PostScript is /usr/lib/lpdfilters/ttops. The name of this program will vary depending on your system.

• Line 10

The printer device is opened for both reading and writing.

• Line 11 – 14

Finally various serial device bits are set or cleared depending on what the attached printer requires. Note that the keywords ending in "c" clear bits, while those ending in "s" set bits. The "fs" and "fc" keywords set or clear the bits of the tty device "flags" field, while the "xs" and "xc" keywords set or clear the bits of the tty device "local" mode.

When a job is queued for this printer, the print job is placed in the directory */usr/spool/lp0*. Also placed in that directory is a control file, which the printer spooler uses along with the printcap description in order to send the job to the printer.

A remote printer is described similarly but its description is much simpler because the printer needs only a name, a local spool directory, and the names of the remote host and printer to print on; all the description about devices and filters isn't needed. Figure 9.10 shows a remote printcap entry on host *akasha.tic.com*.

• Line 1

Here the printer name, known locally, is *peaches* or *lp*.

Figure 9.10 A Remote Printcap Entry.

```
(1)  peaches|lp|line printer on beast:\
(2)       rp=peaches:\
(3)       rm=beast.tic.com:\
(4)       sd=/usr/spool/peaches:\
(5)       lf=/usr/adm/lpd-errs
```

- Line 2

  The name of the remote printer (on *beast.tic.com*) is also *peaches*.

- Line 3

  The remote machine with the printer is *beast.tic.com*.

- Line 4

  The local spool directory is */usr/spool/peaches*.

- Line 5

  Errors generated by the local print spooler are written to the file */usr/adm/lpd-errs*.

A print job received for the printer *peaches* is spooled locally and then sent to the print spooler on *beast.tic.com,* where it will be finally printed.

Remote Printer Access

Access to remote printers is controlled by two methods, as follows:

1. A host that sends a print request to a remote host must appear in */etc/hosts.equiv.* Or the hostname can appear in */etc/lpd.equiv.* By placing the hostname in this file, rather than */etc/hosts.equiv,* remote access to printers is allowed, but remote login or command access without a password is denied.

2. If the *rs* capability appears in a printers printcap entry, then only users with accounts on the machine to which the printer is attached can print on that printer.

Printcap Organization

Much like NFS, the line printer system can allow a tangled web of printers to exist and to be accessible on a large network. The result is likely to be an administrative nightmare, for each machine must have a separate printcap file (although some UNIX systems allow printcap entries to be kept in an NIS database, an arrangement that simplifies administration). Because printers don't change very often, a fairly simple scheme can be devised to organize printcap files on multiple hosts. There must be a reasonable printer naming scheme. Printer names should be unique across the network. For example, you could name printers lp0, lp1, etc. More mnemonic names can also be used; PostScript printers could be called ps0, ps1, etc., while true line printers can be named lp0, lp1, etc. Again, the idea is to give all printers unique names. Printer spool files should follow the same naming convention.

Another good approach is to give hosts with printers well-known aliases that describe the printers on that particular host; for example, the machine with ps0 on it could have an alias *ps0.tic.com.* Therefore if the printer moves, only the alias needs to be changed in order to point at the right host. Using the above rules, a generic remote printcap entry can be built into the printcap file for each printer.

For example, following the above conventions, the printer *lp0* would have the generic printcap entry of:

```
lp0|lineprinter 0:\
    rm=lp0.tic.com:\
    rp=lp0:\
    sd=/usr/spool/lp0:\
    lf=/usr/adm/lpd-errs:
```

Other printcap entries for other printers follow the same general format.

For all machines, you can build the printcap file using a simple shell script. Accordingly a default printer could be specified by adding an "lp" keyword to the appropriate printcap entry. Figure 9.11 shows a script that generates a printcap file and also creates the spool directories for each printer. This script should be run as part of a new system installation procedure. The conventions used by this script are as follows:

1. Local printer descriptions are maintained in the */etc/printcap.local* file. The printcap entry in this file is used, instead of building a remote entry.

2. Spool directories for remote printers are given the same file names as the name of the printer.

3. The hosts where the remote printers are attached have aliases with the same name as the printer.

The script also handles locally attached printers by including the */etc/printcap.local* file into the generated printcap file. If the same printer names are used throughout, this approach can greatly simplify printcap maintenance. Remember, however, to always keep the local printcap entries in the file */etc/printcap.local*. Then when new printers are added, the *gen_printcap* script can be run with the names of the existing and new printers.

9.5   USENET news

USENET news, also known as **Network News,** or simply **news,** is a very useful distributed bulletin board system. As of this writing, almost 70,000 machines exchange USENET news. USENET doesn't really need TCP/IP in order to work; it can be carried on any transport medium that supports 7-bit ASCII. But useful features that exploit the interactive nature of a TCP connection have been added to it. For example, the **Network News Transfer Protocol (NNTP)** can transport news using TCP as the transport protocol [Kantor & Lapsley 1986]. NNTP also can interactively retrieve selected news articles for use by a news reader. And it is the preferred method for moving news from one system to another where both systems support TCP/IP.

```
#!/bin/sh
#
# generate /etc/printcap file
#
# argument are names of printers
# -d <name> sets the default printer for this host
DEFAULT=
DOMAIN=tic.com
PRINTCAP_LOCAL=printcap.local
USAGE="usage: gen_printcap [ -d name ] name ..."

if [ $# -eq 0 ]; then echo $USAGE; exit 1; fi

while getopts d: arg; do
    case $arg in
        d) DEFAULT=$OPTARG ;;
            esac
done
shift `expr $OPTIND - 1`
if [ -f $PRINTCAP_LOCAL ]; then
    if [ ! "$DEFAULT" ]; then
        cat $PRINTCAP_LOCAL
    else
        sed "s/^$DEFAULT/&|lp/" $PRINTCAP_LOCAL
    fi
fi
for i do
    if grep "^$i" $PRINTCAP_LOCAL >/dev/null 2>&1; then continue; fi
    line="${i}|"
    if [ "$i" = "$DEFAULT" ]; then line="${line}lp|"; fi
    line="${line}printer ${i}:\"
    echo $line
    echo "    sd=/usr/spool/${i}:\"
    echo "    rm=${i}.$DOMAIN:\"
    echo "    lf=/usr/adm/lpd-errs:"
    if [ ! -d /usr/spool/${i} ]; then
        mkdir /usr/spool/${i}
        chown root /usr/spool/${i}
        chgrp daemon /usr/spool/${i}
        chmod u+rwx g+rx o-rwx /usr/spool/${i}
    fi
done
```

Figure 9.11 A printcap Generator.

USENET news distribution and reading software is freely available. Archi-
tecturally the system is divided into a news transport system and a news reading
and posting system — very similar to the division of mail into MTAs and UAs.
Several transport methods are available, as are a wide variety of news readers.
Space prohibits our explaining the installation details of all the various packages,

so we present instead an overview of a generic USENET news system architecture, particularly in a TCP/IP environment. Still the best reference on setting up and managing news is Todino & O'Reilly 1989.

News System Architecture

A news article is similar to a mail message. Unlike mail, however, which is directed at explicitly selected recipients, a news article can be read by anyone who has a login account on a system that receives news. The format of a news article closely resembles that of an RFC822-format mail message; in fact many of the message headers are the same. Some additional headers have been added specifically for use by the news system. When a news article is received at a site, it's stored in a publicly accessible directory, usually */usr/spool/news,* where it can be retrieved and read not only by any user on the system but also by a remote user using NNTP.

Articles are divided into **newsgroups.** A newsgroup is identified by a series of identifiers separated by periods. For example the newsgroup *comp.unix* is a group in the top-level *comp* group (short for Computer Science) with a specific subtopic about the UNIX operating system. The newsgroups form a hierarchy that can extend to any depth. As a practical matter, though, the depth is usually deepest at about five levels. When an article is stored locally, it is placed in the */usr/spool/news* directory. Within that directory, it is placed in a subdirectory with the same name as the name of the newsgroup to which it belongs (note, the periods in the newsgroup name are replaced with slashes). The article itself is stored in a numeric filename. Each time a new article is posted to a group the number is incremented by one.

The first level of the news hierarchy articles into general categories of interest, such as the *comp* group. There also are groups about biology (*bionet*), business (*biz*), GNU software (*gnu*), and many others. Under these top-level groups are over 1,000 individual newsgroups. New newsgroups are created all the time. Some groups are created using a rather anarchic voting system; others are created unilaterally by individuals. In keeping with the totally decentralized philosophy of USENET, a site can chose to subscribe or not subscribe to any newsgroup. Further, in addition to being divided into general categories, newsgroups can be distributed locally, within a group of related machines, within a defined geographic boundary, and worldwide.

The news system uses a flooding algorithm with loop detection to distribute articles from the article origination point to all USENET sites. Each site defines in a configuration file its own set of news neighbors; most sites end up being leaf nodes with a single neighbor. Actual links between the sites range from slow-speed dialup connections to very high-speed links using NNTP over TCP. News can be transported using any transport protocol which supports 7-bit ASCII; not surprisingly, the two most common transport methods are UUCP and TCP/IP. The relationship between news sites is not limited to a tree; multiple paths may exist between news sites. In practice, however, the USENET structure is mostly a tree, with a number of redundant connections at the core of the system added for increased reliability.

The basic flooding algorithm, that is, one without loop detection, works as follows. Suppose site A has three news feeds, one each to and from sites B, C, and D. When A posts an article locally, the article also is sent to its neighbors B, C, and D. It also is stored locally in the news spool directory where local users can read the article. A news article received from B is posted locally and sent to C and D; because the article came from B, all of B's neighbors have already received the article so there is no need to send it back to B. All USENET sites follow this simple algorithm. It can be shown, for any arbitrary network structure, that the article will eventually reach every node in the network.

When USENET is organized as a tree, this algorithm is all that is needed to ensure delivery of the article to all remote systems. The origin of the article is the root of the tree and the article is distributed to all the child nodes of the origin and then to their children, until every system has received the article. With an arbitrary network structure with loops, the flooding algorithm without loop detection alone will lead to articles moving endlessly around the network. So a simple duplicate detection system is used, as follows.

Whenever a USENET article is posted, it has a **message-id** associated with it. The message-id is a unique identifier that is kept in the **article-header** sent with every article. Figure 9.12 shows an example article-header. The message-id comprises an integer and the sitename of the article's origin. It is guaranteed to be unique because the sitename is unique. The integer, too, is unique within that site because each time a news article is posted the message-id number for that site is incremented by 1. Message-ids enable the system to detect duplicate articles;

Figure 9.12 Article-Header.

```
Xref: tic.com austin.forsale:206 austin.general:437
Path: tic.com!cs.utexas.edu!ut-emx!ccwf.cc.utexas.edu!ifav473
From: ifav473@ccwf.cc.utexas.edu ([])
Newsgroups: austin.forsale,austin.general,tx.general,tx.wanted
Subject: Terminal wanted (again)
Message-ID: <64389@ut-emx.uucp>
Date: 29 Dec 91 19:30:25 GMT
Sender: news@ut-emx.uucp
Reply-To: ifav473@ccwf.cc.utexas.edu ([])
Followup-To: austin.forsale
Distribution: tx
Organization: The University of Texas at Austin, Austin TX
Lines: 2
Originator: ifav473@happy.cc.utexas.edu

<message text here>
```

every time an article is received by the news system, the system checks the article's message-id against those of articles that have already been received by the system. These latter id's are kept in a list called the **history file.** A new message-id not on the history-list is added to the list, posted locally, and forwarded to neighboring sites using the flooding algorithm. An article with a message-id that is already on the list means the article has been seen before, so the system drops the article.

Because the history-list can become very large and is accessed frequently, it's ordinarily kept as a keyed file. The software trims this file periodically by deleting very old entries representing articles that are unlikely to be still circulating in the network. The combination of the flooding algorithm and the history-list guarantees an article will be received by every USENET site without duplication.

The flow of news is further controlled by each system's **sys file.** and **active file.** The *sys* file consists of a list of neighboring sites with which news is exchanged, as illustrated in Fig. 9.13. This example is taken from the C News distribution, one type of news transport software. As the figure shows, the file is divided into fields separated by colons, as follows:

1. The sitename of each neighboring news system. A special sitename, ME, is used to denote the local news site. An entry for the local site must be present in this file.

2. The names of the newsgroups to forward to the site. A specific newsgroup can also be disallowed from being forwarded by preceding its name with an exclamation point. Note that for the local site, the newsgroup list is the newsgroups which will be locally posted to the site.

Figure 9.13 News sys File.

```
ME:rec.aviation,rec.games.fr, to::

huey:news.config,to.huey/all::uux - -r -gd huey!rnews

gladstone:comp.protocols.tcp-ip,rec.aviation/all:f:

dewey:comp,news,sci,rec,misc,soc,talk,can,ont,tor,ut,\
    to.dewey/all:f:dewey/togo

donald.angry.duck:comp,news,sci,rec,misc,soc,talk,\
    to.donald/all,!ut:f:

scrooge:comp,news,sci,rec,misc,soc,talk,to.scrooge/all:Lf:
```

3. The method by which news is distributed to a neighboring site. The first field within this group is a series of internally understood flags; the second is the command to invoke for sending news to the remote site.

The active file is a list of currently active newsgroups. Articles can only be posted to active groups. After an incoming article is checked against the history-list and the articles newsgroup appears in the active file, the *sys* file is consulted. The article is only forwarded to the sites in the *sys* file where the article's newsgroup is allowed to be forwarded.

Obtaining a News Feed

News feeds can be obtained from a friendly neighboring site that is already receiving news. A feed can be either a UUCP link or a full-blown TCP/IP connection. Dialup feeds from a neighbor are usually transmitted via UUCP, while if you can get a TCP/IP connection, the preferred transport mechanism is NNTP. When you obtain permission from a neighbor to obtain a news feed, you should register a USENET site name, especially if you are going to post news. Doing this guarantees your message-ids will be unique. The installation instructions that accompany most news software explains the registration procedure.

Batching and Compression

A full news feed can consume considerable bandwidth, especially on a slow speed link. So the news system usually offers you several methods both for batching news articles and for compressing the batches. Batching involves tagging but not sending each outgoing news article destined for a remote site. Tagging usually consists of appending the pathname of the news article to a batch file. Periodically, the batch file is read and then each article is read and all the articles are sent to the remote site as a single file. Also, the entire batch can be compressed using the UNIX *compress* utility. The batch file is then deleted and the batching process starts anew.

News and Mail

Mail and news articles share similar formats, therefore it's possible to forward news articles to specific mail addresses and forward mail messages to a specific newsgroup. Relaying news articles to and from mail lets Internet-style mailing-lists be cross-posted to USENET newsgroups. This is a very common practice. The mail relay also lets a user without news read specific newsgroups. Some very complex cross-posting systems can be developed with this feature.

NNTP

As we said earlier in this section. NNTP is the preferred way to send and receive news on systems that support TCP/IP. NNTP is closely modeled after SMTP, except it's used to transport news articles rather than mail messages. The traditional news transport mechanism uses UUCP over dialup serial lines. While it's possible to run UUCP on top of TCP/IP and retain this traditional mechanism, doing so has proved to be inefficient and cumbersome. Also, NNTP has facilities that enable an end user to read selected news articles on a remote server. While this was totally impractical when the news transport mechanism was UUCP, with a high-speed LAN it became a desirable feature.

Traditionally, reading news required the news article of interest to be on the same system as the user. To read news from a workstation, all news articles had to be either stored locally or remotely mounted from the news server. The first choice meant that a lot of disk storage had to be added to the workstation; the second meant the workstation needed NFS support, which was not always available. NNTP solved the first problem by letting a user on a remote system query a server on the system where the news articles resided and have it download interactively only the articles of interest to the user.

The NNTP dialogue is very simple, as illustrated in Fig. 9.14 and explained in part as follows:

• Lines 1 – 5

The user connects to the NNTP server port and receives a banner message.

• Lines 6 – 12

The user uses the HELP command to obtain a list of valid NNTP commands.

• Line 13

The user then uses the GROUP command to see which articles are available in the newsgroup *comp.unix.admin.*

• Line 14

The server replies that 54 articles are available for reading: the first is number 9756 and the last is number 9809. The 221 is the NNTP reply code that indicates the request was successfully replied to. Note that the article numbers are the spool file names under which the server stored the files.

• Line 15 – 16

The user issues an ARTICLE command followed by the number of the article of interest, in this case 9756. The article is then retrieved and displayed.

• Line 17 – 18

The NEXT command increments the current article number. The server returns the name of the next article.

• Line 19 – 20

At this point, an ARTICLE command is issued without a number and the next article in the newsgroup is retrieved.

• Line 21 – 22

The user issues a QUIT command to terminate the session.

```
(1)   csh> telnet akasha nntp
(2)   Trying 192.135.128.129 ...
(3)   Connected to akasha.tic.com.
(4)   Escape character is '^]'.
(5)   200 akasha.tic.com NNTP[auth] server version 1.5.11\
      (10 February 1991) ready at Wed Jan  6 10:00:48 1993.

(6)   HELP
(7)   100 This server accepts the following commands:
(8)   ARTICLE      BODY           GROUP
(9)   HEAD         LAST           LIST
(10)  NEXT         POST           QUIT
(11)  STAT         NEWGROUPS      HELP
(12)  IHAVE        NEWNEWS        SLAVE

(13)  GROUP comp.unix.admin
(14)  211 54 9756 9809 comp.unix.admin

(15)  ARTICLE 9756

(16)  <article header and text listed>


(17)  NEXT
(18)  223 9759 <1992Dec31.170925.7351@welchgate.welch.jhu.edu>\
      Article retrieved; request text separately.

(19)  ARTICLE

(20)  <article header and text>


(21)  QUIT
(22)  205 akasha.tic.com closing connection.  Goodbye.
```

Figure 9.14 Example NNTP Dialogue.

Of course, an end-user is unlikely to use NNTP in this raw form. Rather, the NNTP protocol is imbedded into a friendlier newsreader that allows the user to simply request the articles of interest.

An NNTP client also can distribute news articles to its neighbors by issuing the command IHAVE. Doing this asks a server if it has a specific article. The server then determines if it has received the article; if not it asks the client to send the article. The IHAVE protocol is commonly used to transfer news between news systems. Further a client can ask a server if it has new news in any specific newsgroup since a certain date and time. This is done using the NEWNEWS command with a newsgroup tag and a date and time.

Setting Up C News

Several news implementations exist. The original was known as **A News.** A replacement with enhanced functionality was called **B News,** which was in turn enhanced to create **C News.** Another news software package called **Internet News** is also available. You should either use C News or Internet News because they are the most up-to- date implementations available as of this writing. We discuss C News next, which is the more seasoned version.

C News Architecture. The general C News operational architecture is shown in Fig. 9.15. All incoming news articles from remote systems enter the local system via the *rnews* command, which queues up the incoming news in the directory */usr/spool/news/in.coming.* Locally posted articles use the *inews* program to pass the article to *relaynews* for posting. Periodically, relaynews takes the queued-up news articles and with help from the *sys, history,* and *active* files, determines whether the article should be posted locally, be sent to remote neighbors, or both.

Figure 9.15 C-News Architecture.

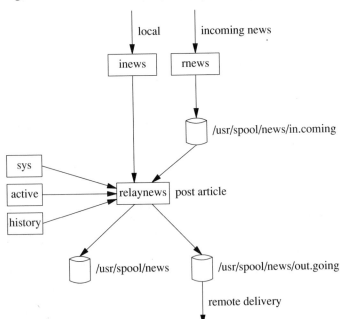

Relaynews in the normal C news distribution is wrapped in a script called *newsrun* that checks to be sure there is enough disk space to post the news articles.

For a local machine, news articles are placed in the appropriate spool directory. The article filename is determined by the second field in the *active* file. Note that posting an article means updating the *active* file as well, so arbitrarily editing the *active* file while news is being posting can have dire consequences. For a remote system, the method of delivery is obtained from the *sys* file. The */usr/spool/news/out.going* directory holds files that are lists of news article filenames. Each file is periodically processed by the appropriate batcher, which reads the files and sends the actual articles to the remote site.

In the meantime, usually daily, various administrative chores are being handled in the background. For example, the *doexpire* program calls on *expire* to discard old article-ids from the history-list file. Otherwise this file will grow without bound. The discard policy is set in the *explist* file. Another administrative chore is truncating the logging file, usually on a weekly basis. This file logs all article postings. If your site has a full news feed, this file can grow by several megabytes a week.

C News Directories. C News installs in the following three directory trees:

1. The article storage, typically */usr/spool/news.*

2. The news library directory, typically */usr/local/lib/news.* for compatibility with old news software this directory is linked to */usr/lib/news.*

3. The utility directory, typically */usr/local/lib/newsbin.*

All three directory names may be redefined; however, most news readers expect news articles to be found in */usr/spool/news* and configuration files in */usr/lib/news.* So if you relocate these directories, be sure to add symbolic links to the real directories from the default locations.

NNTP and C News. NNTP doesn't come as part of the C News distribution but must be installed separately. Fortunately, the NNTP distribution contains the necessary hooks to interact properly with C News. When an NNTP server receives an IHAVE command from a client, it creates a batch file in the */usr/spool/news/in.coming* directory and appends articles to this batch file. When the client closes the session, the server renames the batch file to a numeric name that newsrun understands as a batch file. Newsrun then unbatches the articles. The server alternatively can call *rnews* directly after reading each article from the client. In this manner, incoming news received via NNTP is passed to C News in a straightforward way.

Outbound news to be sent to a remote NNTP server is queued in the */usr/spool/news/out.going* file. Within that file, the news is placed within a separate file, one for each remote system that is typically named for the remote host. The *nntpxmit* command is then run periodically, implementing an NNTP client and using the IHAVE command to send each article to the remote system.

9.6   Anonymous FTP

Anonymous FTP enables a remote user to communicate with an FTP server without any user authentication, hence allowing the usual FTP commands to be invoked by the anonymous user. Because of the lack of any kind of authentication, an anonymous FTP server must be set up very carefully. This is accomplished usually by allowing anonymous FTP access only to a subtree of your filesystem. The anonymous FTP server controls this by exploiting the UNIX *chroot()* system call, which restricts access by a user to just a subtree of the entire filesystem. After the *chroot()* call, a logged-in user sees only the subtree.

In order to list UNIXfiles, an FTP server needs access to the *ls* command. Because the anonymous FTP directory is divorced from the rest of the file system by the *chroot* system call, you will need to place a copy of *ls* within the subtree. You also should include in this subtree an abbreviated copy of the */etc/passwd* file and the */etc/group* file. This let's the *ls* command show the owner and group field with a name, rather than the userid or groupid. These files can be very short and should not be copies of your real *passwd* and *group* files. Building the *passwd* file with an entry for the *root* and the *ftp* user is usually sufficient. The *group* file can contain an entry for the group the *ftp* user is a member of. The layout for the anonymous FTP directory is as follows:

```
/etc/group
/etc/passwd
/bin/ls
/pub - public files
```

This subdirectory can be placed anywhere within your filesystem; */usr/spool/ftp* or a similar location is usually a good choice. Further, you should set the *etc* and *bin* subdirectories so that they are only searchable. You make the *pub* directory world readable and searchable. It should also be owned and writeable by the anonymous FTP administrator. Then if you choose to allow users to place files within your anonymous FTP area, you can make a subdirectory of *pub* world writeable. Be aware, however, that doing this is not entirely safe because you won't have control over what is placed within your anonymous area. It also enables a remote user to fill up your filesystem and gives mischievous users the opportunity to spread programs containing possibly serious bugs or security holes.

Next, an *ftp* user account should be created that sets the home directory for the anonymous FTP user to the above created subdirectory. The line in the real *passwd* file should look like the following:

```
ftp:*:123:65534:FTP:/usr/spool/ftp:!
```

Note that this entry does not contain a valid encrypted password and also sets the shell field (the last field) to an illegal value. This is to prevent remote access to this account via the RSH or RLOGIN protocols.

Once you have set up the anonymous FTP account and built the basic subdirectory layout, you may place files within the anonymous FTP area. Most sites organize related files into separate subdirectories under the anonymous FTP *pub* directory and place README files with succinct information about the contents of each subdirectory. Be careful about what you put within this area. With anonymous FTP access and Internet connectivity, any user anywhere can copy files from your server to their own system. Anonymous FTP is a useful tool for distributing public information to remote users. It is not very useful for distributing proprietary information to a select set of users.

9.7   User Validation

Usually UNIX system security involves using passwords to validate logins. A user is associated with an internal userid and with one or more groupids. These id's determine the user's system privileges, that is, which files the user can read, write to, and/or execute. This simple system was designed for a single timesharing system. Under networking, however, multiple systems can be attached to the same network and can share resources such as filesystems; for example, the basic TCP/IP remote services — TELNET and FTP — rely on password authentication. But this arrangement is inconvenient; a user must type a password when logging in from one system to another. FTP does allow usernames and passwords to be placed in the *.netrc* file in a user's home directory, but the password is very vulnerable because it's kept in an unencrypted form. To alleviate the inconveniences associated with using passwords, several extensions to basic password authentication have been implemented to provide users more convenient network access. We discuss some of these next.

R* Authentication

One widely used authentication extension called **R* authentication** was introduced by the BSD UNIX system and has since been well accepted and made available on most UNIX systems [Kantor 1991]. BSD UNIX added several useful network protocols in the 4.2BSD and all subsequent releases of the operating system, including the following:

• RLOGIN allows remote logins to another UNIX system.

• RSH allows remote execution of shell level commands.

• RCP allows files to be copied to and from a remote system or between two remote systems.

All of these protocols use an authentication strategy that eliminates having to type a password each time a remote system is accessed. This strategy is based two notions: **secure ports** and IP address validation. Port addresses ranging from 1 to 1023 are considered secure on UNIX systems because a process cannot create a socket with a port address within the secure range unless the process is running with superuser privileges. IP address validation assumes that the IP source address found in any IP packet is believable. As an example of how the user validation strategy works, we will step you through how the RLOGIN protocol works.

1. The RLOGIN client process is run setuid to the superuser. This allows the client to use a secure port.

2. The client process finds an unused secure port (it tries port 1023 and counts down from there until it finds an unused port) and, using the secure port, makes a TCP connection to an RLOGIN server on a remote system. The client process then reverts back to running as an unprivileged process. It only uses the setuid capability to get an unused secure port.

3. The RLOGIN server uses the *getpeername()* system call to obtain the IP address and source port of the client. This information is saved as part of the unique connection address. See Chapter 4 for more details.

4. The server checks that the port number is within the secure range; if it is, the server then maps the IP address to a hostname by using the *gethostbyaddr()* library routine. This value is the remote hostname. If the port is not in the secure range, then the server closes the connection, assuming that the client was not running setuid to the superuser and is an ordinary user attempting to spoof the server.

5. The client sends three arguments to the server over the established connection: The login name of the user on the client (the remote username); the login name of the user on the server (the local username); and the type of the client user's terminal. Each of these arguments is sent as an ASCII string, separated by a <NULL> character.

6. The server then checks if the local username is the superuser. If so, the next step is skipped.

7. For a local username that is not the superuser, the server checks the */etc/hosts.equiv* file. Each line of this file consists of a hostname followed by a username. The hostname on each line is checked against the remote hostname. If a match is found then the following is checked. If a username is found on the matched line, the remote user is allowed to log in without a password as any local user, if the remote username matches the username on the line. This feature should be used with extreme care, for obvious reasons. If the username is missing, the remote user is allowed to log in without a password only if the local username is the same as the remote username.

8. If the preceeding check fails, the server now looks up the home directory of the local user. The home directory of the local user is searched for a file called *.rhosts*. This file has the same format as the */etc/hosts.equiv* file — each line is a hostname followed by a username. As a precaution the file must be owned and only writeable by the local user or owned by the superuser. If not the

following check is skipped. If there is in this file a line in which the hostname and username match the remote hostname and username, then the remote user is allowed to log in as the local user without a password.

9. Finally, if all the above validation checks fail, the remote user is prompted for a password. Note that for the RSH or RCP protocols the command will not prompt for a password, but simply fail.

Some UNIX systems have added extensions to the above validation system. One such extension allows a "+" to be substituted for a hostname or username in both the /etc/hosts.equiv and .rhosts files. The "+" stands for "any" in this context. So an entry like

```
xfrsparc.tic.com +
```

in a local user's .rhost file allows any remote user from the machine xfrsparc.tic.com to access the system as the local user. A line with a single "+" in the /etc/hosts.equiv file let's any user on any remote system have access, provided the remote username matches one of the local username. This is in general a bad idea, although some systems come from the factory with this entry. Also net-groups (discussed later in this section) can be used in place of the standard entries on some systems. These extensions are convenient notational shorthands, but they do not alter the fundamental validation strategy.

This validation strategy is convenient, particularly when the networked machines share the same /etc/passwd files. All that is needed to allow remote logins without a password is the inclusion of all the machine names in the /etc/hosts.equiv file. It's important that the names in the file be the official names of the hosts because that is what is compared. For systems without a shared password file, a user can access remote systems by placing an .rhosts file in the user's home directory; the user then can log in without having to type a password.

This form of remote user validation doesn't require the use of consistent user or group ids. NFS one the other hand requires a common set of userids to avoid userid mismatches between systems. NFS validates file access based on user and group ids; the R* method validates access based on usernames. So if both R* and NFS validation are used, a consistent mapping between userids and usernames is the easiest to manage. As you can see, a convenient method of distributing the password and group files is essential, which we discuss next.

Password and Group File Distribution

Password and group file distribution can be handled in several ways. One of the simplest is to copy the a master password and group file to all hosts. Then all users within a single administration can access all systems within the network. Copying password and group files on a system that has only a few machines is fairly easy. When the size of the system reaches more than 30 or so machines, copying the entire password and group files is burdensome, particularly if frequent changes are made to the file. You can avoid this by using NIS to distribute the password file.

Doing this has the added advantage of NIS being able to implement a two-level access hierarchy as well. The NIS system enables a common password file database to be shared among many hosts. Username searches are always started using the regular password file. Adding a line with a "+" at the end of this file tells the search mechanism to continue looking for a matching username in the NIS database. Accordingly, accounts specific to a particular host can be added to that host's password file and left out of the NIS database. This method is commonly used for system-related accounts such as *root* where a separate password for each system is desirable.

An extension to the standard password lookup mechanism is **netgroups.** A netgroup is a named group of users or hosts associated with a specific NIS domain. A netgroup entry is a triple *<host,user,domain>*, where if any component is empty it is interpreted as "any." If a components is a "-" then it is interpreted as "none." For example, to create a list of users that are in the netgroup "accounting" a line is entered in the file */etc/netgroup* as follows:

```
accounting (,sam,) (,fred,) (,sally,)
```

The name *accounting* now can stand for the list of three usernames — *sam, fred,* and *sally.* Netgroups also can be looked up using NIS, therefore it's not necessary to distribute the */etc/netgroup* file to all hosts within a particular NIS domain.

Using netgroups, you can easily customize particular password files to restrict access to sensitive systems. This is done using a convenient shorthand netgroups provide for building password file entries. For example, an entry of the form

```
+@accounting
```

tells the system to add the usernames *sam, fred,* and *sally* as valid password file entries. Other entries in the NIS password database are not added to the file. A netgroup entry starting with a "-" means to disallow those entries from the password file. So an entry of the form

```
-@accounting
```

would disallow access to the host. The netgroup mechanism is not supported on all UNIX systems. It is, again, a convenient shorthand for tailoring system access.

Kerberos

For the truly security minded, the Kerberos authentication system is a big step up from the standard UNIX password authentication or the R* authentication method already described [Miller *et al.*]. The standard UNIX password authentication has a major weakness: passwords are typed in cleartext over the network, which might be wiretapped by an intruder, thus leaving the password vulnerable to improper use by unauthorized users.

The R* authentication method eliminates the user having to type passwords in cleartext over the network. However, it relies on the software's ability to authenticate IP addresses and map them correctly back to hostnames. This procedure assumes an intruder can't spoof a server machine into thinking it's another machine. Unfortunately, such spoofing can be done all too easily, particularly on a broadcast medium like Ethernet. If you have extremely sensitive data or are concerned about tight network security, then you might consider using the Kerberos authentication scheme. Kerberos was developed at MIT for a very specific environment: a university computing environment with open access to workstations where an individual workstation could be compromised. In developing the scheme, the Kerberos developers made the following assumptions:

- Wiretapping for passwords could happen.

- Most workstations would be used by more than one user and so might not be physically secure.

- A server machine with the authentication database can be physically secured.

Accordingly, the Kerberos authentication strategy was devised based on encryption technology. In choosing this method, the developers made two other assumptions: that cryptographic attacks either weren't possible; or if possible, would take longer than the time interval a user used the same password. These assumptions meant that users should use passwords that can't be guessed easily. As it turns out, easily guessed passwords are probably the biggest security risk on any system. Kerberos for all its strengths cannot do anything about easily guessed passwords.

Kerberos Architecture. The Kerberos architecture consists of an authentication service on a physically secured server machine that validates all user's identities by means of a password mechanism. A user that is authenticated is issued a **ticket** that is used to access a network service on other machines. A ticket is a unique message encrypted in such a way that a server can genuinely identify the user requesting service. It's valid for only a specific time period, after which the user must be reauthenticated by the authentication service, which is also known as the **ticket-granting service.**

Figure 9.16 shows a diagram of the ticket system. Off-line, a user registers with the ticket server and obtains a password, which in Kerberos is called a user's **secret key.**

When the user logs in to a workstation, the user sends an initial message in cleartext to the ticket server to obtain a **ticket-granting ticket.** This message contains the name of the ticket-granting server, the name of the user — who is the client of the Kerberos system — and the time of day. (The client name is usually just the login name of the user.) Note that this message could be sent by anyone and can be intercepted by anyone on the network with enough knowledge on how the system works. The user's secret key is not sent with this message.

Getting a Ticket-Granting Ticket

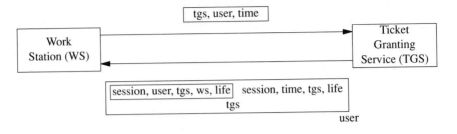

Getting Another Services Ticket

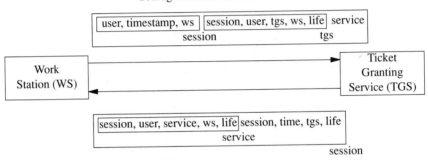

Figure 9.16 Getting Kerberos Tickets.

The ticket server takes the message and returns a response, which contains the following five parts:

• Ticket-granting ticket
  A unique message that uniquely identifies the client to the ticket-granting server.

• Session key
  An encryption key for use by the client when it later wants other tickets from the ticket-granting server for the duration of the user's login session.

• Timestamp
  The time the response was returned.

• Ticket-granting server's name

• Lifetime
  The time the ticket is valid.

Unlike the initial message, the response isn't sent in cleartext. Rather it is encrypted using the user's secret key. Presumably only the user and the ticket server know the user's secret key, therefore only they can interpret the message contents. (We show encryption in the figure by enclosing the encrypted values within a box with the owner of the secret key subscripted under the box.) The timestamp within the encrypted message is used to detect a replay of an earlier response from the ticket service. If the time is within a few minutes of the current time, the ticket is considered to be authentic. Note that anybody who intercepts this message must know the user's secret key, so it does an intruder no good to intercept the encrypted message. The ticket within the message is also encrypted using the key of the ticket-granting service. This prevents the user from tampering with the ticket. The encrypted ticket contains the following fields:

• Session key
  The same temporary session key as in the response. This is the way the session key is passed back to the ticket-granting server in a secure fashion.

• User's name
  The user's unique name.

• Ticket-granting service name

• Timestamp indicating the current time.

• Workstation
  The IP address of the workstation the user logged in on.

• Lifetime
  The time the ticket is valid.

Only after receiving the response from the server does the user type the secret key that will decrypt the response from the ticket-granting server. Note that the user must decrypt the message in order to verify the response. Verification is achieved by the user's comparing the value of the ticket-granting service name, the client name, and the timestamp with what was sent in the original message. The user also saves the session key for later use. So now the user has a legitimate ticket-granting service ticket that can be used to obtain tickets for other services. Tickets for these other services are obtained, as follows:

The user sends to the ticket-granting service a message with the following fields:

• *authenticator*
  Authenticates the user to the ticket granting service. (We explain how this is done later on in this section.)

• *TGST*
  The ticket-granting server's ticket. This is the ticket obtained from the service in the initial authentication transaction.

• *Service Name*
  The name of the service being requested.

This message is sent without further encryption because the TGST is already encrypted using the ticket-granting services key and the *authenticator* is encrypted using the previously obtained session key.

The authenticator contains the following fields:

• Client name

• Timestamp
The current time.

• WS
The IP address of the workstation.

When the ticket-granting server receives the request, it decrypts the enclosed ticket using its own private key and then decrypts the authenticator using the session key found inside the ticket. As we mentioned earlier, the server can verify the identity of the sender by comparing the username found inside the ticket with the username inside the authenticator. As before it uses the timestamp to prevent a replay of a previous message. At this point, the ticket-server sends a response exactly like the original ticket-granting response, except the ticket-granting ticket is replaced with a ticket for the requested service. This response also is encrypted, but using the temporary ticket-granting session key rather than the user's secret key. Note that a new session key is included in the reply for the requested service. The new session key appears in the response and also appears in the service ticket, so the server can use it to encrypt replies, if desired. The user can verify this ticket came from the ticket-granting service as before.

Now when the user wants to use the service, it sends the service ticket to a server for that service and builds an authenticator encrypted with the temporary session key for that service. The service authenticates the user just as the ticket-granting server did, that is, by using the temporary session key found in the encrypted ticket. With this procedure in place, authentication proceeds without the user having to send passwords in cleartext across the network or without dependence on the accurate mapping of IP addresses found in IP packets sent to hostnames.

Kerberos Installation on UNIX. Installing Kerberos on a system that doesn't have built-in support for it isn't easy. First the Kerberos ticket-granting service must be installed on a secure host. Note that if a secure host isn't available, then there isn't much point in using Kerberos; usually you need a dedicated machine that can be locked up and physically secured and this machine shouldn't have general user accounts installed on it.

Second, each service must be "kerberized" for use with Kerberos authentication. The most common UNIX commands that have Kerberos implementations are the BSD R* services. The latest BSD network release has the kerberized versions of these commands. However, if you are not running BSD UNIX then building these programs can be difficult since the BSD *make* command also must be installed. Also there are compile-time differences when building these commands on a non-BSD system. In this case, unless you have considerable time to dedicate to its implementation or have a very clear need for Kerberos, it's probably best to learn if your vendor supports Kerberos and if so, to use your vendor's implementation. In a mixed vendor environment in which not all machines support Kerberos, you need to install it on all systems to take full advantage of its benefits. If you have a server with Kerberos authentication and yet still allow some non-Kerberos machines to have access to the server, then you will have defeated the purpose of the system.

9.8   Syslog in a Network Environment

The System Logging facility, known as **syslog,** is a very useful logging tool. Found on most BSD-based UNIX systems, syslog can be thought of as an error message multiplexor. Many UNIX servers and systems have their own specific logging schemes. Normally this involves each program opening an application-specific logging file. This means the location of log files isn't consistent. As the number of applications doing their own logging grows, it becomes much more difficult for the system administrator to remember where all the logging information is kept. Syslog is intended to modularize and logically organize logging file placement and maintenance.

The general syslog architecture consists of a logging daemon, *syslogd,* that runs on all machines with syslog support. This daemon listens on a local UNIX address family socket called */dev/log* as well as on the UDP port number 514. Client programs that use syslog send logging messages to their own local syslog daemon, usually via the */dev/log* device. Each message is tagged with a **facility** and a **log level,** both of which are selectable by the client. A facility code is a manifest constants that is hard-wired into the syslog system. This hard-wiring possibly will be changed in the future so you can add your own facility codes, thus making the system more extensible. The message itself is simply an ASCII string that the client generates with *syslog()* — a *printf()*-like function. Logging is enabled with the *openlog()* function where options are specified that allow the output of the process-id of the process that generated the message, as well as the mnemonic name of the program that generated the message. When syslogd receives a message, it looks up the facility code and the log level and then uses the information read from its configuration file to determine where the message needs to be delivered. A message can be written to a local logfile or forwarded to another syslogd process running on a remote host. The forwarding function lets client machines with possibly limited disk space log their messages to a more capable server.

Syslog Configuration

The syslog configuration file describes where specific messages are to be logged, as shown in Fig. 9.17 and explained as follows. As the figure shows, each line in the file comprises two tab-separated fields. The first is a list of *facility.level* with each item separated by semi-colons. The second field is the target log and is the name of a file, a user, or a remote syslog host. A file is written as a full UNIX pathname; the remote logger is the remote system's name preceded by an "@." A user is simply the user's login name.

```
*.err;kern.debug;user.none                    /dev/console
*.err;kern.debug;daemon,mail.crit;user.none /var/adm/messages
lpr.debug                                     /var/adm/lpd-errs
mail.debug                                    @loghost.tic.com
*.alert;kern.err;daemon.err;user.none         operator
*.alert;user.none                             root
*.emerg;user.none                             *
```

Figure 9.17 Syslog Configuration File.

For each message's facility code and log level, syslogd examines the configuration and for all lines that match the facility code of the message, the log levels are compared. All messages with a log level greater than or equal to the log level found in the configuration file are sent to the specific log. Note that a message is sent to more than one log, if the message's *facility.level* is found in more than one line.

The legal facility codes are shown in Table 9.2. The table shows the processes that generate messages with the specific codes. Note that these coding conventions are just that. There is no enforcement of facility codes. If you write applications that use syslog, you should try to follow this convention.

Level numbers have descending priority and are intended to indicate the the severity of a particular message. The legal levels are as follows:

Table 9.2 Syslog Facility Codes.

Code	Generated by
user	a user process
kern	the operating system
mail	The mail system, usually the *sendmail* daemon
daemon	user-level system servers
auth	user authentication processes such as login and su.
lpr	the line printer spooling system
news	the USENET news system
uucp	the UUCP system
cron	the cron system
mark	syslogd's internal timestamp generator
local0-7	other local processes
*	stands for any facility except the mark facility

- emerg

- alert

- crit

- err

- warning

- notice

- info

- debug

As with facility codes, legal level numbers are again hard-wired into the syslog implementation as manifest constants.

How to Use Syslog

The usual default syslog configuration logs all messages on the machine from which the messages were generated. For kernel messages and other critical conditions, this is probably appropriate. However, in a system with many machines it can be very inconvenient to have to log in to all machines periodically to see whether any errors have occurred or whether events have happened that require attention. Syslog's ability to log messages to a remote host is a convenient feature. If you have a set of clients that use the same server, it's easy to configure syslog to send most client messages to the server for logging. Because each remote message contains the name of the machine that generated the message, messages can be distinguished easily.

Finally keep in mind that logfiles can grow without bound, so you should periodically run a script to truncate or delete old logfiles. A convenient technique for doing this is to keep weekly logs and rotate the logs each week to progressively older logfiles. A common convention is to append a number on the end of the old logfiles that is incremented each time the log is moved. Fig. 9.18 is a simple shell script that performs this task. The first argument to the script is the name of the logfile. The second argument is the number of old copies to keep before discarding them. You can use this script to rotate any logfile. Note that syslog expects a logfile to already exist. Otherwise it will not write any messages to the logfile. So be sure and create a new empty logfile when you rotate it to an old logfile.

9.9   Uses of RSH and RCP

RSH and RCP protocols are two very useful protocols. To use them successfully, the user must be able to be authenticated on the remote system without a password.

```
#!/bin/sh

LOGDIR=/var/log

cd $LOGDIR

if [ $# -ne 2 ]; then
    echo usage logrot log number
    exit 1
fi

log=$1
n=$2

rm -f ${log}.$n
while [ $n -gt 0 ]; do
    n1=`expr $n - 1`
    if [ -f $log.$n1 ]; then
        mv -f $log.$n1 $log.$n
    fi
    n=$n1
done

mv -f $log $log.1
cat >$log </dev/null
chmod 664 $log
```

Figure 9.18 Example Logfile Rotation Script.

RSH allows the remote execution of a UNIX command. The client side UNIX command is called *rsh*. It takes a set of arguments that is passed as a shell command to the remote system and executed. The rsh command associates the stdin and stdout file descriptors with the TCP port to the remote system, so input supplied by the client is sent to the remote command executing on the server and output from the remote command appears on stdout on the client system. Using rsh has advantages in that it follows the UNIX paradigm for a filter program and can be used as part of a pipeline of commands. That rsh executes the command executed remotely in a manner transparent to the rest of the pipeline. This setup is useful for example when you have a computer-intensive application that can be more effectively run on a faster machine, but you want the output to appear on a slower workstation.

The implementation of the RCP protocol, *rcp,* is simply a special case of rsh that executes the rcp command itself on the remote system. Although rcp has been superseded in many cases by NFS, it's still useful in simple scripts where you must copy files from one machine to another without NFS support. It's also useful over slow-speed lines, where NFS is less efficient.

Once you have properly set up the R* command authentication, there is little you need to configure to get RSH and RCP working. Both RSH and RCP use the remote shell server (TCP port 514), which differs from the remote execution server REXEC (TCP port 512) that does not do R* authentication and always requires a password.

9.10 A Simple Client/Server

Under some circumstances, authentication is not needed for a user to access a remote service. For example, a server that looks up telephone numbers should be accessible by any user regardless of whether the user has RSH access to the server that maintains the phone list database. Probably the level of security needed is no more than identifying the user as part of the organization. A special phone list server could be written to perform this task using the normal client/server tools provided by the socket or TLI interface. However, given the nature of the problem and its extensibility to other simple services, a better approach is to write generic client/server software, such as a simple client/server, that handles the connection setup with a simple interface reminiscent of the rsh command interface.

The simple client/server consists of the *client* command that receives requests from a user and the *server* command that processes the request on the remote system. The client command is easy to use, as shown in the following example:

```
client remote.tic.com who
```

The first argument to this program is the remote host's name. The next one is the name of the command to execute on that host. Client establishes a TCP connection with the remote host's server. The program sends to the remote server a single line that consists of the command to execute and its arguments. It then waits for the response from the remote server and writes the response to its own stdout. This output can, of course, be piped to other UNIX utilities in the usual way.

Execution of the client program itself can be embedded in a shell script to make it easier to use, as shown in Fig. 9.19. The example script uses the client program to call a series of hosts and returns the output of the *who* command from each of them.

The server command is a bit more complicated because it does some simple validation as well as some logging. Its general algorithm is shown in Fig. 9.20. Note that user verification is much looser than it is with R* validation. The only type of verification performed is whether the client host is "local," where local is defined to be a machine within the same DNS domain as the server. The server program uses a single support file called *server.cmds* located in the */usr/local/etc*

```
#!/bin/sh
#
# rwhosit
#
# remote who client
#
# arguments are names of the remote hosts to query
#
PATH=/usr/local/bin:/bin:/usr/bin:
if [ $# = 0 ]; then
    echo "usage rwhosit host ..."
    exit 1
fi
for h do
    client $h who
done
```

Figure 9.19 Example Client Program.

directory. Each line of this file describes a single valid command that the server will execute on behalf of the client. The format of each line is

```
command_name [login] [local]
```

This is handy for limiting the number of directories that are searched for commands to execute. Using the PATH variable, the environment for the remote command execution can be completely controlled. The command name is the name of the command to execute. The "login" keyword tells the server to log the command in the *wtmp* so the accounting system can record that the command was used and from which host it was executed. The "local" keyword says to only allow this command from a machine within the local domain. Both keywords are optional.

The server also can be used as a generic framework for other simple protocols such as FINGER. This is allowed by replacing *fingerd* (the server side of FINGER) with the server code. If the server sees that its own name ends in "d" and is not "serverd," then the command to execute is that name, that is, in this case *finger* without the trailing "d". This is a useful extension since many servers simply set up the network connection and then execute the actual service provider.

For the rest of this chapter, we discuss some examples of how to use the simple client/server. All are written as Bourne shell scripts, and as you will see the programming task for each borders on the trivial. The usual script error checking is not shown for the sake of brevity.

```
Listen for a connection from remote clients
  (this is done in inetd)

Upon receiving a connection, read command name
  and arguments sent from remote client as a single line.

Verify that command name exists in /usr/local/etc/server.cmds

Validate that connection is from a valid host

Log connection to wtmp if required

Executes command with stdout from command
  redirected to the network connection.
```

Figure 9.20 Server Algorithm.

Remote Man Server

Conserving disk space taken up by manual pages was the original motivation for writing the simple client/server software. Note that for systems having NFS support, manual pages can be distributed by using NFS and remotely mounting the manual page directory on the client systems. However, the simplified server method has the advantage of quickly timing out or refusing the connection when the server is down, thus avoiding a hanging NFS call to a hung server. The manual page client is a one-line script as follows:

```
client man_server man $*
```

The hostname *man_server* is expected to be an alias for the machine on which the manual pages reside in the current domain. On the server side, the following line is added to the *server.cmds* file:

```
man login local
```

Phone Server

A phone server allows a user on a client system to look up phone numbers from a central database. This facility is very useful in a department that lacks a central phone operator. The arguments to the client are the names of the persons for whom to search. The client side is again a one-line script, as follows:

```
client phone_server phones $*
```

Again the hostname *phone_server* is expected to be an alias for the host where the phone number database resides.

The server side executes a program that looks up phone numbers in a database. The database can be sophisticated or as simple as a text file with names followed by phone numbers. An example of the latter searchable using an *awk* script is shown in Fig. 9.21.

Although this program can be improved, it gives you an idea of the ease of using the client/server code as a framework for developing interesting and useful applications. Note that the phone lookup program itself doesn't require the user to know about the network or the fact it can be accessed in a networked environment. All the user sees is a program that returns telephone numbers.

Redundant Servers

A redundant server also can be implemented using this system. Its execution is somewhat complicated but not overwhelming. The client side of a phone service with redundant servers is shown in Fig. 9.22. Note that the *ping* command is used to determine whether a server is available. Also if a connection fails to a server, the client program returns a non-zero return code that the script can check.

Security

The simple client/server mechanism is somewhat more secure than R* validation. With the R* method both the system administrator and an individual user can decide from whom and from what systems remote access is allowed to an account on a given system. However, with the simple client/server, the system administrator alone decides where access can be made, at least at the granularity of the local domain. Further RSH allows remote execution of any command, while the simple

---

Figure 9.21 Phone Server.

```
#!/bin/sh
#
# phone server
#
# the phone database consists of:
# <last_name> <first_name> <tab> <phone_no>
# line for each person
PHONE_DB=/usr/local/lib/phones

for a do
    awk "/$a"'/ { print $0 }' ${PHONE_DB}
done
```

```sh
#!/bin/sh

# phone client

PRIMARY=phone_server.tic.com
SECONDARY=back_up_phone_server.tic.com

# try each host in turn
for h in $PRIMARY $SECONDARY; do

# ping the host to see if it's up at all
# this will need modification depending on the ping used
    response=`ping $h`
    if [ "$response" = "host not responding" ]; then
        continue
    fi
    client $h phones $* 2>/dev/null

# success
    if [ $? -eq 0 ]; then
        exit 0
    fi
done

# failure
echo "phone server not responding - try again"
exit 1
```

Figure 9.22 Redundant Phone Servers.

client/server permits execution only of a specific list of commands that is under the control of the server's system administrator. The simple client/server actually is more analogous to a shell-level RPC mechanism than to the RSH protocol, which is a more general remote command execution facility.

As an administrator, you should not list just anything in the *server.cmds* file, for example, programs that permit a shell escape from command line arguments. Also, care should be taken when allowing shell scripts as remote commands. Also avoid setuid programs unless their functions are strictly limited.

Note that the code of the server command itself has been carefully checked for the most obvious problems, such as buffer overflows, and so appears to be reasonably safe. However, any program can have one last bug that could be exploited by system crackers. See Appendix A for where this code can be obtained using anonymous FTP.

References

Kantor 1991.   Kantor, B., *BSD rlogin (RFC1282)*, December 1991.

Kantor & Lapsley 1986.   Kantor, B., & Lapsley, P., *Network News Transfer Protocol (RFC977)*, February 1986.

McLaughlin 1990.   McLaughlin, L., *Line Printer Daemon Protocol (RFC1179)*, August 1990.

Miller et al..   Miller, S. P., Neuman, B. C., Schiller, J. I., & Saltzer, J. H., *Kerberos Authentication and Authorization System*.

Sun 1991a.   Sun, *Network Interface Programmer's Guide,* Sun Microsystems, Inc, Mountain View, CA (1991).

Sun 1991b.   Sun, *System and Network Administration,* Sun Microsystems, Mountain View, CA (1991).

Todino & O'Reilly 1989.   Todino, Grace, & O'Reilly, Tim, *Managing UUCP and USENET,* O'Reilly & Associates, Sebastopol, CA (1989).

PART 3

Advanced Topics

## CHAPTER 10

Macintosh and PC Integration

You will find Macintosh computers and DOS personal computers (PCs) in almost every computing environment and integrating them into TCP/IP networks is becoming more popular and commonplace. Integration levels range from simple terminal access using terminal emulator software to more complicated filesharing using Sun NFS or Appleshare. With the rapid decline in the cost of Ethernet adapter cards for both PCs and Macintosh computers, better and more complete integration of these systems has become affordable in most environments.

In this chapter, we describe several common methods of integrating PCs and Macintosh computers into a TCP/IP network. A wealth of public domain software that covers the range of integration options is currently available from Internet and UUCP archive sites. Generally, we discuss this freely available software, but the techniques described here apply equally well to supported commercial software. Note also that we generically refer to both IBM compatible PCs and Macintoshes as PCs and distinguish between them only when needed.

10.1 Terminal Emulators

Terminal emulators for PCs are very common and many are freely available. If simple remote terminal access to a networked UNIX system is all you need, this option is by far the easiest and the least expensive. The PC is simply connected to a networked UNIX system using one of its built-in serial communications ports and is treated by the UNIX system as an ordinary terminal. If the PC user wants only to read mail or use the UNIX system as a gateway to remote systems connected to the TCP/IP network, terminal emulator software on the PC is usually all that is required. Figure 10.1 shows a PC connected to a UNIX system using a simple serial line. The user must have an account on the UNIX system and can read mail and news on that system or use TELNET or FTP to access other systems on the network.

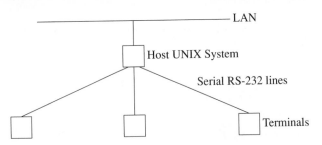

Figure 10.1 Dumb Terminal Connection.

Rather than directly connecting the PC to a UNIX host, you also could connect it to a **terminal server.** A terminal server is a dedicated machine that multiplexes several serial devices and allows them to communicate with remote hosts over a high-speed network, such as Ethernet. Servers designed for TCP/IP environments run TELNET and sometimes RLOGIN clients for each connected serial device. It in effect becomes an access point to the network for simple terminal devices. One convenient feature of this setup is that the server is usually optimized for use with terminal devices. Also several servers can be connected to the network at different places to serve different clusters of terminals.

The biggest advantage of using a terminal emulator only is that all that need be added to the PC is the emulator software. No changes to its hardware configuration are required and the PC can be for other tasks. The user can copy files between the UNIX host and PC using a standard serial line protocol. For example, you can use the **kermit** protocol. You would need to add a kermit server on a UNIX host. However, this presents no problem as kermit is in the public domain and reliable kermit software for all PCs and UNIX systems is freely available.

The most significant drawback of having only a terminal emulator on the PC is the serial interface's slow speed, which is typically no more than 19.2 kbps for directly connected terminals. While this speed is acceptable for normal interactive access, it's insufficient for expeditious transport of large files between the PC and the UNIX host. Also a file transfer using kermit takes up all of the bandwidth of the connection, which means the user usually can't do anything else while the file is being transferred. Further, a user wanting to print to a remote printer must manually download the file to the remote UNIX system and print the file from there. This is very awkward for most PC users.

Regardless of the drawbacks, if you need only occasional access to network services installing a terminal emulator is easy to set up and administer. The hardest part is dealing with the serial line communication. Some of the subtle nuances of RS-232 communication can be very frustrating since not all computer vendors follow the exact same serial communication conventions. Dealing with these issues is beyond the scope of this book, however, most computer manufacturers supply sufficient information to enable you to connect terminals using serial lines without too much trouble.

10.2 LAN Connectivity

Connecting your PCs directly to your LAN offers the highest level of network functionality. For example, if you need higher bandwidth access to hosts on your network, direct LAN connectivity has become, with the rapid price decline of network interface cards, very cost effective. Public domain software is available that implements TELNET, FTP, and other TCP/IP applications for PCs. Commercially supported software is also available. See the access list in Appendix A.

Direct LAN connectivity is more complex than using only a serial line. For the PC to able to use TCP/IP services, you must assign the PC an IP address and treat the PC just like any other networked host system. You also must install a network interface card in the PC and add the appropriate network driver with TCP/IP support.

However, a direct network connection is better that a serial line connection for integrating many of the more interesting TCP/IP network services. Even if you just run a TELNET client on the PC, you'll find the speed of the connection significantly greater; with an Ethernet, for example, you can access a 10-mbit/sec pipe rather than just, at most, a 19.2-kbit/sec serial line.

Macintosh Configuration

To establish a LAN connection to a Macintosh, you must install a network interface card and the appropriate low-level device driver software in your machine. You then must configure the Macintosh for TCP/IP communication. Apple supplies a TCP/IP driver, **MacTCP,** that is shipped as a part of all Macintosh applications that use TCP/IP services. MacTCP coexists with the built-in Appletalk network driver that is an integral part of MacOS, the standard Macintosh operating system (OS). In Macintosh terminology, MacTCP is a **system extension** that is installed in the Macintosh System Folder and loaded by the operating system when the Macintosh is booted. It talks to the low-level network interface device driver and gives any application that uses TCP/IP services a standard way of interfacing to the network.

MacTCP's user interface is a Macintosh Control Panel in which you set the IP address and subnet mask for the Macintosh. MacTCP also supports hostname-to-IP address mapping using either a local static host table or DNS. Also, it supports only the DNS resolver and not the server. Thus if you use DNS you must have a DNS server configured on another machine. You further must configure a default route to any network beyond the locally attached network.

MacTCP also lets you use RARP or BOOTP to dynamically configure the host IP address. Use of RARP or BOOTP requires you to have a server that can handle the datalink address-to-IP address translation; in a large environment with many Macintoshes, this setup gives the administrator complete control over IP address assignments. It also allows a single MacTCP configuration to be used for many machines since the IP address is acquired dynamically from the RARP server.

MacTCP has two Control Panel interfaces; MacTCP and AdminTCP. AdminTCP lets you change the various configuration parameters and lock in some or all of the configuration values. Once you have set up the specific configuration, you delete the AdminTCP control panel. Accordingly, the locked configuration parameters can't be changed by a user unless another copy of MacTCP is installed with the AdminTCP Control Panel. This procedure is an administrative convenience for a site with many machines. For example, you can lock all the parameters and have the Macintosh use RARP to obtain a valid IP address. Or you can just lock the network address and let Macintosh users set their own IP host addresses.

Once MacTCP is installed properly, any application that uses TCP/IP and is written against the MacTCP interface will function properly. Keep in mind that while most Macintosh TCP/IP applications use the MacTCP driver, some might use their own network drivers.

DOS Configuration

Setting up direct LAN connectivity on a PC is somewhat more complex and less standardized than in the Macintosh environment. Unlike the Macintosh, which has a single network interface standard, DOS has several. As a result, if you are running only one TCP/IP based network application, such as TELNET, then you can get an application with the network device driver built into the application. If at a later time, you change out your network interface, you must also change the driver used by the program. If you have different network interface cards on different PCs, you must install a different application configuration on each machine. Also if a PC also uses other network layer protocols, such as Novell Netware or NetBios, then all the protocols must coexist and not interfere with each other. Finally there is no standard DOS equivalent of MacTCP, therefore much of the TCP/IP protocol stack must be written as a part of every application.

Fortunately, several standard hardware driver interface specifications exist that allow different higher-level protocols to coexist and use the same datalink interface. Five different types of specifications have been defined for use on the PC, as follows:

• Packet Driver

• Network Driver Interface Specification (NDIS)

• Adapter Support Interface (ASI)

• Open Datalink Interface (ODI)

• The Datalink Layer (DLL)

Each of these defines a standard method of writing a network application against the actual device interface. It also defines how a specific network interface device driver must interact with the driver interface specification. In essence each defines a virtual network interface for the application writer and a specific higher-level

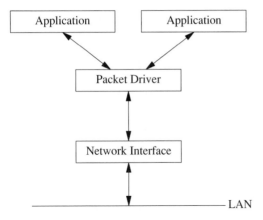

Figure 10.2 Packet Driver.

communications interface for the device driver programmer. A good source book for how these interfaces work is found in [FTP Software 1991].

Descriptions of these specifications are beyond the scope of this book. Fortunately, describing how one interface works pretty much covers the others as well — the differences are in the details and not the general philosophy — so we present next a common driver specification.

A Common Device Interface Specification. The most common specification used with TCP/IP applications today is the Packet Driver specification. This specification is written as a DOS **terminate and stay resident (TSR)** program and defines a sharable device interface specification. The TSR it is loaded into memory by instructions in the DOS *autoexec.bat* file.

Fig. 10.2 shows the Packet Driver architecture. As the figure illustrates, each application shares a common logical network interface. The Packet Driver sits between the hardware device (LAN) and the application. The application communicates with the Driver through a standard network interface, telling the Driver what packets it expects to be passed to it from the network device. The Driver then demultiplexes each frame received from the network interface and uses the value of various frame fields to determine if the encapsulated packet is, for example, an IP packet. An application can even tell the Driver which IP application it wants, down to the port number found in the TCP or UDP header. The Driver itself handles all the details about how the specific communication device works to send and receive frames from the network. More than a single application can run using the same Packet Driver; the interface specification keeps applications from stepping on each other.

Note that if you are running other applications that use the network and you also are using a Packet Driver, all other applications, even those that use NetBios or Netware, must use the Packet Driver interface. An application that uses an NDIS interface can't be running or loaded at the same time as an application that uses a Packet Driver. If this does occur, the two separate device drivers will interact with each other as they access the same device and cause unexpected results.

Another problem arises when using a Packet Driver with Novell Netware. When using Ethernet, Novell originally employed a variation of the 802.2 frame format. As in an 802.2 frame format, the *type* field in the frame header of the Novel variation is treated as a *length* field. With a Packet Driver that understands 802.2 formats, this normally doesn't pose a problem. Unfortunately, Novell decided on its own internal format, which doesn't conform to the 802.2 specification. The result is a DOS Novell client machine that uses a Packet Driver and Novell Netware won't work. To solve this problem, you must modify the frame format the Novell systems generate to comply with Ethernet framing. You do this by setting the *type* field in the Ethernet header for Novell packets to 0x8137, which is assigned to Novell, and then configure the DOS client machine to use the Packet Driver interface. In this way, a Novell client and server can work with TCP/IP-based services. See Appendix A for where this fix is available from.

Appendix A also tells you the FTP sites where the collection of Packet Drivers can be obtained. It is very likely a Packet Driver is available for your particular network interface card in the collection. Also many network interface card manufacturers freely supply a Packet Driver with their products.

To properly load the Driver, add the correct commands to your *autoexec.bat* file. This usually means you must select a software interrupt address plus some board-specific parameters for the device. The Packet Driver collection comes with more complete instructions about how to initialize these TSRs. The software interrupt address that DOS expects for a TSR is in the range 0x60 through 0x80. To load the Driver, pick a software interrupt that is not already in use and start the Driver. The Driver responds with the software interrupt address and appears to terminate; however, it remains memory resident and responds to application and network driver requests.

Once the Packet Driver is loaded, any application that needs network services can use the Driver's services to send and receive packets. Be aware that the Packet Driver is a very low-level interface. It has no TCP/IP functionality; rather it simply passes IP packets to an application when it determines that a frame encapsulates an IP packet. All the higher-level TCP/IP protocol functionality must be built into the various applications. This means in practice that unlike the Macintosh case, every application has a large part of the TCP/IP protocol stack built into it. What this means in practice that only a single TCP/IP application can be run at a time.

10.3 Setting UP NCSA Telnet

A popular public domain TCP/IP system for use on both PC and Macintosh is the NCSA Telnet package. Developed by the National Center for Supercomputing Applications, NCSA Telnet is an integrated TELNET and FTP client program that allows a user to use the TELNET and FTP protocol from the user's PC.

Appendix A explains how to get this software. Once you obtain the software, copy it to your DOS or Macintosh system. The easiest way to perform the latter function the first time is either to copy it to a floppy disk or to use serial line file transfer program such as *kermit*. You must get the NCSA Telnet package in the native file format for the target system. Note that the DOS version is bundled up and archived with the ZIP archive utility that is a standard PC archival tool. It is functionally a combination of the UNIX *tar* and *compress* utilities. Copies of this utility are available from most archive sites. The Macintosh version is distributed in what is called "binhex" format. A Macintosh utility called *binhex4* is used to read this archive. The file is then processed with the *stuffit* utility to expand the file and unarchive it into its final format.

Once the program is unbundled and installed, it's a relatively straightforward matter to configure the program itself. We describe the DOS configuration first — it's more complex because of the lack of a DOS equivalent of MacTCP — and follow with the Macintosh configuration.

DOS Configuration for NCSA Telnet

The configuration file for NCSA Telnet is called *config.tel*. The file, a sample of which is shown in Fig. 10.3, is largely self-explanatory and the example supplied with the distribution is heavily annotated. This file sets the various operating parameters used by the system. All the parameters are a keyletter followed by an equal sign (=) and then the value of the keyletter. Following are the meanings of the various parameters:

• Line 1 – *myname*
The name of the local system. It isn't essential and is used only by the associated *lpr* program to identify print jobs.

• Line 2 – *myip*
The IP address of the PC. It can be set to either a specific address or one of the keywords RARP or BOOTP. If the value is RARP or BOOTP, IP address lookup is handled dynamically.

• Line 3 – *netmask*
The IP subnet mask.

• Line 4 – *domain*
The default domain that is added to simple names when a DNS query is sent.

• Line 5 – *hardware*
The type of network interface used. In this case, the keyword *packet* means that a Packet Driver interface is installed.

• Line 6 – *ioaddr*
The software interrupt address of the Packet Driver. This number is interpreted as a hexadecimal number but is not written in the standard hexadecimal format, that is, with a leading "0x."

```
(1)   myname="pc.tic.com"
(2)   myip=192.135.128.67
(3)   netmask=255.255.255.0
(4)   domain="tic.com"
(5)   hardware=packet
(6)   ioaddr=60
(7)   arptime=8
(8)   contime=20
(9)   retrans=7
(10)  mtu=1500
(11)  maxseg=2048
(12)  rwin=512
(13)  termtype="vt100"
(14)  tek=yes
(15)  video=cga
(16)  bios=yes
(17)  ftp=no
(18)  rcp=no
(19)  passfile="c:\ncsa\password"
(20)  services="c:\sys\services"
(21)  capfile="c:\xx"
(22)  beep=yes
(23)  name=default
(24)  scrollback=400
(25)  erase=backspace
(26)  vtwrap=yes
(27)  crmap=4.3BSDCRNUL
(28)  nfcolor=white
(29)  nbcolor=black
(30)  bfcolor=red
(31)  bbcolor=blue
(32)  rfcolor=black
(33)  rbcolor=white
(34)  ufcolor=red
(35)  ubcolor=cyan
(36)  name=akasha.tic.com
(37)  hostip=192.135.128.129
(38)  nameserver=1
(39)  name=gw.tic.com
(40)  hostip=192.135.128.65
(41)  gateway=1
```

Figure 10.3 NCSA Telnet Configuration File.

• Line 7 – *arptime*
The timeout interval when an ARP request is sent. If no reply is received within this timeout, the target host is presumed to be down or nonexistent.

• Line 8 – *contime*
The number of seconds TCP will try a connection before timing it out and returning an error message to the user.

- Line 9 – *retrans*

  The retransmission timer in intervals of 1/18 second. This is the time TCP will wait before retransmitting a message that has not been acknowledged.

- Line 10 – *mtu*

  The MTU of the interface hardware. This is the maximum IP packet size that will be sent out on the interface by the program. Some versions of NCSA Telnet limit this to a maximum of 1024 bytes.

- Line 11 – *maxseg*

  The largest TCP message that can be received by the program.

- Line 12 – *rwin*

  The TCP receive window size. Note that larger is not necessarily better.

- Line 13 – *termtype*

  The type to use for the terminal emulation. This is most commonly *vt100*.

- Line 14 – *tek*

  A determination of whether Tektronics graphics support is desired. This is an option that allows the PC to act as a Tektronics graphics terminal.

- Line 15 – *video*

  The type of video card installed in the PC.

- Line 16 – *bios*

  An indication of whether screen updates should use the standard BIOS system or write directly to the screen.

- Line 17 – *ftp*

  An indication of whether an FTP server on the PC is activated when the program is run. Use this parameter carefully since a server will let any network user access files on your PC. The server can be protected by setting up a password file with the *passfile* keyword.

- Line 18 – *rcp*

  Indicates whether an RCP server on the PC is activated when the program is run. Use this parameter carefully because it allows unlimited access to the PCs files.

- Line 19 – *passfile*

  A password file for the FTP server that contains usernames and encrypted passwords. Unfortunately, the encryption algorithm is different from the encryption used by all UNIX systems, so encrypted UNIX passwords can't be used in this file. A separate utility, *telpass,* supplied as part of the distribution, is used to maintain the password file on the PC.

- Line 20 – *services*

  The name-to-port mappings of IP services. This file contains the same information as the */etc/services* file found on a UNIX system.

- Line 21 – *capfile*
  The scrollback capture file. Lines scrolled off the screen are saved in this file.

- Line 22 – *beep*
  A notice to the user regarding which session generated a bell character. Because the program can run multiple sessions simultaneously but doesn't have window support, this parameter is convenient for notifying the user which session needs attention.

Following the general parameters are specific ones for each session, the more important of which are listed next:

- Line 23 – *name*
  The name of a session. Each session is given a name. Note, the name *default* is reserved and should include all the default parameters used by all other sessions. Many of these defaults relate to color displays.

- Line 24 – *scrollback*
  The number of lines of display scrollback. Lines of scrollback are saved in *capfile*.

- Line 25 – *erase*
  The erase character.

- Line 26 – *vtwrap*
  The determination of whether automatic linewrapping is enabled on the terminal emulator.

- Line 27 – *crmap*
  An indication of how TELNET carriage returns are mapped. These should be set to 4.3BSDNUL for compatibility with most BSD UNIX hosts.

- Lines 28 – 35 nfcolor, nbcolor, bfcolor, bbcolor, rfcolor, rbcolor, ufcolor, ubcolor
  Respectively, normal foreground color, normal background color, blinking foreground color, blinking background color, reverse foreground color, reverse background color, underlined foreground color, and underlined background colors on color displays. These parameters can be set for each session.

- Line 36 and 39 – *name*
  The name of a specific session. The session inherits all the default session parameters, unless they are changed. Additional parameters for each session may follow, until a new session definition is started. In this example we show two session definitions.

- Lines 37 and 40 – *hostip*
  The IP address of the host for each session.

- Lines 38 – *nameserver*
  The IP address of the host for this session is a DNS nameserver. More than a single nameserver may be listed. The lookup order is denoted by the numeric argument from lowest to highest.

Telnet Batch File

```
echo off
if .%1 == . goto defh
telbin -h config.tel %1 %2 %3 %4 %5 %6
goto exith
:defh
telbin -h config.tel yoyodyne
:exith
```

FTP Batch File

```
ftpbin -h config.tel %1 %2 %3 %4 %5 %6 %7 %8 %9
```

Figure 10.4 Telnet and FTP Batch Files.

• Line 41 – *gateway*

The host for this session is a router to nonlocal networks. IP packets for a nonlo-cal network are sent to the router. More than one gateway can be specified and each gateway is tried, like nameservers, in a round-robin fashion.

Note that it is not essential to list all hosts you may want to access in the configu-ration file. If you connect to a host without a session, the parameters of the default session are used. But you must have at least one session with the *nameserver* key-word in order to perform hostname to IP address translation.

Once you have set up the configuration file, you can install the executables on the PC. The actual TELNET client program is in the file *telbin.exe* and the FTP client program is in the file *ftpbin.exe*. Each program is front-ended with config-urable DOS batch filed called *telnet.bat* and *ftp.bat,* respectively. Shown in Fig. 10.4, these files can be customized for your particular operating environment. The *-h* option (line 3 of Fig. 10.4) is followed by the name of the configuration file that is read when each program is started.

Several support programs also come with the NCSA Telnet package. They include DOS implementations of some familiar UNIX utility programs, such as *finger, lpq, lpr, lprm, rexec,* and *rsh.* These utilities can be run concurrently with the basic NCSA Telnet package.

Macintosh Configuration for NCSA Telnet

The Macintosh version of the program is functionally almost identical to the DOS version. It has support for both MacTCP as well as its own internal TCP/IP stack and is shipped as a single program with both types of interface support. We describe here the MacTCP version since it is the standard way to interface with a network using TCP/IP.

```
(1)   myname="mac.tic.com"
(2)   domain="tic.com"
(3)   contime=20
(4)   domaintime=2
(5)   domainretry=4
(6)   termtype="vt100"
(7)   tek=yes
(8)   ftp=no
(9)   rcp=no
(10)  passfile="ftppass"
(11)  name=default
(12)  scrollback=400
(13)  font="Courier"
(14)  fsize=12
(15)  erase=backspace
(16)  tektype=1
(17)  vtwrap=yes
(18)  vtwidth=80
(19)  vtlines=24
(20)  crmap=4.3BSDCRNUL
(21)  nfcolor="{0,0,0}"
(22)  nbcolor="{65434,65535,35286}"
(23)  bfcolor="{0,0,0}"
(24)  bbcolor="{65535,65535,65535}"
(25)  name=akasha.tic.com
(26)  name=gw.tic.com
```

Figure 10.5 NCSA Telnet Configuration File for the Macintosh.

All MacTCP parameters should be set up for the host as described earlier in this chapter. After you have installed the program, you can edit the *config.tel* file, which is nearly identical to the file used on the DOS version of the program. Fig. 10.5 shows an example configuration file for the Macintosh. You should place this file in either the System Folder or the directory in which the program's executable binary is stored.

Note that many TCP/IP-specific parameters are not included in the configuration file. This is because MacTCP takes care of that information. Without MacTCP support, the configuration file closely resembles DOS's. Therefore we explain next only the parameters that are specific to the Macintosh version.

• Line 4 – *domaintime*
  DNS retry interval for the first retry. Subsequent retries take increasingly more time.

• Line 5 – *domainretry*
Number of times to retry a DNS request.

• Line 10 – *passfile*
Password file for FTP. This is kept in the System Folder.

• Line 13 – *font*
Font to use for each separate window.

• Line 14 – *fontsize*
Size of font used in each window.

10.4 Mail Access

PC mail service with only TELNET and FTP access to the network is awkward and inconvenient for PC users. First, a user having mail must read it on a remote system. Also, the user must learn to use a different UA. Finally, the user either must compose mail responses on the remote system or download and edit them on the PC and then upload them for delivery.

Fortunately, direct network connection offers several alternatives to these inconveniences. For example, it's possible to run SMTP on a PC for both mail reception and delivery. In this case, the PC appears to be just another SMTP host on the network and mail is sent and received using SMTP. This solution, while viable, does have some significant drawbacks. First, most PC operating systems are not designed to run multiple programs concurrently. To run an SMTP server in the background under DOS or MacOS is not easy to do. More importantly, most PCs are turned off when not in use, which means mail reception is delayed until the PC is turned back on.

Suppose the PC user goes on vacation for two weeks, turning off the PC before departure. Mail sent to the user will sit in a remote site's mail queue. The MTA on the remote site will repeatedly try to send the mail to its final destination and will repeatedly fail. Eventually after many retries, the queued-up mail will timeout and be returned to the sender. Obviously, this is not reliable mail service.

You can solve this problem by installing a POP client on the PC. With POP installed, mail is delivered to a mailbox for the PC user on a well-known and stable mail server that is up continuously, thus ensuring mail is reliably received by the PC user. When ready to read the mail, the PC user executes the POP client, that is, the user checks with a POP server that in turn reads mail messages from the remote mailbox and transfers them to the PC. The PC user then can read the mail on the PC using a familiar editor. (We explained how a UNIX POP server is set up in Chapter 8.) To reply to an mail message, the user composes the message on the PC and delivers it using SMTP. Usually, the message is transferred first to a well-known local mail server, which then forwards the message to the final destination. This store-and-forward technique lets the mail server do all forwarding operations. The server also queues all outgoing mail, which simplifies the client SMTP implementation on the PC. Otherwise if the PC tried to deliver a message directly to the remote site, the site might be down and the message would need to be queued, an unnecessary complexity for the PC software. Letting the mail gateway handle all mail forwarding is both simpler and more reliable.

For mail to work properly, the fact that mail is sent or received from a PC should be hidden. This means that when a PC user sends an mail message to a remote recipient, the return address should hide the fact the message came from the PC. As we saw in Chapter 8, you should uncouple mail addresses from specific machine names. For example, a PC user, *george,* can send mail from the machine *mypc.tic.com,* but the return address should be *george@tic.com.* Fortunately, most POP software handles this address hiding when it is configured. If it doesn't, the *sendmail* configuration on the POP server can be modified to remove the specific machine name from the return address. The sample POP server configurations in Chapter 8 already do this.

POPMail for DOS

Both commercial software and freeware implementations of POP clients for PCs exist. For example, the University of Minnesota has implemented a freeware POP client for a DOS PC. Called POPMail, it gives the user a full-screen interface with pull-down menus that runs under DOS. The POP client uses the same Packet Driver interface that the NCSA Telnet package uses and is therefore completely compatible with the NCSA package. Setting up this program is very easy, for initial configuration is menu driven and the user is taken step by step through the configuration process. Any POP server that support POP Version 3 is compatible with this program.

Its configuration parameters resemble in many respects the NCSA Telnet package. When POPMail is initially configured, you must supply the following information:

• The IP address of the local host

• The IP address of the POP server on which the user's mailbox resides

• The full mail address of the PC user

• The password for access to the server mailbox

POPMail for the Macintosh

POPMail is also available for the Macintosh. Like the NCSA Telnet package, it is fully compatible with the MacTCP interface. POPMail gives the Macintosh user a familiar interface for reading and replying to mail. And as with the DOS version, setting up this program is very easy. It must be configured just as in the NCSA Telnet case and it can use the same POP server as the DOS version uses. Its configuration parameters also resemble the DOS version. When it is initially configured, you must supply only two parameters: the IP address of the local host and the IP address of the POP server on which the user's mailbox resides. For information on where to get both the Macintosh and DOS versions of this program, see Appendix A.

10.5 File Sharing

The final step up in functionality from TELNET, FTP, and mail connectivity using POP is full remote file sharing with a UNIX host system. File sharing allows a UNIX host to act as a fileserver for a set of PC clients. From a PC's point of view, the shared files look like another local disk on the PC; they are actually accessed over the network. This setup has the advantage of letting PCs access commonly shared files without having to duplicate them on every PC. It also lets the administrator more easily back up the commonly shared files with the more functional UNIX file backup software.

DOS Filesharing

Several proprietary filesharing systems are available for DOS-based machines. By far the most common is Novell Netware. Netware uses an adaptation of the **XNS (Xerox Network System)** protocol suite that is tailored for a LAN environment. However, while XNS is a peer-to-peer protocol, most Netware systems follow a strict client/server model in which a set of PCs remotely share a single fileserver on the same physical network. An extremely popular solution for filesharing across PC clients, Netware originally was implemented as a proprietary operating system (hence we don't go into detail about Netware installation). However, a version of the system called Portable Netware has been ported to several UNIX systems. Netware is frequently found in PC only environments, and is found less often in UNIX and TCP/IP environments, although with the development of Portable Netware, more UNIX-based Novell servers probably will be deployed.

You also can use NFS to fileshare your DOS PCs. Given the wide availability of NFS on UNIX systems, this solution is by far the most popular if you already have a large number of UNIX hosts. A number of commercial client implementations of NFS exist for IBM compatible PCs.

Macintosh Filesharing

For Macintosh to UNIX filesharing, you can use either **Appleshare** or NFS. Appleshare is the filesharing application protocol in the **Appletalk** protocol family that comes bundled with every Macintosh and so is reasonably easy to set up. A freeware UNIX version of an Appleshare file server is available. There also are a number of proprietary implementations of Appleshare fileserver software for UNIX systems that enable a Macintosh client to transparently access files on a UNIX server. We will discuss later in this chapter in detail how to use the most popular freeware version, the **Columbia Appletalk Package (CAP).**

Commercial NFS client implementations are also available for the Macintosh. Remote NFS filesystems can be mounted on them and look to the Macintosh client just like any Appleshare volume. See Appendix A for where you can obtain the CAP package.

DOS PC NFS Clients

PC NFS clients enable a PC to share UNIX files as if those files were mounted as a separate PC filesystem. A PC user accesses the remote filesystem as if it were a PC filesystem, using the familiar DOS filesystem convention. Essentially the NFS client translates PC filesystem calls into NFS RPC calls and retrieves the files across the network.

Several issues arise when using NFS to access a remote UNIX NFS server.

1. The DOS filenaming conventions are different and more limited than are UNIX filenaming conventions, as follow:

   - DOS allows filenames with a maximum of 8 characters and a 3-character extension, while all UNIX systems allow at least 14-character filenames.

   - DOS filenames aren't case sensitive, unlike UNIX filenames.

   - DOS filenames also are identified by a unique disk partition prefix that is a single letter in the range A to Z. UNIX filenames have no notion of a disk partition number; rather, the file's physical location is hidden by allowing a filesystem to be arbitrarily mounted at any point in the UNIX filesystem hierarchy.

   The DOS NFS client must translate a UNIX filename into an equivalent and unique DOS filename. If you are accessing an arbitrary UNIX directory tree with NFS, the translated filenames can become somewhat cryptic. On the other hand, if you set up a subdirectory on the UNIX host and enforce the rule that specific subdirectory should only be accessed by DOS PCs, then the DOS filenames will map nicely into their UNIX equivalents. Because of the limitations of DOS filenames, this is probably the preferred way of using NFS on DOS machines.

2. Another problem is access to text files. Unfortunately, the UNIX and DOS line termination characters are different. DOS uses a carriage-return <CR> followed by a line-feed <LF> character to terminate a line, while UNIX uses only a line-feed character. So editing a DOS text file on a UNIX system, and vice versa, is a problem. Again because of this difference in convention, it's usually best to allow DOS users to create their own text files and to establish specific conventions for translating between the differing formats.

3. The final problem with using NFS on a PC involves access security. The standard UNIX NFS file access method uses UNIX userids and groupids to permit or deny access to specific files. Within an all UNIX environment that has a consistent userid/groupid space, this access methodology works reasonably well. DOS, however, has no notion of a userid or a groupid. A DOS user can access all the machine resources, and no permission checking is mandated or provided. While the standard NFS access mechanism is not the most secure, it does provide some level of protection. However, a DOS user can completely subvert

the entire access control system if the user's machine is allowed access to NFS filesystems via the normal method of adding the hostname to the */etc/exports* file on the UNIX server. Once the filesystem is mounted, the DOS user can masquerade as any UNIX user simply by passing the other user's userid/groupid as part of each filesystem request.

To provide some measure of security, a separate daemon is used to authenticate a DOS NFS user. A public-domain version of such a daemon called *bwnfsd* is available. Using this daemon, the NFS client asks the DOS user for a valid UNIX username and password. The username/password is sent to the daemon, which is running as a normal Sun RPC server. The daemon validates the username/password and returns a valid userid followed by a list of valid groupids. At this point, the NFS client calls on the normal mount daemon to request a remote filesystem be mounted. NFS file requests using the userid/groupids are then sent to the NFS server. While this method can be subverted by a determined system cracker, it does allow some degree of security. As long as the NFS client implementation is not compromised, the procedure lets a remote DOS user be automatically authenticated to the NFS server. Note, each remote DOS user must have a valid UNIX username on the NFS server.

Macintosh NFS Clients

A number of commercial vendors support an NFS client for the Macintosh. The NFS client looks like a Mac Chooser extension, and remote UNIX file volumes can be mounted as if they were Macintosh filesystems. When the Macintosh accesses an NFS volume, the volume appears as an icon on the Mac Desktop. Security measures are similar to those taken with PCs using NFS — the same *bwnfsd* method is used to authenticate Macintosh users.

MacOS uses a directory structure similar to UNIX's, except that each Macintosh file has the following three possible parts:

• *data fork*
Contains normal data that is equivalent to the contents of a UNIX file; that is, the data is a sequence of bytes interpreted by the application.

• *resource fork*
Holds what MacOS calls various resources. A resource can be as simple as the text string of an error message to something as complex as an executable program.

• *finderinfo*
Consists of information about the file that the MacOS finder uses for displaying the desktop and finding files in the filesystem. Also file creation, modification, and backup dates are kept here. This data is loosely equivalent to the UNIX inode information kept for each file, although this information does contain additional items not found in an inode.

An actual MacOS file has both a data and a resource fork. One of these forks can be 0 length. Typically an executable program has a 0 length data fork, while a data file has a 0 length resource fork. The finderinfo is kept separate from the actual file itself and is a part of the Macintosh hierarchical file information. Although the data/resource fork and finderinfo extension is a nice feature, it does cause some filename translation problems when a Macintosh file is stored on a UNIX system. On a UNIX server, there are several methods for storing the three parts of a Macintosh file. One method shadows each directory with a separate subdirectory that contains the resource fork and the finderinfo for each file. Alternatively, the resource and finderinfo can be stored in the same file that includes a unique prefix indicating it contains resource and finderinfo data and not user data. Finally, all three parts of a Macintosh file can be stored in a single UNIX file. Note that the NFS client code handles access to each of these files by translating the normal MacOS filesystem calls into their appropriate NFS counterparts.

Macintosh filenames are also incompatible with UNIX filenames because they can contain 8-bit characters. UNIX filenames contain only 7-bit characters. Therefore these 8-bit characters must be mapped to an appropriate sequence of 7-bit characters. This character mapping is handled by the specific NFS client software. Special characters lengthen filenames, which then might be longer than allowed by the particular version of UNIX. On UNIX systems with very long filename support (up to 255 characters), however, this rarely presents a problem. Note also that *tar* archives of a deeply nested Macintosh filesystem might not work when very long Macintosh filenames combined with a lot of special characters are used.

Access to UNIX text files is generally supported by Macintosh applications. However, care should be taken if these text-only files are edited on the Macintosh. A resource fork is usually created, resulting in the files being transformed to the point where they are unreadable on the UNIX system. NFS on the Macintosh is particularly useful when used to support user files that are accessed only by the Macintosh user or for text-only UNIX that don't have a resource fork. Some implementations of NFS for the Macintosh will automatically translate the UNIX text line-terminator (the line-feed character <LF>) to the Macintosh line-terminator (the carriage-return character <CR>). This is convenient when sharing read-only files between the two types of systems.

UNIX Appleshare Server

As an alternative to an NFS client, you can use a UNIX system as an Appleshare server. Macintosh computers are shipped with a built-in Appleshare client implementation that allows Macintosh computers to share files with any computer that supports an Appleshare server. The freeware CAP package mentioned earlier turns a UNIX system into an Appleshare server. CAP also includes in addition to a fileserver, applications that allow a UNIX-connected Laserwriter to be used transparently by Macintosh applications over the network. CAP implements most of the Appletalk protocol suite. Before delving into its specifics, let's first become better acquainted with the Appletalk protocol family.

Overview of Appletalk. Appletalk supports an Internet-style architecture. Each Appletalk node is uniquely identified by a 2-byte network number and a 1-byte node number. An Appletalk internetwork is connected using Appletalk routers ("bridges" in Appletalk parlance). Each bridge is initially configured with the network and node address of each interface. Then as other Appletalk nodes are started up, they are dynamically assigned an unused node address.

Appletalk is a layered protocol similar to IP. At the lowest layer of the stack is a **Link Access Protocol (LAP).** The LAP indicates to which node on the local network to send a packet. A LAP header is 3 bytes long: 1 byte is the destination address, 1 is the source address, and 1 is a type field that tells the type of the encapsulated packet. The original LAP is called **Localtalk,** which sends and receives packets over one of the serial interfaces found on all Macintosh computers.

The next most popular LAP is **Ethertalk Phase I.** Here, packets are encapsulated within Ethernet frames with a type field of 0x809b. Other LAPs are also defined for 802.3 and 802.5 networks.

An integral part of Ethertalk and other broadcast LAN LAPs is the **Apple Address Resolution Protocol (AARP)** which is similar to IP ARP. AARP maps the LAP destination node addresses to the datalink address for delivery.

Above LAP is the **Datagram Delivery Protocol (DDP).** DDP has two header formats — long and short. A long DDP header contains the following data:

• The source and destination network and node numbers

• The total length of the DDP packet and a checksum

• The source and destination socket numbers

• The type of the encapsulated higher-level protocol

An Appletalk socket resembles the functionality of a TCP/IP socket. Appletalk has a set of well-known sockets for each of the higher-level protocols. Each socket address is 1 byte long. A short DDP header contains only a length, a destination and a source socket, and a type field. This type of header assumes the node address is the same as that found in the LAP header and that the network is the same as the sending host's.

On top of the DDP are various support and application protocols. These include those for data delivery as well as support protocols that are integral to Appletalk and that handle naming and routing in an Appletalk internet:

• The **Apple Transaction Protocol (ATP)** is a reliable delivery mechanism similar to TCP.

• The **Apple Filing Protocol (AFP)** is a remote file system protocol, resembles the functionality of NFS and is used to transfer files to and from an Appleshare server.

• The **Printer Access Protocol (PAP)** defines how to send output to and control access to printing devices on the network. Its closest equivalent is the Berkeley Print Spooler Protocol used by the UNIX *lpd* daemon. Most Laserwriters are attached to Macintoshes using Appletalk and PAP, where the Macintosh and the Laserwriter talk to each other using the PostScript page description language. As we see later, it's possible to configure a UNIX machine to pretend it's an attached Laserwriter and therefore to spool Macintosh printer jobs to a printer attached to the UNIX system.

• The **Zone Information Protocol (ZIP)** distributes information about Appletalk zones. An **Appletalk zone** is analogous to a DNS domain but with some important differences.

• The **Name Binding Protocol (NBP)** is Appletalk's nameservice for locating resources on the network. Its closest equivalent in the IP world is DNS or perhaps NIS. Table 10.1 shows the general parallels between IP and Appletalk.

Appletalk internetwork resources are identified by a network number and a node number. They also are given names that are registered with the NBP and that Appletalk clients use to request resources. A **resource name** is a alphanumeric identifier and a zone name separated by an "@". Zone names are arbitrary and can span Appletalk networks. An example resource name is

```
Peaches:Laserwriter@tic
```

Table 10.1 Appletalk and IP.

ISO Layer	IP	Appletalk
Application	NFS	AFP
	DNS	NBP
	RIP	RMTP
	BSD Print Spooler	PAP
	—	ZIP
Presentation	RFC822	—
Session	Sun RPC	-
Transport	TCP	ATP
	UDP	—
Network	IP	DDP
Datalink	Ethernet	Ethertalk
	—	Localtalk

which identifies the resource named Peaches to be a Laserwriter in the *tic* zone. Associated with the resource will be the network and node number where the resource is located.

Setting up a single Appletalk network that uses LAP is simple since Appletalk dynamically assigns node addresses to each connected system. This dynamic address assignment makes simple Appletalk networks easy to install.

An Appletalk internetwork requires a little more work since each separate network needs to be assigned a unique number. Usually this network number need to be configured only on the routers that connect the separate networks. When systems come up on each separate network, they are dynamically assigned node numbers. File servers and other resources identify themselves by broadcasting their own resource names, resulting in the naming tables on all systems being updated.

Appletalk currently supports two different phases of internetworks. Phase I networks are called **nonextended.** This means each physical network cable identifies a single Appletalk network. Although zone names can span networks, only one zone is associated with each network cable. Phase II networks are called **extended.** In this case, a single physical network can have more than one logical Appletalk network and each network can have more than one zone associated with it. CAP currently supports only Phase I networks, but can be used in a Phase II environment if Phase I restrictions are followed. For more information on Appletalk, see [Apple 1986].

CAP Implementation. Theoretically a complete Appletalk implementation could be incorporated into a UNIX kernel much as TCP/IP is. Because Appletalk frames can be distinguished from IP frames, they could be carried over the same datalink interface. The full Appletalk protocol family could be implemented as a part of the UNIX kernel's networking code, although this method would require a great deal of work and the implementation would not be very portable across a range of UNIX systems. Other problems also would arise. For example, source OS code would be required, which often is not possible. Also the original Localtalk serial LAP interface was not supported by most UNIX system serial ports. CAP was developed as a piece of software to help integrate Macintoshes which were attached to Localtalk networks. An obvious use of a UNIX system would be as a server to a cluster of Macintoshes. Since UNIX did not have Appletalk support nor the serial protocol support, this integration was not possible without some assistance.

Most UNIX systems did support TCP/IP rather well. UNIX systems also supported Ethernet hardware. One approach to adding a UNIX system as a part of an Appletalk network is to put Appletalk LAP packets inside UDP packets for transport to and from the UNIX host. Software on the UNIX system which implemented Appletalk would send and receive UDP encapsulated Appletalk packets. Hardware and software was developed which allowed the linkage between a Localtalk network and an Ethernet. A machine that does this is called an **Appletalk IP bridge** and they encapsulate Appletalk packets inside UDP packets in a specific way which is called **Kinetic's IP (KIP).**

KIP encapsulation avoids the problem of sending all Appletalk packets to a single UNIX process which then has to demultiplex the packet types and socket numbers which then sends each demultiplexed stream to a specific UNIX process which uses Appletalk. This method would be extremely inefficient unless Appletalk was implemented as part of the UNIX kernel.

Instead KIP defines some rules about how Appletalk applications can map a set of UDP ports, so each UNIX Appletalk process can talk directly to the remote Appletalk process. KIP maps each well-known Appletalk service to a specific UDP port. Since each Appletalk services uses an Appletalk socket number, the mapping of the well-known services to a UDP port number is trivial. A specific range of UDP ports has been set aside for this purpose. They are shown in Table 10.2 For non well-known services an algorithm is used to map the Appletalk socket to the IP port. Basically a starting range of UDP ports is defined and each port in the range is tried in sequence until a free one is found.

Using this method the Appletalk IP bridge can simply forward an incoming Localtalk packet to the correct IP address and UDP port number. The IP address of the server is mapped from the Appletalk network and node numbers and the UDP port is mapped from the destination Appletalk socket number. This methodology lets Appletalk be implemented as a set of library calls which at the lowest layer read and write from and to UDP sockets.

When a new service, say an Appleshare server, is created, it advertises itself using the NBP protocol to other nodes on the network. The advertisements address which includes the Appletalk socket number is tucked away by each client. An Appletalk client simply sends a request to that socket on that particular node to obtain the service. The KIP bridge does the translation of the <network, node, socket> triple to the appropriate <IP address, UDP, port> triplet. Using this system an Appletalk network can be transparently routed across an IP network and UNIX systems can act as servers for Macintosh clients.

CAP is an implementation of the user level library of basic Appletalk calls. Applications which use Appletalk can be written against this library. CAP supports both KIP encapsulation and has functions which provide the Appletalk to UDP interface. CAP also supports native Ethertalk on UNIX systems which

---

Table 10.2 Appletalk Socket to IP Port Numbers.

Appletalk Socket	UDP Port
RMTP	201
NBP	202
ECHO	204
ZIS	206

support direct access to Ethernet frames. In this implementation each Ethernet frame is examined and sent to the Appletalk application if it meets the filtering criteria specified. Currently only SunOS and Ultrix support for native Ethertalk exists.

Setting Up CAP. Appendix A tells you where the CAP sources are available on the Internet. CAP supports both Ethertalk and KIP. The KIP interface calls for no special host requirements. Native Ethertalk, however, requires a frame-level Ethernet interface. If you have kernel sources, CAP also supports the generic *enet* driver code that is found in BSD UNIX systems.

Simply follow the installation instructions and compile and load the CAP library and applications. CAP applications use two configuration files. For KIP, it examines the file *atalk.local,* which contains up to four configuration lines. An example *atalk.local* file is shown in Fig. 10.6 and described as follows:

• Line 1

A required line, this line contains the Appletalk network number and node address of the CAP host and the host's Appletalk zone. Appletalk network numbers are written as decimal numbers separated by a period; a node address is written as a single decimal number. For example, in the figure the Appletalk address of the CAP host is network 10.1, node 6 in zone *tic*.

• Line 2

Also a required line, it comprises the Appletalk address of the Appletalk-to-IP bridge followed by the KIP bridge's IP address in dotted quad notation. The IP address assignment for the bridge is a special mapping. In that case the last byte of the IP address must match the Appletalk node number.

• Line 3

An optional line, it identifies the host that is running the Appletalk Network Information Server. This server acts as a registry for Appletalk resources. It also runs the Appletalk echo protocol, which is a required protocol. In the figure, it's the CAP machine that must be running the CAP *atis* application.

• Line 4

Also an optional line, it gives the network address of the Asynchronous Appletalk Network. This network requires either special hardware or running

---

Figure 10.6 atalk.local File.

```
55.1    6    "MY ZONE"
55.1    5    128.254.1.5
55.1    6
170.32 "Async Zone"
```

the **UNIX Appletalk Bridge (UAB),** an application that turns a UNIX host into an Appletalk router. The UAB routes Appletalk packets between Ethernet interfaces. It also supports Asynchronous Appletalk, a network that allows a UNIX host to attach to another Appletalk network via a serial line interface. This has since been superseded by **Apple Remote Access (ARA).**

You can write your own Appletalk applications using the CAP library, but several useful applications are included with the distribution. Two of the most useful are *aufs* and *lwsrv,* both of which we discuss next.

Setting Up aufs. *aufs* is a server implementation of AFP. It lets a UNIX host act as an Appleshare server. If you are using KIP, simply set up the *atalk.local* file and add aufs to your OS startup script. Note that unless another host is already running as a Network Information Server, you must start up atis before you start aufs. Aufs requires no special options for normal use; however two of its options are useful, as follows:

• *-l*

Enables logging. Following the *-l*, you specify the name of a logfile.

• *-U*

Sets the number of concurrent sessions allowed. The default is 10 and each session takes up one process slot.

From the user's standpoint, aufs looks like any other Appleshare server. Security is provided via the normal UNIX password mechanism. An aufs user must have a userid and login account with a password on the UNIX system. Also supported is an optional look-aside password validation mechanism that lets the Macintosh username be longer than the 8-character limit imposed by the length of UNIX usernames. The longer Macintosh username is mapped to a UNIX username and validated with a separate password. If an invalid password is assigned to the UNIX username, the Macintosh user can have file access, but is denied login access to the UNIX system. You might want to consider this option if for security reasons, login access to the fileserver is undesirable.

Setting Up lwsrv. Another popular CAP application is a UNIX Laserwriter server called *lwserv.* The lwserv program appears to a Macintosh client like it's a directly attached Laserwriter. Macintosh users can access the Laserwriter through the Chooser dialogue. Lwserv spools PostScript files to a real Laserwriter through the standard Berkeley Print Spooler protocol. Because the Berkeley Print Spooler supports remote spoolers, the real Laserwriter need not be on the host that is acting as the proxy Laserwriter.

Lwserv includes a number of options that take into account the differences between the output of a Macintosh PostScript and that which a Laserwriter attached to a UNIX system expects. One difference is the end-of-line terminator.

For a PostScript file to produce proper output, the printer must be able to access **Procedure Sets (ProcSets)** that are contained in a typical PostScript program. ProcSets are functions called by the PostScript program to produce output on a printer. On a Macintosh, they are found on the Macintosh client in the LaserPrep file. A printer that speaks PostScript over an Appletalk network requests these ProcSets as they are needed. The ProcSets are included as they are encountered in the PostScript program. Lwserv will ask for these ProcSets from the Macintosh client.

References

Apple 1986.   Apple, *Inside Macintosh,* Addison-Wesley, Reading, MA (1986).
FTP Software 1991.   FTP Software, *PC/TCP Interoperability Guide,* FTP Software, Inc., Wakefiled, MA (1991).

CHAPTER 11

Managing the Network

A TCP/IP network is not a static system. Because it is intentionally an internetworking protocol suite, you can design and construct very large, complex networks that cross administrative boundaries and cover large geographic areas. The ability of TCP/IP to scale up to large networks means separate networks can be interconnected; they don't remain islands of computing. As a result administration is more complex. Further, most UNIX systems aren't really designed in a way that they can be administered well in a networked environment. The administrative tools that come as a part of most UNIX systems derive from a timesharing tradition and are therefore designed with that model in mind.

Managing the network invariably takes more time and money than does the initial network installation. Just when you think everything is configured properly, a new application comes along that requires higher bandwidth or a reallocation of existing resources. The network also might expand to outlying offices for mail access or direct interactive connectivity. An isolated network could be interconnected as well. And user accounts will, of course, continue to be added to the system and issues over access privileges will arise.

In this chapter, we focus primarily on how to effectively administer UNIX systems and less on management of the pieces of the network infrastructure, such as routers, bridges, and the network hardware itself. However, we briefly explore network management issues, offering a short guide rather than a panacea with all the solutions. We also examine some useful UNIX tools that help network management and describe SNMP and how it is a useful framework for managing routing nodes. In addition, we examine some of the more mundane issues regarding how managing UNIX systems in a networked environment differs from the traditional timesharing model from which UNIX evolved.

11.1   Rdist as a Management Tool

Rdist is a UNIX tool that automates the distribution of files across a system of networked computers. Most UNIX systems come with rdist as a built-in utility program. It's also freely available in source form from Internet archive sites.

Rdist was designed as a stop-gap way of duplicating common files on networked UNIX systems before networked file systems became generally available. Many people were sure the need for it would disappear once distributed file were deployed. However, rdist has not died and gone away. In fact it's still a useful utility even in a network that relies heavily on a networked file system for filesharing. It turns out that many common files in some cases should be explicitly duplicated rather than shared using a distributed file system in a distributed environment. Replication of critical utilities is still important to prevent the networked system from becoming vulnerable to single points of failure.

Single Server System

It's possible to set up a single NFS server that contains all user files. It's also possible to NFS-mount all the utility and application programs from that single server onto all the client machines. You then configure each client with only a local swap disk or even without any disk space at all. A local swap disk is usually configured, however; doing so improves overall performance because paging and swapping across the network isn't very efficient use of network bandwidth.

Figure 11.1 shows a server with a number of diskless clients. This system is very easy to manage. All operating system and user files reside on the single server. Backups are easy, since the server has all the disks. You need only keep a single copy of all the utility and application programs. Adding an application into this environment also is easy — you simply add it to the server. Management of the system closely resembles that for a timesharing system. You manage UNIX userids and groupids on the single server machine and use NIS to distribute them to clients. Finally, adding or deleting user is trivial.

While easy to manage, the single server model does have drawbacks:

Figure 11.1 Diskless Cluster.

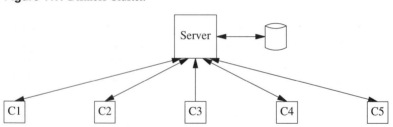

- The server is a single point of failure.
  This means that if the server goes down, all the clients are unusable. Given the high reliability of hardware today, this is not an enormous drawback except for applications that require very high system availability. And the single point of failure is offset by the easier management of the overall system.

- The server and the network might not scale very well.
  Using a single server for more than 5 or 10 client machines on a single Ethernet is not advisable. Eventually network bandwidth is taken up doing file transfers to and from the server. Because all executable programs reside on the server, network bandwidth also is used by initial program loading from the server.

Scaling up a single server architecture requires the addition of a much bigger and faster server. Eventually a larger network bandwidth also is needed between the clients and the server or multiple network interfaces must be provided to keep overall network bandwidth utilization on each network to a reasonable level.

The single server model is really a timesharing system in a more modern guise. The server functions like a large timesharing system with very fast, intelligent terminal nodes. The terminals are no longer just dumb character-mapped devices, yet like a timesharing terminal, they are entirely dependent on the server for their operation. While considerable computing is offloaded to the clients, the server is located where all the other resources of the system are shared. Thus the same single point of failure and scalability problems of the old centralized timesharing model of computing reappear.

Multiple Servers

The alternative to a large centralized server is multiple servers, each with its own set of clients. Figure 11.2 shows a networked system with several servers. As the figure shows, each client/server cluster is configured as a separate network. Client/server traffic is isolated to a single physical network that utilizes network bandwidth more efficiently. Each server contains client user files and copies of all

Figure 11.2 Multiple Servers.

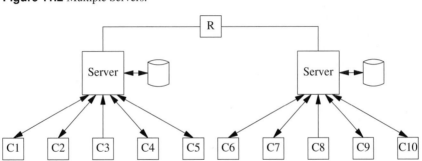

shared utilities. Managing this system is more difficult, however, because the common files on each server must be consistently maintained — an update applied to one server must be propagated to the other servers.

You can use rdist very effectively in this environment to maintain server consistency. Also, as we shall see, rdist can be used to distribute software updates to all servers and to distribute and maintain system configuration files on all the servers as well.

11.2 Managing Userids and Groupids

UNIX system security is based solely on userids and groupids; all system resource access is granted or denied based upon them. On a single timeshared UNIX system, this method has always worked well and is simple to manage. With multiple systems shared by the same user community, however, proper userid and groupid management is more difficult and yet is essential for system usability and security.

Distributing Userids and Groupids

The userid and groupid concept is a very simple and elegant solution to system access on a single timeshared host. Unfortunately, it's not well suited to a distributed heterogeneous computing environment. Some method must be developed to allow all hosts on the network to share the access information contained in the *etc/passwd* and the *etc/group* files. Userids and groupids can be explicitly copied using rdist or accessed by use of NIS. For a small set of hosts, rdist distribution is simple to do; however, it doesn't scale very well. For a larger set of hosts, NIS is the best method today.

Centralized Versus Distributed Authority

When you set up userids and groupids, an important policy issue must be addressed: whether to centrally administer system access or to attempt a rationally distributed userid and groupid authority. Central administration is the easiest to manage because assignment of userids can be strictly controlled. Here, all new userid and groupid additions or deletions are handled by a central administrative authority. You update a centrally maintained copy of the *etc/passwd* and *etc/group* files and then regularly distribute copies of the files to all systems.

Using NIS to distribute userids and groupids involves placing all host systems in the same NIS domain. You maintain a single master NIS server, and on a large network, NIS slave servers periodically copy the master server's information, thus ensuring high availability of the information. Access to specific workstations is controlled under NIS by using netgroups, which we described in Chapter 9. In the absence of NIS with netgroup support, each workstation receives a copy of only the userids and groupids valid on that workstation.

Although centralized administration is reasonably easy to manage on a small network, on a large network, it can quickly become unwieldy. The central authority must be consulted every time a userid or groupid change is requested, while access to each workstation also is handled from the central authority. The alternative to centralized management is distributed userid and groupid management. Yet this system too has its drawbacks. One is userid and groupid duplication and overlap, which can create administrative and security problems. Sun NFS, for example, depends upon userids and groupids in its default configuration for all file access requests; however, NFS doesn't know anything about usernames or NIS domains. In an example, suppose an NFS server exports one of its filesystems. Some files within the filesystem are owned by the user *fred* with userid 382. Then an account on a client machine is created with username *sally* that also has a userid of 382. If the client machine subsequently mounts the server's filesystem, *sally* will have access to *fred*'s files on the server, which Fred might not appreciate.

NFS could employ an alternative authentication system based on public-key cryptography using **Secure RPC,** which is a more secure RPC authentication method. However, this method isn't available on all systems, Most NFS servers still use the simple userid/groupid authentication method.

As the above example illustrates, NFS is unaware of usernames or groupnames; it sees only userids and groupids. Confusion can result if care isn't taken when assigning userids across all hosts that share NFS-mounted filesystems. Therefore having a set of organizationally consistent userids and groupids is very important in a networked UNIX environment.

Several reasonable methods exist for distributing userid and groupid authority. First however you must decide whether resource sharing, especially filesharing, will take place between systems in each separate administration. If not, then userid and groupid assignment can be independently done within each administration. But if you think resource sharing might take place in the future, then you should anticipate that eventuality and take measures that will support sharing.

One method to distribute authority is to divide the userid and groupid space into ranges of id's and manage the space in a hierarchical manner. The top-level administrative authority divides the user and group id range into a set of short ranges, which we will call **segments.** When a distributed authority is created, a set of userids and groupids is handed to that new authority, which in turn distributes authority to subordinate authorities.

For example, suppose a segment size of 100 is used. There are a total of 32,768 userids and groupids and therefore a total of 328 segments. The first segment (0–99) is reserved on all systems for essential system userids and groupids. The next is reserved for shared userids and groupids between all authorities; usernames and groupnames within this range are agreed upon by all the authorities involved. The remaining segments are handed out for private userids and groupids within each authority. At first an authority is assigned only a few segments. If new userids and groupids subsequently are needed, then additional segments can be allocated from the central authority. This assignment scheme avoids userid and groupid clashes when using NFS with its default authentication.

An Example of Distributed Authority

Suppose the Acme Company builds a corporate network on which userid and groupid authority is granted to each operating department. No filesharing takes place between the departments, but some resource sharing is anticipated in the future. The initial departments are accounting, engineering, sales, and administration. Each department is assigned the NIS domains *acct.acme.com, eng.acme.com, sales.acme.com,* and *admin.acme.com,* respectively. Each also has exclusive control over userid and groupid range 200–299, 300–399, 400–499, and 500–599, respectively. Userid and groupid range 100–199 is reserved for shared access between all departments. Each department establishes a NIS master server for its own NIS domain, while each machine within each domain uses the same set of userids and groupids; therefore filesharing with NFS proceeds normally.

Now suppose the sales and administration departments want to share information between some of their users. Because their internal userid and groupid name spaces are disjoint, no userid or groupid clashes will occur. Both departments agree to use groupid 100 with group name *share* as a shared groupid for specific information in the filesystem */share,* which is located on the machine *server.admin.acme.com.* Shared files use the groupid *share* and set the appropriate read or write permissions. Users within each department that can access the shared information are placed in the *share* group. The */share* filesystem on machine *server.admin.acme.com* is added to the exported filesystems, thus enabling client machines in both departments to access the shared filesystem and the files without any userid or groupid clashes.

If another department subsequently needs to access the same information, then the shared groupid *share* can be added to that department's NIS configuration and the authorized users added to that group's list. As you can see, using this methodology userids and groupids are assigned in a rational and consistent fashion without conflict.

Consistency among usernames also must be maintained if remote login or shell access between the NIS domains is desirable using the *rlogin* or *rsh* commands. Probably the set of users that need cross-departmental access is relatively small. For example, the core administrative group that maintains the network might need uniform access to all systems, in which case userids in the range 100-199 can be used for these accounts and shared across all NIS domains. The appropriate */etc/hosts.equiv* file would be maintained to allow shared access between the appropriate machines. Alternatively each user can maintain the user's own *.rhosts* file and have a different account within each NIS domain. Regardless of which method is used, multiple accounts must be maintained so changing the password in one NIS domain doesn't affect the other domains.

Superuser Access

Where feasible, superuser access should be used only by the system administration staff, not by ordinary users. Because UNIX workstations often end up on individual user's desks, it is not uncommon for an end-user to demand superuser privileges. After all the system is the user's office, so it is owned by the end user. However, with superuser access an end user could make changes to the system that could severely impact other systems on the network. Although end users usually aren't malicious, inadvertent configuration changes often are more disastrous than deliberate meddling. For example, changing the hostname or the IP address of a workstation could have unforeseen and unfortunate consequences on the overall networked system. In this situation, a machine can masquerade as another machine. Superuser access also allows a user to change the NIS domain, which might result in that machine granting access to information in another NIS domain. Further superuser access enables a user to set up accounts on the user's local machine, with results that might conflict with the overall username and userid policies.

As you can see, allowing superuser access to end users usually creates administrative headaches and gaping security holes within the network. Note also that some UNIX workstations give superuser access to a user that reboots the workstation in single-user mode. If possible this access, too, should be denied by ensuring the *init* process always asks for the superuser password. Further, the superuser privileges should be used sparingly even by administrative staff; such as when installing setuid programs or editing critical system configuration files. However, judicious use of groupids can dramatically reduce the need to become the superuser. Another useful tool for controlling superuser access is the *sudo* utility [Nemeth *et al.* 1989].

Every machine should have a secure superuser password that is changed regularly. However, in a network of UNIX systems, maintaining separate passwords on several hundred or thousands of systems can be an administrative nightmare. And note that a separate password for each machine is not necessarily more secure because all the passwords have to recorded somewhere and must be looked up periodically. Further, typing the password in cleartext on a network, which can be wiretapped, isn't secure.

It's better to maintain a small set of superuser passwords and allow access over the network using either the R* authentication method or, for the more security conscious, Kerberos. Suppose you have the simple network of Fig. 11.2, consisting of a fileserver, end-user client machines, and the administrator's workstation. Superuser access to the client machines should be from the administrative workstation only. This permits the administrator to log in as the superuser on each client machine without a password, while preventing an intruder who breaks into a client machine from gaining superuser access to any other machine. And even if the intruder discovers the client's superuser password, the intruder will be unable to access either the administrator's machine or any of the fileservers without first discovering their passwords. The fileservers in this example should be superuser accessible only from the administrator's workstation. Other systems with critical servers should be equally well protected from intruders. These include the DNS nameserver host or hosts that are NIS servers.

Which superuser password is used on which machine can be determined by the each machine's importance with regard to security, that is, a security breach on a client machine is likely to be less severe than one on a major fileserver. So a fileserver should have a separate password and access should be strictly limited while client machines can share a superuser password. If possible, end-user accounts should be restricted to administrative personnel on fileservers and other critical systems.

Keep in mind that none of these measures will prevent a determined system cracker from breaking into your systems. Rather, they are but one step in access security for your system to help prevent a cracker from jumping from one system to another.

11.3 Adding New Machines

New machines will always need to be added to a network. Doing this involves making the necessary electrical connections, loading local software on the new machine, and changing the appropriate configuration parameters when a new machine is initially installed.

Checklists

A simple checklist can be used to describe the procedure to follow when a new machine is first installed. It should consist of which parameters need to be set before the machine is brought up fully and should include actions that aren't easily automated. An example checklist is shown in Fig. 11.3. Your checklist might be far more lengthy and detailed depending on the types of machines in your configuration.

Configuration Scripts

After the checklist procedure is followed, the machine should be able to successfully communicate with other machines on the LAN. Now is the time to run a local configuration script against the new machine. A simple script can be maintained to install and keep track of local modifications, as shown in Fig. 11.4. This script is designed to be run from the administrator's workstation rather than directly on the new system. It uses *rsh* and *rdist* to run commands with superuser privileges on the new system, so that system must be accessible from the administrator's workstation. In this example, rdist copies the *sendmail* configuration file; using *rdist* maintains the dates and time of file creation so they can be easily checked to determine the version of the file being used. The script also sets up the */etc/fstab* to mount remote file systems, which are added to that file.

The script shown is a simple example; in practice it can be quite complex. Several configuration scripts might be used, depending on the type of machine installed. For example, a script for a new server might copy, rather than remotely mount, locally installed programs. Or different scripts might exist for different OS versions or for different hardware types. The scripts can serve as living procedures that document all the local system changes. Moreover, if carefully managed

New Installation Checklist

1. Unpack machine and check packing list

2. Set up machine

3. Attach to network

4. Determine subnet (if any) machine is connected to

5. Boot single user and standalone

6. Basic information for equipment database
   Machine type _____
   Serial number _____
   Location _____
   Ethernet Address _____
   IP Address _____
   Netmask _____
   Name _____

7. Set name, IP address and network mask and broadcast address in startup scripts.

8. Set NIS domain in startup scripts and be sure NIS services are started

9. Change root password and note what it is

10. Add default route to appropriate router

11. Be sure routed is not running

12. Reboot machine multiuser

13. Login as root

14. Check connectivity by using ping and other tools with hosts on the local network and on the farside of a router.

15. Run configuration script on new machine.

Figure 11.3 Checklist.

and maintained, they can be run against already installed systems when new global changes are incorporated and just update the old systems with the latest changes.

```
#!/bin/sh
#
#
# example configuration script
#



if [ $# -ne 2 ]; then
    echo usage $0 hostname
    exit 1
fi

host=$1
server=$2

if ping $host >/dev/null 2>&1; then
    echo $host reachable
else
echo $host not reachable - check configuration
    exit 2
fi

if rsh $host -l root echo hello >/dev/null 2>&1; then
    echo we can be root on $host
else
    echo root access denied on $host - check configuration
    exit 3
fi

cd /usr/src/local/config

rdist -c sub.cf root@$host
rsh $host -l root "rm -f /etc/sendmail.cf"
rsh $host -l root ln -s /etc/sub.cf /etc/sendmail.cf"
dpid=`rsh $host -l root "ps -ax | awk '/send\mail/ { print $1 }'`
rsh $host -l root kill $dpid
rsh $host -l root /usr/lib/sendmail -bz
rsh $host -l root /usr/lib/sendmail -bd -q1h

rsh $host -l root ex /etc/fstab <<EOF
d/# REMOTE MOUNTS/-$d
w
q
EOF
sed "s/SERVER/$server/" fstab.remote |\
rsh $host -l root "cat >>/etc/fstab"

rsh $host /etc/fastboot
exit 0
```

Figure 11.4 Example Configuration Script.

11.4 Adding a New Network Physical Segment

Adding a new network segment is relatively easy. Most important when adding additional wiring is to update your network map. This map shows the location of all the wiring and network devices that are part of your installation. Amazingly few installations have adequate maps of their installations. When a new segment is installed, it's important to know all the locations that can plug into the network. For example, if you install twisted-pair wiring it's more important to know which offices have wall taps that are connected to the cable than it is to know where the physical wires are located. For example, Table 11.1 shows one way of maintaining network information for each segment. In this case a simple table is used. This information can be kept in text files or, with more elaborate installations, in an online database. The table shows the location and number of each wall tap. For example, the IP subnet network that operates over this hub is shown, as is the location of the hub repeater.

After installing and testing the new wiring, assign an unused IP network number to the new physical segment. If you are using subnets, you must use a separate subnet number on the new segment. Another consideration is where to plug in the new network segment to the existing network. A critical factor affecting this is the type and locality of traffic on the new cable segment. Machines hooked up to the same physical network should exchange most of their network traffic primarily with machines on the same physical segment. If considerable traffic is expected between machines on different segments, be sure to minimize the number of router hops between the communicating systems. If on the other hand traffic between cable segments is minimal, this is a less important consideration.

Software additions might also be needed as new network segments are added. For example, if you are using NIS to distribute resource information, then at least one slave NIS server must exist on the segment. Because an NIS client uses IP

Table 11.1 Network Segment Table.

Segment Number: 10
IP Network Number: 131.135.10.0
Hub: Phone Closet 140
Hub No: 10

Tap	Room	Wall
1	100	N
2	110	S
3	110	N
4	120	E
5	135	S

---

broadcast packets to discover the location of a server, a client on a network segment without a NIS server will hang when trying to bind to a server. The intervening router consequently will prevent distribution of the broadcast packet to the other cable segments. Therefore every new network segment should have at least one NIS server.

Other broadcast-based services also will need local servers. For example, if you use RARP to boot diskless workstations, then an RARP server must also exist on the local network segment. BOOTP on the other hand can send requests through intervening routers, but only if the routers are configured to pass BOOTP packets.

Services that aren't broadcast based, such as DNS, might work better when a local server is available rather than their having to depend on a remote server. It's good practice to add a secondary DNS server when a new network segment is added. DNS requests from the local hosts then will stay on the local network. Given the speed and reliability of routers these days, doing this might seem like overkill. However, remember that each new network segment means additional hosts on the network, which in turn adds load on various resource services such as DNS and NIS.

11.5 Network File System Backups

Even though disk technology continues to become extremely reliable, a good filesystem backup system remains one of the most important and often overlooked management tasks. Even with disk mirroring and other techniques to improve the reliability and availability of data, a good backup system is still an absolute requirement for both disaster recovery and archival storage. Therefore when planning your network also plan to buy and install a good backup system.

Backing up a set of networked hosts, when compared with that of a single host filesystem, is more a problem of scale and volume than anything that is intrinsically different. Today various cartridge tape systems provide compact storage systems for archiving disk data. Since it's impractical to put a tape system on every computer, the network itself is often used to access remote tape systems. With a relatively small network, one tape system might be adequate; with a large installation, several tapes might be needed because of the time involved to dump every file system periodically. A good strategy is to make a full backup of every host's volatile file systems on a regular schedule, say once a month, while running incremental backups periodically, with the frequency dependent on the data's volatility and importance. Because there are many more filesystems on a set of networked hosts and tape drives tend to be relatively scarce resources, try to minimize the number of filesystems which need to be backed up by standardizing many of the host filesystems. For example, the *root* and *usr* filesystems have numerous files that never change. We suggest you move as many volatile files off of these filesystems as possible and standardize them for as large a set of machines as possible. Obviously, you won't be able to do this completely; in some cases, some system configuration files in /etc will differ between systems. If a disk crash results in one of these filesystems needing to be restored, these differences can be minimized and a common configuration script developed to recreate the changes. With this methodology, a single template filesystem can be copied and used as an archival copy for a large number of client filesystems.

You also can minimize the number of filesystems to backup by using NFS to place most user generated files on one or more fileservers. The client machines end up with the *root* and *usr* filesystems, which are configured to be relatively nonvolatile except for a few key directories such as the *mail spool* directory. Using the *tar* utility, you can automatically copy these relatively small volatile directories to a special directory on one of the fileservers. Then when the fileserver is backed up, every client's volatile files also are backed up.

Using the UNIX dump and rdump Utilities

While there are many good commercial backup utilities available, the *dump* and *rdump* utilities found on most UNIX systems, if used judiciously, are quite adequate for backing up filesystems. Dump copies filesystems to a local tape drive or even to another disk, while rdump copies filesystems to a remote tape drive.

Performing a backup with rdump has some potential security and access problems. Rdump uses the R* authentication method to give access to a remote tape drive through the *rmt* utility program. Unfortunately, this means that to allow a dump from a remote host, the superuser must have superuser privileges on the system with the tape drive. Usually this system is a fileserver that shouldn't be accessible from any client system. Rdump from one fileserver to another is usually reasonable, since allowing superuser access from one fileserver to another is ordinarily less of a security problem.

If the remote system is a client machine with disks that need periodic backups, use a script that runs the dump program on the remote system and pipes the output back to the server. The dump then can be saved on a local disk and backed up when the server's filesystem is dumped or the client's filesystem dump can be directed to the server's local tape drive. Figure 11.5 shows an example of such a script. In this figure, the filesystems are saved to a disk file on the server on which the command is run. Note that the remote client must be up and running for this to work properly.

11.6 SNMP Monitoring

The **Simple Network Management Protocol (SNMP)** defines a common low-level query interface to network devices. Usually you use it to retrieve information from dedicated network devices such as bridges or routers. SNMP uses a **Management Information Base (MIB)** that defines the objects of interest you want to retrieve. Other books explain SNMP in much more detail [Leinwand & Fang 1993] and in particular the standard MIB definitions. Here, however, we briefly discuss SNMP and describe how it can be used to monitor network devices.

```
#!/bin/sh
# @(#) remdump.sh 1.1 92/01/01 @(#)
#
# remotely dump a filesystem to disk
#
# arguments
# $1 - name of remote system
# $2 - directory to put dump images in
# $3 - dump level
# $4... - directories to dump on remote system

umask 007
if [ $# -lt 4 ]; then
    echo usage: remdump host dir level filesystem...
    exit 1
fi

host=$1
dir=$2
level=$3
shift 3
cd $dir
for i do
    out="${host}"`echo $i | sed "s//./g"`
    rsh $host -n dump ${level}uf - $i | compress >$out.${level}.Z
done
exit 0
```

Figure 11.5 Example Dump Script.

SNMP Overview

An interesting hybrid, SNMP is defined using the OSI **Abstract Syntax Notation One (ASN.1)** presentation protocol. ASN.1 is a powerful description language used to describe networking protocols. Used in combination with a set of **Basic Encoding Rules (BER)** it can completely describe the format of any network message. It's similar in functionality to Sun's XDR but much more elaborate. While SNMP uses ASN.1 and the BER, it is not an OSI protocol. Rather, SNMP uses UDP transport.

SNMP lets you query or modify system tables kept on dedicated network devices in an unambiguous way. Usually a single machine, called a **management station** generates a query. The actual query protocol is very simple. An SNMP query with the unique name of the value desired is sent to a network device. The device then responds to the query either by returning the value desired or by updating the field. Because it's common to step through a table of values in order, SNMP also let's you specify the next value in a table by putting the unique identifier of the previous value in the query and asking the SNMP agent to return the next value. With this method, you can easily step sequentially and unambiguously through a large table.

Security is minimal and is based on a **community name** sent with each query. Also network devices that respond to SNMP queries can limit queries or update commands to only specific IP addresses. There are plans to upgrade this minimal security mechanism. A network node with SNMP support can also generate traps. A **trap** is a method of asynchronously notifying an SNMP management station of an unusual event on a network device, such as a reboot or a warmstart.

The name of each value that can be queried is defined by a MIB. A MIB defines a tree-structured database, as shown in Fig. 11.6. Each node of the tree has a number — an object identifier — and a name associated with it. Like the DNS hierarchy, each parent node's child must have a unique object identifier. Each node is uniquely identified by the set of object identifiers on the path to the node of interest from the root. This setup is the reverse of DNS (which traverses

Figure 11.6 SNMP MIB.

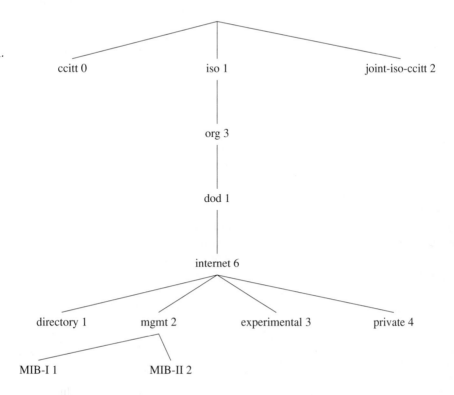

from the node to the root), but very similar to a UNIX pathname. Each node also is given a unique text name that is shorthand for the node traversal to that point in the tree.

SNMP uses two MIBs — MIB-1 and MIB-2. MIB-1 has the unique object identifier of 1.3.6.1.2.1 or {mgmt-1}; MIB-2 has the identifier 1.3.6.1.2.2 or {mgmt-2}. Under each of these subtrees are the names of the managed objects. Most SNMP implementations today use the MIB-2 subtree. Other subtrees define other MIBs; for example, under 1.3.6.1.3 {experimental} are experimental MIBs and under 1.3.6.1.4 {private} are private MIBs. Many network device vendors use this subtree to define their own private MIB extensions. These extensions, because they are private, are implemented only by and under the control of the specific vendor. In effect, the vendor is given naming authority over its own sub-tree. However, while these MIBs are private, you can use SNMP to retrieve data named by each MIB, provided you know the path to the object of interest. MIB-2 information is specific to the TCP/IP protocol suite. For a TCP/IP network, this MIB and the objects it contains will be queried the most.

Using SNMP

SNMP can be very confusing to people accustomed to TCP/IP networking. The ASN.1 syntax and MIB definitions can be daunting initially. Even though SNMP is really very simple, the generalized MIB interface appears unfamiliar to those who know both UNIX and TCP/IP. When should you use SNMP? It depends on the size and the complexity of your network. SNMP's greatest strength is its common interface to a common set of information. It's most useful when your network is fairly large, has a complex topology, and uses systems from many different vendors. Therefore on a small LAN with, for example, a single physical network and no outside connectivity, SNMP is clearly overkill. All network device vendors usually have their own proprietary management interface, which can be as simple as a console monitor program. If you have a network with, say, routers from a variety of vendors, then SNMP can greatly simplify the monitoring of those heterogeneous devices.

To use SNMP effectively, you must have one or more workstations that serve as a management station for the network and then install management station software that makes the workstation an SNMP management node. Most management software is graphically oriented and is designed to allow interactive queries to be sent to network devices. Also, on critical devices, traps can be generated that are captured by the management station. On a small network, a single management station usually suffices. Remember, the SNMP query processing itself places a load on the network because all queries are sent using the network medium itself. Because SNMP uses UDP, it's inefficient when retrieving a large table; for example, to fully retrieve a table with 10 lines requires 10 queries. There has been some discussion about updating the querying mechanism for greater efficiency.

On a large network, it's usually a good idea to create more than a single management node, as illustrated in Fig. 11.7. This is particularly true when the network is widely distributed and parts of it are under different management

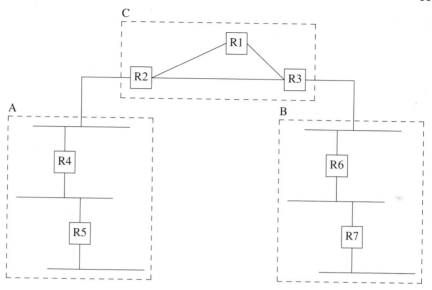

Figure 11.7 Large SNMP Network.

authority. As this figure shows, network administration is split among several groups. The equipment each group manages is shown within the dotted boxes. Group A controls a large LAN installation with several routing nodes; Group B controls another large installation that is still within a LAN environment; and Group C handles the WAN interconnections. In this figure, each group maintains an SNMP management station. The devices and station within each administration has its own community name, which are shown as part of the diagram. With this separation, management traffic is contained within each large installation. The only management traffic on the WAN links is that required to monitor the WAN links and routing nodes themselves.

References

Leinwand & Fang 1993.   Leinwand, Allan, & Fang, Karen, *Network Management A Practical Perspective,* Addison-Wesley, Reading, MA (1993).

Nemeth et al. 1989.   Nemeth, Evi, Synder, Garth, & Seebass, Scott, *UNIX System Administration Handbook,* Prentice Hall, Englewood Cliffs, NJ (1989).

## CHAPTER 12

Network Debugging

Debugging TCP/IP network problems and finding the proper fix can be very time-consuming and frustrating. Some people still believe you need specialized network analyzers to properly debug an errant network. You can only solve some cabling and some physical network problems using specialized equipment such as a protocol sniffer or a cable fault analyzer, which are useful tools especially in a large complex installation. However, you can track down and isolate many more common problems using the built-in UNIX network management tools such as *netstat* and *ifconfig*.

In this chapter, we discuss at length these invaluable UNIX debugging tools and discover that they are surprisingly useful and easy to use.

12.1 Tools for Debugging

Most of the tools described here are on the majority of UNIX systems that support TCP/IP. A few, like *traceroute* and *dig,* are publicly available from Internet archive sites. Still others, such as *etherfind,* are found only on specific vendor systems. We describe them all because in many cases they are commonly found on at least a few machines on your network.

ping

The *ping* program is a simple yet valuable network debugging tool. It sends an ICMP *echo request* message to a remote host, which in turn returns an ICMP *echo reply* message to the sender. Sending an echo request is called "pinging." Pinging is a good baseline test of connectivity. If a ping succeeds, then the two hosts can successfully send and receive IP packets. If the two hosts are on different IP networks, the network routing configuration is also tested.

```
% ping akasha.tic.com
akasha.tic.com is alive

% ping ticmac.tic.com
no response from ticmac.tic.com

% ping beast.tic.com 5
no response from beast.tic.com
```

Figure 12.1 Short ping Examples.

There are two major ping variants. The first sends a single echo request message and waits for a reply. If the reply is not received within one second, another echo request is sent. This process continues until at least one affirmative reply is received. Figure 12.1 shows how this variant is used and the reply messages that are generated. In the first example, a reply was received before the timeout interval (the default is 20 seconds). In the second, no reply was received within the timeout period. You can use this command to very quickly determine whether a host system is up enough to respond to ICMP requests. The timeout period can also be specified, as shown in the figure's third example. If the host *beast.tic.com* hasn't responded after five seconds, this command will timeout.

The second ping variant (or in some by using the *-s* option) sends an echo request message every second and records the time it takes for each reply to be received. It does this by placing a timestamp as part of the echo request. When the echo reply is received, the time difference is calculated. This time difference is a very good measure of the round-trip time between the two hosts. Every echo request also contains a unique sequence number, so the replies can be matched with a specific request. Figure 12.2 shows the output from this ping variant. Here, an echo request packet is sent once per second, each with a monotonically increasing sequence number. When the reply is received, the round-trip time is recorded. The program will continue to run indefinitely unless a total number of request packets is included as an argument. When the program terminates, a set of simple statistics is displayed that shows the total packets sent and received; the loss rate; and the minimum, average, and maximum calculated round-trip times.

A high but not complete packet loss rate is a good indicator of intermittent hardware problems or network congestion. Remember that a host or router can throw away IP packets if it is too busy to process them. While ping gives you no definitive answers regarding the specific cause of packet loss, it can give you some important clues. For example, if you can successfully ping hosts on the same network cable but can't ping hosts reachable via a router, then the problem is very likely at the router. If only a few ping packets receive successful replies, then the router might be experiencing congestion. On the other hand, if you can't ping a specific host on the same network cable, then the problem is with that host.

```
% ping -s aahsa.tic.com
PING aahsa.tic.com: 56 data bytes
64 bytes from aahsa.tic.com (192.12.23.130): icmp_seq=0. time=6. ms
64 bytes from aahsa.tic.com (192.12.23.130): icmp_seq=1. time=5. ms
64 bytes from aahsa.tic.com (192.12.23.130): icmp_seq=2. time=6. ms
64 bytes from aahsa.tic.com (192.12.23.130): icmp_seq=3. time=6. ms
64 bytes from aahsa.tic.com (192.12.23.130): icmp_seq=4. time=5. ms

----aahsa.tic.com PING Statistics----
5 packets transmitted, 5 packets received, 0% packet loss
round-trip (ms)  min/avg/max = 5/5/6
```

Figure 12.2 Output of ping.

Ping also lets you send different message sizes. As a default, it sends a 64-byte message. This is the size of the echo request message itself and does not include the IP header or the datalink frame header or trailer. In Fig. 12.3 a ping command sends a 1,000-byte message to a remote host. With this option, you can easily check IP fragmentation and reassembly because the packet size can exceed the MTU of the network interface. Note that the actual message size is 8 bytes larger than the size specified on the command line; the first 8 bytes of an ICMP message are the required ICMP header. You also can specify a message size of 0 bytes, in which case no round-trip time is computed since ping puts the timestamp in the first 8 bytes of the message following the header.

Because echo request and echo reply are part of ICMP, ping doesn't depend upon any application server running on the remote host. If the network interface is properly configured and is up and running, then ping should work. A UNIX host in single-user mode with its network interfaces configured and running will respond to pings. Thus you can use ping to remotely diagnose several types of

Figure 12.3 Altering Ping Message Size.

```
% ping -s aahsa.tic.com 1000
PING aahsa.tic.com: 1000 data bytes
1008 bytes from aahsa.tic.com (192.12.23.130): icmp_seq=0. time=11. ms
1008 bytes from aahsa.tic.com (192.12.23.130): icmp_seq=1. time=10. ms
1008 bytes from aahsa.tic.com (192.12.23.130): icmp_seq=2. time=11. ms

----aahsa.tic.com PING Statistics----
3 packets transmitted, 3 packets received, 0% packet loss
round-trip (ms)  min/avg/max = 10/11/11
```

network problems. For example, if telnetting to a remote host fails but ping works, the problem is probably a TELNET configuration problem. You would know that it's not a problem with either IP packet or datalink frame delivery because if a ping packet can be replied to, then the remote host is able to receive, process, and send IP packets.

Ping checks connectivity at the IP level. In particular, when used with IP addresses instead of hostnames, it's very effective for checking basic connectivity between hosts on the same network and routing between hosts on different networks. Let's consider the following example to illustrate this point. A server that stops responding to NIS requests is a common NIS problem; NIS clients will hang waiting for a response from the server. Suppose the message

```
NIS: server not responding for domain tic.com; still trying
```

appears on a NIS client's console. This indicates that *ypbind* on the client machine is attempting to contact a NIS server, but no server for the domain *tic.com* is responding. You can use ping to determine if the server has crashed. If ping works, then the problem is probably in the NIS configuration; if ping fails, then either a problem at the IP level exists or the server has crashed.

Ping uses the services of IP directly and does not depend upon TCP or UDP transport. On a LAN that supports broadcasting, such as Ethernet, ping relies only on ARP to map the destination IP address to the correct datalink address. If you ping a machine on the same physical network that has been down for a while, the echo request message might never be sent. This occurs only when there is no ARP entry for the off-line machine in the local ARP cache. Rather than the echo request packet being sent, four ARP packets are sent and the ping eventually times out. If there is an ARP cache entry for the remote machine on the local machine, then the echo request message will be sent, but no echo reply will be received from the remote machine since it is turned off.

The remote Script

The *remote* script found in Appendix B is a simple script that permits any arbitrary command to be run on a set of remote machines. Useful for collecting valuable debugging information from a set of remote machines, remote takes a single command followed by a list of hosts. This command can have any number of arguments and is executed using the RSH remote execution protocol. The list of hosts follows the -*h* option on the command line. Remote uses ping with a short timeout to quickly timeout machines that are down, thus eliminating annoying and time-consuming TCP connection timeout delays. Other programs can easily use the output generated by remote to create reports or do other post-processing. (Remote assumes you have proper authority to execute commands on remote machines.)

A simple example using *remote* is shown in Fig. 12.4. In this figure, the *uptime* command is run on the remote system. Remote displays a line indicating the name of the machine on which the command was executed.

```
% remote uptime -h aahsa akasha
Host:aahsa
 10:50am  up 1 day, 15:01,  2 users,  load average: 1.42, 1.10, 1.16
Host:akasha
 10:50am  up 5 days, 20:34,  2 users,  load average: 0.91, 0.29, 0.19
```

Figure 12.4 Remote Example.

Generating Hostnames. One problem on a relatively large network is deter-mining the list of active local hosts to pass as arguments to remote. It can be hard to remember all the hostnames. If you use a static */etc/hosts* table or have a single NIS domain, you can generate a host list from the table or from the output of *ypcat*. The *getstatic* found in Appendix B can be used to extract hostnames from either of these sources. By default, getstatic reads the */etc/hosts* file; with the *-yp* option, it uses the output of ypcat. The loopback interface (127.0.0.1) name is ignored and only the canonical names of the hosts are listed.

If you use DNS for hostname lookup, generating hostnames is somewhat harder. The *getdns* script found in Appendix B uses the output of *nslookup* to extract the hostnames within a particular domain. Getdns takes a single domain name as an argument and uses nslookup to generate a host list for the domain. The script first determines the servers that are authoritative for the domain of interest by looking up all the DNS NS records for the domain. Each server is queried in turn until one generates the host list. Extraneous lines are edited from the output stream and the hostnames are output in alphabetical order (duplicates are deleted).

With either the getstatic or the getdns scripts, you can run the same command on all active hosts on your network. Figure 12.5 shows an example of how to use remote with the getdns script. In this example, the *date* command is run on each remote system. We see in a later section how remote can be used to help debug an errant network.

Figure 12.5 Remote Using Getdns.

```
% remote date -h `getdns tic.com`
Host: aahsa.tic.com
Fri Dec 20 11:43:34 CST 1991
Host: akasha.tic.com
Fri Dec 20 11:43:36 CST 1991
```

netstat

netstat is the "jack-of-all-trades" tool for displaying host-specific network information. Different options display the contents of network-related operating system tables that track the state of network connections, interfaces, routing tables, and traffic statistics. We examine each of the major suboptions of the netstat command in the following sections.

Active Connection Display. Netstat without any options displays all currently active TCP and UDP connections and active UNIX Protocol Domain connections. The **UNIX Protocol Domain** is an interprocess communications facility for processes on a single UNIX host. (We don't discuss it here because its details aren't pertinent to this book.) Figure 12.6 shows the default output of netstat run on host *akasha.tic.com*. However, you can limit the output to just active TCP and UDP connections by specifying the *-f* option followed by the *inet* keyword.

Figure 12.7 shows netstat output limited to only the TCP and UDP connections. Each connection is displayed in a single line that comprises the following fields:

• *Proto*
The transport protocol used, either udp or tcp.

• *Recv-Q*
The number of bytes in the socket input queue.

• *Send-Q*
The number of bytes in the socket output queue.

• *Local Address*
The local socket address, shown as a pair of period-separated names. The first name is that of the local interface and is usually displayed as the name of the local host with the local domain stripped off. The second is the name of the local port the connection is using. If the port has no name, then the port number is displayed instead.

Figure 12.6 Active Connections.

```
Active Internet connections
Proto Recv-Q Send-Q  Local Address        Foreign Address    (state)
tcp        0   4096  akasha.2684          aahsa.smtp         ESTABLISHED
tcp        0      0  akasha.1023          aahsa.login        ESTABLISHED
udp        0      0  akasha.domain        *.*
udp        0      0  localhost.domain     *.*
Active UNIX domain sockets
Address  Type   Recv-Q Send-Q    Vnode    Conn   Refs Nextref Addr
ff64998c dgram       0      0  ff0a35a8       0      0       0 /dev/log
```

```
% netstat -f inet
Active Internet connections
Proto Recv-Q Send-Q  Local Address        Foreign Address    (state)
tcp         0   4096  akasha.2684          aahsa.smtp         ESTABLISHED
tcp         0      0  akasha.1023          aahsa.login        ESTABLISHED
udp         0      0  akasha.domain        *.*
udp         0      0  localhost.domain     *.*
```

Figure 12.7 netstat Limited to TCP/IP Connections.

• *Foreign Address*
The remote socket address given in the same format as the local address.

• *(state)*
The current state of each TCP connection. This field is always empty for UDP connections.

The figure shows host *akasha* with an active connection from local port 2684 to the SMTP port (25) on host *aahsa*. Also shown is an active RLOGIN session from local port 1023 on *akasha* to the RLOGIN port on *aahsa*. Finally, a domain nameserver is listening for packets on the UDP domain port of both the local network interface and the loopback (localhost) interface.

For TCP connections, it's easy to tell which side of the connection is the server and which is the client: The server side port is the name of the well-known-port for that service; the client side port is an arbitrary port number that is usually greater than 1023. In this figure, a local SMTP client is talking to a remote SMTP server. The status of each active TCP connection is shown. For UDP services, the remote *host.port* is shown as the wildcard "*.*" for services that are actively waiting for UDP packets from any remote port. Because UDP services are connectionless, a UDP server can be configured to receive packets from any remote port.

The names of the well-known ports are found in the */etc/services* file or, if NIS is active, by using the NIS map derived from the same file. The names of the hosts are mapped from their corresponding IP addresses using whatever IP address-to-hostname lookup service is running. (The internal operating system tables store IP addresses and port numbers, not hostnames or portnames.) If possible, netstat translates the internal port numbers and IP addresses to their corresponding names.

To see the IP addresses and port numbers rather than names, use the -*n* option, as illustrated in Fig. 12.8. This option also works for all the other netstat output displays that show hostnames or portnames. The output produced with it is better for debugging purposes, since the IP address-to-hostname mapping and the port number-to-port name mapping are bypassed.

```
% netstat -f inet -n
Active Internet connections
Proto Recv-Q Send-Q  Local Address         Foreign Address     (state)
tcp       0      0   192.12.23.129.2684  192.12.23.130.25   ESTABLISHED
tcp       0      0   192.12.23.129.1023  192.12.23.130.513  ESTABLISHED
udp       0      0   192.12.23.129.53      *.*
udp       0      0   127.0.0.1.53          *.*
```

Figure 12.8 Netstat Connection Display with Addresses.

Using the -a option to netstat, you can display all servers listening for connections in addition to currently active connections. This option is a good check
on inetd's configuration, since most services are started up out of inetd. Netstat
output with the -a option is shown in Fig. 12.9. Here, a state field of LISTEN
indicates the server is waiting for connection requests from clients. The local
socket address is bound only to the well-known port of the service, while the "*"
in the local host field indicates the service is listening and will accept connections
on any network interfaces. The foreign address field is always "*.*."

On a machine running Sun RPC services, the number of listening servers can
be quite large, since most RPC services listen on a TCP port as well as on a UDP
port. Because arbitrary local port numbers are associated with most RPC servers,
it's difficult to tell from just the netstat output which RPC servers are running.
However, active RPC servers can be found by using the rpcinfo command, which
we described in Chapter 9. You can determine whether the RPC portmapper is
running by noting if a server is listening on port 111.

Figure 12.9 netstat Showing Servers.

```
% netstat -a -f inet
Active Internet connections (including servers)
Proto Recv-Q Send-Q  Local Address       Foreign Address     (state)
tcp       0      0   localhost.1557    localhost.sunrpc   TIME_WAIT
tcp       0      0   akasha.1023       aahsa.login        ESTABLISHED
tcp       0      0   akasha.login      aahsa.1023         ESTABLISHED
tcp       0      0   *.4350            *.*                LISTEN
tcp       0      0   *.6000            *.*                LISTEN
tcp       0      0   *.2000            *.*                LISTEN
tcp       0      0   *.3222            *.*                LISTEN
tcp       0      0   *.telnet          *.*                LISTEN
tcp       0      0   *.login           *.*                LISTEN
tcp       0      0   *.nntp            *.*                LISTEN
```

The connection display is a very useful check on the status of active TCP connections. A TCP connection that appears hung can have any number of failure points. As you recall, every TCP connection is initiated by a three-packet hand-shake, which we described in Chapter 4. The client sends a SYN to the server, to which the server replies with a SYN_ACK. Finally the client replies with an ACK and the connection is established. If the client has sent the first SYN, but the server hasn't yet acknowledged it, the state of the connection will be SYN_SENT and the line in the netstat output for a connection in this state on a client host looks like the following:

```
tcp  0   0  akasha.3603      aahsa.telnet  SYN_SENT
```

If the SYN_SENT state is persistent, the most likely causes of the waiting connec-tion are the following:

• The server host is not running. Note, if the server host is running but the server process is not, then the hosts IP module will indicate the connection is refused because there is no process waiting for requests on that port.

• A routing problem prevents the SYN from reaching the server or the SYN_ACK from returning to the client. In this case, the server is running but IP packets can't be exchanged. This can be tested by pinging the remote host.

If the server never receives the initial SYN, no connection exists on the remote server for this client. If the server does receive the initial SYN, then the server state for the connection will be SYN_RCVD and a netstat on the server will show a line like:

```
tcp  0   0  aahsa.telnet     akasha.3603   SYN_RCVD
```

You know this is the same connection because the host.port addresses are reversed and the protocol is the same. A server connection to a remote client that persists in the SYN_RCVD state is probably caused by one of the following:

• The server has a bad route back to the client. The server received the client's SYN packet, so the client can send packets to the server, but the server can't send packets to the client. This problem can occur only between hosts on sepa-rate IP networks.

• The server's ARP cache has a bad entry for the client. This can happen if the network interface card on the client is replaced and the datalink address of the client changes. If the server had already cached the client's old datalink address, then the server will continue to try sending packets to the old address. You can solve this problem by rebooting the server or manually clearing its ARP cache. Later in this section, we show you how the *arp* command is used to display and manipulate the ARP cache.

Under normal circumstances, TCP connection handshaking should take a very short time to complete. If it takes more than a few seconds, then either a high packet loss rate between the client and server is indicated or the server is running under very high loads. We show you later in this section how you can use other tools to determine a high packet loss or error rate.

Another common problem that can indicate network problems occurs when a TCP connection is closing. A connection close can be initiated by either side of the connection. When one end of a TCP connection initiates a close, it stops sending data and sends a FIN, which is the last TCP message received by the remote host. If the local side has closed the connection, but the remote side has not closed the connection, the netstat output looks like the following:

```
tcp  0   0  akasha.3603      aahsa.telnet  FIN_WAIT_1
```

In this case, the remote host can continue to send packets and the local host will continue to receive and process the data. The connection is half-open, since the remote can continue to send data indefinitely. When the remote host sends an ACK in response to the FIN, then the state of the local side goes to FIN_WAIT_2, as follows:

```
tcp  0   0  akasha.3603      aahsa.telnet  FIN_WAIT_2
```

and at this point the remote is in the CLOSE_WAIT state. Note that the remote can continue to send data even after acknowledging the FIN. Finally, when the remote finishes sending data and initiates closing its side of the connection, it sends a final ACK with a FIN and enters the LAST_ACK state. The local side then enters the TIME_WAIT state, as follows:

```
tcp  0   0  akasha.3603      aahsa.telnet  TIME_WAIT
```

The local side next sends its final ACK in response to the FIN and enters the CLOSED state. Thus if the connection termination is initiated locally, the state changes are ESTABLISHED, FIN_WAIT_1, FIN_WAIT_2, TIME_WAIT, and finally CLOSED. If the remote side of a connection initiates a close, then the state changes are ESTABLISHED, CLOSE_WAIT, LAST_ACK, and finally CLOSED.

It's possible for a connection to be closed simultaneously by both ends, in which case the state changes on both sides are ESTABLISHED, FIN_WAIT_1, CLOSING, TIME_WAIT, and finally CLOSED.

Because a successful close depends on the exchange of data across the network, a connection can hang while closing. A common problem with some early TCP implementations is hanging during the FIN_WAIT_2 state, caused by a bug in the implementation. The underlying problem is the different semantics of a UNIX file descriptor and a TCP socket-based connection. Because network communication using sockets map onto UNIX file descriptors, this creates a problem.

A close in the TCP sense is really a half-close. Data can still be received on the connection, but no more data can be sent. On the other hand, a close in the UNIX sense means a full-duplex close. When a normal UNIX close is performed on a file descriptor, both sending and receiving are disallowed. The FIN_WAIT_2 problem occurs when a UNIX process closes the descriptor associated with a socket and then exits, thus leaving the socket structure with no way to receive data, since all the receive buffers are also deallocated. Therefore the state of the connection on the local side is FIN_WAIT_1. The remote side received a FIN (sent when the connection was closed), but if it still wants to send data it can. However, the local side's TCP sets its window size to 0, since it cannot receive any data, while the remote side continues to probe the local side waiting for the window to open, which it never will. Consequently, the connection will stay open forever or until either the client or server is rebooted. If you see this kind of persistence half-closed connection, then you probably have TCP code with the FIN_WAIT bug in it. All newer TCP implementations that we know of have fixed this problem.

Statistics Display. Netstat with the -s option displays network statistics. The statistics are cumulative since the last system boot and give an overall idea of total network usage by specific protocol. Netstat displays statistics for the two transport protocols — UDP and TCP — and then for ICMP and IP. On some systems, the order of the display is different and there may be some additional or different statistics reported. This is due to slight variations in the TCP/IP implementation on each system.

The UDP display shown in Fig. 12.10 displays the following four statistics:

- *incomplete headers*
  The number of incomplete UDP headers received. Incomplete headers indicate some type of frame corruption.

- *bad data length field*
  the length of the data doesn't correspond to the actual size of the received data, meaning there is a mismatch between the IP length field and the UDP data length field.

Figure 12.10 netstat UDP Statistics.

```
udp:
    0 incomplete headers
    0 bad data length fields
    0 bad checksums
    0 socket overflows
```

• *bad checksums*
The count of UDP checksum failures. A large number indicates excessive transmission errors.

• *socket overflow*
An indicator that UDP reception overflowed the socket data buffer. UDP has no flow control mechanism, therefore a very fast host can overflow a slow receiver, although this should happen infrequently.

Much more extensive than the UDP statistics are the TCP statistics, shown in Fig. 12.11, which follow next:

• *packets sent*
The total count of TCP messages sent from the last reboot. This count is subdivided as follows:

  • *data packets*
  The total number of unique data packets sent. The byte count is the number of bytes in each TCP message including the TCP header.

  • *data packets retransmitted*
  The count of messages that were transmitted more than once. Multiple counting of packages results from acknowledgements not being received in time. This count should be low relative to the total packet count, and a high ratio indicates excessive network loss rate or congestion.

  • *ack-only packets*
  TCP messages with no data and just the ACK bit set. The delayed count means the ACK wasn't sent immediately but rather was delayed in an unsuccessful attempt to piggyback some outgoing data.

  • *URG-only packets*
  Messages with only the URG bit set and no data.

  • *window probe packets*
  Messages that are sent asking the remote TCP to open its window. A **window probe** is a message with a single byte of data that is sent when the remote TCP's window is 0. The remote TCP will ACK the single byte and if it can, send a new window size; otherwise the single byte is unacknowledged.

  • *window update packets*
  Messages containing only an update to the TCP window size. This message is usually just an ACK with a new window.

  • *control packet*
  Messages containing only the SYN, FIN, or RST bit set.

• *packets received*
The total number of TCP messages received. The total message count is further subdivided into the following types:

```
tcp:
    3628052 packets sent
        3489730 data packets (138566227 bytes)
        27 data packets (31203 bytes) retransmitted
        102074 ack-only packets (61215 delayed)
        27 URG only packets
        146 window probe packets
        5995 window update packets
        30053 control packets
    3707611 packets received
        3513675 acks (for 138619871 bytes)
        19823 duplicate acks
        0 acks for unsent data
        3495755 packets (53851387 bytes) received in-sequence
        717 completely duplicate packets (714 bytes)
        0 packets with some dup. data (0 bytes duped)
        11581 out-of-order packets (130826 bytes)
        33 packets (20 bytes) of data after window
        20 window probes
        2012 window update packets
        0 packets received after close
        0 discarded for bad checksums
        0 discarded for bad header offset fields
        0 discarded because packet too short
    9993 connection requests
    10074 connection accepts
    20067 connections established (including accepts)
    20168 connections closed (including 3 drops)
    0 embryonic connections dropped
    3513638 segments updated rtt (of 3523642 attempts)
    11 retransmit timeouts
        0 connections dropped by rexmit timeout
    38 persist timeouts
    19 keepalive timeouts
        0 keepalive probes sent
        0 connections dropped by keepalive
```

Figure 12.11 netstat TCP Statistics.

* *acks*

    The count of ACK messages received without any data. Also the total number
    of bytes acknowledged by these ACKs.

* *duplicate acks*

    The count of duplicate ACKs received. This number should relatively low
    compared to the total bytes transmitted, since it indicates the remote receiver
    had to retransmit an ACK even though the first ACK was received successfully.

- *acks for unsent data*
  An indication of an acknowledgement sequence number problem. ACKs for unsent data should happen only rarely.

- *packets received in sequence*
  The total number of TCP messages received in the correct order. This number should be a very high percentage of the total number of bytes received, thus indicating good flow control and stable routing.

- *completely duplicate packets*
  The count of duplicate TCP messages and the total number of bytes duplicated. This number should be small compared to the total number of bytes received. Otherwise, it indicates a TCP flow control problem.

- *packets with some dup. data*
  The count of messages that overlap previously sent messages. Again the total should be small in comparison to the total number of bytes received.

- *out-of-order packets*
  The count of messages received out of sequential order. A number that is a high percentage of total messages received can indicate unstable routing or intermittent hardware failure where messages are periodically dropped.

- *packets of data after window*
  The count of messages received that are greater than the current window size. These are messages already in flight when the local window size was adjusted downward. With consistent flow control, this event should happen only rarely.

- *window probes*
  The count of window probe messages received. A large number in this field results from buffer space shortfalls.

- *window update packets*
  The count of messages that change the remote host's receive window size.

- *packets received after close*
  The count of messages received after the remote side of the connection has closed. The data in this case is discarded (this should happen only infrequently).

- *discarded for bad checksum*
  The count of TCP messages discarded because of a checksum error. This number should be small compared to the total number of messages received. A high ratio indicates a high rate of network transmission errors.

- *discarded for bad header offset fields*
  The count of messages dropped because the offset field in the TCP header is wrong. Dropped messages can result from transmission errors; however, this will happen only very rarely.

- *discarded because packet too short*
  The count of received messages shorter than the TCP header length. This event is caused by data corruption.

- *connection requests*
  The count of total connections attempted to remote servers by clients on this host. This number is a good measure of client TCP activity.

- *connection accepts*
  The count of connections accepted from remote clients, signifying the server has sent a SYN_ACK in response to a client's SYN.

- *connections established (including accepts)*
  The count of connections fully established by all clients and servers.

- *connections closed*
  The count of all connections closed. Included in this count are servers that are listening only for connections that have terminated, which means the total count can exceed the total number of connections established. The drop count is of connections that were closed either because of a connection reset from a remote peer or because the host is about to initiate a reset.

- *embryonic connections dropped*
  The count of connections dropped before the TCP received a SYN from a remote peer. A connection is dropped when a client initiates a connection and no response is received from the remote server.

- *segments updated rtt*
  The count of times the round-trip time estimate was updated. Also, the number of attempts to get a round-trip time estimate.

- *retransmit timeouts*
  The count of retransmission timeouts. This number indicates the TCP retransmission timer expired and had to be set to a longer interval for this connection.

- *connections dropped by rexmit timeout*
  The count of connections dropped because the retransmission interval reached its largest possible value and the connection had to be dropped.

- *persist timeouts*
  The count of persistence timeouts, that is, when a window probe times out.

- *keepalive timeouts*
  The count of keepalive timeouts that require the host to send a message to the remote peer to keep the connection open. This is further subdivided into the following two counts:

  - *keepalive probes sent*
    The count of probe messages sent to keep the connection active.

- *connections dropped by keepalive*
  The count of times the connection was dropped because the keepalive interval
  was exceeded.

As you can see, the TCP statistics are extensive and in some cases require intimate
knowledge of how the protocol implementation works. A limitation of many of
the TCP statistics is they are cumulative and don't distinguish between connections. The statistics would be more useful if collected for each connection.

The ICMP statistics are shown in Fig. 12.12 and are explained as follows:

- *calls to icmp_error*
  The count of ICMP error replies sent. These are error responses to incoming IP
  packets, such as *destination unreachable*. This counter doesn't count nonerror
  ICMP responses, such as *routing redirect* or *echo reply.*

- *errors not generated 'cuz old message too short*
  The count of dropped error responses to a too-short IP packet.

- *errors not generated 'cuz old message was icmp*
  The count of dropped error response because the incoming IP packet was an
  ICMP error message. ICMP doesn't generate error messages for error messages.

- *output histogram*
  A histogram of ICMP messages by type.

Figure 12.12 netstat ICMP Statistics.

```
icmp:
    25 calls to icmp_error
    0 errors not generated 'cuz old message too short
    0 errors not generated 'cuz old message was icmp
    Output histogram:
        echo reply: 31
        destination unreachable: 25
    0 messages with bad code fields
    0 messages < minimum length
    0 bad checksums
    0 messages with bad length
    Input histogram:
        echo reply: 62
        destination unreachable: 91
        echo: 31
    31 message responses generated
```

- *messages with bad code fields*
  The count of ICMP messages with an invalid *code* fields in the ICMP headers. The code field is used to further describe the contents of an ICMP message. Each message type has a specific number of valid values for the code field.

- *messages < minimum length*
  The count of ICMP messages shorter than the required length.

- *bad checksums*
  The count of ICMP messages that failed the checksum test. Along with the TCP and UDP checksum statistics, this number can indicate network transmission problems.

- *messages with bad length*
  The count of ICMP messages in which the length of the message is incorrect.

- *input histogram*
  The count of received ICMP messages by type. A very high count of *destination unreachable* messages can indicate a routing configuration problem. Also, a high number of *time-exceeded* messages can indicate a routing loop. But as we will see later in this section, *traceroute* utility also can generate these messages.

- *message responses generated*
  The count of response messages sent. This count includes responses to *echo request, information request, timestamp request,* and all error responses that return the packet in error.

IP statistics are shown in Fig. 12.13 and are explained as follows:

- *total packets received*
  The count of the total number of IP packets received.

- *bad header checksums*
  The count of packets received that failed the header checksum calculation. A large number here relative to the total packets received indicates network transmission problems.

- *with size smaller than minimum*
  The count of IP packets smaller than the size of the expected header size. A large count here also can indicate transmission or framing errors.

- *with data size < data length*
  The count of IP packets in which the packet data length is less than the IP *length* field. This number also can indicate transmission or framing errors.

- *with header length < data size*
  The count of packets in which the header length is less than the total packet length.

```
ip:
    3855476 total packets received
    7 bad header checksums
    0 with size smaller than minimum
    0 with data size < data length
    0 with header length < data size
    0 with data length < header length
    45940 fragments received
    0 fragments dropped (dup or out of space)
    3 fragments dropped after timeout
    0 packets forwarded
    7 packets not forwardable
    0 redirects sent
    0 ip input queue drops
```

Figure 12.13 netstat IP Statistics.

- *with data length < header length*
  The count of packets in which the total packet length is less than the header length.

- *fragments received*
  The count of total IP fragments received by this host. The figure gives a good estimate of the total reassembly work done by the host. NFS exploits reassembly to send large UDP messages, so an active NFS server will receive many fragments.

- *fragments dropped (dup or out of space)*
  The count of fragments dropped because either they are duplicates or the host ran out of buffer space. If an NFS server has a large number of dropped fragments, its performance will suffer. So if your NFS server is slow, examine this counter to ensure the problem is not excessive fragment loss.

- *fragments dropped after timeout*
  The count of fragments dropped because the reassembly timer expired. A large number of dropped fragments indicates packet loss in the network; for example, because of congestion a router could be dropping them before they get to the host. Transmission errors also can cause fragment loss.

- *packets forwarded*
  The count of packets forwarded by this host. An end-node with one network interface shouldn't forward packets. Only routing nodes should have a nonzero value in this field. If an end-node is forwarding frames, you should turn off its ability to do so. When we discuss broadcast storms in Section 12.5, you'll see why this is important.

- *packets not forwardable*
  The count of packets that couldn't be forwarded. These are packets with a final destination not on this host that weren't forwarded. Either the host is configured to not forward packets or an error occurred when the host attempts to forward the packet.

- *redirects sent*
  The count of ICMP *route redirect* messages sent. These messages should be seen only on a routing node.

- *ip input queue drops*
  The count of packets dropped from the input queue because of buffer space shortage. This statistic occurs on some but not all systems.

Interfaces. Netstat with the *-i* option displays the status of all network interfaces, as shown in the example interface display in Fig. 12.14. This display shows valuable information about the state of all the network interfaces. Note that the *-n* option suppresses the address-to-name translation of IP addresses; for debugging purposes, using this option is preferred. The following fields are displayed:

- *Name*
  The logical name of the network interface. An inactive interface displays the name followed by an "*."

- *MTU*
  The size in bytes of the interfaces MTU.

- *Net/Dest*
  Either the IP network address of the network to which the interface is attached or the IP host address of the remote end of a point-to-point link.

- *Address*
  The local IP address of the interface.

- *Ipkts*
  The count of datalink frames received on the interface since the last bootstrap.

- *Ierrs*
  The datalink frames received with errors and dropped by the interface.

Figure 12.14 netstat Interface Display.

```
% netstat -i -n
Name Mtu   Net/Dest       Address         Ipkts    Ierrs Opkts   Oerrs Collis
le0  1500  192.12.23.128  192.12.23.129  8141881  0     7902647 0     61
lo0  1536  127.0.0.0      127.0.0.1      245772   0     245772  0     0
```

• *Opkts*

The count of datalink frames sent on the interface since the last bootstrap.

• *Oerrs*

The count of frames not sent due to output errors.

• *Collis*

The count of collisions detected by this interface. This figure is meaningful only for Ethernet or other CSMA/CD networks. On an Ethernet, the collision rate should be less than 1% of the total packets sent successfully on the interface. Keep in mind that this field reflects only the collisions seen by the interface on the designated machine. On a machine that sends relatively few packets, the collision rate can be misleadingly low. This is because the machine records collisions only when trying to transmit an Ethernet frame. The only sure way to see the overall collision rate is to use a network sniffer. If the collision rate is greater than 1% on any machine, then serious network problems are indicated which bear further scrutiny.

You can write a simple script using the *remote* script, described earlier in this section, that allows some simple and automated analysis of network traffic on each host and that indicates some abnormal conditions. For example, the *coll_rate* script found in Appendix B passes the output of remote to display the collision rate on each machine on the network. An example use of this script is shown in Fig. 12.15.

Routing. Netstat uses the *-r* option to display the kernel routing tables, as shown in Fig. 12.16. For debugging purposes, the *-n* option bypasses the IP address-to-hostname lookup, which might itself depend on proper routing. Each line of the output describes one routing table entry. The output is divided into the following fields:

• *Destination*

The destination IP network number or host IP address for a route to a host. A default route present is always displayed as "default." This route is to destination network 0.0.0.0, which is interpreted to mean the route of last resort.

Figure 12.15 Collision Rate Script Example.

```
% remote netstat -in -h `getdns` | coll_rate
Host              Interface Address        Collisions Rate(%)
aahsa.tic.com     qe0       192.135.128.130        42   0.00
akasha.tic.com    le0       192.135.128.129        40   0.00
beast.tic.com     en0       192.135.128.132         0   0.00
```

```
Routing tables
Destination     Gateway           Flags    Refcnt Use        Interface
127.0.0.1       127.0.0.1         UH       12     244780     lo0
default         192.12.23.132     UG       0      51         le0
192.12.23.128   192.12.23.129     U        16     8248341    le0
```

Figure 12.16 Routing Table Display.

• *Gateway*

The IP address of the next hop to which to send the packet.

• *Flags*

The status of each route. One or more of the following letters is used to represent the status:

  • *U*

  An indication that the route is useable. All directly connected networks appear with only this single-letter flag value. In this case, the *Gateway* field is the address of the local interface attached to the directly connected network.

  • *G*

  An indication that the route is through an intermediate router on a locally attached network. In this case, the *Gateway* field is the address of the intermediate router.

  • *H*

  The route is to a host rather than to a network. A host route is seen only on the loopback interface or on point-to-point interfaces.

  • *D*

  The route was added by an ICMP *routing redirect* message. In this case, no route to the destination existed before the ICMP message. This can happen when a default router sends a redirect to a better route for a particular network. If you are using default routes but better routes to a specific destination exist, then this flag shows you how the better route came into existence.

  • *M*

  The route was modified by an ICMP *routing redirect* message. This is the same action taken using *D* flag except a route to the destination already existed in the routing table.

• *Refcnt*

The current number of active TCP connections using the route. A TCP connection does an initial routing table lookup when it first establishes a connection. The route selected is then used throughout the life of the connection. Performing this initial lookup saves time in looking up a route. The total of the *Refcnt* field is the total number of active TCP connections.

- *Use*
  The total number of IP packets sent using the route.

- *Interface*
  The logical name of the local network interface.

Adding an -*s* flag to the routing display command displays routing statistics, as shown in Fig. 12.17. The following statistics are displayed:

- *bad routing redirects*
  The count of invalid ICMP *route redirects.* A valid redirect must be from the route's destination and specify a new destination on a locally attached network.

- *dynamically created routes*
  The count of routes created dynamically by redirects.

- *new gateways due to redirects*
  The count of routes modified by redirects.

- *destinations found unreachable*
  The count of routing lookups that result in no routing entry found.

- *uses of a wildcard route*
  The count of the number of times the default route is used.

The -*s* option gives some indication of the health of the routing tables. Many instances of *destination unreachable* indicate a misconfigured routing table or possibly a bad IP address for a destination host.

A simple script that takes the routing table output can be used with the *remote* script to obtain routing information on all machines on the local network and to check the overall configuration. Generally the routing tables on all systems should be similar and have at least a route to the local network. The *route_check* script found in Appendix B checks each routing table for a route to the directly connected network and to the loopback interface (network 127) and also checks for a *default* route. Output from this script is shown in Fig. 12.18.

Figure 12.17 Routing Statistics.

```
% netstat -r -s
routing:
     0 bad routing redirects
     0 dynamically created routes
     0 new gateways due to redirects
     13709 destinations found unreachable
     0 uses of a wildcard route
```

```
% remote netstat -r -n -h `getdns` | route_check
Host            Def    Local    This
aahsa.tic.com          no     yes     yes
akasha.tic.com         no     yes     yes
beast.tic.com          no     yes     yes
```

Figure 12.18 Route Check Output.

ifconfig

Another very useful tool, *ifconfig* is used primarily to configure the network interfaces at boot time. You also can use it to check the interface configuration and, in particular, the interface broadcast address and network mask; a misconfigured broadcast address and/or network mask can create some seemingly mysterious network problems.

The *remote* script can run ifconfig on all remote hosts to check the interface specifications for the local interface. In a heterogeneous network environment, possibly not all local interfaces will have the same name. Therefore in order to obtain the proper network interface name, netstat needs to be run with the *-i* option and the proper interface name plugged into ifconfig as shown in the *getconfig* script found in Appendix B. The output from getconfig is displayed in Fig. 12.19.

The output of getconfig can be used in the script, chkbrdmask found in Appendix B to check the netmask and broadcast address for all local network interfaces. The output from this script is shown in Fig. 12.20. A helper script *ddtohex* also found in Appendix B converts dotted decimal to hex.

Figure 12.19 Getconfig Output.

```
% getconfig `getdns`
Host: aahsa.tic.com
qe0: 192.135.128.130 netmask fffffff0\
     flags=0x463<DYNPROTO,RUNNING,NOTRAILERS,BROADCAST,UP>
     broadcast: 192.135.128.143
Host: akasha.tic.com
le0: flags=63<UP,BROADCAST,NOTRAILERS,RUNNING>
    inet 192.135.128.129 netmask fffffff0 broadcast 192.135.128.143
Host: beast.tic.com
en0: flags=2000063<UP,BROADCAST,NOTRAILERS,RUNNING,NOECHO>
    inet 192.135.128.132 netmask 0xfffffff0 broadcast 192.135.128.143
```

```
% getconfig `gendns` | chkbrdmask fffffff0 `ddtohex 192.135.128.143`
mask:fffffff0 broadcast:c087808f
Host:           Netmask    Broadcast
aahsa.tic.com   fffffff0   c087808f
akasha.tic.com  fffffff0   c087808f
beast.tic.com   fffffff0   c087808f
```

Figure 12.20 chkbrdmask Output.

---

traceroute

traceroute traces the route an IP packet takes to a destination host. It doesn't come as a part of any UNIX OS and so must be retrieved from a public archive site. See Appendix A for where to obtain a copy of this useful utility. In its simplest form, traceroute takes a single hostname argument and lists all the intermediate routers in the path to the final destination, as shown in the example of Fig. 12.21. Here, each line of the output lists the name and IP address of an intermediate router. By default traceroute sends three UDP messages encapsulated in an IP packet and records the round-trip time in milliseconds for each message sent to each intermediate router. A lost message or a router that doesn't respond to a message is denoted with an "*."

Traceroute works by exploiting the IP time-to-live algorithm. Recall from Chapter 3 that the *ttl* field in the IP header is used to keep IP packets from looping forever within the Internet. Traceroute sends a UDP message to an unused port on the target host. However, because the *ttl* field is initially set to 1, when the message reaches the first router, the *ttl* field is decremented. The router notices the value is 0 and so returns an ICMP *time exceeded* message. Traceroute then sees these messages, notices which router they are from (found in the source IP address of the message), and prints the results. The *ttl* field is then set to 2, the message is retransmitted, and the results recorded. Both the UDP port number and the *ttl* field are incremented, the latter until the UDP message reaches its intended destination. At that point, the target host receives the message, but because it doesn't have a server listening on that UDP port, it returns an ICMP *service unavailable* message.

arp

The *arp* command enables you to examine and modify the local ARP cache. You must be the superuser to modify the table, but any user can examine the cache. With the *-a* option, Arp displays the entire ARP table on the local host, as shown in Fig. 12.22. Here, each ARP entry is displayed on a single line and shows the host's name, IP address, and Ethernet address. Systems that support 802.3 or Token Ring also display the type of the datalink address.

The following options let you limit the display or manipulate the cache:

```
% traceroute cs.utexas.edu
traceroute to cs.utexas.edu (128.83.139.9), 30 hops max,\
 40 byte packets
 1  * * *
 2  38.145.245.1 (38.145.245.1)   69 ms   511 ms   77 ms
 3  38.145.244.1 (38.145.244.1)   119 ms   497 ms   101 ms
 4  38.145.169.1 (38.145.169.1)   100 ms   518 ms   105 ms
 5  38.145.166.1 (38.145.166.1)   148 ms   502 ms   136 ms
 6  38.1.2.5 (38.1.2.5)   268 ms   236 ms   210 ms
 7  ENSS.TN.CORNELL.EDU (192.35.82.101)   299 ms   310 ms   299 ms
 8  t3-1.cnss49.t3.nsf.net (140.222.49.2)   419 ms   406 ms   379 ms
 9  t3-3.cnss48.t3.nsf.net (140.222.48.4)   309 ms   321 ms   301 ms
10  t3-2.cnss32.t3.nsf.net (140.222.32.3)   298 ms   446 ms   400 ms
11  t3-1.cnss40.t3.nsf.net (140.222.40.2)   860 ms   257 ms   258 ms
12  t3-2.cnss24.t3.nsf.net (140.222.24.3)   249 ms   327 ms   329 ms
13  t3-2.cnss80.t3.nsf.net (140.222.80.3)   330 ms   297 ms   199 ms
14  t3-1.cnss64.t3.nsf.net (140.222.64.2)   249 ms   357 ms   239 ms
15  t3-0.cnss65.t3.nsf.net (140.222.65.1)   229 ms   236 ms   390 ms
16  t3-0.enss139.t3.nsf.net (140.222.139.1)   359 ms   317 ms   309 ms
17  RICE2-E1.sesqui.net (128.241.0.83)   270 ms   357 ms   268 ms
18  UT1-S1.sesqui.net (128.241.3.130)   270 ms   477 ms   359 ms
19  ser1->dmz.gw.utexas.edu (128.83.5.250)   360 ms   248 ms   289 ms
20  ens->ser1.gw.utexas.edu (128.83.6.2)   269 ms   299 ms   288 ms
21  tay.gw.utexas.edu (128.83.7.135)   359 ms   448 ms   389 ms
22  * backbone-gw.cs.utexas.edu (128.83.213.2)   458 ms   245 ms
23  cs.utexas.edu (128.83.139.9)   241 ms   288 ms   268 ms
```

Figure 12.21 traceroute Output.

- arp *hostname*
  Displays an entry for a single host. This option is particularly useful in very large networks where the ARP cache is very long. The hostname can be either a host's name or address.

- arp -a *kernel core*
  Lets you use a different kernel image and core image. This facility is in addition

---

Figure 12.22 arp Command Output.

```
# arp -a
aahsa.tic.com (192.135.128.130) at 8:0:2b:e:eb:95
xfrwf.tic.com (192.135.128.134) at 0:0:a2:1:2c:b0
```

to displaying the entire ARP table on the local host and is useful for examining kernel dumps and seeing the state of the cache at the time the system crashed.

- arp -d *hostname*
Deletes the cache entry for a host. It's used to clear up invalid cache entries, for example, when a network interface card is changed and the host's datalink address changes. After the entry is deleted, the next IP packet sent to the remote host causes an ARP request packet to be generated.

- arp -s *hostname datalink_address* [temp] [pub] [trail]
Lets you install an ARP cache entry by hand. This needs to be done rarely; however, it's useful if you have a host that doesn't support ARP. In this case, another host can install an ARP cache entry using the *pub* option for the target host. The *pub* option tells the host to respond for requests not only for itself but also for the target host. When we discuss broadcast storms in Section 12.5, we will show you a creative use of this command for reducing errant broadcast traffic.

The *temp* option indicates that the entry is temporary and should time out like a normal cache entry. Without this option, the entry is considered permanent and will never time out. The *trail* option is an old and now obsolete type of encapsulation and should never be used.

- arp -f *filename*
Lets you add multiple ARP cache entries listed in a file. Intended to batch ARP updates, it's rarely used today.

etherfind

etherfind is a specific Sun tool for tracing Ethernet frames on your local network. While etherfind is not found on all UNIX systems, it's so useful that it bears mention as a debugging tool. In essence, etherfind performs many of the monitoring functions of a dedicated network analyzer. It has the added advantage that its output can be massaged by common UNIX tools such as *grep, awk,* and *sed.*

Etherfind lets you monitor traffic on your Ethernet and selectively display Ethernet frames as they are received by the host's network interface. By using Sun's **NIT** low-level device interface, etherfind can display all traffic on the network. This is done by setting the hardware interface to what is called "promiscuous" mode, which allows for the reception of all traffic and not just frames bound for the specific host.

A syntax reminiscent of the *find* command is used by etherfind to limit the types of packets that will be displayed. The find-like syntax can be difficult to remember; fortunately most etherfind applications don't need it in all its ugliness. If you have predetermined types of frames you want to examine, it's better to set up a shell script to produce the output desired rather than attempt to remember this syntax.

Generally the etherfind command uses a number of options followed by the type of frames to display. Etherfind is optimized to scan and decode TCP/IP packets. Thus, it's not very useful for debugging other protocols. Rather than describe all the various options available with etherfind, we explore a sampling of examples that will give you a sense of how it works.

Note that etherfind requires superuser privileges; an ordinary user should not be able to run it, since that allows network eavesdropping. If you use etherfind extensively, you might find it convenient to set its permissions to run setuid to the superuser and allow only selected users in an administration or staff group to execute the command, and disallow any ordinary user from using the command.

The etherfind example in Fig. 12.23 displays all frames on the network. Note the use of the *greater* keyword, which causes all frames to be displayed. Etherfind requires at least one selector to be put on its command line, so to select all frames, the example simply selects those that have a frame length greater than zero. Each frame is displayed as a single line that has the following fields:

- *lnth*
The length of the frame, which includes the Ethernet frame header and trailer.

- *proto*
The protocol encapsulated within the frame. In the case where an IP packet is encapsulated, the name of the transport protocol used is displayed. ICMP messages are also identified, in which case the *src port* or *dst port* fields have no meaning and the type of the ICMP message is displayed. ARP packets are also identified. If the received frame is an IP fragment, only the encapsulated protocol preceded by an "*" is shown.

- *source*
The source node of the IP packet.

Figure 12.23 Default etherfind Output.

```
% etherfind -i le0 greater 0
 lnth proto          source      destination    src port    dst port
   60  tcp xfrsparc.tic.co  akasha.tic.com      1023        login
   60  tcp xfrsparc.tic.co  akasha.tic.com      1023        login
   60  type 8102 0:0:a2:1:2c:b0 -> 0:0:a2:1:2c:b0
   42  arp akasha.tic.com   xfrwf.tic.com
   60  arp   xfrwf.tic.com  akasha.tic.com
   98 icmp xfrsparc.tic.co  akasha.tic.com      echo reply
   98 icmp xfrsparc.tic.co  akasha.tic.com      echo
 1514  udp    aahsa.tic.com xfrsparc.tic.co     2049        1020
*1514  udp
*1514  udp
*1514  udp
*1514  udp
*  934 udp
```

• *destination*
The destination node of the IP packet.

• *src port*
The source port number from which the message was sent. If the port number appears in */etc/services,* then the mnemonic name of the port is displayed.

• *dst port*
The destination port number for which the message was bound.

Etherfind has some limited knowledge of other network protocols. For example, it will properly identify DECNet and Appletalk packets but give very little information about their contents. If etherfind encounters a frame encapsulating an unknown protocol, it simply displays the decimal *ethertype* field value and the source and destination Ethernet addresses.

While the default display is useful, etherfind allows you to use the -*v* option to display more specific and detailed information about each frame. Also, with the -*t* option, each frame can be timestamped. Figure 12.24 shows output using these options. Here, each frame is displayed on a single line, but the amount of information about the contents of each frame is much more detailed.

nslookup

nslookup is a simple tool for querying DNS servers. Without arguments, nslookup prompts the user for nameserver queries. Simply typing a name asks nslookup to compose a query for a DNS address type record for the domain name. You can set

---

Figure 12.24 More detailed etherfind Output.

```
csh> etherfind -i le0 -v -t greater 0
 0.00    68  type 8102 0:0:a2:1:2c:b0 -> 0:0:a2:1:2c:b0
 0.64 TCP from xfrsparc.tic.com.1023 to akasha.tic.com.login\
    seq 50286B, ack 1A1D98EE,  window 4380,
 1.44 TCP from xfrsparc.tic.com.1014 to akasha.tic.com.login\
    seq 7A21C1C, ack 2167F185,  window 4380, 1 bytes data
 1.45 TCP from xfrsparc.tic.com.1014 to akasha.tic.com.login\
    seq 7A21C1D, ack 2167F186,  window 4379, 1 bytes data
 4.88 ICMP from xfrwf.tic.com to akasha.tic.com echo reply 64 data bytes
20.03 UDP from c.nyser.net.domain to akasha.tic.com.domain  198 bytes
20.69 UDP from ns.psi.net.domain to akasha.tic.com.domain  75 bytes
33.13 TCP from cs.utexas.edu.smtp to akasha.tic.com.4592\
    seq 284D6200, ack 2D0D3401, SYN,  window 4096,
33.64 TCP from xfrsparc.tic.com.1023 to akasha.tic.com.login\
    seq 50286B, ack 1A1DD936,  window 4380,
```

various options to change the type of lookup or change to which server each query
is sent. Figure 12.25 shows an example usage of nslookup.

Figure 12.25 nslookup Example.

```
% nslookup
Default Server:  akasha.tic.com
Address:  192.135.128.129
> akasha
Server:  akasha.tic.com
Address:  192.135.128.129
Name:    akasha.tic.com
Address:  192.135.128.129
> ls tic.com
[akasha.tic.com]
Host or domain name              Internet address
 tic                             server = akasha.tic.com
 akasha                          192.135.128.129
 aahsa                           192.135.128.130
 ticmac                          192.135.128.131
> set type=ptr
> 129.128.135.192.in-addr.arpa.
Server:  akasha.tic.com
Address:  192.135.128.129
129.128.135.192.in-addr.arpa    host name = akasha.tic.com
129.128.135.192.in-addr.arpa    host name = tic.com
> set type=any
> tic.com
Server:  localhost
Address:  127.0.0.1
Aliases:  localhost.tic.com
tic.com origin = akasha.tic.com
        mail addr = root.tic.com
        serial=921112, refresh=86400, retry=3600, expire=3600000, min=604800
tic.com nameserver = akasha.tic.com
tic.com nameserver = ns2.psi.net
tic.com inet address = 192.135.128.129
tic.com CPU=SUN4        OS=SUNOS
tic.com preference = 10, mail exchanger = aahsa.tic.com
tic.com preference = 5, mail exchanger = akasha.tic.com
akasha.tic.com  inet address = 192.135.128.129
ns2.psi.net     inet address = 192.35.82.1
aahsa.tic.com   inet address = 192.135.128.130
% nslookup akasha
Server:  akasha.tic.com
Address:  192.135.128.129
Name:    akasha.tic.com
Address:  192.135.128.129
```

Note here that the syntax is a somewhat peculiar in that nslookup knows that certain strings are the names of commands and not unqualified hostnames. For example, if you have a host named "help," then you must use the fully-qualified name, since "help" is a built-in nslookup command. If a single argument is given on the command line, then as a shortcut nslookup returns the address type record for the single host and then exits. This command is useful for single-shot queries.

dig

dig is a public-domain tool for querying DNS nameservers. See Appendix A for where this useful utility can be obtained. It resembles nslookup, but many administrators find it the easier to use of the two. In its simplest form, dig takes a single domain name as an argument and returns the associated address type record as a result. By default, dig gives the result plus significant amounts of debugging detail about the actual query processing.

Figure 12.26 shows some common ways to use this tool. The first example in the figure shows how to use dig to get a host's address type record. The second shows getting an alternative record type; in this case, the first argument is the type of the DNS record. The third shows the built-in shortcut for doing an inverse query. The *-x* option tells dig to construct an inverse query using the next argument as an IP address.

Conclusion

The simple tools described here are certainly not as sophisticated as a network management system based on SNMP. Even so they are invaluable for debugging misconfigured networks and finding simple configuration errors that lead to an unstable and unusable network. More importantly, these tools are found on nearly all UNIX systems and are generally portable across those systems. And as demonstrated, some simple shell scripts can be built that enhance the basic network debugging tools. Let's see how they can be used to debug network problems.

12.2 Diagnosing Routing Problems

Improperly configured routing tables are a major source of network communication problems on TCP/IP networks. IP makes routing decisions based upon the network or subnetwork part of the destination address. If that part of the address is the same as that of the locally attached and configured network, then the packet is sent directly to its final destination (for example, the destination interface on the same physical network). If the network is not locally attached, then the packet is sent to an intermediate router on the locally attached network. In the first case, IP generates an ARP packet (if the network supports ARP) to get the destination IP address, provided it has not already been cached. In the second case, IP looks for a routing table entry to the destination network and ARPs for the address of the first hop router on the local network, provided the routers datalink address is itself not already cached.

```
% dig akasha
; <<>> DiG 2.0 <<>> akasha
;; ->>HEADER<<- opcode: QUERY , status: NOERROR, id: 6
;; flags: qr aa rd ra ; Ques: 1, Ans: 1, Auth: 0, Addit: 0
;; QUESTIONS:
;;      akasha.tic.com, type = A, class = IN
;; ANSWERS:
akasha.tic.com. 604800  A       192.135.128.129
;; Sent 1 pkts, answer found in time: 1 msec
;; FROM: akasha.tic.com to SERVER: default -- 127.0.0.1
;; WHEN: Thu Dec 10 09:41:48 1991
;; MSG SIZE  sent: 32  rcvd: 48


% dig mx tic.com
; <<>> DiG 2.0 <<>> mx tic.com
;; ->>HEADER<<- opcode: QUERY , status: NOERROR, id: 6
;; flags: qr aa rd ra ; Ques: 1, Ans: 2, Auth: 0, Addit: 1
;; QUESTIONS:
;;      tic.com, type = MX, class = IN
;; ANSWERS:
tic.com.        604800  MX      10 aahsa.tic.com.
tic.com.        604800  MX      5 akasha.tic.com.
;; ADDITIONAL RECORDS:
aahsa.tic.com. 604800  A       192.135.128.130
akasha.tic.com. 604800  A       192.135.128.129
;; Sent 1 pkts, answer found in time: 1 msec
;; FROM: akasha.tic.com to SERVER: default -- 127.0.0.1
;; WHEN: Thu Dec 10 09:41:55 1991
;; MSG SIZE  sent: 25  rcvd: 101


% dig -x 192.135.128.129
; <<>> DiG 2.0 <<>> -x
;; ->>HEADER<<- opcode: QUERY , status: NOERROR, id: 6
;; flags: qr aa rd ra ; Ques: 1, Ans: 2, Auth: 0, Addit: 0
;; QUESTIONS:
;;      129.128.135.192.in-addr.arpa, type = ANY, class = IN
;; ANSWERS:
129.128.135.192.in-addr.arpa.   604800  PTR     akasha.tic.com.
129.128.135.192.in-addr.arpa.   604800  PTR     tic.com.
;; Sent 1 pkts, answer found in time: 1 msec
;; FROM: akasha.tic.com to SERVER: default -- 127.0.0.1
;; WHEN: Thu Dec 10 09:42:09 1991
;; MSG SIZE  sent: 46  rcvd: 88
```

Figure 12.26 dig Example.

When a network is connected to the outside world using a router, it's all too common to have routes improperly configured or not disseminated to hosts on the local network. Given the simple network shown in Fig. 12.27, if Host A wants to send a packet to a host with IP address 131.133.2.1 then Host A must have a

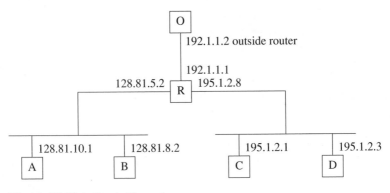

Figure 12.27 A Simple Network.

routing table entry for network 131.133.0.0 that points at the Router R. Either an explicit route to that network exists in the hosts routing table or a default route exists that has a destination of R's IP address. If a user on A tries

```
telnet 131.133.2.1
```

and gets the message

```
telnet: connect: Network is unreachable
```

then Host A's routing table is not properly configured. Using the *netstat* command you can display the contents of A's routing tables, as follows:

```
% netstat -r -n
Routing Tables
Destination      Gateway         Flags    Refcnt   Use        Interface
127.0.0.1        127.0.0.1       UH       8        55906      lo0
195.81.10.0      195.81.10.1     U        14       4099214    le0
```

In this case, no routing table entry exists for network 131.133.0.0. Thus the failure to connect results from the absence of a correct routing table entry on the local host. However, a route to the destination network can be manually added using the route command

```
route add 131.133.0.0 195.81.5.2 1
```

or a default route can be added as follows:

```
route add 0 195.81.5.2 1
```

A default route is one of last resort; that is, absent a route entry for a particular network in the routing table, the default route is used.

In both of these cases, the source of the routing problem still has not been determined. When Host A is rebooted, the routing problem might recur since any route added manually disappears across system boots. At this point, it's a good idea to determine whether you are using default routes to the nearest router or whether the router should be advertising and broadcasting routing updates to hosts on the local network.

If the router is suppose to be advertising routes on the local network, then find out what routing protocol is being used. If it's RIP, which is very common for distributing routing local information, then ensure *routed* is running on Host A. You can check this by using the *ps* command to determine if the routed daemon is running. If it is, then check whether the router is sending routing updates. Do this by manually running routed with the *-t* option, as follows:

```
% routed -t
RESPONSE from 195.81.5.2.520:
    dst 195.1.2.0 metric 1
    dst 0.0.0.0 metric 1
```

The output shows routing updates being received and sent by routed.

Ensure you kill the routed process running as a daemon before starting routed manually. Each routing update's source is identified; in this example, a routing update was sent from IP address 192.135.128.130 from port 520 (the RIP well-known port). The destination networks are listed along with the metric to the destination; in this case, network 192.135.128.0 is one hop away and network 0.0.0.0 (the default route) is also one hop away.

RIP sends updates every 30 seconds, therefore if no updates show up after that amount of time, your router is not advertising its routes. At this point, check your router configuration and ensure its routing tables are correct and that it's sending routing updates on the local network. Keep in mind that the router itself can receive routing updates from other routers on the Internet, so it must be configured to receive those additional routes. You also can configure a router with a single connection to the Internet to distribute a default route rather than routes to all the networks for which it receives routing updates. Because only a single router is the gateway to all outside networks, this is a convenient way to reduce the size of the routing tables on all your hosts.

Finally, after verifying that updates are being properly distributed, be sure that routed is run when the host is booted.

If you are using a default route to a single router, then add the correct *route* command in the machine's startup script so the default route will be properly configured when the machine reboots. At this point, retry the *telnet* command to the remote network. If you still get "Network unreachable" or if the connection times out, then probably something is wrong with the router's configuration. First, check the connectivity with the router itself by pinging the router's interface address on the local network using the *ping* utility with the router's IP address as an argument, as follows:

```
% ping 195.81.5.2
195.81.5.2 is alive
```

Next, try pinging the interface address of the serial interface on the router that connects it to a WAN, as follows:

```
% ping 192.1.1.1
192.1.1.1 is alive
```

These two steps will give you a good indication of whether the router is properly configured and properly routing IP packets. Finally, ping the address on the other side of the serial interface from the router, as follows:

```
% ping 192.1.1.2
ping 192.1.1.2 is alive
```

Doing this will tell you whether your connectivity to the outside is correct and working.

If the results of the above three steps are positive and the routing problem persists, then the problem probably exists outside your local environment. So try to ping another known IP address outside your local environment. If this doesn't work, then track down the routing problem with the *traceroute* utility. Run a traceroute to the remote destination. If a remote router isn't responding or is routing incorrectly, no response will be returned beyond a certain number of hops.

12.3 Nameservice Problems

A network communication that works when using IP addresses but not when using hostnames means hostname-to-IP address translation is misconfigured. Methods for tracking down nameservice problems depend largely on what method or combination of methods — static tables, NIS, or DNS — you use for name-to-address translation.

Static Tables

If you use static tables alone and can't ping a hostname but can ping its IP address, then ensure an entry for the remote host exists in */etc/hosts*. If it doesn't, add the entry and then retry. Also ensure you really are configured to use only static tables. Different UNIX systems decide which nameservice to use based upon certain configuration options and the contents of various files. Not all systems are consistent in their approach to this problem.

For example, Sun OS 4.1.x uses static host tables if the *ypbind* process is not actively running; however, if ypbind is present NIS is used. When *ypserv* on a NIS server is run with the *-i* option and NIS can't handle the translation, it passes the hostname on to a DNS nameserver configured in the */etc/resolv.conf* file. SUNs can also be configured to use DNS only by replacing the C library routines *gethostbyname()* and *gethostbyaddr()* with routines that do direct DNS lookups.

DEC Ultrix systems use the file */etc/svcorder* to determine hostname lookup order. With this system, all three methods — static tables, NIS, and DNS — can be used simultaneously. IBM RS6000 systems use DNS exclusively if the file */etc/resolv.conf* exists, falling back to static host lookup if DNS fails. However, if *ypbind* is running and */etc/resolv.conf* doesn't exist, NIS is used for hostname lookup. SVR4 uses the */etc/netconfig* file, which indicates which shared library to load for host-to-address mappings. Static table lookups are used, unless the resolver library is included in the configuration setup, in which case DNS is used.

NIS

Because NIS is a means of distributing static host table information across a LAN, ensure an entry for the remote host exists in the NIS hostname map. Do this using a *ypcat* or a *ypmatch,* as follows:

```
% ypcat hosts | grep akasha
192.135.128.129 akasha.tic.com akasha
% ypmatch akasha hosts
192.135.128.129 akasha.tic.com akasha
```

Both ypcat and ypmatch exercise the NIS systems and so are good programs for checking proper NIS configuration. When they work, NIS is properly configured. However, if the remote host's name doesn't show up in either the ypcat or ypmatch output, add an entry for it in the correct map input file. A ypcat or ypmatch that hangs or shows it's not bound to a server means your NIS server has probably hung or crashed. In this case, try the ypwhich command to determine if the machine is bound to a NIS domain. If ypwhich then appears to hang, you know either that the NIS server has definitely failed or it can't be contacted. A third possibility, however, is that the server has an incorrect NIS domain on the client, in which case, check the NIS domain with the *domainname* command, as follows:

```
% domainname
tic.com
```

If your domain is correct but NIS services are still hung, then determine whether the server has crashed and there are any alternative servers available. If services are restored when the server comes back up, then consider adding an NIS slave server for redundancy on the network.

For an NIS server that is functioning normally when NIS services are being handled properly on other hosts, check the errant machine's broadcast and network addresses. A misconfigured broadcast address will cause a NIS client never to bind to an NIS server, since NIS depends on broadcasting on the local network to find an available server. Also check whether an NIS server is on the same datalink network; NIS doesn't work across routers.

DNS

When running DNS only, try pinging or telnetting to a host on your local network, in this case, exercising the nameserver using the hostname instead of the IP address. If this fails, try the same command from another host that uses the same nameserver. Success at this point means the problem is isolated to the one host; failure indicates the nameserver on the server machine might be failing. You can check the server by using *nslookup* or *dig,* as shown in Fig. 12.28. Another possible error is a misconfigured */etc/resolv.conf* file. Here, ensure the correct nameserver entry is used and the default domain is spelled correctly.

Figure 12.28 DNS Server Debugging.

```
% nslookup akasha.tic.com
Server:   akasha.tic.com
Address:  192.135.128.129

Name:     akasha.tic.com
Address:  192.135.128.129


% dig akasha.tic.com

; <<>> DiG 2.0 <<>> akasha.tic.com
;; ->>HEADER<<- opcode: QUERY , status: NOERROR, id: 6
;; flags: qr aa rd ra ; Ques: 1, Ans: 1, Auth: 0, Addit: 0
;; QUESTIONS:
;;   akasha.tic.com, type = A, class = IN

;; ANSWERS:
akasha.tic.com.     604800  A    192.135.128.129

;; Sent 1 pkts, answer found in time: 1 msec
;; FROM: akasha.tic.com to SERVER: default -- 127.0.0.1
;; WHEN: Thu Dec 10 09:15:00 1991
;; MSG SIZE   sent: 32   rcvd: 48
```

```
(1) Debug turned ON, Level 1

(2)  datagram from 127.0.0.1 port 1761, fd 8, len 31
(3)  req: nlookup(akasha.tic.com) id 6 type=1
(4)  req: found 'akasha.tic.com' as 'akasha.tic.com' (cname=0)
(5)  req: answer -> 127.0.0.1 9 (1761) id=6 Local

(6)  datagram from 127.0.0.1 port 1766, fd 8, len 46
(7)  req: nlookup(129.128.135.192.in-addr.arpa) id 6 type=255
(8)  req: found '129.128.135.192.in-addr.arpa' as\
            '129.128.135.192.in-addr.arpa' (cname=0)
(9)  req: answer -> 127.0.0.1 9 (1766) id=6 Local

(10) datagram from 127.0.0.1 port 1771, fd 8, len 28
(11) resp: nlookup(purdue.edu) type=1
(12) resp: found 'purdue.edu' as 'purdue.edu' (cname=0)
(13) resp: forw -> 128.10.2.5 8 (53) nsid=6 id=6 0ms

(14) datagram from 128.10.2.5 port 53, fd 8, len 44
(15) send_msg -> 127.0.0.1 (UDP 9 1771) id=6

(17) Debug turned OFF, Level 1
```

Figure 12.29 Sample BIND Debugging Output.

If all else fails, you can examine the nameserver's debug output while a client is querying for an answer. To do this, use the *poke_ns* command, described in Chapter 6, with the "debug" option and look at the output in the file /usr/etc/named.run. This output is rather cryptic and was not designed with system level debugging in mind; however, there are some things you can look for and check that will help in this area. In Fig. 12.29, an excerpt from the nameserver debugging output shows several successful queries. Each set of debugging statements is a single query/response sequence and shows you what the nameserver did with each of them. The parts of the line for each are described as follows:

• Line 2
This line gives the IP address and the port the query was received on, which UNIX file descriptor the UDP port is associated with, and the length of the UDP message.

• Lines 3 – 5 and 7 – 9
These lines all begin with "req" and illustrate the query processing.

• Lines 3, 7, and 11
These "req" lines include "nlookup" and indicate the domain name being searched for, the unique query id of the query, and the type of query. The unique

query id is useful for tracking the query, especially when it is forwarded to another nameserver. The type of query unfortunately is displayed numerically and not with the mnemonic record type; however, the mnemonic name can be looked up in the */usr/include/arpa/nameser.h* file.

- Lines 4 and 8
These "req" lines include "found" and indicate which part of the domain was found in the local database.

- Lines 5 and 9
These "req" include "answer" and give the replies sent back to the query originator.

For example, the first set shows a query coming from a remote IP address that can be answered locally. Here, the domain name in the query is *akasha.tic.com,* the query id is 6, and the type of query is 1 (an address type record). The answer was found in the local database and returned to the sender. The debugging output always emerges in this format, since BIND itself is single-threaded, that is, it decides what to do with each query before receiving the next query.

The next set shows an inverse query, which also is answered locally. Note that the query type in this case is 255 (ANY) and not 12 (PTR). In this case, however, it really doesn't matter which it is since the query will return only a PTR record for this particular query.

The final two sets show a query from the local host that can't be answered locally. In the first, the lookup partially succeeded in that the nameserver for the *purdue.edu* domain was found in the local cache. However, the query is still forwarded to another server, in this case to the nameserver for the *purdue.edu* domain. This nameserver remembers it still has to process this query and so places it in a queue, thus freeing itself up to answer other queries in the meantime. Note that the query id was reused since the previous query with this id had already been completely answered. The final query set shows the response from the nameserver to which the request was forwarded. On a busy nameserver, other queries could have been processed, so the sequential ordering of the response is simply a matter of no other queries being received.

Another common mistake with nameservers is failure to boot up properly because of an error in one of the configuration files. If this happens, reboot the nameserver with the *-d 1* option on and check the output of the debugging file, */usr/tmp/named.run.*

Mixed Nameservers

Complex networks might use a combination of name services for hostname-to-address translation. For example, NIS could be used for local lookup and DNS for nonlocal lookups. Debugging can be very complicated in this kind of environment. If nonlocal lookups fail, but local lookups work, then the probable source of the problem is DNS. If the inverse is true, then look to NIS or the static tables. It's important in a heterogeneous environment that you be aware of how your hosts are doing name lookups; different vendors have different defaults. Also many PC and Mac TCP/IP applications have full DNS support. If you aren't using DNS locally, these applications will fail unless hostname-to-address mappings are added to their own private host tables.

12.4 Network Snooping with ping and traceroute

You can learn a great deal about the health of your network simply by using *ping* and *traceroute*. The IP connectivity of every host on your network can be determined quickly with ping and the routing can be easily checked with traceroute.

You can run ping with the *remote* script described in Section 12.1 to determine if machines are up and have IP connectivity. You also can use ping with the -*s* option to collect round-trip time statistics to key hosts on your network, thus providing you with an indication of both the network load and the load on the remote system. Running such a script periodically and collecting the statistics can give you a good idea of your network load over a long time. With a complex network topology, particularly those including WAN links, you'll find traceroute to be an invaluable debugging aid for tracking down most routing problems, such as routing loops and routers out of commission.

We offer next some simple ways to determine the general health of your network and also to check overall connectivity. Refer to the network shown in Fig. 12.30 and note that it comprises a number of interconnected LANs and WANs

Figure 12.30 Example Network Topology.

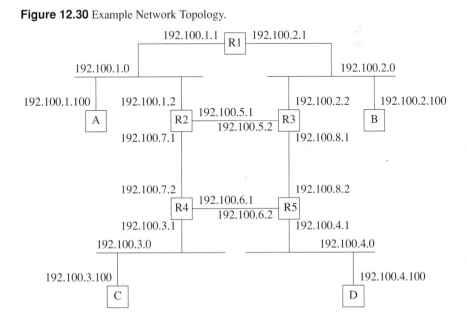

with redundant paths. We assume that RIP is used to maintain the routing tables. To simplify this diagram, we show only one host per network plus the routers. We determine full network connectivity by pinging from Host A. Here, we use a short version of ping and receive back only a connectivity message, as shown in Fig. 12.31. All machines respond, so we can feel confident that the network is functioning properly. However, because we have redundant routes, it's possible that a link from one router to another might be down. We can get a better idea of the paths IP packets are taking by using traceroute.

Figure 12.32 shows the output from traceroute run from Host A to the remote hosts. We are using RIP, therefore if all the routers and links are functional we should see packets being sent along the shortest paths. So the path from Host A to Host B should go through R1; from Host A to Host C through R2 and R3; and from Host A to Host D through R2, R3, and R5 or R2, R3, R5 or R2, R4, R5.

Based on the output shown, we know that the link from Network 192.100.1.0 to both R1 and R2 is functioning and the link from R2 to R4 is functioning, since that is the route shown when tracing the route from Host A to Host C. The link from R1 to Network 192.100.2.0 also is functional, as is that from R4 to Network 192.100.3.0 and that from R5 to Network 192.100.4.0. The links from R2 to R3 and R3 to R5 are also functioning, since that is the route taken from Host A to Host D. The only unknown data here is whether the link from R4 to R5 is up, that is, we know the R4 and R5 routers are working, but we don't know if the link between them is up. We can check this by running a traceroute from Host C to Host D and discovering what routing path is shown.

Figure 12.31 Pinging Remote Hosts.

```
% ping B
B is alive
% ping C
C is alive
% ping D
D is alive
% ping R1
R1 is alive
% ping R2
R2 is alive
% ping R3
R3 is alive
% ping R4
R4 is alive
% ping R5
R5 is alive
```

```
% traceroute B
traceroute to B (192.100.2.100), 30 hops max, 40 byte packets
 1  R1 (192.100.1.1)   2 ms   2 ms   2 ms
 2  B (192.100.2.100)   3 ms   3 ms   3 ms


% traceroute C
traceroute to C (192.100.3.100), 30 hops max, 40 byte packets
 1  R2 (192.100.1.2)   2 ms   2 ms   2 ms
 2  R4 (192.100.7.2)   100 ms   105 ms   95 ms
 3  C (192.100.3.100)   104 ms   106 ms   99 ms


% traceroute D
traceroute to D (192.100.4.100), 30 hops max, 40 byte packets
 1  R2 (192.100.1.2)   3 ms   2 ms   4 ms
 2  R3 (192.100.5.2)   5 ms   6 ms   6 ms
 3  R5 (192.100.8.2)   110 ms   111 ms   108 ms
 4  D (192.100.4.100)   112 ms   113 ms   110 ms
```

Figure 12.32 traceroute Output.

This simple example obviously isn't an exhaustive analysis of all network topologies; however, it does illustrate some of the useful output you can obtain by the judicious use of both ping and traceroute. Using these tools, you can learn much about the general state of both simple and complex networks.

12.5 Broadcast Storms on Ethernets

Broadcast storms occur not only on Ethernet LANs but also can appear in a similar guise on other network hardware that supports broadcasting and uses ARP. Because today most LANs use Ethernet technology, we describe next the phenomena as they occur on an Ethernet.

A **broadcast storm** occurs when a LAN is overwhelmed by a large number of broadcast datalink frames that are transmitted nearly simultaneously by several hosts. A broadcast storm on an Ethernet causes a dramatic increase in the collision rate because usually many machines are trying to access the network at the same time. In normal LAN operation, on the other hand, broadcast frames should occur only infrequently. How do broadcast frames get generated almost simultaneously and in large numbers? To understand this, you first must understand the normal uses for broadcast frames on a LAN.

Uses of Broadcast Frames

As a first step in comprehending the broadcast storm phenomenon, let's review when broadcast frames are normally generated. On an Ethernet one use of a broadcast frame is to send a message to all hosts on the LAN asking for a resource for which the sender doesn't know the location. All hosts receive and process the broadcast frame, but usually only the hosts that have the resource are expected to respond; all other hosts simply ignore the message. This is a very reasonable and efficient system. With it, a host can send a message to all other hosts on an Ethernet by sending only one Ethernet frame to the broadcast address. To send a message to all hosts without broadcasting requires the sending host to transmit as many frames as there are hosts on the network. It also demands that the sending host to know beforehand the addresses of all machines on the network, an unnecessary requirement when broadcasting.

ARP is a very good example of this method of resource discovery. Only a single host will respond to the ARP request — the one whose IP address matches the destination IP address in the ARP packet — thus demonstrating a very effective use of broadcasting.

Another example of using broadcasting to discover resources is the NIS protocol. When an NIS client boots, it doesn't know the address of an NIS server. So it sends a UDP message to the IP broadcast address. This UDP message is encapsulated in a datalink broadcast frame and sent to all hosts. Machines that are not NIS servers do nothing with the UDP message; those that are NIS servers respond, thus enabling the NIS client to discover the address of one or more NIS servers. If there is more than a single server, the client binds to the server that responds the fastest.

As mentioned earlier, you also can use broadcasting to disseminate information to all hosts on a LAN without your having to know the address of every host. For example, *routed* broadcasts a UDP message that contains routing information. The IP broadcast packet is encapsulated in a broadcast frame and sent out on the network. All hosts receive the broadcast frame, process the encapsulated UDP message, and update their own routing tables with the information in the message. In this case, no host responds to the broadcast message; they simply use it to update their own routing tables. As you can see, this is a very efficient way to distribute information on a LAN.

Note, however, that if some hosts are misconfigured this mechanism can lead to serious network performance degradation, especially when using Ethernet.

A Broadcast Storm Generator

Suppose a host broadcasts a message and many hosts on the network respond. Pinging the network broadcast IP address is an example of such a message. When the message is received, an ICMP *echo reply* message is returned to the sending host. The timing sequence is shown in Fig. 12.33. The ICMP *echo request* is received by all machines almost simultaneously. Each then generates an *echo reply* message encapsulated in an IP packet. On a network having many

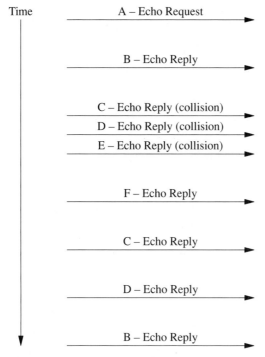

Figure 12.33 Broadcast Storm Timing.

machines, all this reply activity probably will result in quite a few collisions. Interfaces that collide will backoff and retry later at a random interval of time. However, if a sufficiently large number of hosts collide then further collisions will again occur.

In the small-scale example shown in Fig. 12.33, there are six hosts on the network; however, a single ICMP echo request has generated not five, but eight, replies, resulting in a collision rate that increases slightly for a very short period. Now suppose the echo request is sent every 0.1 seconds. Consequently each host will try to reply to every request. Again, the collision rate will rise slightly over the period of time during which the echo requests are being sent. This is a broadcast stormlet.

Now suppose that the host sending the echo request modifies the request so the source IP address is the address of a nonexistent IP host on the same network. A host receiving the request that then attempts to reply will see that the sending host is on the same network and so will construct a reply. Not finding the Ethernet address of the sender in its ARP cache, it will ARP for the nonexistent address. Naturally, the ARP will eventually fail, but not before being tried four times. Therefore in this scenario, the number of replies has been multiplied by four for each host, thus further increasing the chances of collisions.

On a small network with only a few hosts, the performance degradation would probably go unnoticed. The collision rate will be perceptibly higher, but performance will be only slightly affected. But suppose there are several hundred hosts on the LAN and all machines attempt to reply to each echo request. The result is that each echo request generates many hundreds of replies, some of which collide and cause further retransmissions. Collisions on a network of this size will cause a noticeable degradation in network performance and a significant increase in the collision rate.

For example, we conducted an experiment on a network with fewer than 200 hosts in which we sent a broadcast echo request message every 0.1 seconds. The result was an increased collision rate to over 40% within 30 seconds. Of course, nobody would deliberately generate such an ICMP message to which all hosts on the network respond. However, because of misconfigured broadcast addresses and hosts, scenarios similar to this one can and do occur. Next, let's put together a few more pieces of the puzzle to understand how this can happen.

Broadcast Address Mismatching and IP Forwarding

Suppose a broadcast frame encapsulates a nonbroadcast IP address. Each host receives the broadcast frame and starts to look at the encapsulated IP packet. The IP input process looks at the packet's destination address. If the address is its own address or the IP broadcast address, it will process the encapsulated message; if the IP address is something other than these two cases, it will do one of two things with the IP packet, depending on whether IP forwarding is enabled on the host.

IP forwarding is the algorithm used by a router to forward an IP packet that is not destined for the router itself. This algorithm looks at the network part of the IP address. If it finds there a routing table entry that matches the network part of the address, it sends out the packet either on the interface to the host that is the next hop found in the routing table or, if the network is directly connected, directly to its final destination. In either case, the packet will be reencapsulated in a new frame with the destination Ethernet address of the router or of the final destination, whichever applies. (The destination Ethernet address is obtained using ARP before the frame is sent.)

IP forwarding optimizes the routing algorithm. If the packet is to be sent out on the same interface it was received on, then the original sender of the packet should send future packets directly to the destination computed by the router. In this case, the router not only forwards the packet to the destination but also generates an ICMP *redirect message* to the originating host telling the host to send future packets directly to the computed destination. This mechanism is illustrated in Fig. 12.34 and each step is described as follows:

1. Host A sends to Host B a packet with the destination of IP address Host C.

2. Host B sees the packet is really for Host C and so forwards it to C. Host B also sends an ICMP redirect to Host A telling A to thereafter send directly to C since C is on the same network as A.

IP forwarding coupled with mismatched broadcast addresses is the source of most broadcast storm events. How are broadcast addresses mismatched? Early versions of TCP/IP shipped with the 4.2BSD system indicated a broadcast address by using all 0's in the host part of an IP address, whereas newer versions use all 1's. Consequently, an older-version implementation thinks newer-version broadcast addresses are just host addresses. Further, some versions of TCP/IP don't understand subnet addressing. Thus even if all hosts used the newer broadcast address convention, very often some machines didn't understand these addresses as broadcast, since they don't understand subnet broadcast addresses. This problem also can happen when a machine's subnet mask is not configured correctly.

A LAN with both 4.2BSD and more modern TCP/IP implementations has a mismatched set of broadcast addresses. While most newer versions understand the older broadcast format, the older versions don't understand the newer format. Rather they think a newer-styled broadcast address is just another host. To make matters worse, old systems often have IP forwarding on by default even if they have only a single network interface. A newer system usually has IP forwarding turned off, unless it had multiple network interfaces.

Consider what happens when an older-styled host receives a newer-styled IP broadcast packet. The older-styled host receives the Ethernet broadcast frame and passes the encapsulated IP packet to the IP input process. IP looks at the destination address and sees it does not match either its own address or its notion of a broadcast address. It assumes the address is just another host address. Thinking the packet is misdirected, it sends an ICMP redirect back to the sender and attempts to forward the packet to the "real" host. Since the packet is on a directly connected network, an ARP request is generated, but the ARP is for a host that doesn't exist since the destination address is the misinterpreted broadcast address. Therefore the ARP request is retransmitted four times and eventually times out.

Figure 12.34 IP Forwarding.

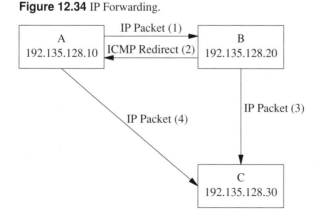

Ether Dest	Ether Source	IP Dest	IP Source	
ff:ff:ff:ff:ff:ff	80:12:1:2:5:6	192.135.128.255	192.135.128.10	→

◄ Redirect	Ether Dest	Ether Source	IP Dest	IP Source
	80:12:1:2:5:6	80:10:13:14:10:8	192.135.128.10	192.135.128.15

◄ ARP Request	Ether Dest	Ether Source	Ether Hardware	IP Proto Addr
	ff:ff:ff:ff:ff:ff	80:12:1:2:5:6	0:0:0:0:0:0	192.135.128.255

◄ ARP Request	Ether Dest	Ether Source	Ether Hardware	IP Proto Addr
	ff:ff:ff:ff:ff:ff	80:12:1:2:5:6	0:0:0:0:0:0	192.135.128.255

◄ ARP Request	Ether Dest	Ether Source	Ether Hardware	IP Proto Addr
	ff:ff:ff:ff:ff:ff	80:12:1:2:5:6	0:0:0:0:0:0	192.135.128.255

◄ ARP Request	Ether Dest	Ether Source	Ether Hardware	IP Proto Addr
	ff:ff:ff:ff:ff:ff	80:12:1:2:5:6	0:0:0:0:0:0	192.135.128.255

Figure 12.35 Bad ARP for Broadcast Address.

This sequence is diagrammed in Fig. 12.35. If only a few hosts do this, relatively little harm is done. However, if your network has several hundred hosts, half of which have older-styled broadcast addresses, then all the older-styled machines will respond to a newer-styled broadcast packet with one ICMP redirect and four ARP requests. These responses will likely cause quite a few collisions. With just a small amount of broadcast traffic, an Ethernet can "melt down" and in a very short period of time become essentially unusable.

Services That Contribute to Broadcast Storms

Services that generate broadcast packets most likely to cause the broadcast storm problem include *routed*. Although routed usually doesn't generate much traffic, if it is misconfigured and is run actively on hosts that are nonrouting nodes, problems can arise. Another source is the *rwho* protocol, a service that broadcasts hosts' status messages every three minutes. A large network with many hosts that run rwho can generate a considerable amount of broadcast traffic. On a network with 100 machines running rwho, a broadcast frame is generated about every two seconds. With 200 machines, a frame is generated every second, which is more than enough to generate storm events.

If you suspect a broadcast storm, monitor your network for excessive ARP traffic. etherfind is useful for monitoring of this type. If you see ARP requests for

```
% etherfind -i le0 -v -t arp
0.10 ip arp request from akasha.tic.com(8:0:20:d:ca:13) for 192.135.128.25
0.15 ip arp request from aahsa.tic.com(8:0:2b:e:eb:95) for 192.135.128.25
0.20 ip arp request from akasha.tic.com(8:0:20:d:ca:13) for 192.135.128.25
0.25 ip arp request from aahsa.tic.com(8:0:2b:e:eb:95) for 192.135.128.25
0.30 ip arp request from akasha.tic.com(8:0:20:d:ca:13) for 192.135.128.25
0.35 ip arp request from aahsa.tic.com(8:0:2b:e:eb:95) for 192.135.128.25
0.40 ip arp request from akasha.tic.com(8:0:20:d:ca:13) for 192.135.128.25
0.45 ip arp request from aahsa.tic.com(8:0:2b:e:eb:95) for 192.135.128.25
```

Figure 12.36 ARP Packet Output with Etherfind.

the IP broadcast address, you know you have some misconfigured hosts. Figure 12.36 illustrates etherfind output of ARP packets on a network with some misconfigured machines. Alternatively, if you have a sniffer that can capture all packets, a broadcast storm signature is shown in Fig. 12.37.

Fixing Storms

Ideally you solve a broadcast storm problem by fixing the misconfigured hosts. Turning off IP forwarding on these misconfigured hosts will clear up most of the problems. In this case, misunderstood broadcast packets are simply dropped with no response. UNIX systems that use the BSD networking code have a kernel variable called *ip_forwarding* that can be turned off in a running kernel by using *adb*. On IBM AIX systems, the *no* command will give the same result. Also, most kernel configurations can be built with IP forwarding turned off. If you can't reconfigure hosts because they are locked up somewhere, have old software that can't be changed, or are in another administration, then attempt to turn off the broadcast services, such as rwho, that are triggering the storm events.

Another useful technique is to sponge up the unnecessary ARPs sent out by the misconfigured hosts. Because ARP requests are transmitted four times before timing out, they generate the largest amount of traffic in a storm. However, if the

Figure 12.37 Broadcast Storm Signature.

```
Host · Packet
A   Broadcast
B   ICMP redirect to A ·
B   ARP request for the broadcast IP address
B   ARP request for the broadcast IP address
B   ARP request for the broadcast IP address
B   ARP request for the broadcast IP address
```

first ARP request receives a reply, retransmissions are eliminated and no further
ARP requests will be generated, since a cache entry will be created on the misconfigured host. The forwarded IP packet then is sent to host that acts as a packet
sink and simply drops the packet. Let's see how this works. Suppose Host A is
an older-styled host with IP forwarding turned on. If an entry is made in A's ARP
cache as follows:

```
arp -s 192.135.128.255 8:0:3:2:1:f
```

then when A receives an IP packet with 192.135.128.255 as the destination
address, it attempts to forward the packet and encapsulates it in an Ethernet frame
with destination address 8:0:3:2:1:f. If this Ethernet address corresponds to the
address of Host B, B receives the forwarded packet and processes it. Since the
destination IP address is the broadcast address, B processes the IP packet as it normally would. As this packet is probably a duplicate of the broadcast packet that B
has already received, so no harm is done. In this scenario, host A generates only
two packets — the ICMP redirect and the forwarded IP packet — instead of five
packets — the ICMP redirect and four ARP requests. This results is a significant
traffic reduction. Note that for this to work effectively, Host B must have IP forwarding turned off.

    If you can't add a manual ARP cache entry on all misconfigured hosts then
add an entry on a single machine that supports publishing ARP requests, as follows:

```
% arp -s 192.135.128.255 8:0:3:2:1:f pub
```

A published arp entry causes this machine to respond to ARP requests intended
for the indicated IP address, and a response is sent with the Ethernet address found
in the published entry. In this case, the misconfigured host's ARP requests are
responded to and an entry is added to the host's ARP cache.

Access

This appendix contains basic information about how to use anonymous FTP, archie, and several mail document servers. It tells where to get all the software mentioned in this book, except for the source code that is included directly in the following appendix. The present appendix also contains templates for registration of domains and IP network numbers.

A.1 Anonymous FTP

To use **anonymous FTP,** use the FTP user client program on your host to connect to the anonymous FTP server host, and log in as user *anonymous*, with password *guest*, before retrieving files.

The exact commands to use will depend on your local operating system. Figure A.1 is an example using the 4.3BSD FTP client to connect to the server *ds.internic.net*, and log in as the anonymous FTP user. The text in italics is what you, the user, would type. The password you type does not echo, but we have shown it here anyway. The example then shows the user changing to the subdirectory *rfc*, turning off verbose mode, getting a long directory listing of the RFC index, which is file *rfc-index.txt*, and then actually retrieving the file. The user then quits the FTP session.

Many hosts also accept the username *ftp* in place of *anonymous*. Most UNIX hosts accept this alternate convention.

The "anonymous" adjective is a historical relic when applied to FTP. Years ago, most users used timesharing systems and were anonymous in the crowd. But workstations and PCs are common on the Internet now, and it is usually easy to guess who you are even on a timesharing system. But large systems are still sufficiently anonymous that some people abuse them by transferring spurious files from them to anonymous FTP servers. For this reason, some anonymous FTP servers are now requiring an electronic mail address as a password.

```
% ftp ds.internic.net
Connected to ds.internic.net.
220 ds FTP server (SunOS 4.1) ready.
Name (ds.internic.net:jsq): anonymous
331 Guest login ok, send ident as password.
Password: guest
230 Guest login ok, access restrictions apply.
ftp> cd rfc
250 CWD command successful.
ftp> verbose
Verbose mode off.
ftp> dir rfc-index.txt
-rw-r--r--  1 101      1       170812 Mar  8 01:50 rfc-index.txt
ftp> get rfc-index.txt
ftp> quit
%
```

Figure A.1 Anonymous FTP.

Popular Anonymous FTP Servers

Here are some popular anonymous FTP servers. This list includes servers for all
the software mentioned in this book, except for that which is included directly in
the following appendix.

- prep.ai.mit.edu
  The home of the **GNU (GNU's Not UNIX)** free software collection, mentioned
  in Chapter 9. The **FSF (Free Software Foundation)** is the creator of GNU.
  The GNU collection has freely available replacements for most of the common
  UNIX utilities. All are available in source tree form complete with instructions
  for building the software on your UNIX platform. The GNU collection includes
  gcc, a C compiler; gas, a hardware independent assembler; bash, a Bourne shell
  replacement; groff, a troff-like text formatter; and much much more.

- ics.uci.edu
  The MH mail user agent software described in Chapter 7 and Chapter 8.

- ftp.tic.com
  The client/server software discussed in Chapter 9.

- cert.org
  Computer Emergency Response Team (CERT) information, plus the
  tcp_wrappers or **tcpd** software that can provide protection per port and foreign
  domain name or IP address.

- sumex-aim.stanford.edu
This archive contains perhaps the largest collection of Macintosh software in the world. You can find many useful tools for the Macintosh here, including the common utilities for transferring Mac files to and from a UNIX system. Complete instructions for downloading files to your Macintosh are described.

- rutgers.edu
The **Columbia Appletalk Package (CAP)** described in Chapter 10. CAP is an implementation of the Appletalk protocol suite for UNIX. One CAP application lets you set up an Appletalk server using a UNIX system. CAP also allows Macintosh and UNIX systems to share printers. Other very useful tools are also a part of the CAP package.

- wsmr-simtel20.army.mil
This site is the major archive site for the SIMTEL-20 collection of PC (MS-DOS and other) software. The archive is mirrored on the following archive servers: oak.oakland.edu, wuarchive.wustl.edu, ftp.uu.net, nic.funet.fi, src.doc.ic.ac.uk, archie.au, or nic.switch.ch. You will find a wealth of freely distributed IBM PC software at these sites. Most of the software comes in both source and binary format. Look at the README.finding-files for information on obtaining an archive index. The PC software is divided by subject area and ranges from small utilities to full-blown application programs.

- ftp.ncsa.uiuc.edu
The **NCSA TELNET** package, which implements IP for MS-DOS PCs and Macintoshes, and is described in Chapter 10. For DOS, the archival file is */PC/Telnet/tel23b.zip*; while */Mac/Telnet/Telnet2.5/Telnet2.5sit.hqx.* is the file for the Macintosh. Both versions are periodically updated and also are available in source code.

- boombox.micro.umn.edu
All the interesting software is in the *pub* directory, mostly under subdirectories with obvious descriptive names. The **POPMail** software for DOS and the Macintosh, described in Chapter 10, plus a **POP2** daemon for UNIX; see Chapter 8. The source for the **Packet Driver,** and the Brigham Young University fixes to the Novell NetWare MS-DOS client software to use the Packet Driver interface (see *pub/netware/readme.byu*); both these packages are described in Chapter 10. Also, **SLIP** software for most common platforms; see Chapter 6. And the source for the gopher software mentioned in Chapter 2.

- quake.think.com
Source for the **WAIS** (Wide Area Information Servers) mentioned in Chapter 2.

- ftp.cs.colorado.edu
Source for the **netfind** software mentioned in Chapter 2, plus source for another useful service, called essence.

- ftp.ripe.net
RIPE (European IP Networks), RARE (Associated European Research Networks), and EBONE (European Backbone) files.

• nic.ad.jp
Information about Japanese networks, such as WIDE, TISN, JAIN, JUNET, and
BITNET-J.

• archie.au
Information about AARNET (Australian Academic and Research Network).

Commercial Anonymous FTP Sites

Several commercial IP networking organizations run large FTP servers.

• **CERFNET (California Education and Research Federation Network)** uses
this server to provide information about: CERFNET (their IP and UUCP network); the **Commercial Internet Exchange (CIX),** of which CERFNET, PSI,
UUNET, and others are members; the **Federation of American Research Networks (FARNET); FrEDMail (Free Educational Mail network),** a network
for **K–12 (kindergarten to twelfth grade)** networking; and other subjects.

• ftp.psi.com
Performance Systems International (PSI) uses this server to provide information about: PSINet (their IP and UUCP network); SNMP (Simple Network Management Protocol), described in Chapter 11; X.500 White Pages information,
mentioned in Chapter 1 and xC_Unknown .xC services; **ISODE (ISO Development Environment)** software to permit OSI applications to run under IP; and
other subjects.

• ftp.uu.net
UUNET Technologies (UUNET) uses this server to provide information about:
UUNET (their UUCP network); AlterNet (their IP network); ClariNet (a commercial news service); Supreme Court decisions; book publishers; some trade
magazines; and other subjects. A number of the other archives mentioned above
are mirrored on this machine. Several useful debugging utilities can be found
here, such as *traceroute,* (in */networking/ip/trace/traceroute_pkg.tar.Z.*), and *dig*
(in */networking/ip/dns/dig.2.0.tar.Z*).

A.2   Archie

Archie is an application that collects indexes of anonymous FTP servers (by
polling them approximately monthly) and provides search access to those indexes
to clients [Deutsch *et al.* 1992]. Archie is a good example of a widely used Internet service that was developed by essentially volunteer labor, and that has no organized means of support [Deutsch 1991; Barron 1992].

To try archie, TELNET to one of the archie server machines, such as
archie.sura.net, and log in as archie. Try to pick a server close to you; there are
currently servers on at least three continents and many countries. The archie command *servers* lists all archie servers. Archie has a help command that tells you

how to actually use it. For real use, it's best to get an archie client. The source for the archie client may be retrieved by anonymous FTP to one of the archie servers. Look in the directory **/archie/clients** or **/pub/archie/clients**. Comments and bug reports may be sent to archie-admin@bunyip.com.

A.3   The InterNIC

The **InterNIC** is a **Network Information Center (NIC)** service sponsored by the U.S. National Science Foundation (NSF) to provide and coordinate services for the NSFNET community. InterNIC also provides services to the Internet at large. InterNIC services are provided by three companies, listed below. The servers listed here each support anonymous FTP service, and sometimes other services.

- is.internic.net
  InterNIC information services, provided by General Atomics/CERFnet. The same host also supports a gopher server and a WAIS server. If you don't have a gopher client, TELNET to is.internic.net and log in as the user *gopher*. General Atomics provides a general referral service, as well:

info@internic.net	InterNIC Information Services
800-444-4345	General Atomics
+1-619-455-4600	P.O. Box 85608
fax: +1-619-455-3990	San Diego, CA 92186-9784

- ds.internic.net
  InterNIC directory and database services, including RFCs and Internet Standards, provided by **American Telephone and Telegraph (AT&T).** The same host supports a WAIS server, which can be accessed by TELNET with login as username **wais**, or by other WAIS clients. The host also supports various other services, such as archie and netfind.

  admin@ds.internic.net
  +1-908-668-6587
  fax: +1-908-668-3763

- rs.internic.net
  InterNIC registration services, including DNS domain and IP network registration templates, and WHOIS service, provided by **Network Solutions, Inc. (NSI).**

hostmaster@rs.internic.net	Network Solutions
+1-703-742-4777	Attn: InterNIC Registration Services
7AM through 7PM EST	505 Huntmar Park Drive
	Herndon, VA 22070

• nic.ddn.mil

This server is *not* part of InterNIC. Instead, it provides MILNET information, that is, public information related to U.S. military IP networks. For general Internet information, instead use is.internic.net, ds.internic.net, or rs.internic.net.

A.4   Mail Document Servers

Many hosts on the Internet, and some on other networks, such as BITNET, support mail document servers. These facilities allow remote users to retrieve information by electronic mail. This kind of facility is usable even by people who are not on the Internet, as long as they can send mail to the Internet. Here are examples of mail servers, at the InterNIC, and at ISI.

Each of the three InterNIC providers supports a mailserver. To get details on InterNIC information services, send a HELP command, like this:

```
To: mailserv@is.internic.net

HELP
```

For directory and database services, send this:

```
To: mailserv@ds.internic.net

HELP
```

Most of the servers in these examples expect commands to be in the body of the message, and ignore the Subject: header. The exception is the InterNIC registration server, rs.internic.net, which expects commands in the Subject: header, not in the message body. For example, you can get any RFC by sending a message with headers like this:

```
To: mailserv@rs.internic.net
Subject: RFC 791
```

That is, the *Subject:* header line contains the keyword RFC, a space, and the RFC number. The RFC will be returned by mail to the address in the From: header of your message. The rest of the message is ignored. To get an index of RFCs, use

```
To: mailserv@rs.internic.net
Subject: RFC Index
```

ISI supports a mail server that expects queries in the body of the message; the contents of the *Subject:* is ignored. The ISI server permits searches by organization or date, and keyword searches with wildcards. To get details on other commands, send the server a request for help:

```
To: RFC-INFO@ISI.EDU
Subject: anything

HELP
```

A.5   Registration Templates

To connect to the Internet, you must register at least one domain name and at least one IP network number, and you must register an inverse mapping from each network number to a domain. Here are condensed versions of the necessary templates. We have not included the entire actual texts of the templates, because they duplicate many references and contextual comments, and are formatted with much white space for reading in ASCII text online; those features would be superfluous in this book.

What to Register

To connect a host or network to the Internet, you must register:

What	Example	Template
domain	bigco.com	domain-template.txt
IP network number	192.143.13	internet-number-template.txt
inverse domain	13.143.192.in-addr.arpa	in-addr-template.txt

These registrations are intertwined. For example, you need to specify two DNS servers for your domain. If one of those servers is on your network, you must wait until the network registration is completed before the domain registration can be completed. You may have register several network numbers, and you need to register an inverse domain for each of them. You must also get connected status for networks.

You do not need to register subdomains, e.g., if you're registering bigco.com, you do not need to register eng.bigco.com. Nor do you need to register subnets, e.g., if you are registering 192.143.13, you do not need to register 192.143.13.100.

Getting Templates

You can get authoritative copies of all necessary registration templates by anonymous FTP from rs.internic.net, in the directory *templates*. Completed templates should be sent to hostmaster@internic.net, except as noted below. You can also get the templates by electronic mail, through the rs.internic.net mail server described in the previous section. If you do not have access to either FTP or electronic mail, you can get the templates by paper mail from the InterNIC registration

services, using the contact information given in the section on the InterNIC, and
you can return completed templates by paper mail.

If the domain you are registering is not under one of the top level domains
EDU, COM, MIL, GOV, NET, or ORG, you are registering under a national top
level domain, and you will need to contact your national domain registry, which
may be found through the WHOIS service, or by asking hostmaster@internic.net
or, if you are in Europe, by asking hostmaster@ripe.net.

If you are registering an IP number for use in Europe, use *european-ip-
template.txt* instead of *internet-number-template.txt*, and send the completed template to hostmaster@ripe.net, rather than to hostmaster@internic.net.

Registration Information

Registration procedures and information for domains and for network numbers are
similar. Registration depends on the identification of key administrative and technical people for each domain and network number registered. Each key person
must have an electronic mailbox and a **handle,** which is a unique identifier used in
NIC databases. If you have one, you can find it using the WHOIS service. For
each key person who does not have one, when filling out the template, instead of
that person's handle, fill in the person's name, paper mailing address, telephone
number, organization, and electronic mail address. That person will then be
assigned a handle on registration.

Domain Registration

The information for registering a domain may vary slightly according to the top
level domain you want to join. The example here is from the InterNIC *domain-
template.txt* template.

From domain-template.txt

(1) The name of the top-level domain to join (EDU, COM, MIL, GOV, NET,
ORG).

    1. Top-level domain:

(2) The name of the domain (up to 12 characters). This is the name that will be
used in tables and lists associating the domain with the domain server addresses.
[While, from a technical standpoint, domain names can be quite long we recommend the use of shorter, more user-friendly names.]

    2. Complete Domain Name:

(3) The name and address of the organization establishing the domain.

    3a. Organization name:

3b. Organization address:

(4) The date you expect the domain to be fully operational.

4. Date operational:

(5) The handle of the administrative head of the organization — or this person's name, mailing address, phone number, organization, and network mailbox. This is the contact point for administrative and policy questions about the domain. In the case of a research project, this should be the principal investigator.

NOTE: Both the Administrative and the Technical/Zone contact of a domain MUST have a network mailbox, even if the mailbox is to be within the proposed domain.

5a. Handle (if known) :
5b. Name (Last, First) :
5c. Organization:
5d. Mail Address:

5e. Phone Number:
5f. Net Mailbox :

(6) The handle of the technical contact for the domain or the person's name, mailing address, phone number, organization, and network mailbox. This is the contact point for problems concerning the domain or zone, as well as for updating information about the domain or zone.

Technical and Zone Contact
6a. Handle (if known):
6b. Name (Last, First):
6c. Organization:
6d. Mail Address:

6e. Phone Number:
6f. Net Mailbox:

(7) Domains must provide at least two independent servers on Government-sponsored networks that provide the domain service for translating names to addresses for hosts in this domain.

* If you are applying for a domain and a network number assignment simultaneously and a host on your proposed network will be used as a server for the domain, you must wait until you receive your network number assignment and have given the server(s) a netaddress before sending in the domain application.

Sending in the domain application without complete information in Sections 7 and 8 of this template will result in the delay of the domain registration.

Also, establishing the servers in physically separate locations and on different PSNs and/or networks is strongly recommended.

> 7a. Primary Server Hostname:
> 7b. Primary Server Netaddress:
> 7c. Primary Server Hardware:
> 7d. Primary Server Software:

(8) The Secondary server information.

> 8a. Secondary Server Hostname:
> 8b. Secondary Server Netaddress:
> 8c. Secondary Server Hardware:
> 8d. Secondary Server Software:

(9) If any currently registered hosts will be renamed into the new domain, please specify old hostname, netaddress, and new hostname.

> For example:
>
> BAR-FOO2.XYZ.COM (26.8.0.193) -> FOO2.BAR.COM
> BAR-FOO3.XYZ.COM (192.7.3.193) -> FOO3.BAR.COM
> BAR-FOO4.ARPA (34.6.0.193) -> FOO4.BAR.COM

(10) Please describe your organization briefly.

> For example: Our Corporation is a consulting organization of people working with UNIX and the C language in an electronic networking environment. It sponsors two technical conferences annually and distributes a bimonthly newsletter.

IP Network Number Registration

The example here is from the InterNIC *internet-number-template.txt* template. The part about a military or governmental sponsor being required is archaic, and will probably be corrected soon.

From internet-number-template.txt

1) If the network will be connected to the Internet, you must provide the name of the governmental sponsoring organization, and the name, title, mailing address, phone number, net mailbox, and NIC Handle (if any) of the contact person (POC) at that organization who has authorized the network connection. This person will serve as the POC for administrative and policy questions about authorization to be

a part of the Internet. Examples of such sponsoring organizations are: DISA DNSO, the National Science Foundation (NSF), or similar military or government sponsors.

NOTE: If the network will NOT be connected to the Internet, then you do not need to provide this information.

    1a. Sponsoring Organization:
    1b. Contact name (Lastname, Firstname):
    1c. Contact title:
    1d. Mail Address :

    1e.Phone :
    1f. Net mailbox :
    1g. NIC handle (if known):

2) Provide the name, title, mailing address, phone number, and organization of the technical POC. The online mailbox and NIC Handle (if any) of the technical POC should also be included. This is the POC for resolving technical problems associated with the network and for updating information about the network. The technical POC may also be responsible for hosts attached to this network.

    2a. NIC handle (if known):
    2b. Technical POC name (Lastname, Firstname):
    2c. Technical POC title:
    2d. Mail address :

    2e. Phone :
    2f. Net Mailbox :

3) Supply the short mnemonic name for the network (up to 12 characters). This is the name that will be used as an identifier in internet name and address tables.

    3. Network name:

4) Identify the network geographic location and the responsible organization establishing the network.

    4a. Postal address for main/headquarters network site:

    4b. Name of Organization:

5) Question #5 is for MILITARY or DOD requests, ONLY.

If you require that this connected network be announced to the NSFNET please answer questions 5a, 5b, and 5c.

    5a. Do you want MILNET to announce your network to the NSFNET? (Y/N):

    5b. Do you have an alternate connection, other than MILNET, to the NSFNET? (please state alternate connection if answer is yes):

    5c. If you've answered yes to 5b, please state if you would like the MILNET connection to act as a backup path to the NSFNET? (Y/N):

6) Estimate the number of hosts that will be on the network:

    6a. Initially:

    6b. Within one year:

    6c. Within two years:

    6d. Within five years:

7) Unless a strong and convincing reason is presented, the network (if it qualifies at all) will be assigned a class C network number. If a class C network number is not acceptable for your purposes state why. (Note: If there are plans for more than a few local networks, and more than 100 hosts, you are strongly urged to consider subnetting. [See RFC 950])

    7. Reason:

8) Networks are characterized as being either Research, Defense, Government - Non Defense, or Commercial, and the network address space is shared between these four areas. Which type is this network?

    8. Type of network:

9) What is the purpose of the network?

    9. Purpose:

IP Number to Domain Registration

The example here is from the InterNIC *in-addr-template.txt* template.

From in-addr.arpa.txt

The Internet uses a special domain to support gateway location and Internet address to host mapping. The intent of this domain is to provide a guaranteed method to perform host address to host name mapping, and to facilitate queries to locate all gateways on a particular network in the Internet.

The following information is needed for delegation of registered networks in your domain for inclusion in the IN-ADDR.ARPA zone files:

• the IN-ADDR.ARPA domain

• the Network name

• the Hostnames of the two hosts on networks that will be acting as servers

IN-ADDR domains are represented using the network number in reverse. Network 123.45.67.0's IN-ADDR domain is represented as 67.45.123.IN-ADDR.ARPA. For example:

IN-ADDR domain	Network Name	IN-ADDR Servers (Hostname) (NetAddress) (CPUType/OpSys)
41.192.IN-ADDR.ARPA	NET-TEST-ONE	BAR.FOO.EDU 123.45.67.89 VAX-II/VMS ONE.ABC.COM 98.76.54.32 SUN/UNIX

Please have the Network Coordinator complete and return the following information for those networks needing IN-ADDR registration.

IN-ADDR domain	Network Name	IN-ADDR Servers

European IP Number Registration

All IP network number registrations were previously centralized, in a single **Internet Registry (IR).** But the global registry, currently InterNIC, now delegates registration for regions to regional IRs, which may then delegate subregions, such as countries, to local IRs.

The regional IR for Europe is the RIPE (see Chapter 1) **Network Coordination Center (NCC),** which has been delegated blocks of IP numbers. The RIPE NCC has in turn delegated blocks of IP numbers to local IRs. These local providers are of two types.

• service provider
An organization that provides Internet connectivity and handles IP number registration requests. If you are a customer of such a service provider, you should register your network number through them.

• non-service provider
An organization (currently one per European country) that handles IP number
registration requests from other organizations that have no Internet connections.
If you are not currently a customer of a service provider, you should contact your
national non-service provider. To find it, contact the RIPE NCC.

hostmaster@ripe.net   RIPE NCC
+31-20-592-5065   Kruislaan 409
fax: +31-20-592-5090   1098 SJ Amsterdam
                                    The Netherlands

Here is a condensed version of the notes from the RIPE NCC *european-ip-
template.txt* template, which is acceptable to any local IR in Europe.

Supporting Notes for the European IP Request Form

Part A - Administrative Details.
The information supplied for this section together with the assigned network numbers will be entered into a database of European network numbers and their contact information which is accessible by the whole Internet community.
Network Template

netname: Please complete with an appropriate network name for the network to
           be numbered which is short and meaningful. The 'netname' is used
           mainly for administrative purposes like consistency checking of the
           Internet Registry. You will most likely not see this name appear any-
           where, but on forms like this. The network name should be written in
           capital letters eg:

                       netname: TBIT

descr: Please complete with a short description of the organisation, including
           the location. The full postal address is not needed as this is required in
           the person template eg:

                       descr: Terabit Labs Inc.
                       descr: Network Bugs Feeding Facility
                       descr: Northtown

country: Please give the two letter country code (ISO 3166) which is appropri-
           ate for the organisation. We know this gives problems for networks
           crossing national boundaries, so choose the most appropriate country,
           based on the location of the admin contact. If you do not know the
           appropriate code for your country, please complete with the full name
           of the country eg:

                       country: NL

admin-c: Please complete with the name or NIC handle of the person who is the administrative contact for the network. The NIC handle (if known) is preferred. Please do not use formal titles like 'Dr' or 'Prof' or 'Sir'. Please specify as in the example below (or with the NIC handle). Do not add full stops between the names or initials eg:

> admin-c: John E Doe or
> use the NIC handle (if applicable)
> admin-c: JD58

tech-c: Please give the name of technical contact person (or NIC handle as mentioned above). There can be more than one name specified for the technical contact. NOTE: please give names for both the administrative AND the technical contact. If two different names are not appropriate, then the same name for both contacts is fine. Example as above.

changed: Email address of the person who is completing the template, followed by the current date. If you do not have email connectivity please leave blank and we will complete it. Please add the date in the format shown below eg:

> changed: johndoe@terabit.nl 930225

source: Source of the information. It will always be RIPE. This is information which is always required in the database, so it has been added already.

Person Template

For each different person specified in the network template, please complete a separate person template, unless the data about those persons is already in the RIPE database.

person: Please give the full name of the admin-c contact and the tech-c contact. There must be a person template completed for each different name specified. The names must be written identically to those given above in the "admin-c:" and "tech-c:" attributes above (but must not be the NIC handle) or official titles like "Dr, Prof or Sir" eg:

> person: John E Doe

address: Please complete with the full postal address, and write as you would for ordinary postal mail using one line for each part of the address as shown below eg:

> address: Terabit Labs Inc.
> address: North Perpendicular Road 12
> address: NL-1234 Northtown
> address: The Netherlands

phone: Please give the work telephone number of the person specified above.
            Please specify the telephone number with + <country code> <area
            code> <telephone number> Most countries should drop the leading zero
            when specifying their area code. More than one telephone number is
            fine. Each telephone number should be put on a separate line and writ-
            ten in order of the most appropriate number for the contact person eg:

                        phone: +31 20 1233 4676
                        phone: +31 20 1233 4677 ext. 4711

fax-no: Please complete with the telefax number of the person specified above.
            Follow with the same rules as specified for telephone number above eg:

                        fax-no: +31 20 12334678

e-mail: Please supply the appropriate electronic mail address for the contact. If
            you DO NOT have e-mail connectivity, please insert <none>. Please
            ensure that this is a valid domain address eg:

                        e-mail: johndoe@terabit.nl or
                        e-mail: <none>

nic-hdl: This refers to a NIC handle which is a unique identifier assigned and
            used by the US NIC to unambiguously refer to Internet people. If you
            do not have a NIC handle, then please leave blank eg:

                        nic-hdl: JD0401

changed: Who and when changed this last. Please complete with your e-mail
            address followed by the current date in the format which is shown
            below. If you do not have e-mail connectivity, please leave blank and
            we will complete this on your behalf eg:

                        changed: johndoe@terabit.nl 930225

source: Source of the information. This will always be RIPE and is a required
            field so it has been added.

Part B - Technical Details.

Information supplied below helps us to evaluate and process your request.It will
be kept IN CONFIDENCE by us for internal use only. It will NOT be entered into
the RIPE Network Management Database.

Technical Template

request-type: Please specify the quantity and class of your request for network
                numbers.

In making the application, please be guided by the following EXAMPLES of number of hosts which relate to the quantity of network numbers requested eg:

1 class C number	(maximum 254 hosts)
2 class C numbers	(maximum 508 hosts)
4 class C numbers	(maximum 1016 hosts)
8 class C numbers	(maximum 2032 hosts)
16 class C numbers	(maximum 4064 hosts)
32 class C numbers	(maximum 8128 hosts)
a single class B number	
other (please specify)	

machine-0:   Please state the number of machines in your organisation that currently require a unique IP address. Do not forget to include terminal servers and network numbers needed for transit networks when calculating this figure eg:

machine-0: 100

machine-1:
machine-2:   As above for machine-0 but estimate for 1 and 2 years time.

subnet-0:   Please state the number of subnets required for the current network. A subnet refers to the physical parts of the network which need a unique (sub)net number eg:

subnet-0: 10

subnet-1:
subnet-2:   As above for subnet-0 but estimate for the number of subnets in 1 and 2 years time.

inet-connect: Please state whether you plan to connect to the Internet. Please answer with whichever of the following options most closely describes the position of your organisation eg:

• will never connect

• already connected <through whom>

• plan to connect <date> <through whom>

If you are "already connected" to the Internet, please state which service provider you are connected to. If you answer with "plan to connect" then please make an estimation on the date that you hope to connect, specifying the month, the year (if possible) and through whom if known eg:

inet-connect: plan to connect 930401 Net-Provider Inc

exist-IP-net: Has your organisation already obtained an IP network number or numbers? If so, please give the network number(s) and the network name if known. If not, then please complete with <no>.Format: complete with the network number only - four numbers separated by dots, as shown below. If known, please also add the network name entry as shown below. This must be specified in exactly the same way as it appears below eg:

> exist-ip-NET: 193.87.45.0 TBIT or
> exist-IP-net: <none>

net-country: Please give the ISO 3166 country code which describes where the network will be located. If more than one country applies, then give the names of the countries which will be covered by the network. Format: complete with the country name(s) using the ISO 3166 country code. If you are unsure about the code, write the name of the country in full.

> net-country: NL SE

Part C - Technical Details.

Please complete this section on a separate page if you are applying for more than 2 Class C network numbers. The more numbers you are requesting, the more detailed your technical description will need to be. Furthermore, the more detail you provide, the quicker we will be able to process your application. Please include an overview of the size of your subnets, ensuring that you do not forget transit networks, terminal servers etc. when calculating your needs.

Before you complete this section you should read the 'Helpful Hints' document (currently being updated) which will guide you. It is particularly important to read this document if you are applying for a class B network number, as it provides additional hints. Until this document has been updated, the "Additional Hints" will be appended.

If you are applying for a Class B network number please send your completed application to the local registry who will review your case. If it is felt that a Class B network number is justified, your application will be forwarded to the RIPE NCC who will review your application. Please be reminded that Class B network numbers are extremely scarce and are rarely allocated.

Part D - Contact Details.

This section should be completed *ONLY IF* you are making an application on behalf of another organisation. Please indicate who the application is being made by and on behalf of whom, giving all the contact details requested.

A.6 More Online and Registration Information

Much more information is available online on the Internet, and you may need to know more to register your particular host, router, or network configuration and to connect it to the Internet. See our next book for more details ...

References

Barron 1992.   Barron, Billy, "The Left Hand Doesn't Know What the Right Hand Is Doing," *Matrix News* **2**(4), Matrix Information and Directory Services, Inc. (MIDS) (April 1992).

Deutsch 1991.   Deutsch, Peter, "On the Need to Develop Internet User Services," *Matrix News* **1**(4), Matrix Information and Directory Services, Inc. (MIDS) (July 1991).

Deutsch et al. 1992.   Deutsch, P., Emtage, A., & Heelan, B., "Archie: An Internet Electronic Directory Service," *ConneXions—The Interoperability Report* **6**(2), pp. 2–9, Interop, Inc. (February 1992).

Program Listings

B.1   Nameserver Database Programs

The following scripts and programs may be obtained via anonymous ftp from the host *ftp.tic.com* as the pathname */pub/dns.tar.Z*.

readinfo

```
#!/bin/sh
# @(#) readinfo 1.1 91/12/29 @(#)
# reads a host database file
#
# input from stdin
# output to stdout
#
# arguments are names of fields in the file
#
# fields in a file are defined by a comment line of the form
# #FIELDS <field_description> ...
#
# where <field_description> is the name of the field followed by optional
# keyword parameters of the form parameter=<value>
# two paramaters are supported in this script
#    prefix - prefix added to value of the field
#    suffix - suffix added to value of field
#    no - character to prevent adding a prefix or suffix to a field
#
# fields in the file are separated with white space.  Embedded blanks in fields
# are either escaped with a '\' or the entire field is quoted with double quotes
# The prefix or suffix can be overridden by prepending or following the value
# with the ''no='' character
```

```
# get the fields from the command line - will be funnelled to awk
fields="$*"
# change whitespace to tabs and handle quoted fields and escaped blanks
# also remove comment lines, except the #FIELDS line
awk '
BEGIN {
    # get around double quote bug
    dq = sprintf("%c", 34)
}
/^#FIELDS/ || ( ! /^#/ && ! /^$/ && ! /^[ ][   ]*/ ) {
# line has double quotes or backslashes
    if ($0 ~ /"/ || $0 ~ /\\/) {
        # print everything up to field with double quote or backslash
        l = length($0)
        n = 0
        for (i=1; i<=NF; i++) {
            if ($i !~ /"/ && $i !~ /\\/) {
                printf("%s\t", $i)
            }
            n += length($i)
            n++
        }
        remainder = substr($0, n+1, l-n)
        l -= n
        quoted = 0
        escaped = 0
        for (i=1; i<=l; i++) {
            sub = substr(remainder, i, 1)
            if (sub == dq) {
                if (quoted) {
                    quoted = 0
                }
                else {
                    quoted = 1
                }
            }
            else if (sub == "\\") {
                escaped = 1
            }
            else if (quoted) {
                printf("%s", sub)
            }
            else if (escaped) {
                printf("%s", sub)
                escaped = 0
            }
            else if (sub == " ") {
                printf("\t")
            }
            else {
                printf("%s", sub)
            }
        }
    }
```

```
        # line is just a bunch of normal fields
        else {
            for (i=1; i<=NF; i++) {
                printf("%s", $i)
                if (i < NF) {
                    printf("\t")
                }
            }
        }
        printf("\n")
}' |
# read file and output fields wanted
awk -F' ' '
# get the fields from the command line
BEGIN {
    EXTRACT="'"$fields"'"
    nextract = split(EXTRACT, extract, " ")
}
# extract field definition info from file
/^#FIELDS/ {
    nfields = 0
    for (i=2; i<=NF; i++) {
        # field is a paramter
        if ($i ~ /\=/) {
            n = split($i, part, "=")
            keyword = part[1]
            value = part[2]
            # prefix
            if (keyword == "prefix") {
                prefix[nfields] = value
            }
            # suffix
            else if (keyword == "suffix") {
                suffix[nfields] = value
            }
            else if (keyword == "no") {
                no[nfields] = value
            }
        }
        #field name
        else {
            nfields++
            fields[nfields] = $i
            prefix[nfields] = ""
            suffix[nfields] = ""
            no[nfields] = ""
        }
    }
}
# process a record
! /^#/ && ! /^$/ && ! /^[    ][    ]*/ {
    # scan the list of fields to extract and compare them with the
    # list in the file and print as they are encountered
    for (i=1; i<=nextract; i++) {
```

```
        for (j=1; j<=nfields; j++) {
            if (fields[j] == extract[i]) {
                break
            }
        }
        if (j > nfields) {
            printf("***ERROR*** field not found - %s\n", extract[i])
            continue
        }
        if (i > 1) printf("  ")
        # no overide character for this field
        if (no[j] == "") {
            printf("%s%s%s", prefix[j], $j, suffix[j])
            continue
        }
        # overide character exist - split up the field
        n = length($j)
        first = substr($j, 1, 1)
        last = substr($j, n, 1)
        # no overide character in field value
        if (first != no[j] && last != no[j]) {
            printf("%s%s%s", prefix[j], $j, suffix[j])
            continue
        }
        middle = ""
        if (n >= 3) {
            middle = substr($j, 2, n-2)
        }
        if (first != no[j]) {
            printf("%s%s", prefix[j], first)
        }
        printf("%s", middle)
        if (last != no[j]) {
            printf("%s%s", last, suffix[j])
        }
    }
    printf("\n")
}'
```

updatehosts

```
#!/bin/sh
# @(#) updatehosts 1.9 92/08/31 @(#)
#
# update the host tables and DNS files
#
# arguments are the files to edit

EDITOR=${EDITOR-vi}
DNS_PARAMETERS=${DNS_PARAMETERS-dns_parameters}
NAMED_DIR=${NAMED_DIR-/etc/named}
cd ${NAMED_DIR}
```

```
# if no arguments display options
if [ $# -eq 0 ]; then
    echo "Usage: -u | file..."
    exit 1
fi

# shift off the update option and proceed
if [ "$1" = "-u" ]; then
    shift
fi

# set umask to group read and write
umask 2
# check if the files exist and are under SCCS control and are readable
okay=1
for i do
    if [ ! -f SCCS/s.$i ]; then
        echo "file $i is not under SCCS control"
        okay=0
    elif [ ! -r SCCS/s.$i ]; then
        echo "file $i is not readable by you"
        okay=0
    elif [ -f SCCS/p.$i ]; then
        echo "file $i is already checked out under SCCS"
        okay=0
    elif [ -f $i ]; then
        rm -f $i
    fi
done
if [ $okay -eq 0 ]; then
    exit 1
fi

# checkout and edit the files
for i do
    sccs edit $i
    $EDITOR $i
    sccs delget $i
done

# update the serial file
sccs edit serial >/dev/null 2>&1
sccs delget -s -y "" serial

# generate the static tables
echo "generating static hosts table..."
genstatic

# generate the dns map
echo "generating the DNS database..."
gendns
poke_ns reload
```

genstatic

```
#!/bin/sh
# @(#) genstatic 1.4 92/08/31 @(#)
# generate the static hosttable from database files
# called from updatehosts
#
# files used
#    hosts.local
#    hosts.main
#    hosts.cname

# this cannot be /etc/hosts
HOSTS=hosts.static
SERIAL=serial
PATH=.:$PATH

# put the serial number of this table as the first line
serial=`cat $SERIAL`
echo "# $serial" >$HOSTS

# extract host name and IP address from hosts.main
readinfo ip host <hosts.main  | awk '
{
    # split up the domain name
    n = split($2, domain, ".")
    printf("%s %s %s\n", $1, $2, domain[1])
}' >>$HOSTS

# build edit script for aliases
readinfo host alias <hosts.cname | awk '
{
    # extract simple alias name from domain name
    n = split($2, alias, ".")
    # split up the domain name
    n = split($1, domain, ".")
    # build the edit command for this line
    # will look like /<domain>/s/$/<alias> <alias.domain>/
    edcmd = "/" domain[1]
    # replace "." with "\."
    for (i=2; i<=n; i++) {
        edcmd = edcmd "\\." domain[i]
    }
    edcmd = edcmd "/s/$/ " $2 " " alias[1] "/"
    print edcmd
}
END {
    print "w"
    print "q"
}' | ed >/dev/null 2>&1 $HOSTS
```

gendns

```sh
#!/bin/sh
# @(#) gendns 1.16 92/11/12 @(#)
# generate the DNS database files from generic database files
#
# files used
#    hosts.main
#    hosts.aliases
#    hosts.mx
#    hosts.ns
#    hosts.wks
#
# this script assumes that a subdomain is always delegated to
# another nameserver and hosts for the subdomain except for the
# glue records do not exist in the base host database files

# make the forward database files

makeforw() {

    # extract host name and IP address from hosts.main
    # and make A records out of it,
    # but only for hosts within this domain
    # add NS and A records for the servers
    # add HINFO from hardware and os

    ( readinfo host ip hard os <hosts.main | awk -F'    '
    BEGIN {
        nservers = split("'"$servers"'", servers, " ")
        for (i=1; i<=nservers; i++) {
            printf("'$domain'. IN NS %s.\n", servers[i])
        }
    }
    {
        for (i=1; i<=nservers; i++) {
            if ($1 == servers[i]) {
                printf("%s. IN A %s\n", $1, $2)
                if ($3 != "X") {
                    printf("%s. IN HINFO %s %s\n", $1, $3, $4)
                }
                next
            }
        }
        if ($1 ~ /'$escape_domain'$/) {
            printf("%s. IN A %s\n", $1, $2)
            if ($3 != "X") {
                printf("%s. IN HINFO %s %s\n", $1, $3, $4)
            }
        }
    }'
```

```
    # make cname records out of the aliases
    # again only for this domain

    readinfo alias host <hosts.cname | awk -F' ' '{
        if ($1 ~ /'$escape_domain'$/)
            printf("%s. IN CNAME %s.\n", $1, $2)
    }'

    # and the MX records the same way

    readinfo domain priority host <hosts.mx | awk -F'  ' '{
        if ($1 ~ /'$escape_domain'$/)
            printf("%s. IN MX %s %s.\n", $1, $2, $3)
    }'

    # and WKS records
    # sort them and concatenate the application protocol mnemonics

    readinfo host ip proto wks <hosts.wks | sort | awk -F' ' '{
        if ($1 ~ /'$escape_domain'$/) {
            if ($1 != host || $2 != ip || $3 != proto) {
                if (host != "") {
                    printf("%s. IN WKS %s %s %s\n", host, ip, proto, wks)
                    wks = ""
                }
            }
            host = $1
            ip = $2
            proto = $3
            wks = wks " " $4
        }
    }
    END {
        if (host != "")
            printf("%s. IN WKS %s %s %s\n", host, ip, proto, wks)
    }' )
}


makerev() {

    # extract host name and IP address from hosts.main
    # and make inverse PTR records out of it
    # but only for IP addresses which match the IP addresses in this domain

    readinfo host ip <hosts.main | awk -F' ' '
    BEGIN {
        nrev = split("'$unreverse'", unreverse, ".")
        nservers = split("'"$servers"'", servers, " ")
        for (i=1; i<=nservers; i++) {
            printf("'$domain'. IN NS %s.\n", servers[i])
        }
    }
```

```
        {
            # check for servers and output glue A records
            for (i=1; i<=nservers; i++) {
                if ($1 == servers[i]) {
                    printf("%s. IN A %s\n", $1, $2)
                }
            }
            n = split($2, ipparts, ".")
            for (i=1; i<=nrev; i++) {
                if (ipparts[i] != unreverse[i])
                    break
            }
            if (i <= nrev)
                next
            for(; i<=n; n--)
                printf("%s.", ipparts[n])
            printf("%s. IN PTR %s.\n", "'$domain'", $1)
        }'
}


SERIAL=serial

serial=`cat $SERIAL`
dateserial=`date +%y%m%d`

# read SOA info for each domain
readinfo domain server contact refresh retry expire min <hosts.soa |\
while read domain server contact refresh retry expire min; do

    # get the domain name with escaped "."

    escape_domain=`echo $domain | awk -F. '{
        for (i=1; i<NF; i++) {
            printf("%s", $i)
            printf("\\.")
        }
        printf("%s", $NF)
    }'`


    # get servers for this domain

    servers=`readinfo domain server <hosts.ns | awk -F' '{
        if ($1 ~ /'$escape_domain'$/)
            printf("%s ", $2)
    }'`

    case $domain in
    *.in-addr.arpa)
        rev=true
        # get the filename fo reverse domains
        # unreverse the domain name for matching IP addresses
        unreverse=`echo $domain | awk -F. '{
            for (i=NF-2; i>1; i--)
                printf("%s.", $i)
```

```
            printf("%s", $1)
        }' `
        filename=f.$unreverse ;;

    *)
        rev=
        filename=$domain ;;
    esac

    # print the header and SOA record

    ( echo "; $serial"
    echo '$ORIGIN'" ${domain}."
    echo "@ SOA ${server}. ${contact}. ( $dateserial $refresh $retry $expire $min )"

    # scan the input file and extract info depending on whether this
    # is a forward or reverse domain file

    if [ $rev ]; then
        makerev
    else
        makeforw
    fi |\

    # get rid of extraneous domain info

    sed -e 's/\(.*\)\(\.'${escape_domain}'\.\)/\1/g' \
    -e 's/\(.*\)\(\.'${escape_domain}'\. \)/\1 /g' \
        -e 's/^'${escape_domain}'\./@/g' ) >$filename
done
```

poke_ns.c

```c
char sccs_id[] = "@(#) poke_ns.c 1.4 92/08/31 @(#)";

/*
 * simple front-end for sending signals to the bind process
 * run setuid to root with appropriate group permission
 * for your installation
 */

#include <stdio.h>
#include <sys/types.h>
#include <sys/stat.h>
#include <sys/wait.h>
#include <signal.h>
#include <errno.h>

#define PIDFILE "/etc/named.pid"
#define NAMED "/usr/etc/in.named"
#define DB_DUMP "/usr/tmp/named_dump.db"
#define DEBUG "/usr/tmp/named.run"
```

```
struct {
    char *name;  /* command name */
    int sig; /* signal to send to bind */
} commands[] = {
    "restart",   SIGTERM,
    "reload",    SIGHUP,
    "debug", SIGUSR1,
    "nodebug",   SIGUSR2,
    "dump",      SIGINT,
    "terminate", SIGTERM,
    NULL,        0
};

main(argc, argv)
int argc;
char **argv;
{
    FILE *fd;
    int cmd, pid;
    struct stat status;
    void usage(), execute();
    int lookup();
    int uid, gid;

    if (argc != 2) {
        usage();
        exit(1);
    }

    /* match one of the commands */
    if ((cmd = lookup(argv[1])) == -1) {
        fprintf(stderr, "command %s not found\n", argv[1]);
        exit(1);
    }


    /* check permissions on /etc/named.pid */
    if (stat(PIDFILE, &status) == -1) {
        fprintf(stderr, "%s cannot stat\n", PIDFILE);
        exit(2);
    }
    if (status.st_uid != 0) {
        fprintf(stderr, "%s not owned by root\n", PIDFILE);
        exit(2);
    }
    if (status.st_nlink > 1) {
        fprintf(stderr, "%s has more than one link\n", PIDFILE);
        exit(2);
    }
    if (status.st_mode&(S_IWGRP|S_IWOTH)) {
        fprintf(stderr, "%s can be written by others\n", PIDFILE);
        exit(2);
    }
```

```
        /* if it is safe - then read pid */
        if ((fd = fopen(PIDFILE, "r")) == NULL) {
            fprintf(stderr, "%s cannot be read\n", PIDFILE);
            exit(3);
        }
        if (fscanf(fd, "%d", &pid) != 1) {
            fprintf(stderr, "%s does not contain an integer\n", PIDFILE);
            exit(3);
        }

        /* execute appropriate command */
        execute(cmd, pid);

        /* change ownership to real user of debugging files */
        uid = getuid();
        gid = getgid();
        chown(DB_DUMP, uid, gid);
        chown(DEBUG, uid, gid);
        exit(0);
}

void
usage()
{
        int i;

        fprintf(stderr, "usage: poke_ns ");
        for (i=0; commands[i].name != NULL; i++) {
            fprintf(stderr, commands[i].name);
            if (commands[i+1].name != NULL) {
                fprintf(stderr, " | ");
            }
            else {
                fprintf(stderr, "\n");
            }
        }
}

int
lookup(cmd)
char *cmd;
{
        int i;

        for (i=0; commands[i].name != NULL; i++) {
            if (strcmp(commands[i].name, cmd) == 0) {
                return i;
            }
        }
        return -1;
}
```

```
void
execute(cmd, pid)
int cmd;
int pid;
{
    int newpid, wstat;

    /* some sanity checking on pid */
    if (pid <= 2) {
        fprintf(stderr, "pid (%d) must be greater than 2\n", pid);
        exit(4);
    }

    /* send the signal to the process */
    if (kill(pid, commands[cmd].sig) == -1) {
        /* let restart work if no named process is running */
        if (!(cmd == 0 && errno == ESRCH)) {
            fprintf(stderr, "signal failed\n");
            exit(4);
        }
    }

    if (cmd != 0) {
        return;
    }
    /* special case of "restart" */

    /* wait and be sure process is dead */
    while (kill(pid, 0) != -1) {
        sleep(1);
    }
    /* restart named */
    newpid = fork();
    if (newpid == -1) {
        fprintf(stderr, "fork failed\n");
        exit(5);
    }
    if (newpid == 0) { /* child */
        execl(NAMED, "in.named", NULL);
        /* only if execl failed */
        fprintf(stderr, "execl failed\n");
        exit(5);
    }
    /* parent */
    wait (&wstat);
    if (WEXITSTATUS(wstat) != 0) {
        exit(5);
    }
    return;
}
```

B.2   Debugging Program Listing

The following scripts and programs may be obtained via anonymous ftp from the host *ftp.tic.com* as the pathname */pub/debug.tar.Z.*

remote
```
#!/bin/sh
#
# run a command on remote systems
# the -h delimits the hosts

USAGE="usage: remote command -h host ...."
TIMEOUT=2

if [ $# -lt 3 ]; then
    echo $USAGE
    exit 1
fi

while [ $# -gt 0 -a "$1" != "-h" ]; do
    command="$command $1"
    shift
done

if [ $# -eq 0 ]; then
    echo $USAGE
    exit 1
fi

shift
for h do
    if ping $h $TIMEOUT >/dev/null 2>&1; then
        echo "Host: $h"
        rsh $h $command
    fi
done
```

getstatic
```
#!/bin/sh
#
# getstatic - get hostnames from static host table or ypcat output
USAGE="usage: getstatic [-yp]"

cat="cat /etc/hosts"
if [ $# -eq 1 ]; then
    if [ $1 = -yp ]; then
        cat="ypcat hosts"
    else
        echo $USAGE
        exit 1
    fi
fi
```

```
# eliminate the cruft
$cat | sed '/^#/d
    /^127\.0\.0/d
    /^$/d' |\
# extract the hostnames, sort and uniq them
awk '{ print $2}' | sort | uniq
```

getdns

```
#!/bin/sh
#
# use nslookup to get DNS hostname list
USAGE="usage: getdns domain"

if [ $# -ne 0 ]; then
    domain=$1
elif [ -f /etc/resolv.conf ]; then
    domain=`awk '/^domain/ { print $2 }' /etc/resolv.conf`
else
    echo $USAGE
    exit 1
fi

# first find the servers
# these are output of nslookup with lines starting with the target domain
servers=`echo "set type=ns
$domain" | nslookup 2>&1 | grep "^$domain" | awk '{ print $4 }'`

if [ "$servers" = "" ]; then
    echo no hosts in domain $domain
    exit

fi
# try each server in turn
# exit when a server is successful
for s in $servers; do
    if echo "set server $s
        ls $domain" | nslookup 2>&1 |\
        sed '/>/d
            /^$/d
            /^Default Server:/d
            /^Address:/d
            /Host or domain/d
            /server = /d' |\
        awk '{ printf("%s.'$domain'\n", $1) }'\
            | sort | uniq |\
        if grep ".*"; then
            exit 0
        else
            exit 1
        fi; then
        exit
    fi
done
```

coll_rate

```sh
#!/bin/sh
#
# get collision rate for each host on a network

awk '
BEGIN {
    printf("Host                  Interface Address\
        Collisions Rate(%)\n")
}
# get host name
/^Host:/ { host = $2; next }
# ignore header line
/^Name/ { next }
# ignore loopback interface (lo0)
/^lo0/ { next }
# other lines must be real interface
{
    interface = $1
    address = $4
    output = $7
    collisions = $9
    rate = collisions*100/output
    printf("%-16.16s %-9s %-15s %10d %7.2f\n",\
        host, interface, address, collisions, rate)
}'
```

route_check

```sh
#!/bin/sh
#
# check routing tables
#
# input is remote command output with netstat -rn
#
# argument is network number in dotted decimal notation

if [ $# -ne 1 ]; then
    echo usage: route_check localnet
fi

awk '
BEGIN {
    no = "no"
    yes = "yes"
    host = ""
    default = no
    local = no
    thisnet = 0
    printf("Host\t\t    Def   Local    This\n")
}
/^Host:/ {
    if (host != "") {
        printf("%-15s %8s%8s%8s\n", host, default, local, thisnet)
        default = no
```

```
            local = no
            thisnet = no
    }
    host = $2
}
/^Routing tables/ { continue }
/^Destination/ { continue }
/^127/ {
    if ($2 == "127.0.0.1")
        local = yes
    else
        local = no
}
/'$1'/ {
    thisnet = yes
}
/^default/ {
    default = yes
}
END {
    printf("%-15s %8s%8s%8s\n", host, default, local, thisnet)
}'
```

getconfig
```
#!/bin/sh
#
# get remote interface configuration
#

# argument list is hosts to get info from
if [ $# -eq 0 ]; then
    echo "usage: getconfig host ..."
    exit 1
fi

# the '\'' sequence adds a single-quote to the argument string
remote '/etc/ifconfig `netstat -i -n |
    awk '\''/^Name/ { next }; /^lo0/ { next }; { print $1 }'\''`' \
    -h $*
```

chkbrdmask
```
#!/bin/sh
#
# check consistency of broadcast address to netmask
#
# assume we are reading output of getconfig command with Host: lines
# delimiting hosts on same network
#
# arguments
# $1 - what the netmask should be in hex
# $2 - what the broadcast address should be in hex

if [ $# -lt 2 ]; then
    echo usage: chkbrdmask mask broadcast
```

```
        exit 1
fi

awk '
BEGIN {
    n = 0
}

/^Host/ {
    n++
    host[n] = $2
    next
}


{
    for (i=1; i<NF; i++) {
        if ($i ~ /broadcast/) {
            i++
            m = split($i, broad, ".")
            if (m != 4) {
                printf("bad broadcast address - %s\n", host[n])
                exit
            }
            broadcast[n] = sprintf("%2.2x%2.2x%2.2x%2.2x",\
                    broad[1], broad[2], broad[3], broad[4])
            continue
        }
        if ($i ~ /netmask/) {
            i++
            if ($i ~ /^0x/)
                netmask[n] = substr($i, 3, 8)
            else
                netmask[n] = $i
            continue
        }
        if ($i ~ /inet/) i++
        if ($i ~ /[0-9][0-9]*\./) {
            m = split($i, address, ".")
            if (m != 4) {
                printf("bad ip address - %s\n", host[n])
                exit
            }
            address[n] = sprintf("%2.2x%2.2x%2.2x%2.2x",\
                address[1], address[2], address[3], address[4])
        }
    }
}

END {
    # check the mask and broadcast address - they should all be the same
    mask = "'$1'"
    broadaddr = "'$2'"
    printf("mask:%s broadcast:%s\n", mask, broadaddr)
    printf("Host:          Netmask   Broadcast\n")
```

```
     for (i=1; i<=n; i++) {
          printf("%-16.16s", host[i])
          printf("%-8.8s", netmask[i])
          if (netmask[i] != mask)
              printf("* ")
          else
              printf("  ")
          printf("%-8.8s", broadcast[i])
          if (broadcast[i] != broadaddr)
              printf("*")
          printf("\n")
     }
}'
```

ddtohex
```
#!/bin/sh
#
# dotted decimal to hex converter

echo `echo "obase=16;$1" | sed 's/\./;/g' | bc | tr "A-F" "a-f"` | sed 's/ //g'
```

Glossary

10Base2   An Ethernet specification with a throughput of 10 mb/sec and a maximum single cable length of 200 meters.

10Base5   The original Ethernet specification with a throughput of 10 mb/sec with a single cable distance of up to 500 meters.

10BaseT   An Ethernet specification with a throughput of 10 mb/sec that uses twisted pair wiring.

AARP (Apple Address Resolution Protocol)   Appletalk equivalent of ARP that maps the datalink address to the Apple Link Access Protocol address.

Abstract Syntax Notation One   *See* ASN.1.

active file   USENET News file that lists all the currently active newsgroups.

address   A symbol (usually numeric) that uniquely identifies the interface of a host attached to a network.

Address Resolution Protocol   *See* ARP.

Advanced Research Projects Agency   *See* ARPA.

AFP (Apple Filing Protocol)   The Appletalk remote filesharing protocol on top of which Appleshare is built.

AFS (Andrew File System)   A transparent file access system.

American Telephone and Telegraph   *See* AT&T.

Andrew File System   *See* AFS.

anonymous FTP   A form of FTP that allows any user to access a restricted set of files without authentication.

Apple Address Resolution Protocol   *See* AARP.

Apple Filing Protocol   *See* AFP.

Apple Remote Access   *See* ARA.

Apple Transaction Protocol   *See* ATP.

Appleshare   The remote filesharing system that uses Appletalk.

Appletalk   The network protocol family that comes as a part of every Apple Macintosh computer.

Appletalk IP bridge   Hardware device that links an Appletalk Localtalk network to a TCP/IP network.

Appletalk zone   A logical subdivision of an Appletalk internetwork used to help name the attached nodes.

Applicability Specification   *See* AS.

ARA (Apple Remote Access)   A serial line protocol for attaching two Appletalk networks over a serial line. Very similar in functionality to SLIP.

archie   An Internet archive resource discovery protocol.

ARP (Address Resolution Protocol)   The protocol used to map from an interface's IP address to its corresponding datalink address.

ARP cache   The list of recent IP to datalink address mapping kept by a host operating system in response to ARP replies.

ARPA (Advanced Research Projects Agency)   A research agency of the US Department of Defense.

article   The name of a USENET news message.

AS (Applicability Specification)   A specification of applicability of protocol specifications, used in Internet Standardization. *See* TS and IAB.

AS (autonomous system)   A collection of routers under a single administration.

ASN.1 (Abstract Syntax Notation One)   The OSI standard presentation protocol.

ATP (Apple Transaction Protocol)   The Appletalk equivalent of TCP.

AT&T (American Telephone and Telegraph)   The provider of InterNIC directory and database services.

automounter   A daemon process that fields remote filesystem requests and only mounts remote filesystems that are currently used.

autonomous system   *See* AS.

Baseband   A signalling method used by Ethernet and IEEE 802.3 networks.

Basic Encoding Rules   *See* BER.

BBN 1822   The protocol used to communicate between a host an and IMP in the ARPANET.

Because It's Time Network   *See* BITNET.

BER (Basic Encoding Rules)   A set of rules used to encode an ASN.1 structure.

Berkeley Internet Name Daemon   *See* BIND.

Berkeley sockets   *See* sockets.

BGP (Border Gateway Protocol) An implementation of an inter-AS routing protocol.

big-endian Machine architectures that store numbers from high-order byte to low-order byte in memory.

BIND (Berkeley Internet Name Daemon) A UNIX implementation of the DNS.

BITNET (Because It's Time Network) A network formed in 1981 to interconnect educational and research institutions.

Border Gateway Protocol *See* BGP.

bridge A device that forwards datalink layer frames.

broadcast address An address that is recognized and processed by all nodes on the same network.

broadcast storm A phenomena on Ethernet networks where the network is overwhelmed by a large number of broadcast datalink frames.

brouter A device that combines the functionality of a bridge and a router.

bus A network where the topology of the network is a graph where at most one path exists between every node on the network.

California Education and Research Federation Network *See* CERFNET.

CAP (Columbia Appletalk Package) A freeware implementation of Appletalk for UNIX systems.

capabilities Entries in a printcap file that defines the attributes of a printer.

carrier sense multiple access/collision detection *See* CSMA/CD.

CCITT (International Consultative Committee on Telegraphy and Telephony) A committee for telecommunications standards.

CD (Committee Draft) The first state of ISO standardization.

CDDI (Copper Distributed Digital Interface) A version of the FDDI protocol that works over twisted-pair wiring.

CERFNET (California Education and Research Federation Network) A commercial Internet access provider based in San Diego.

CERT (Computer Emergency Response Team) A group charged with disseminating information about Internet security.

cheapernet *See* **thinwire.**

circuit switching A method of data communication where a complete path is constructed between two entities that wish to communicate.

CIX (Commercial Internet Exchange) An association composed of commercial Internet access providers.

class A sendmail variable whose value is one or more strings of characters.

Client/Server Computing A form of computing where server processes reside on a separate computer from the computers used by an end-user.

CLNP (Connectionless Network Protocol)   The OSI network protocol that is very similar to IP.

CLNS (Connectionless Network Service)   The OSI network layer service that provides an unreliable packet-oriented service to a transport protocol.

CMC (Computer Mediated Communication)   Communication among people that is aided by computer systems.

collision   An event on an Ethernet where two nodes attempt to transmit at the same time.

Columbia Appletalk Package   *See* CAP.

Commercial Internet Exchange   *See* CIX.

Committee Draft   *See* CD.

community name   Used by SNMP to grant an SNMP server access rights to a MIB.

Computer Emergency Response Team   *See* CERT.

Computer Mediated Communication   *See* CMC.

Computer Science Network   *See* CSNET.

Computer Systems Research Group   *See* CSRG.

Connectionless Network Protocol   *See* CLNP.

Connectionless Network Service   *See* CLNS.

connectionless protocol   A protocol where the switching nodes of the network attempt to deliver the packet without any guarantees.

Connection-oriented Network Protocol   *See* CONP.

Connection-oriented Network Service   *See* CONS.

connection-oriented protocol   A protocol that requires the setup of a complete path between two nodes before data can be exchanged.

CONP (Connection-oriented Network Protocol)   The traditional OSI network protocol, X.25, which provides the CONS.

CONS (Connection-oriented Network Service)   The OSI network layer service that provides a reliable connection-oriented service to a transport protocol.

Copper Distributed Digital Interface   *See* CDDI.

core AS   An autonomous system that serves as a central routing switch for all other attached autonomous systems.

CREN (Corporation for Research and Education Networking)   The organization that was the merger of BITNET and CSNET.

CSMA/CD (carrier sense multiple access/collision detection)   The access protocol used by baseband networking technologies to arbitrate network access.

CSNET (Computer Science Network)   A network established in 1981 to facilitate research in computer science and engineering.

CSRG (Computer Systems Research Group) The research group at the University of California at Berkeley that developed the 4.2BSD version of the UNIX operating system.

data service unit/channel service unit *See* DSU/CSU.

datagram A discrete chunk of data with sufficient addressing information that it can be routed independently in an internetwork.

Datagram Delivery Protocol *See* DDP.

DCA (Defense Communications Agency) The early name of DISA.

DDP (Datagram Delivery Protocol) Appletalk equivalent of IP.

default routing A simple routing paradigm where all packets not bound for the local network are sent to a well-known router for further processing.

Defense Communications Agency *See* DCA.

Defense Information Systems Agency *See* DISA.

Department of Defense *See* DoD.

Digital Signal Level 0 *See* DS0.

Digital Signal Level 1 *See* DS1.

Digital Signal Level 3 *See* DS3.

DIS (Draft International Standard) The middle state of ISO standardization.

DISA (Defense Information Systems Agency) The DoD agency that oversees the operation of the military portion of the Internet.

distance vector protocol A routing protocol that grades the quality of the all the paths to a given network and selects the best path.

distributed naming system A naming system where the mapping information is stored on many hosts scattered around the network.

DNS (Domain Name System) The resource naming system of the Internet.

DNS Mail System All hosts that interexchange electronic mail using domain names.

DNS resolver Software code in an application that communicates with a DNS server to answer resource mapping requests.

DoD (Department of Defense) The U.S. Department of Defense.

domain A node in the DNS naming tree and all of its descendant nodes.

domain name A unique identifier for a single node in the DNS naming tree.

Domain Name System *See* DNS.

domain-based addresses Electronic mail addresses of the form user@domain.

dotted-decimal Notation where each 8-bit byte of a number is represented as a decimal integer and separated from the next byte in the number by a period.

Draft International Standard *See* DIS.

DS0 (Digital Signal Level 0) A U.S data signalling standard with a throughput of 56 kb/sec.

DS1 (Digital Signal Level 1)   A U.S. data signalling standard with a throughput of 1.544 mb/sec.

DS3 (Digital Signal Level 3)   A U.S. data signalling standard with a throughput of 44.736 mb/sec.

DSU/CSU (data service unit/channel service unit)   An interface device that allows a customer to attach to a leased common carrier line.

EARN (European Academic and Research Network)   The European academic community equivalent of BITNET.

EC (European Commission)   The council of the European Community.

EGP (Exterior Gateway Protocol)   A specific implementation of an inter-AS routing protocol.

EGP (exterior gateway protocol)   Another name for an inter-AS routing protocol.

electronic mail   A protocol for interperson communication on a computer network.

e-mail   Another name for electronic mail.

Ethernet I   The original Ethernet specification with a throughput of 3 mb/sec.

Ethernet II   The current Ethernet specification with a throughput of approximately 10 mb/sec.

Ethertalk Phase I   The Appletalk datalink protocol over Ethernet.

European Academic and Research Network   *See* EARN.

European Commission   *See* EC.

extended Ethernet   *See* **wide-area Ethernet.**

Exterior Gateway Protocol   *See* EGP.

external data representation   *See* XDR.

facility   In syslog, a number given to each message that directs what type the message is and where it should be logged.

FDDI (Fiber Distributed Digital Interface)   A fiber optic token passing network media which supports speeds of up to and beyond 100 mb/sec.

Federal Networking Council   *See* FNC.

Fiber Distributed Digital Interface   *See* FDDI.

Fido   The protocol suite used by FidoNet.

FidoNet   Network of mostly DOS machines that use a store and forward protocol very similar to UUCP.

File Transfer, Access, and Manipulation   *See* FTAM.

File Transfer Protocol   *See* FTP.

filtering bridge   A bridge that selectively filters out frames from being needlessly forwarded to another connected network where the bridge has learned the frame's destination is not attached.

FNC (Federal Networking Council)   A council that coordinates networking activity among different U.S. Federal agencies.

forward query   A DNS query that is forwarded from one server to another server with better information.

FQDN (fully qualified domain name)   A domain name that completely traverses the path from anode in the DNS tree to the root of the tree.

fragment   A piece of an originally larger IP packet.

fragmentation   The process of splitting an IP packet into several smaller packets for transport on a network which cannot accommodate the larger size of the of the original packet.

frame   A common name for the data unit exchanged by datalink peers.

frame relay   An access protocol for building private dedicated virtual circuits over a common-carrier public network.

FrEDMail (Free Educational Mail network)   A network for K–12 (kindergarten to twelfth grade) networking.

FSF (Free Software Foundation)   Creator of GNU.

FTAM (File Transfer, Access, and Manipulation)   The OSI file transfer protocol.

FTP (File Transfer Protocol)   The remote file transfer protocol in the TCP/IP suite.

fully qualified domain name   *See* FQDN.

GNU (GNU's Not UNIX)   A free software collection.

gopher   A menu-oriented Internet resource discovery protocol.

GOSIP (Government OSI Profile)   The U.S. government OSI procurement profile specified by NIST; FIPS 146-1.

handle   A unique identifier used in NIC databases.

HDLC (High-level Data Link Control)   A standard datalink encapsulation method for point-to-point network links.

High Performance Computing Act   *See* HPCA.

High-level Data Link Control   *See* HDLC.

history file   A list of recently posted USENET news articles maintained to detect duplicate postings.

hop count   The number of intermediate nodes a packet will pass through on its way to its final destination.

host   A computer system used for application processing on a network.

host number   The part of an IP address that uniquely identifies the host on a specific IP network.

hostname   A simple mnemonic identifier for a network node.

HPCA (High Performance Computing Act)   The U.S. government act that authorized the NREN.

IAB (Internet Activities Board)   The old name of the IAB.

IAB (Internet Architecture Board)   The technical policy board of the Internet.

ICMP (Internet Control Message Protocol)   The protocol that enables in-band control, diagnostic, and error messages to be passed between nodes in an IP internetwork.

IEEE 802.2   A standard framing format for the 802.x series of network standards.

IEEE 802.3   A standard for baseband networks that is very similar to Ethernet.

IEEE 802.4   A standard for a baseband network that uses a form of token passing for access control.

IEEE 802.5   A standard for a network that uses a ring topology with token passing for access control.

IEEE/CS TCOS-SS   *See* POSIX.

IESG (Internet Engineering Steering Group)   The coordinating body for the IETF.

IETF (Internet Engineering Task Force)   The committee that oversees the development and deployment of TCP/IP protocols.

IGP (interior gateway protocol)   A routing protocol that keeps all routes updated within a single autonomous system.

IMP (Interface Message Processor)   The original name given to an internal switching node in the ARPANET.

indefinite patterns   A special pattern that appears on the left-hand side of a sendmail rule that can match many input strings.

inetd   A short name for the Internet Daemon.

inter-AS routing protocol   A routing protocol that maintains the routing tables between two or more autonomous systems.

Interface Message Processor   *See* IMP.

interior gateway protocol   *See* IGP.

International Consultative Committee on Telegraphy and Telephony   *See* CCITT.

International Organization for Standardization   *See* ISO.

International Standard   *See* IS.

on the Internet   A host that has direct IP connectivity to any well-known Internet host.

the Internet   The worldwide interconnected collection of networks that predominantly use the TCP/IP protocol suite.

Internet Activities Board   *See* IAB.

Internet Architecture Board   *See* IAB.

Internet Control Message Protocol   *See* ICMP.

Internet Daemon   A daemon process that multiplexes many TCP or UDP network connections.

Internet Engineering Steering Group   *See* IESG.

Internet Engineering Task Force   *See* IETF.

Internet Mail System   Another name for the DNS mail system.

Internet News   A USENET news software system with enhanced functionality for hosts with TCP/IP connectivity that process a very large volume of news.

Internet Protocol   *See* IP.

Internet Registry   *See* IR.

Internet Research Steering Group   *See* IRSG.

Internet Research Task Force   *See* IRTF.

Internet Society   *See* ISOC.

internetwork   Any interconnected set of networks. The little "i" distinguishes this term from the specific instance of an internet, called the Internet.

InterNIC   A NIC service sponsored by the U.S. National Science Foundation (NSF) to provide and coordinate services for the NSFNET community (and by default to the Internet at large).

interprocess communications facility   *See* IPC.

inverse query   A DNS query that does the inverse map from a resource record to a domain name

IP (Internet Protocol)   The single protocol at the internet layer of the TCP/IP protocol model.

IP forwarding   The algorithm used by a routing node to forward an IP packet not destined for the routing node itself.

IPC (interprocess communications facility)   A system that allows two or more processes to exchange information using an underlying transport mechanism.

IR (Internet Registry)   A registry for IP numbers. InterNIC is the global IR; the RIPE NCC is the European regional IR; there are local IRs for many countries; and many Internet connectivity providers are also local IRs.

IRSG (Internet Research Steering Group)   The coordinating body for the IRTF.

IRTF (Internet Research Task Force)   The committee that oversees research related to the TCP/IP protocols. *See also* IETF and IAB.

IS (International Standard)   The final state of ISO standardization.

ISO (International Organization for Standardization)   The international standards body.

ISO Development Environment   *See* ISODE.

ISOC (Internet Society)   An international nonprofit membership organization to promote the use of the Internet for research and scholarly communication and collaboration.

ISODE (ISO Development Environment)   Software to permit OSI applications to run under IP.

K–12 (kindergarten to twelfth grade)   Primary and secondary educational institutions.

kermit   A file transfer protocol typically used over slow-speed serial lines with implementations for almost every brand of computer or operating system.

kindergarten to twelfth grade   *See* K–12:

KIP (Kinetic's IP)   A method for encapsulating Appletalk DDP packets inside UDP messages for transport over a TCP/IP network.

LANs (local area networks)   A network that spans a small geographic area like a building or a campus.

LAP (Link Access Protocol)   The name of the various datalink protocols in the Appletalk protocol family.

left-hand side   The pattern-matching side of a sendmail rule.

Line Printing Protocol   *See* LPR.

link   A communication path between two network nodes.

Link Access Protocol   *See* LAP.

literal tokens   A sendmail token that appears in the left-hand side of a rule.

little-endian   Machine architectures that store numbers from low-order byte to high-order byte in memory.

LLC (Logical Link Control)   The protocol used in the IEEE 802.x family for establishing, maintaining, and terminating a logical link between two network peers on the same 802.x network.

local area networks   *See* LANs.

local traffic   Packets that are bound for nodes within an autonomous system.

Localtalk   The original Appletalk datalink protocol.

lockstep   A protocol where every message must be acknowledged before the next message is sent.

log level   A number given to each syslog message that subdivides the message into a severity class.

Logical Link Control   *See* LLC.

LPR (Line Printing Protocol)   A network print spooling protocol developed as a part of the 4.2BSD operating system.

MacTCP   Apple's implementation of TCP/IP for its Macintosh computer.

mail   The common name for electronic mail.

mailbox   A repository (usually just an ordinary file) for incoming electronic mail.

mailer   In the context of sendmail, a user-defined program that takes a mail message and delivers it.

mailing list   A list of mail addresses where a message sent to the name of the list is redistributed to all the addresses in the list.

MAN (metropolitan area network)   A network that covers a large urbanized area with more of the characteristics of a LAN.

Management Information Base   *See* MIB.

management station   A node on a network that generates SNMP queries and displays their results.

in the Matrix   A host that can exchange electronic mail with a host on the Internet.

the Matrix   All computer networks that exchange electronic mail or news.

maximum transmission unit   *See* MTU.

message   A common name for the data unit exchanged by Transport Layer peers of the Internet protocol model.

Message Handling System   *See* MHS.

message transfer agent   *See* MTA.

message-id   A unique identifier given to every USENET news article. It is the concatenation of the unique site name and an integer number.

metropolitan area network   *See* MAN.

MHS (Message Handling System)   The standard third party messaging system in the OSI protocol suite.

MIB (Management Information Base)   The information structure that defines the type of information accessible on a managed SNMP node by an SNMP management station.

MIME (Multipurpose Internet Mail Extensions)   Extensions to Internet electronic mail that permit sending non-ASCII documents over a 7-bit ASCII channel by using specific encoding standards.

mixed-mode addresses   A combination of UUCP and domain-based mail addresses.

MTA (message transfer agent)   The software system that moves mail messages from one host system to another.

MTU (maximum transmission unit)   The maximum number of bytes that can be contained within the data portion of a datalink frame.

multihomed AS   An autonomous system with multiple paths to outside networks, but which disallows any transit traffic from crossing its boundaries.

Multipurpose Internet Mail Extensions   *See* MIME.

Name Binding Protocol   *See* NBP.

nameserver   A software system that maps user-friendly names into numbers usable by lower layer protocols.

National Institute of Standards and Technology   *See* NIST.

National Research and Education Network   *See* NREN.

National Science Foundation   *See* NSF.

NBP (Name Binding Protocol)   The Appletalk nameservice protocol. Closest IP equivalent is DNS.

NCC (Network Coordination Center)   The regional Internet Registry for Europe.

NCP (Network Control Protocol)   The precursor to TCP/IP on the ARPANET.

netgroups   A method used to name groups of hosts or users.

Network Control Protocol   *See* NCP.

Network Coordination Center   *See* NCC.

Network File System   *See* NFS.

Network Information Center   *See* NIC.

Network Information Service   *See* NIS.

Network Job Entry   *See* NJE.

network mask   A 32-bit mask used to determine which part of an IP address covers the network number and any subnet number.

Network News   Another name for USENET News.

Network News Transfer Protocol   *See* NNTP.

network number   The part of an IP address that is the number of the IP network the host is attached to.

Network Solutions, Inc   *See* NSI.

Network Time Protocol   *See* NTP.

A News   The original USENET news software.

B News   A replacement for the original A News USENET news software.

C News   A currently popular USENET news system package.

news   A short name for USENET news.

newsgroups   A topic name in the USENET News system.

NFS (Network File System)   A popular implementation of a transparent file access system developed by Sun Microsystems.

NIC (Network Information Center)   An organization or service that provides information about networks.

NIS (Network Information Service)   A resource mapping protocol developed by Sun Microsystems.

NIS map   A file that maps an NIS key to its corresponding value for a specific resource.

NIST (National Institute of Standards and Technology) The U.S. federal agency that promotes standards in the U.S.

NIT A low-level interface to a network device driver that let's you read and write datalink frames found on Sun workstations.

NJE (Network Job Entry) The remote job entry protocol used on the IBM VM/370 operating system. It was the original underlying transport protocol used by BITNET.

NNTP (Network News Transfer Protocol) The standard protocol for transporting USENET News articles between TCP/IP systems.

node Any computer attached to a network.

NREN (National Research and Education Network) The follow on network to NSFNET.

NSF (National Science Foundation) The U.S. agency that took over funding of the major U.S. Internet backbone, NSFNET. Also seed-funded a number of regional networks that all tied into the backbone network.

NSFNET The backbone network funded by the National Science Foundation.

NSI (Network Solutions, Inc.) The provider of InterNIC registration services.

NTP (Network Time Protocol) A network time synchronization protocol.

ODA (Office Documentation Architecture) The OSI application protocol for storing and retrieving documents.

Open Shortest Path First *See* OSPF.

Open Systems Interconnection *See* OSI.

operator character A set of special characters in a sendmail input string that are scanned as a single token.

OSI (Open Systems Interconnection) The basic reference model for the ISO networking protocols.

OSPF (Open Shortest Path First) The emerging standard interior gateway protocol for the Internet community.

packet A discrete chunk of data, usually no more than a few thousand bytes long. Each packet is self-contained and holds all the information required to send it to its final destination. *See also* packet switching.

Packet Switch Node *See* PSN.

packet switching A method of data communication where one entity divides data sent to another entity into discrete chunks or packets. Each packet travels to its destination independently of all other packets.

PAP (Printer Access Protocol) Appletalk's protocol for talking to printers.

path The route taken by a data packet through a network.

Performance Systems International *See* PSI.

Point-to-Point Protocol *See* PPP.

policy routing   Routing that takes into account more information than just the destination of a given packet.

POP (Post Office Protocol)   A protocol that allows mail to be retrieved from a mailbox on a server host for viewing on a workstation.

portmapper   A process that maps Sun RPC program numbers to TCP and/or UDP ports.

POSIX (IEEE/CS TCOS-SS)   Committees and their standards for interfaces related to the UNIX operating system.

Post Office Protocol   *See* POP.

PPP (Point-to-Point Protocol)   A standard datalink protocol that allows the encapsulation of multiple higher layer protocols over the same point-to-point interface.

primary nameserver   The DNS server that loads and maintains the authoritative zone database.

Printer Access Protocol   *See* PAP.

ProcSets (Procedure Sets)   A set of PostScript functions called by a PostScript program to produce output on a printer.

profiles   Sets of protocols and related options. *See* AS.

Prospero   A resource discovery protocol that allows transparent access to many FTP sites.

protocol   The set of rules that govern the way a service is provided.

protocol stack   A selection of protocols from a protocol suite that supports a specific application.

Protocol Standards Steering Group   *See* PSSG.

protocol suite   The entire set of protocols that are a part of a protocol model.

protocol tunnelling   A method where one network protocol's packets are encapsulated in another network protocol for forwarding over a network that does not directly support the first network protocol.

Proxy ARP   A protocol that allows a router to stand-in or act as a proxy for a host that does not understand subnets and lets the host successfully communicate with hosts on the same network, but not on the same physical subnet.

pseudo-header   A header which serves as a skeleton IP header for a TCP message. It is used to calculate the TCP checksum, but is not carried as a part of the TCP message.

PSI (Performance Systems International)   A commercial Internet access provider based in Reston, Virginia.

PSN (Packet Switch Node)   The later name given to an internal switching node in the ARPANET. *See also* IMP.

PSSG (Protocol Standards Steering Group)   A U.S. military joint group chaired by DISA.

R* authentication   An remote user authentication protocol introduced by the 4.2BSD UNIX operating system. Used by the *rlogin, rsh, rdist, and rcp. commands.*

RARE (Reseaux Associés pour la Recerche Européenne)   Associated European Research Networks, a coordinating body for European networking.

RARP (Reverse Address Resolution Protocol)   The protocol used to map a datalink address to its corresponding IP address.

RCP (Remote Copy Protocol)   A remote file copying protocol for a network of UNIX systems.

Rdist (Remote Distribution)   A remote file distribution system for a network of UNIX systems.

reachability protocol   A routing protocol that simply tells whether a network can be routed to, without regard to the quality of the path to the network.

reassembly   The process of rejoining a previously fragmented IP packet.

reference model   A common model for talking about how the components of a complex system fit together.

regular expression   A pattern matching language used by most common UNIX text processing utilities.

relative address   An address that specifies the entire path taken by a message from its source to its destination.

relative domain name   A domain name that only traverses part of the path from a node to the root of the DNS naming tree.

Remote Copy Protocol   *See* RCP.

Remote Distribution   *See* Rdist.

Remote Login Protocol   *See* RLOGIN.

remote procedure call   *See* RPC.

Remote Shell Protocol   *See* RSH.

Request for Comments   *See* RFC.

Reseaux Associés pour la Recerche Européenne   *See* RARE.

Reseaux IP Européens   *See* RIPE.

resource name   A unique identifier for a node on an Appletalk internetwork

resource record   A record that contains the mapping from a domain name to a specific type of resource.

Reverse Address Resolution Protocol   *See* RARP.

reverse query   A special inverse DNS query that maps from an IP address to a domain name using the special in-addr.arpa domain.

RFC (Request for Comments)   The set of documents that for the most part describes the standard specifications for the TCP/IP protocol suite. Also includes other material, ranging from network demographics to poetry.

RFC-822 message format   The Internet standard format for electronic mail messages.

right-hand side   The pattern-transformation side of a sendmail rule.

ring   A network where each node on the network is connected to exactly one other node and the last node is connected top the first node.

RIP (Routing Information Protocol)   A popular routing distribution protocol found on most UNIX systems.

RIPE (Reseaux IP Européens)   The coordinating body for Internet activity in Europe.

RLOGIN (Remote Login Protocol)   A virtual terminal protocol specific to UNIX systems.

route   Same as a path. Also used as a verb to describe what a router does.

router   A device that forwards network layer packets.

Routing Information Protocol   *See* RIP.

routing protocol   A protocol used to keep each node's routing table up-to-date.

routing table   A table of routes kept by a node's operating system and used to direct where the next destination for each IP packet is.

Royal Signals and Radar Establishment   *See* RSRE.

RPC (remote procedure call)   A network service where a remote client program can make a procedure call that is possibly executed on a remote server.

RSH (Remote Shell Protocol)   A protocol that allows execution of commands on a remote UNIX host.

RSRE (Royal Signals and Radar Establishment)   The research organization in the U.K. that developed an early implementation of the TCP retransmission algorithm.

rule   The basic rewriting language construct used by sendmail.

ruleset   A collection of sendmail rules.

secondary nameservers   A DNS server that maintains a redundant copy of the authoritative zone database.

secret key   A user's password in the Kerberos authentication system.

secure ports   The TCP and UDP port range 1-1023 that are considered secure on UNIX systems, since they can only be assigned to a process by the superuser.

Secure RPC   A more secure RPC mechanism developed by Sun Microsystems.

Serial Line IP   *See* SLIP.

server   A process that offers a service to a client. Sometimes refers to an entire machine that offers a specific service, such as filesharing.

service   In the OSI model, something that a program or a user actually gets from a communications system.

SGML (Simplified Generic Markup Language)   A standard method of specifying keywords and other features of a document.

Simple Mail Transfer Protocol   *See* SMTP.

Simple Network Management Protocol   *See* SNMP.

Simplified Generic Markup Language   *See* SGML.

slave nameserver   A DNS nameserver that only caches answers from other authoritative servers.

sliding window   A protocol that allows several messages to be in flight before any of the messages are acknowledged.

SLIP (Serial Line IP)   A standard protocol for encapsulating IP packets over low-speed serial interfaces.

SMTP (Simple Mail Transfer Protocol)   The Internet standard protocol for moving mail messages from one host to another.

SNAcP (Subnetwork Access Protocol)   An OSI protocol that identifies what Network Layer protocol is encapsulated within a specific Data Link Layer protocol frame.

SNMP (Simple Network Management Protocol)   The standard Internet protocol for accessing common TCP/IP management information on network nodes.

socket   A communication end-point used by a process to communicate with a transport protocol.

sockets (Berkeley sockets)   A popular applications interface to the TCP/IP protocol suite.

star   A network where each node is interconnected at a central point or hub.

stateless   A client/server system where each defined operation is independent of any previous operation.

stub AS   An autonomous system with a single connection to another autonomous system that handles all routing decisions for traffic bound for non-local networks.

subdomains   The descendants of any node in the DNS naming tree.

subnets   An IP addressing standard where a portion of the host address can be used to create multiple network addresses that are logically a subdivision of the network address.

Subnetwork Access Protocol   *See* SNAcP.

sys file   File used to keep information about how to post USENET news articles both locally and to news system neighbors.

syslog   A network logging facility found as a part of most UNIX systems.

system extension   In the Macintosh world, an extra piece of code that is dynamically added to the operating system when it is bootstrapped.

T-carrier   The framing protocol for a class of point-to-point data communication circuits.

TCP (Transmission Control Protocol)   The reliable two-way byte stream protocol in the TCP/IP protocol family.

TCP slow start   An algorithm used to smoothly increase the transmission rate of a TCP connection at startup to prevent a slower intermediate link from being overwhelmed.

TCP/IP (Transmission Control Protocol/Internet Protocol)   The name of the protocol suite developed for the US Department of Defense and now the dominant protocol in the worldwide Internet. The name is taken from the major transport and internet layer protocols. *See also* Internet, TCP, and IP.

Technical Specification   *See* TS.

TELNET (Virtual Terminal Protocol)   The remote virtual terminal protocol in the TCP/IP suite.

terminal server   A computer dedicated to multiplexing serial devices with access to a LAN. Normally the terminal server only supports TELNET or RLOGIN client programs. Some also have support for SLIP or PPP.

terminate and stay resident   *See* TSR.

TFA (transparent file access)   Filesystem protocols that while they access files from remote servers, the files appear to the end-user application as if they were local.

thickwire   The original 50 ohm cabling used by Ethernet.

thinwire   An alternative Ethernet specification that uses thin 50 ohm cable with twist-on BNC type connectors.

ticket   In the Kerberos authentication system, the unique message that securely validates the identity of a service user to the service.

ticket-granting service   The server in the Kerberos authentication system that issues tickets for other services.

ticket-granting ticket   A ticket in the Kerberos authentication system that is used to securely identify a user, so other tickets may be issued to that user.

time-to-live   The maximum time in seconds that an IP packet is allowed to survive in an internetwork before being unconditionally dropped by a router.

TLI (Transport Layer Interface)   An alternative application interface to the TCP/IP protocol suite.

token   A known signal used by a token passing protocol to arbitrate network access.

tokens   A set of character strings into which sendmail breaks an input string.

top-level domains   The domains that are the immediate descendants of the root node in the DNS naming tree.

transceiver   The device that connects a host to an Ethernet cable.

transit AS   An autonomous system that allows transit traffic.

transit traffic   Packets that simply moves through an autonomous system.

Transmission Control Protocol   *See* TCP.

Transmission Control Protocol/Internet Protocol   *See* TCP/IP.

transparent file access   *See* TFA.

Transport Layer Interface   *See* TLI.

trap   A method for an SNMP client to asynchronously notify an SNMP management station.

TS (Technical Specification)   A protocol specification, used in Internet Standardization. *See* AS and IAB.

TSR (terminate and stay resident)   A stub program that loads into memory and responds when called upon by a hardware or software interrupt. Used as a method to dynamically load network device drivers.

UA (user agent)   A software system that acts as an interface between a mail user and the mail transport system.

UAB (UNIX Appletalk Bridge)   An application program that turns a UNIX system into an Appletalk router.

UCB (University of California at Berkeley)   The university that developed the 4.2BSD version of the UNIX operating system that incorporated full TCP/IP support.

UDP (User Datagram Protocol)   An unreliable packet oriented protocol where ordering or delivery is not guaranteed.

UNIX Appletalk Bridge   *See* UAB.

UNIX Protocol Domain   An interprocess communications facility that allows unrelated processes on a single UNIX system to share information.

UNIX Seventh Edition   An early version of the UNIX operating system first distributed in the late 1970s.

University of California at Berkeley   *See* UCB.

UNIX to UNIX Copy   *See* UUCP.

USENET (Users' Network)   Network of machines that carry a distributed bulletin board system called "news."

USENET news   The distributed bulletin board system of USENET.

user agent   *See* UA.

User Datagram Protocol   *See* UDP.

Users' Network   *See* USENET.

UUCP (UNIX to UNIX Copy)   A store and forward protocol used to link together UNIX systems over low-speed serial lines.

UUCP addresses   Electronic mail addresses of the form a!b!c!user that describes the path taken by the message to reach its final destination.

UUCP mail network   Network used to link hosts that exchange electronic mail using the UUCP protocol.

UUNET (UUNET Technologies)   A commercial Internet access provider based in Reston, Virginia.

veronica   A resource discovery protocol that allows indexed searchs across many gopher servers.

virtual circuit   A connection established between two nodes in an internetwork. Differs from traditional circuit switching in that the connection is not physically established, but may be created on top of a packet switched network.

Virtual Terminal   *See* VT.

Virtual Terminal Protocol   *See* TELNET.

VT (Virtual Terminal)   The OSI remote login protocol.

WAIS (Wide Area Information Servers)   A distributed client/server protocol and implementations for searches of documents, with or without prior keyword markup.

WANs (wide area networks)   A network that spans a large geographic area like a state, country or even worldwide.

Wide Area Information Servers   *See* WAIS.

wide area networks   *See* WANs.

wide-area Ethernet   An Ethernet that uses specialized bridging hardware where two or more remote Ethernet segments can appear as if they were a single physical Ethernet.

window probe   A message sent to a TCP that has closed its receive window asking it to open the window.

WWW (World Wide Web)   A hypertext-based resource discovery protocol.

X.500   The ISO-OSI Directory and Naming Service.

XDR (external data representation)   The common data format for data when transmitted on a network.

XNS (Xerox Network System)   A protocol family developed by the Xerox Palo Alto research lab.

XTI (X/Open Transport Interface)   Another name for the TLI.

ZIP (Zone Information Protocol)   Appletalk support protocol that maintains information about Appletalk zones.

zone   A fully connected portion of the DNS tree under the administrative control of a single entity.

zone database   The files that contain the resource records for a DNS zone.

Zone Information Protocol   *See* ZIP.

Index